بسم الله الرحمن الرحيم

KAMIL AL ZIARAT

Abul Qasim Jafar Bin Muhammad Bin Jafar Bin Musa
Bin Quluya Al Qummi

Translated by

Syed Jazib Reza Kazmi

Wilayat Mission® Publications

Kamil al Ziarat

Copyright © 2014 Wilayat Mission® Publications

All Rights Reserved

ISBN-13: 978-0692228043

ISBN-10: 0692228047

Original Author Abul Qasim Jafar Bin Muhammad Bin Jafar Bin Musa Bin Quluya Al Qummi

Translated by Syed Jazib Reza Kazmi

Cover Art by ShiaGraphics (www.facebook.com/ShiaGraphics)

Published by Wilayat Mission® Publications

For full listings of translations available as well as upcoming projects please visit our website, www.wilayatmission.org , and join our mailing list to receive email notifications of all new releases.

.

Wilayat Mission® Publications
Lahore, Pakistan
info@wilayatmission.org
http://www.wilayatmission.org

Dedication

We present this meager offering before Imam e Zamana (atfs) without His help and blessings we would not have been able to complete. It is a great honor and blessing for us to be able to share with all momineen such glorious teachings of Masoomeen (asws).

We pray our offering is accepted and that we move one step closer to fulfilling the oath that we promised to fulfill.

Table of Contents

Chapter 1

The Reward for Performing the Ziarat of RasoolAllah (saw), Ameerul Momineen (asws), Imam Hasan (asws), and Imam Hussain (asws)

HADITH 1

Imam Jafar Sadiq (asws) said:

"One day while Hussain (asws) ibn Ali (asws) was sitting on the lap of RasoolAllah (saw), He (Hussain asws) raised His head and said, "O'Father (saw)! What is the reward for those who perform Your Ziarat after You leave this world?"

RasoolAllah (saw) replied:

"O' My Son (asws)! Those who perform My Ziarat after I leave this world will be rewarded with Paradise; those who perform the Ziarat of Your Father (asws) after His martyrdom will be rewarded with Paradise; those who perform the Ziarat of Your Brother (asws) after His martyrdom will be rewarded with Paradise and those who perform Your Ziarat after Your martyrdom will be rewarded with Paradise."

HADITH 2

Imam Jafar Sadiq (asws) narrates:

Hussain (asws) ibn Ali (asws) asked RasoolAllah (saw), "What is the reward for those who perform your Ziarat?"

RasoolAllah (saw) replied:

"O' My Son (asws)! On the Day of Judgment, it will be My duty to visit those who performed My Ziarat either during My life or after I have departed this world as well as those who have performed the Ziarat of Your Father (asws) and those who performed the Ziarat of Your Brother (asws) and those who have performed Your Ziarat, and to save them from their sins."

HADITH 3

RasoolAllah (saw) said to Ameerul Momineen (asws):

"O' Ali (asws)! I guarantee those who perform My Ziarat during My lifetime or after I depart this world and those who perform Your Ziarat both during Your life or after Your martyrdom and those who perform the Ziarat of Your Two Sons (asws) either during Their lives or after Their martyrdom that I will save them from the terrors and difficulties of the Day of Judgment and that I will raise them alongside Me."

HADITH 4

RasoolAllah (saw) said:

"On the day of judgment I will perform the Ziarat of those who performed My Ziarat or the Ziarat of anyone from My Progeny and I will save them from the afflictions of that day."

HADITH 5

Imam Jafar Sadiq (asws) said:

"Hussain (asws) ibn Ali (asws) asked RasoolAllah (saw), "O' Father (saw)! What is the reward for those who perform Your Ziarat?"

RasoolAllah (saw) replied:

"O' My Son (asws)! On the day of judgment, it will be My duty to perform the Ziarat of those who performed My Ziarat either during My life or after My departure from this world and those who performed the Ziarat of Your Father (asws) and those who performed the Ziarat of Your Brother (asws) and those who performed Your Ziarat and to forgive them of their sins."

Chapter 2

The Reward for Performing the Ziarat of RasoolAllah (saw)

HADITH 1

RasoolAllah (saw) said, "On the Day of Judgment I will intercede for those who have performed My Ziarat."

HADITH 2

ibn Abi Najran narrates:

I asked Imam Muhammad Taqi (asws), "May I sacrifice myself for You! What is the reward for those who perform the Ziarat of RasoolAllah (saw)?"

Imam (asws) replied, "Jannah (paradise)."

HADITH 3

ibn Abi Najran narrates:

I asked Abu Jafar (Imam Muhammad Taqi asws) about the reward for those who perform the Ziarat of RasoolAllah (saw) with the niyyat (intention) of simply performing the ziarat (visitation) of RasoolAllah (saw)?"

Imam (asws) replied, "Jannah (paradise)."

HADITH 4

See Hadith 3

HADITH 5

Abu Bakr ibn al Hadrami narrates:

Abu Abdullah Imam Jafar Sadiq (asws) ordered me to perform prayer in the Masjid al Nabwi as much as you are able to because you are not always able to pray there whenever you desire.

Imam (asws) asked me, "Do you perform the ziarat of RasoolAllah (saw)?"

"Yes," I replied.

Imam (asws) replied, "RasoolAllah (saw) hears the voices of those who perform His Ziarat from near and those who perform His Ziarat from afar. "

HADITH 6

Ameer ibn Abdullah narrates:

I said to Abu Abdullah (Imam Jafar Sadiq asws), "I paid two or three extra gold coins to my cameleer to take me through Medina."

Imam (asws) replied, "Now you can visit the tomb of RasoolAllah (saw) and say "salam" to Him." Then the Imam (asws) continued, "RasoolAllah (saw) hears the voices of those who perform His Ziarat regardless if they are nearby or far away."

HADITH 7

See Hadith 3

HADITH 8

See Hadith 7

HADITH 9

Imam Jafar Sadiq (asws) narrates:

RasoolAllah (saw) said, "On the day of Judgment, I will deny those who came to Mecca for Hajj but did not come to Medina for My Ziarat. My intercession is wajib (obligatory) upon those who performed My Ziarat and Jannah is wajib (obligatory) upon those for whom My intercession is wajib. Those who die in one of the two Harams, either in Mecca or Medina, will not have to face Hasab (accountability) on the Day of Judgment. They will be counted as those who died while traveling towards Allah and will be resurrected with the companions of the Battle of Badr on the Day of Judgment."

HADITH 10

Abu Abdullah Imam Jafar Sadiq (asws) narrates:

RasoolAllah (saw) said, "On the Day of Judgment, I will intercede for those who have performed My Ziarat."

HADITH 11

RasoolAllah (saw) said:

"Those who perform My Ziarat during My life or after I leave this world will be My neighbors on the Day of Judgment."

HADITH 12

Ali (asws) ibn Abi Talib (as) narrates:

RasoolAllah (saw) said, "Those who perform My Ziarat after My departure from this world are the same as those who visited Me during My lifetime and I will be their witness and intercede for them on the Day of Judgment."

HADITH 13

See hadith 10

HADITH 14

RasoolAllah (saw) said:

"On the day of judgment, I shall intercede for those who came to Medina to perform My Ziarat seeking the pleasure of Allah".

HADITH 15

ibn Abi Najran narrates:

I asked Masoom Imam (asws), "What is the reward for those who perform the Ziarat of RasoolAllah (saw) with the niyyat (intention) of simply performing Ziarat?"

Imam (asws) replied, "Allah will take them to Jannah (paradise)."

HADITH 16

Abu Abdullah Imam Jafar Sadiq (asws) narrates:

RasoolAllah (saw) said:

"On the day of judgment, My shifaat (intercession) shall be for those who have performed My Ziarat."

HADITH 17

Abul Hasan Musa ibn Ismael ibn Musa ibn Jafar who narrated from his father who narrated from his grandfather (Imam Musa Kazim asws) who narrated from His Father Jafar (asws) ibn Muhammad (asws) who narrated from His Father (Imam Muhammad Baqir asws) who narrated from Ali (asws) ibn Hussain (asws) (Imam Zainul Abideen asws) who said:

RasoolAllah (saw) said:

"Those who perform the Ziarat of My grave after I have left this world are like those who had—during My lifetime—immigrated to live near to Me. However if you are unable to perform My Ziarat, then send your Salam to Me and it will reach Me."

HADITH 18

Abu Abdullah Imam Jafar Sadiq (asws) said:

Imam Hussain (asws) ibn Ali (asws) asked RasoolAllah (saw), "O' Father (saw)! What is the reward for those who perform Your Ziarat?"

RasoolAllah (saw) replied, "O' My Son (asws)! On the day of judgment it will be My duty to perform the ziarat of those who performed My Ziarat either during My life or after I leave this world and to protect from the punishment of their sins."

HADITH 19

Abu Jafar (Imam Muhammad Baqir asws) said:

"The reward for performing the Ziarat of the grave of RasoolAllah (saw) is equal to performing a Hajj with RasoolAllah (saw)."

HADITH 20

Zaid al Shahham narrates:

I asked Abu Abdullah (Imam Jafar Sadiq asws), "What is the reward for those who perform the Ziarat of the grave of RasoolAllah (saw)?"

Imam (asws) replied, "They are like those who perform the Ziarat of Allah on His Arsh (throne)."

Chapter 3

Ziarat of RasoolAllah (saw) and Duas to be Recited Near His Grave

HADITH 1

Abu Abdullah Imam Jafar Sadiq (asws) said:

"Perform ghusl before going to or entering in Medina. Then proceed to the grave of RasoolAllah (saw) and say salam to Him. Then proceed to the pillar that is on the right side by the head of the grave. Stand there with your left shoulder towards the grave, your right shoulder towards the pulpit of the Prophet (saw), and face qiblah. This is the spot nearest to the head of RasoolAllah (saw). "

Then recite:

أَشْهَدُ أَنْ لاَ إِلَهَ إِلاَّ اللَّهُ وَحْدَهُ لاَ شَرِيكَ لَهُ

I testify that there is no god save Allah; He is One; there is no partner with Him.

وَ أَشْهَدُ أَنَّكَ رَسُولُهُ وَ أَنَّكَ مُحَمَّدُ بْنُ عَبْدِ اللَّهِ وَ أَشْهَدُ أَنَّكَ قَدْ بَلَّغْتَ رِسَالاَتِ رَبِّكَ وَ نَصَحْتَ لِأُمَّتِكَ

I testify that You are His Messenger, and You are Muhammad (saw) son of Abdullah; and I testify that You had delivered the Message of Your Lord, advised and warned Your Ummah like a sincere friend,

وَ جَاهَدْتَ فِي سَبِيلِ اللَّهِ بِالْحِكْمَةِ وَ الْمَوْعِظَةِ الْحَسَنَةِ وَ أَدَّيْتَ الَّذِي عَلَيْكَ مِنَ الْحَقِّ

and strived, leaving no stone unturned, against heavy odds, in the way of Allah, with wisdom, and good advice. Strong and powerful support was put at Your disposal from al Haq (Allah),

وَ أَنَّكَ قَدْ رَؤُفْتَ بِالْمُؤْمِنِينَ وَ غَلُظْتَ عَلَى الْكَافِرِينَ وَ عَبَدْتَ اللَّهَ مُخْلِصاً حَتَّى أَتَاكَ الْيَقِينُ

and You were kind and compassionate to the momineen (believers), but were harsh with the kafireen (disbelievers), and had sincerely served Allah, until what was certain came to You.

فَبَلَغَ اللَّهُ بِكَ أَشْرَفَ مَحَلِّ الْمُكَرَّمِينَ

Therefore, Allah made You reach the highest stage of glory and honor.

الْحَمْدُ لِلَّهِ الَّذِي اسْتَنْقَذَنَا بِكَ مِنَ الشِّرْكِ وَ الضَّلَالِ

All praise is for Allah alone who saved us through You from the shirk and deviation

اللَّهُمَّ صَلِّ عَلَى مُحَمَّدٍ وَ آلِهِ وَ اجْعَلْ صَلَوَاتِكَ وَ صَلَوَاتِ مَلَائِكَتِكَ وَ أَنْبِيَائِكَ وَ الْمُرْسَلِينَ

O Allah! Send blessings on Muhammad (saw) and on the Progeny of Muhammad (asws). Your blessings, and the blessings of Your Angels, and of Your Prophets and Messengers,

وَ عِبَادِكَ الصَّالِحِينَ وَ أَهْلِ السَّمَاوَاتِ وَ الْأَرَضِينَ

And of Your pious servants, and of the people of the heavens and the earths,

وَ مَنْ سَبَّحَ لَكَ يَا رَبَّ الْعَالَمِينَ مِنَ الْأَوَّلِينَ وَ الْآخِرِينَ عَلَى مُحَمَّدٍ عَبْدِكَ وَ رَسُولِكَ

and of those who glorify Thee, O the Lord of the worlds, from times of old and the present times, be upon Muhammad (saw), Your servant and Messenger,

وَ نَبِيِّكَ وَ أَمِينِكَ وَ نَجِيبِكَ وَ حَبِيبِكَ وَ صَفِيِّكَ وَ صِفْوَتِكَ وَ خَاصَّتِكَ وَ خَالِصَتِكَ وَ خِيَرَتِكَ مِنْ خَلْقِكَ

Your Prophet, Your trustee, Your complier, Your beloved, Your chosen, purified by Thee, Your preferred, the best essence from Thee, Your best from amongst the creation,

وَ أَعْطِهِ الْفَضْلَ وَ الْفَضِيلَةَ وَ الْوَسِيلَةَ وَ الدَّرَجَةَ الرَّفِيعَةَ وَ ابْعَثْهُ مَقَاماً مَحْمُوداً يَغْبِطُهُ بِهِ الْأَوَّلُونَ وَ الْآخِرُونَ

and gave him surpassing superiority and eminence in wisdom and character, subtle ways and means, highest stations, and put him on the pedestal of praiseworthy fame and fortune; the men of old and the men of later time were envious of His status.

اللَّهُمَّ إِنَّكَ قُلْتَ وَ لَوْ أَنَّهُمْ إِذْ ظَلَمُوا أَنْفُسَهُمْ جَاءُوكَ فَاسْتَغْفَرُوا اللَّهَ وَ اسْتَغْفَرَ لَهُمُ الرَّسُولُ لَوَجَدُوا اللَّهَ تَوَّاباً رَحِيماً

O Allah! Thou said, *"And if, when they had wronged themselves, they had but come unto you and asked forgiveness of Allah, and asked forgiveness of the Messenger, they would have found Allah Forgiving, Merciful."* (Quran Sura Nisa ayah 64)

إِلَهِي فَقَدْ أَتَيْتُ نَبِيَّكَ مُسْتَغْفِراً تَائِباً مِنْ ذُنُوبِي فَصَلِّ عَلَى مُحَمَّدٍ وَ آلِهِ وَ اغْفِرْهَا لِي

O Allah, therefore I turn repentant to Your Prophet (saw), asking pardon for my sins, send blessings on Muhammad (saw) and on His Progeny (asws) and forgive me.

يَا سَيِّدَنَا أَتَوَجَّهُ بِكَ وَ بِأَهْلِ بَيْتِكَ إِلَى اللَّهِ تَعَالَى رَبِّكَ وَ رَبِّي لِيَغْفِرَ لِي

O my Master, we turn towards the Most praised Allah, our Lord and Your Lord and ask forgiveness through You so that our sins may be forgiven.

Then the Imam (asws) continued:

"Place your back towards the grave and face towards the direction of qiblah, raise your hands and ask for your request. If you do this, then inshaAllah your request will be granted."

HADITH 2

Abu Abdullah Imam Jafar Sadiq (asws) said:

"After you have finished reciting your duas beside the grave of RasoolAllah (saw), go to the Mimbar and place your hands on it. Hold its two bottom pillars. Rub your face and eyes on them for they are a cure for the eyes.

After that, stand near the Mimbar, praise and glorify Allah, and then ask for the fulfillment of your needs.

RasoolAllah (saw) has said:

"There is a garden from the gardens of Jannah between My Mimbar and My grave. The door of My Mimbar is from one of the doors of Jannah (paradise). My Mimbar is placed over an oasis from the Oasis of Jannah and its pillars were built in Jannah".

Imam (asws) then said:

"Then go to Babul Sagheer, the place where RasoolAllah (saw) use to pray and offer as many rakats of prayer as you desire. Send blessings on Muhammad (saw) and His Family whenever you enter or exit Masjid al Nabwi and pray as much as you can while you are in Masjid al Nabwi."

HADITH 3

Ali (asws) ibn Jafar (asws) ibn Muhammad (asws) who narrated from his brother Abul Hasan Musa (asws) ibn Jafar (Imam Kazim asws) who narrated from His Father Imam Sadiq (asws) who said:

Imam Muhammad Baqir (asws) said:

Ali (asws) ibn Hussain (asws) (Imam Zainul Abideen asws) used to stand next to the grave of RasoolAllah (saw). He would say salam to RasoolAllah (saw) and testify that RasoolAllah (saw) had delivered the message of Allah. Then He would perform prayer and afterwards He would touch the green marble that is connected to the grave of RasoolAllah (saw).

With His back towards the grave, He would face the qiblah and recite:

اللهم إليك ألجأت أمري، و إلى قبر محمد عبدك ورسولك أسندت ظهري و القبلةالتي رضيت لمحمد استقبلت

O Allah! I entrust all of My affairs to You. The grave of RasoolAllah (saw) is at My back and I am facing towards that qiblah which You chose for Muhammad (saw)

اللهم إني أصبحت لا أملك لنفسي خير ما أرجو لها ولا أنقع عنها شر ما أحذر عليها وأصبحت الامور بيدك ولا فقير أفقر مني إني لما أنزلت إلي من خير فقير

O Allah! I do not have the ability to obtain the good that I desire for myself nor do I have the ability to avert the harm I fear. O Allah! I am aware that everything is in Your Hand and that there is no one needier than I am. I am in need of that good which You have decreed for Me.

اللهم أردني منك بخير فلاراد لفضلك

O Allah! I ask You to bestow upon Me that which is good because no one can keep away Your grace

اللهم إني أعوذ بك من أن تبدل اسمي أو أن تغير جسمي أو تزيل نعمتك عني

O Allah! I seek refuge with You from replacing My name, from changing my body or from removing Your blessings upon me

اللهم زيني بالتقوى وجملني بالنعم و امرني بالعافيةوارزقني شكر العافية

O Allah! Bestow upon me piety and glorify me with Your blessings. Grant me a long, healthy life and provide me with my rizq (sustenance).

HADITH 4

Muhammad ibn Masood narrates:

I saw Abu Abdullah Imam Jafar Sadiq (asws) going to the grave of RasoolAllah (saw). Upon arriving at the grave, He would place His hands upon it and recite:

أسأل الله الذي اجتباك واختارك وهداك وهدي بك أن يصلي عليك

I ask Allah who chose You, guided You and guided the creation through You to send His blessings upon You

Then He would recite:

إِنَّ اللَّهَ وَمَلَائِكَتَهُ يُصَلُّونَ عَلَى النَّبِيِّ يَا أَيُّهَا الَّذِينَ آمَنُوا صَلُّوا عَلَيْهِ وَسَلِّمُوا تَسْلِيمًا

Surely Allah and His angels bless the Prophet; O you who believe! ask for Divine blessings on him and greet him with a worthy greeting. (Quran 33:56)

HADITH 5

Ibrahim ibn Abul Bilad narrates:

Abul Hasan (Imam Musa Kazim asws) asked me, "What do you say when you recite tasleem of RasoolAllah (saw)?"

I replied, "I say that which is known and commonly recited."

Imam (asws) asked, "Would you like for Me to teach you that which is better than which you recite?"

I replied, "Yes. May I be sacrificed for You."

As I sat there, Imam (asws) wrote the following by His own hand and then He read it to me:

"Recite the following whilst standing near the grave of RasoolAllah (saw):

أشهد أن لا إله الله وحده لا شريك له وأشهد أن محمداً عبده ورسوله

I testify that there is no god except Allah who is One and has no partners and I bear witness that Muhammad is His servant and messenger

وأشهد أنك محمد بن عبدالله و أشهد أنك خاتم النبيين وأشهد أنك قد بلغت رسالات ربك ونصحت لامتك

I testify that You are His Messenger, and You are Muhammad (saw) son of Abdullah; and I testify that You had delivered the Message of Your Lord, advised and warned Your Ummah like a sincere friend,

وجاهدت في سبيل ربك وعبدته حتى أتاك اليقين وأديت الذي عليك من الحق

and strived, leaving no stone unturned, against heavy odds, in the way of Allah, with wisdom, and good advice. Strong and powerful support was put at Your disposal from al Haq (Allah),

اللهم صل على محمد ﷺ عبدك ورسولك ونجيك وأمينك وصفيك وخيرتك من خلقك أفضل ما صليك على أحد من أنبيائكورسلك

O Allah! Send Your Blessings on Muhammad (saw), Your servant, Your messenger, Your confidant and Your trustee, Your chosen one, and the best from amongst Your creation, blessings greater than You sent on any of Your prophets or messengers

اللهم سلم على محمد ﷺ و آل محمدّ كما سلمت على نوح العالمين، و امنن على محمد وآل محمد كما مننت على موسى و هارون، وبارك على محمد ﷺ وآل محمدّ كما باركت على إبراهيموآل إبراهيم إنك حميد مجيد

O Allah! Send Your salam on Muhammad (saw) and on the Family of Muhammad (asws) just as You sent Your salam on Nuh from *"amongst the people"* (Quran 37:79) and bestow Your grace upon Muhammad (saw) and the Family of Muhammad (asws) the way You bestowed Your grace upon *"Musa and Haroon"* (Quran 37:114) and bless Muhammad (saw) and the Family of Muhammad (asws) the way You blessed Ibrahim (as) and the Family of Ibrahim (as). You are the Praised and the Glorified

اللهم صل على محمد ﷺ وآل محمدّ وترحم على محمد ﷺ وآل محمدّ

O Allah! Send blessings upon Muhammad (saw) and the Family of Muhammad (asws) and send mercy on Muhammad (saw) and the Family of Muhammad (asws)

اللهم رب البيت الحرام ورب المسجد الحرام، ورب الركن والمقام، ورب البلد الحرام، ورب الحل والحرام، ورب المشعر الحرام، بلغ روح نبيك محمد مني السلام

O Allah! O Lord of Sacred House! O Lord of Masjid al Haram! O Lord of Rukn and Maqam! O Lord of the Sacred City! O Lord of Halal and Haram (lawful and unlawful)! O Lord of Mashir al Haram! Send salams from me upon the ruh (soul) of Muhammad (saw)

HADITH 6

Ahmad ibn Muhammad ibn Abi Najran narrates:

I asked Abul Hasan (Imam Reza asws), "How should I say salam to RasoolAllah (saw) by His grave?"

Imam (asws) replied:

السلام على رسول الله ﷺ ،

Salam be upon RasoolAllah (saw)

السلام عليك يا حبيب الله

Salam be upon You, O Habeebullah (Beloved of Allah)

السلام عليك يا صفوة الله و السلام عليك يا أمين الله

Salam be upon You, O Chosen one of Allah and salam be upon You O Trustee of Allah

أشهد أنك قد نصحت لامتك وجاهدت في سبيل الله، وعبدته مخلصا حتى أتاك اليقين

I testify that You advised and warned Your Ummah and strived, leaving no stone unturned, against heavy odds, in the way of Allah and that You worshipped Allah with absolute certainty

فجزاك الله أفضل ما جزى نبيا عن امته

May Allah grant You a reward that is greater than any reward given to any other prophet for guiding his nation

اللهم صل على محمد ﷺ وآل محمدّ أفضل ما صليت على إبراهيم و آل إبراهيم إنك حميد مجيد

O Allah! Send blessings on Muhammad (saw) and the Family of Muhammad (asws), blessings that are greater than the blessings You sent upon Ibrahim (as) and the Family of Ibrahim (as). For You are the Praised and the Glorified

HADITH 7

Ali ibn Hasan narrated from a companion who said:

I saw Abul Hasan the First (Imam Musa Kazim asws), Haroon the caliph, Isa ibn Jafar, and Jafar ibn Yahya in Medina. All were next to the grave of RasoolAllah (saw). Haroon said to Imam Musa Kazim (asws), "Say salam to RasoolAllah (saw)."

Imam (asws) refused so Haroon went and said salam to RasoolAllah (saw). Then he stood off to the side.

Then Isa ibn Jafar asked Imam (asws) to go and say salam to RasoolAllah (saw). Imam (asws) again refused so Isa ibn Jafar went forward, said salam to RasoolAllah (saw) and then stood off to the side.

Then Jafar ibn Yahya asked Imam (asws) to go and say salam to RasoolAllah (saw). Again, Imam (asws) refused so Jafar ibn Yahya went forward, said salam to RasoolAllah (saw), and then stood off to the side where Haroon was stood.

Then Imam (asws) came forward and said:

السلام عليك يا أبة أسأل الله الذي اصطفاك واجتباك وهداك وهدى بك أن يصلي عليك

"Salam be upon You, O My Father (saw)! I ask Allah who selected and chose You, who guided You, and guided the creation through You to send His blessings upon You"

Haroon turned to Isa ibn Jafar and said, "Did you hear what he said?"

Isa ibn Jafar replied, "Yes".

Haroon said, "I testify that RasoolAllah (saw) truly is His Father."

HADITH 8

See hadith 3

HADITH 9

Ali ibn Hussain narrated from Ali ibn Ibrahim ibn Hashim who narrated from Muhammad ibn Isa ibn Ubaid who narrated from Abu Abdullah Zakariya al Mumin who narrated from Ibrahim ibn Najiyah who narrated from Ishaq ibn Ammar who said:

I said to Abu Abdullah Imam Jafar Sadiq (asws), "Teach me a short salam that I can say to RasoolAllah (saw)."

Imam (asws) replied, "Recite:

أسأل الله الذي انتجبك واصطفاك واختارك وهداك و هدى بك أن يصلي عليك صلاة كثيرة طيبة

I ask Allah—who selected and choose You, who guided You, and guided the creation through You—to continuously increase His blessings upon You

HADITH 10

Sa'ad ibn Abdullah narrated from Ahmad ibn Muhammad ibn Isa, Yaqoob ibn Yazid and Musa ibn Umar who narrated from Ahmad ibn Muhammad ibn Abu Nasir who said:

I asked Abul Hasan (Imam Reza asws), "How should I say salam when I am beside the grave of RasoolAllah (saw)?"

Imam (asws) replied, "Recite the following;"

السلام على رسول الله ﷺ

Salam be upon RasoolAllah (saw)

السلام عليك ورحمة الله وبركاته

Salam be upon You and the blessings and mercy of Allah

السلام عليك يا رسول الله ﷺ

Salam be upon You O RasoolAllah (saw)

السلام عليك يا محمد ﷺ بن عبدالله

Salam be upon You O Muhammad (saw) son of Abdullah

السلام عليك يا خيرة الله

Salam be upon You O the Best of the Creation of Allah

السلام عليك يا حبيب الله

Salam be upon You O the Beloved of Allah

السلام عليك يا صفوة الله

Salam be upon You O the Chosen of Allah

السلام عليك يا أمين الله

Salam be upon You O Trustee of Allah

أشهد أنك رسول الله وأشهد أنك محمد بن عبدالله وأشهد أنك قد نصحت لامتك وجاهدت في سبيل ربك و عبدته حتى أتاك اليقين

I testify You are the Messenger of Allah and I testify that You are Muhammad (saw) son of Abdullah and I testify that You advised Your nation and strived in the way of Your Lord and You worshipped Him with absolute certainty

فجزاك الله أفضل ما جزى نبيا عن امته

May Allah reward You with such reward that is greater than any reward bestowed upon a prophet for guiding his nation

اللهم صل على محمد ﷺ وآل محمدّ أفضل ما صليت على إبراهيم وآل إبراهيم انك حميد مجيد

O Allah! Send blessings upon Muhammad (saw) and the Family of Muhammad (asws), blessings greater than that which You sent upon Ibrahim (as) and the Family of Ibrahim (as). You are the Praised and the Glorified

Chapter 4

Rewards for performing prayers in Masjid al Nabwi

HADITH 1

Ammar ibn Musa al Sabati narrates:

I asked Abu Abdullah Imam Jafar Sadiq (asws), "Is praying in Masjid al Nabwi the same as praying anywhere else in Medina?"

Imam (asws) replied, "No. One prayer in Masjid al Nabwi is equal to one thousand prayers prayed elsewhere. Praying anywhere else in Medina is the same as praying in any other city."

HADITH 2

Murazim narrates:

I asked Abu Abdullah Imam Jafar Sadiq (asws) about praying in Masjid al Nabwi.

Imam (asws) replied, "RasoolAllah (saw) said, "One prayer in My masjid is equal to one thousand prayers elsewhere and one prayer in Masjid al Haram is equal to one thousand prayers in My masjid."

Imam (asws) then said, "Allah has preferred Mecca over other cities and He has preferred certain areas within Mecca over others made clear through His saying, *"Appoint for yourselves a place of prayer on the standing-place of Ibrahim"* (Quran 2:125) Allah has also preferred certain people over others. In His Book He has ordered the people to follow those He has preferred and to love Them (Quran 42:23)."

HADITH 3

Abu Abdullah Imam Jafar Sadiq (asws) said:

"One salat in Masjid al Nabwi is equal to ten thousand salat performed anywhere else."

HADITH 4

Abu Abdullah Imam Jafar Sadiq (asws) said to ibn Abi Yafoor:

"Pray as often as you can in Masjid al Nabwi for RasoolAllah (saw) said, "One prayer in My masjid is equal to one thousand prayers in another masjid except Masjid al Haram. One prayer in Masjid al Haram is equal to one thousand prayers in My masjid."

HADITH 5

Abu Abdullah Imam Jafar Sadiq (asws) narrates:

RasoolAllah (saw) said, "One prayer in My masjid is equal to one thousand prayers elsewhere."

HADITH 6

See hadith 1

HADITH 7

See hadith 5

HADITH 8

See hadith 5

Chapter 5

Ziarat of Hamzah (as) and the other Martyrs of Uhud

HADITH 1

Masoom Imam (asws) narrates:

The following should be recited next to the grave of Hamzah (as):

السلام عليك يا عم رسول الله ﷺ و خير الشهداء

Salam be upon You O Uncle of RasoolAllah (saw) and best of the martyrs

السلام عليك يا أسدالله وأسد رسوله ﷺ

Salam be upon You O Lion of Allah and Lion of His Messenger

أشهد أنك قد جاهدت في حق جهاده ونصحت لله ولرسوله ﷺ وجدت بنفسك وطلبت ما عند الله ورغبت فيما وعد الله

I testify that you strived truthfully in the way of Allah, you faithfully served Allah and His Messenger, and willingly sacrificed yourself in the way of Allah. You sought after only that which lead to Allah and desired only that which He had promised

After you have completed reciting, enter and perform prayer, but do not face the grave while you are praying. After you have completed your prayers, cling to the grave and recite the following:

اللهم صل على محمد و على أهل بيتة

O Allah! Send Your blessings upon Muhammad (saw) and His Ahlul Bayt (asws)

اللهم إني تعرضت لرحمتك بلزوقي بقبر عم بنيك صلواتك عليه و على أهل بيته التجيرني من نقمتك وسخطك ومقتك و من الأزلال في يوم تكثر فيه الأصوات والمعرات وتشتغل كل نفس بما قدمت وتجادل كل نفس عن نفسها فان ترحمني اليوم فلا خوف علي ولا حزن وان تعاقب فمولاي له القدرة على عبده

O Allah! I throw myself upon Your mercy by clinging to the grave of the Uncle of Your Prophet, may Your blessings be upon Him (saw) and His Ahlul Bayt (asws), so that I may find protection against Your wrath, vengeance, and abhorrence, and to keep me from slipping on that day when there will be much clamor and humiliation when every soul will be busy defending that which it has brought forward for itself. If today I am included in Your mercy, then I shall not have any fear or any grief, but if I am included in Your wrath, it is because You are My Master who has power over His slave.

اللهم فلا تخيبني اليوم ولاتصرفني بغير حاجتي فقدلزقت بقبر عم نبيك وتقربت به اليك ابتغآء مرضاتك ورجاء رحمتك فتقبل مني وعد بحلمك على جهلي وبرأفتك على جناية نفسي فقد عظم جرمي وما أخاف أن تظلمني و لكن أخاف سوء الحساب

O Allah! Do not disappoint me on this day and do not allow me to leave without fulfilling my needs for I am clinging to the grave of the Uncle of Your Prophet (saw). I have come seeking to gain the nearness of Allah and His pleasure and mercy. Please accept this deed from me and turn towards my ignorance with Your patience and with Your kindness to the crimes that I committed against myself. For my sins are great. I have no fear that You will oppress me. I only fear the Hasab (accountability).

فانظر اليوم إلي تقلبي على قبر عم نبيك صلواتك على محمد و أهل بيته فيهم فكني ولا تخيب سعي و لا يهون عليك ابتهالي ولا تحبب منك صوتي ولا تقلبني بغير حوائجي

Therefore take into consideration my restless movement on the grave of the uncle of Your Prophet, may Your blessings be upon Him and His Ahlul Bayt (asws) and release me from hell through them. Do not make my efforts futile do not disgrace my supplication, do not prevent my voice from reaching You and do not send me back without fulfilling my needs

يا غياث كل مكروب ومحزون

O savior of all those who are distressed and anguished

و يا مفرج عن الملهوف الحيران الغريب المشرف على الهلكة

O the comforter of the heartbroken, perplexed, and the stranger who is on the verge of perishing

صل على محمد و أهل بيته الطاهرين، وانظر إلي نظرة لا أشقى بعدها أبداً

Send blessings on Muhammad (saw) and His Pure and Pious Ahlul Bayt (asws) and look upon me in such a way that afterwards I shall never be afflicted

وارحم تضرعي وغربتي وانفرادي فقد رجوت رضاك وتحريت الخير الذي لا يعطيه أحد سواك ولا ترد أملي

Have mercy upon me through my supplication and my loneliness for I have hoped to gain Your pleasure. I seek that good which can only be given by You. Do not disappoint me

HADITH 2

Uqbah ibn Khalid al Asadi narrates:

I asked Abu Abdullah Imam Jafar Sadiq (asws), "Which masjid should I visit first when I go to visit the masjids in Medina?"

Imam (asws) replied, "Begin with Quba. Pray as much as you can within it for it is the first masjid RasoolAllah (saw) prayed in. Then proceed to the well of Umm Ibrahim (sa) for that is where RasoolAllah (saw) use to live and pray. Afterwards go to Masjid al Fazeekh and pray two rakats of prayer there for RasoolAllah (saw) has prayed there.

When you have finished visiting the masjids in this area of the city, then proceed to the area of Uhud. Begin with the masjid that is below Harrah and perform prayers there. Then go to the grave of Hamza (as), the son of Abdul Muttalib (as) and say salam to him. Then to the graves of the other martyrs of the Battle of Uhud. While standing at their graves, recite the following:

السلام عليكم يا أهل الديار، أنتم لنا فرط وإنا بكم لاحقون

Salam be upon you O inhabitants of the graves. You have gone before us and soon we shall join you

Afterwards, go to the masjid that is on the right side of the mountain of Uhud and pray there because RasoolAllah (saw) this is the place where RasoolAllah (saw) waited until the time of prayer and then prayed in before going forward in the Battle of Uhud to fight the mushriks (polytheists).

Then return to the graves of the martyrs of the Battle of Uhud and pray next to their graves as many times as Allah compels your heart to so do. Then go to Masjid al Ahzab and perform prayers there because on the day of the Battle of Ahzab RasoolAllah (saw) prayed in that masjid and said:

يا صريخ المكروبين

O helper of the distressed

و يا مجيب دعوة المضطرين

O answerer of the prayers of the despondent

ويا غياث الملهوفين اكشف همي وكربي وغمي فقد ترى حالي وحال أصحابي

O savior of the sorrowful! Relieve me of my sorrows, sufferings, and grief for You; see the state of my affairs and those of my companions

Chapter 6

Performing the Ziarat of the areas
around Medina and its rewards

HADITH 1

Abu Abdullah Imam Jafar Sadiq (asws) said:

"Do not be negligent in visiting the areas around Medina or Masjid of Quba for it is the *"masjid founded on piety from the very first day"* (Quran 9:108). Also, do not be negligent in visiting the well of Um Ibrahim (sa), Masjid al Fazeekh, the graves of the martyrs and the Masjid of Ahzab, which is the Masjid of Fath.

Whenever RasoolAllah (saw) would visit the graves of the martyrs of the Battle of Uhud He would say:

السلام عليكم بما صبرتم فنعم عقبى الدار

Peace be upon you because you patiently persevered, how excellent then, is the issue of the abode.

Then Imam (asws) continued and said:

"Recite the following supplication in the Masjid of Fath along with the common supplications that are recited there:

يا صريخ المكروبين

O helper of the distressed

ويا مجيب دعوة المضطرين

O answerer of the prayers of the despondent

اكشف عني غمي وكربي و همي كما كشفت عن نبيك همه و غمه وكربه و كفيته هول عدوه في هذا المكان

Remove from me my grief, sufferings, and sorrows just as You removed the grief, sufferings, and sorrows of Your Prophet (saw). You were sufficient for Him against the calamities of His enemies in this place.

HADITH 2

Abu Abdullah Imam Jafar Sadiq (asws) narrates:

RasoolAllah (saw) said:

"Those who come to My masjid, the Masjid of Quba, and pray two rakats in it, will receive the reward of those who performed Umrah".

HADITH 3

Abu Abdullah Imam Jafar Sadiq (asws) said to ibn Abu Yafoor:

"Do not be negligent in visiting the areas around Medina or the Masjid of Quba for it is *the "masjid founded on piety from the very first day"* (Quran 9:108). Also do not be negligent in visiting the well of Umm Ibrahim (ra), the Masjid of Fazeekh, the graves of the martyrs or the Masjid of Ahzab which is also known as the Masjid of Fath."

HADITH 4

It is narrated one of the Masoom Imams (asws) said:

"If you are staying in Medina for three days, then pray your prayers in full. Do the same if you are staying in Mecca.

If you are staying in Medina for three days, then fast three days, starting on a Wednesday. Pray on Tuesday night next to the Pillar of Repentance in Masjid al Nabwi, which is where Abu Lubabah tied himself until his forgiveness was revealed from the heavens.

Then on Wednesday, perform fast and stay seated next to the same Pillar. At night, come near to the grave of RasoolAllah (saw), spend the entire night and next day there.

Perform fast on Thursday day. On Thursday night, come near to the Pillar next to the grave of RasoolAllah (saw) and perform prayers there throughout Thursday night and Friday day. You should also perform fast on Friday.

Do not speak during these three days except for that which is absolutely necessary. Do not leave the Masjid except for that which is also absolutely necessary. Try to sleep at night or during the day as little as you can; for this will increase the goodness of your actions.

Then on Friday, praise and glorify Allah, send blessings on RasoolAllah (saw) and ask for the fulfillment of your needs.

Recite the following along with your other supplications:

اللهم ما كانت لي إليك من حاجة سارعت أنا في طلبها والتماسها أو حاجة لم اسرع سالتكها أو لم أسالكها
فإني أتوجه إليك بنبيك محمد نبي الرحمة في قضاء حوائجي صغيرها وكبيرها

O Allah! I come to You through Your Prophet, Muhammad (saw), the Prophet of Mercy, seeking fulfillment of all of my needs, from the smallest to the greatest, the ones which I made haste in my and the ones which I did not make haste in asking for and the ones I did not even ask to be fulfilled."

HADITH 5

Uqbah ibn Khalid narrates:

I asked Abu Abdullah Imam Jafar Sadiq (asws), "Which masjid should I visit when I go visit the masjids around Medina?"

Imam (asws) replied, "Start with the Masjid of Quba. Pray as many prayers as you can in it for it is the first masjid in this area that RasoolAllah (saw) prayed in.

Then go to the well of Umm Ibrahim (ra) and pray there for that is where RasoolAllah (saw) use to live and pray.

Afterwards go to the Masjid of Fazeekh and pray two rakats there for RasoolAllah (saw) has prayed there. When you have finished visiting the masjids in this area, head to the side of Uhud. Begin with the masjid that below Harrah and pray there.

Then go to the grave of Hamza (as), the son of Abdul Muttalib (as).

Then visit the graves of the rest of the martyrs of the Battle of Uhud and recite the following:

السلام عليكم يا أهل الديار أنتم لنا فرط وإنا بكم لاحقون

Salam be upon you O people of the graves! You have gone ahead of us and soon we shall join you

Then go to the masjid that is on the right side of the mountain of Uhud and perform prayers there for that is where RasoolAllah (saw) waited until the time of prayers and then prayed before proceeding in the Battle of Uhud to fight against the mushriks (polytheists).

Then return to the graves of the martyrs of Uhud and pray as much as Allah compels your heart to. Afterwards go to the Masjid of Ahzab and perform prayer there for RasoolAllah (saw) prayed in that masjid on the day of the Battle of Ahzab and said:

يا صريخ المكروبين

O helper of the distressed

و يا مجيب دعوة المضطرين

O answerer of the prayers of the despondent

ويا غياث الملهوفين اكشف همي وكربي وغمي فقد ترى حالي وحال أصحابي

O savior of the sorrowful! Relieve me of my sorrows, sufferings, and grief for You; see the state of my affairs and those of my companions

Chapter 7

Bidding Farewell after performing Ziarat of RasoolAllah (saw)

HADITH 1

Abu Abdullah Imam Jafar Sadiq (asws) said:

"When you are ready to depart from Medina, perform ghusl. After you have asked for the fulfillment of your needs, go to the grave of RasoolAllah (saw) and bid farewell to Him in the same manner as when you entered.

Then say:

اللهم لا تجعله آخر العهد من زيارتي قبر نبيك،

O Allah! Please do not make this Ziarat my last Ziarat of the grave of Your Prophet (saw)

فإن توفيتني قبل ذلك فإني أشهد في مماتي على ما أشهد عليه في حياتي أن لا إله إلا أنت و أن محمداً ﷺ عبدك و رسولك

If you take me from this world before I am able to perform Ziarat again, then I testify after my death to that which I testified during my life, "There is no god except Allah and Muhammad (saw) is Your servant and messenger"

HADITH 2

Yunus ibn Yaqoob narrates:

I asked Abu Abdullah Imam Jafar Sadiq (asws) about the proper way to bid farewell at the grave of RasoolAllah (saw).

Imam (asws) said to recite the following:

صلى الله عليك السلام عليك لا جعله الله آخر تسليمي عليك

May the blessings of Allah be upon You. Salam be upon You. May Allah not make this the last time I say salam to you

HADITH 3

Hasan ibn Ali ibn Fadhal narrates:

I saw Abul Hasan (Imam Reza asws) bidding farewell to RasoolAllah (saw) when He was going for Umrah.

It was after sunset when He approached the grave of RasoolAllah (saw) from the head. He said salam to RasoolAllah (saw) and clung to the grave. Then He went to the Mimbar of RasoolAllah (saw).

After He returned to the grave and performed prayer. He was so close to the grave that His left shoulder touched the part of the grave next to a pillar, which is on the opposite side of the pillar that is by the head of RasoolAllah (saw).

While wearing His sandals, He performed 6 or 8 rakats of prayer there. The length of His rukoo and sajood were the same as reciting tasbihat 3 or more times. After He completed His prayers, He performed sajda for such a long time the sand under Him became moistened.

Some of our companions added that He was also seen placing His cheek on the ground of the Masjid.

Chapter 8

Reward for performing prayers in the
Masjids of Kufa and Sahlah

HADITH 1

Abu Hamza Thumali narrates:

Ali (asws) ibn Hussain (asws) (Imam Zainul Abideen asws) left Medina with the niyyat (intention) of visiting the Masjid of Kufa. He prayed two rakats of prayer before departing. Then He mounted His camel and departed.

HADITH 2

Abu Abdullah Imam Jafar Sadiq (asws) said:

"Giving one dirham as sadqah in Kufa is equal to giving two hundred dirhams as sadqah elsewhere and praying two rakats of prayer in Kufa is equal to praying one hundred rakats elsewhere."

HADITH 3

Abu Jafar Imam Muhammad Baqir (asws) said:

"If people knew the merits of the Masjid of Kufa, then they would travel even from far distances to it. Praying a wajib (obligatory) prayer in the Masjid of Kufa is equal to performing Hajj and praying a mustahab (recommended) prayer in it is the same as performing Umrah."

HADITH 4

Abu Jafar Imam Muhammad Baqir (asws) said:

"Praying a wajib (obligatory) prayer in the Masjid of Kufa is like performing an accepted Hajj and praying a mustahab (recommended) prayer in the Masjid of Kufa is like performing an accepted Umrah."

HADITH 5

Ali (asws) said:

"Praying a mustahab (recommended) prayer in this Masjid (al Kufa) is equal to performing an Umrah with RasoolAllah (saw) and praying a wajib (obligatory) prayer in it is equal to performing a Hajj with RasoolAllah (saw). 1000 prophets and 1000 successors have prayed in this masjid."

HADITH 6

Haroon ibn Kharijah narrates:

Abu Abdullah Imam Jafar Sadiq (asws) asked me, "Do you pray all of your prayers in the Masjid al Kufa?"

I replied, "No."

Imam (asws) said, "I would not miss performing any prayers in it if I lived close to it. Do you know the merits of Masjid al Kufa?"

I replied, "No."

Imam (asws) said, "Every devoted servant and every prophet has prayed in Masjid al Kufa. On the night of Miraj, Jibrael (as) asked RasoolAllah (saw), "O Muhammad (saw)! Do You know where You are right now?"

RasoolAllah (saw) replied, "No."

Jibrael (as) said, "You are in front of Masjid al Kufa."

RasoolAllah (saw) said, "Ask Your Lord for permission so that I may descend and pray in it."

Jibrael (as) asked for permission and it was granted.

Then RasoolAllah (saw) descended and prayed two rakats of prayer in Masjid al Kufa."

The Imam (asws) continued and said:

"Performing one wajib (obligatory) prayer in Masjid al Kufa is the same as praying 1000 prayers anywhere else and performing one mustahab (recommended) prayer in Masjid al Kufa is the same as praying 500 prayers anywhere else. The front side of Masjid al Kufa is a garden from the gardens of Paradise and on its right side is a garden from the gardens of Paradise and at its back is a garden from the gardens of Paradise. Just sitting in Masjid al Kufa even without praying or praising Allah is considered as a worship of Him. If people knew of its merits, then they would surely come to it even if they had to crawl."

HADITH 7

Khalid al Qalanisi narrates:

I heard Abu Abdullah Imam Jafar Sadiq (asws) say:

"Praying one prayer in Masjid al Kufa is like praying 1000 prayers someplace else. "

HADITH 8

Abu Abdullah Imam Jafar Sadiq (asws) said:

"Mecca is the sanctuary of Allah, the sanctuary of His Messenger (saw), and the sanctuary of Ali (asws). Praying one prayer in its masjids is the same as praying 10,000 prayers in another city and giving one dirham as sadqah in Medina is like giving 10,000 dirhams in another city.

Kufa is the sanctuary of Allah, the sanctuary of His Messenger (saw), and the sanctuary of Ameerul Momineen Ali (asws). Praying one prayer in its masjid is the same as praying 1000 prayers in another masjid."

HADITH 9

Imam Jafar Sadiq (asws) said:

"The edge of the Masjid of Sahlah extends to Rawha."

HADITH 10

AbdulRahman ibn Kuthair narrates:

I heard Abu Abdullah Imam Jafar Sadiq (asws) ask Abu Hamza al Thumali, "O Abu Hamza! Did you see my uncle on the night of his uprising?"

Abu Hamza replied, "Yes."

Imam (asws) asked, "Did he pray in the Masjid of Suhail?"

Abu Hamza replied, "Where is the Masjid of Suhail? Are You referring to the Masjid al Sahlah?"

Imam (asws) replied, "Yes. If he had prayed two rakats there and then sought refuge with Allah, then he would have found protection with Allah for one year."

Abu Hamza asked, "May my mother and father be sacrificed upon You! Are these truly the attributes of the masjid which is known as the Masjid of Sahlah?"

Imam (asws) replied, "Yes."

Then Imam (asws) continued and said,

"The Masjid of Sahlah contains the house of Ibrahim (as) where he rose against the giants. It contains the house of Idrees where he use to sew. It contains the place where the rider ties his camel (Prophet Khizr as). It contains a green rock that has all of the images of the prophets within it and the clay under this rock is the clay from which Allah created all of the prophets. The Miraj (ascension of the Prophet saw) occurred in a part of this masjid known as Farooq e Azm.

Masjid al Sahlah is part of Kufa and the people must pass through it. The trumpet will be blown from it and the people will be called towards it. 70,000 people will be resurrected from the side of Masjid al Sahlah and they will enter Jannah (paradise) without having to face the Hasab (accountability). They are those whom Allah has made righteous and increased His blessings upon. They are the devoted ones who will be rewarded first. They do not like to hear praise about themselves and are terrified of being judged by Allah with His adl (justice). They hasten to the obedience of Allah and in performing good deeds. They are fully aware that Allah sees all that they do. They will not have to face accountability (hasab) or punishment. Allah is the remover of punishment and purifier of the momin (believers).

The mountain of Ahwan, a very old mountain populous in the past, rose up from the middle of this masjid."

HADITH 11

Abu Bakr al Hadrami narrates:

I asked Abu Abdullah Imam Jafar Sadiq (asws), "What is the best place after Masjid al Haram and Masjid al Nabwi?"

Imam (asws) replied, "Kufa. O Abu Bakr! Kufa is a pure and virtuous land. It contains the graves of the messengers, the prophets and the truthful successors. Therein is also the Masjid of Suhail in which every prophet sent by Allah has prayed. The Adl (justice) of Allah (Imam e Zamana atfs) will reappear from this city. Qaim (atfs) and those who will lead after Him shall live in it. Indeed it is the place of the prophets, the successors, and the righteous."

HADITH 12

Hanan ibn Sadeer narrates:

I was with Abu Jafar (Imam Muhammad Baqir asws) when a man entered, said salam to the Imam (asws), and sat down.

Imam (asws) asked the man, "Where are you from?"

The man replied, "I am from Kufa, and am one of Your Muhibb (lovers)."

Imam (asws) asked, "Do you pray all of your prayers in Masjid al Kufa?"

The man replied, "No."

Imam (asws) said, "You are deprived of its goodness."

Then Imam (asws) asked, "Do you perform ghusl once a day with the water of the Euphrates River that is near to you?"

The man replied, "No."

Imam (asws) asked, "At least once a week?"

The man replied, "No."

Imam (asws) asked, "Once a month?"

The man replied, "No."

Imam (asws) asked, "Once a year?"

The man replied, "No."

Imam (asws) said, "You are deprived of its goodness."

Then the Imam (asws) asked, "Do you perform the Ziarat of the grave of Hussain (asws) once a week?"

The man replied, "No."

Imam (asws) asked, "Once a month?"

The man replied, "No."

Imam (asws) asked, "Once a year?"

The man replied, "No."

Imam (asws) said, "You are deprived of its goodness."

HADITH 13

Abu Jafar (Imam Muhammad Baqir asws) said:

"O Abu Ubaidah! Do not be negligent in performing prayers in Masjid al Kufa even if you have to crawl to it because one prayer there is the same as performing 70 prayers in another masjid."

HADITH 14

Imam Reza (asws) said:

"Praying one individual prayer in Masjid al Kufa has more rewards than praying 70 congregational prayers in any other masjid."

HADITH 15

Abu Abdullah Imam Jafar Sadiq (asws) said:

"Praying one prayer in Masjid al Kufa is the same as praying 1000 prayers in any other masjid."

HADITH 16

Fudail al Awar narrates:

I met Laith ibn Abu Sulaim after the people had finished performing the afternoon prayers.

Laith ibn Abu Sulaim said, "Do not keep me for I have not yet prayed the noon prayers. Carry on your way."

I asked him, "Why have you delayed your prayers until now?"

He replied, "I had business in the market to attend to. I delayed my prayers so that I could pray in this masjid due to the merits I have heard about it. It is narrated RasoolAllah (saw) said:

"On the night of Miraj when I ascended to the heavens, I descended in the masjid of My fathers, Nuh (as) and Ibrahim (as), Masjid al Kufa, and I prayed two rakats of prayer there. Praying a wajib (obligatory) prayer in Masjid al Kufa is the same as performing Hajj and praying one mustahab (recommended) prayer in Masjid al Kufa is the same as performing Umrah."

HADITH 17

Malik ibn Dumrah al Anbari narrates:

Ameerul Momineen (asws) asked me, "Do you go and perform prayers in the masjid that is behind your house?"

I replied, "O Ameerul Momineen (asws)! Only women go to that masjid."

Ameerul Momineen (asws) replied, "O Malik! No aggrieved person goes to this masjid, prays in it, and supplicates to Allah without Allah removing his grief from him and granting his request."

Malik added, "I swear by Allah that I did not go to that masjid nor did I pray in it until one night when I was in extreme difficulty regarding a matter. Suddenly I remembered the words of Ameerul Momineen (asws) so I rose in the middle of the night and performed wudhu. When I exited my house, I found a lamp outside of the door of my house. The lamp began to move on its own so I followed it until I found myself at the masjid. The lamp stopped in front of me so I prayed there. After I completed my prayers, the lamp began to move again on its own. I followed it until I found myself back at my home. When I entered into my home, the lamp disappeared. Every night after this, whenever I left my home, I would find this lamp lighting my way and Allah granted my request."

HADITH 18

Abu Abdullah Imam Jafar Sadiq (asws) said:

"A man came to Ameerul Momineen (asws) in Masjid al Kufa and said, "Salam be upon You, O Ameerul Momineen (asws). May the mercy and blessings of Allah be upon You."Ameerul Momineen (asws) replied to his salam.

The man said, "May I be sacrificed upon You! I am leaving for Masjid al Aqsa and I wanted to bid You farewell."

Ameerul Momineen (asws) asked, "What do you hope to gain by going there?"

The man said, "May I be sacrificed upon You! Rewards and blessings."

Ameerul Momineen (asws) said, "Sell your camel, spend your money, and pray in this masjid (Masjid al Kufa) instead for praying wajib (obligatory) prayers in this masjid is like performing Hajj and praying mustahab (recommended) prayers in it is like performing Umrah. The blessings of this masjid extend for twelve miles. Prosperity is on its right side and cunning on its left. In the middle of the masjid, there is a well of oil, a well of milk, a well of water for the momineen (believers) to drink and a well of water to purify the momineen (believers). The ark of Nuh (as) embarked from here. Nasr, Yaghooth and Yaooq were placed here."

Ameerul Momineen (asws) continued and said,

"70 prophets and 70 successors have prayed in this masjid and I am one of them. Then He pointed to his chest. No grieved person asks Allah for his needs in this masjid (Masjid al Kufa) without Allah granting his request and relieving him of his difficulties."

Chapter 9

Grave of Ameerul Momineen (asws)

HADITH 1

Safwan al Jamal narrates:

Amir ibn Abdullah ibn Judhah al Azdi and I were with Abu Abdullah Imam Jafar Sadiq (asws) when Amir said to the Imam (asws), "People believe Ameerul Momineen (asws) was buried in Ruhbat."

Imam (asws) replied, "No."

Amir asked, "Where is He buried?"

Imam (asws) replied, "After the martyrdom of Ameerul Momineen (asws), Hasan (asws) carried Him to an area located behind Kufa close to the sea of Najaf. To the left side was Ghari and to the right was Hirah. He buried Ameerul Momineen (asws) in some white colored gravel."

Sometime later, I (Safwan al Jamal) went to the location that had been described by Imam (asws). I thought I had found the grave. When I returned, I told the Imam (asws) about the location that I had thought to be the grave of Ameerul Momineen (asws).

Imam (asws) replied, "You were right! You were right! You were right! May Allah have mercy on you."

HADITH 2

Hussain al Khallal who narrated from his grandfather who said:

I asked Hussain (asws) ibn Ali (asws), "Where did You bury Ameerul Momineen (asws)?"

Imam (asws) replied, "We carried Him out at night. We passed by the Masjid al Ashath and proceeded towards the area behind Ghari."

HADITH 3

Abdullah ibn Sinan narrates:

One day Umar ibn Yazid came to me and asked me to accompany him. I agreed and we traveled until we came to the house of Hafs al Kunasi.

Umar ibn Yazid asked Hafs to join us. Then we traveled until we arrived at a grave in Ghari where Umar said, "Dismount from your ride for this is the grave of Ameerul Momineen (asws)."

We asked him, "How do you know this?"

Umar replied, "I came here on several occasions with Abu Abdullah Imam Jafar Sadiq (asws) when He was in Hirah. He told me that this is the grave of Ameerul Momineen (asws)."

HADITH 4

Yazid ibn Umar ibn Talha narrates:

When Abu Abdullah Imam Jafar Sadiq (asws) was in Hirah, He asked me, "Do you not want that which I promised you (to go to the grave of Ameerul Momineen asws)?"

I replied, "Yes."

Then the Imam (asws) mounted and we rode. His son, Ismail, accompanied us. We passed Thawiyah and stopped between Hirah and Najaf next to some white colored gravel. Imam (asws) and His son, Ismail, descended from their mounts so I did as well. Then we all performed prayers there.

Imam (asws) said to Ismail, "Stand and say salam to your Grandfather, Hussain (asws) ibn Ali (asws)."

I asked, "May I be sacrificed upon You! Is Hussain (asws) not in Karbala?"

Imam (asws) replied, "Yes, but when His head was being brought back from Shaam, a servant stole it and buried it next to Ameerul Momineen (asws)."

HADITH 5

Aban ibn Taghlib narrates:

I was with Abu Abdullah Imam Jafar Sadiq (asws) when He passed through the area behind Kufa. He stopped and prayed two rakats. Then He went forward slightly and prayed another two rakats. Then He again went forward slightly and prayed another two rakats.

Then Imam (asws) said, "This is the location of the grave of Ameerul Momineen (asws)."

I asked, "May I be sacrificed upon You! What were the other two locations You prayed upon?"

Imam (asws) replied, "The location of the head of Hussain (asws) and the mimbar of al Qaim (atfs)."

HADITH 6

Abu Abdullah Imam Jafar Sadiq (asws) said:

"You shall see two graves when you visit Ghari. One will be large and the other will be small. The large grave is the grave of Ameerul Momineen (asws) and the small one is where the head of Hussain (asws) ibn Ali (asws) was buried."

HADITH 7

Safwan ibn Miran narrates:

Once I traveled with Jafar (asws) ibn Muhammad (asws) (Imam Jafar Sadiq asws) from Qadisiyah. When we arrived in Najaf, Imam (asws) said:

"This is the mountain on which the son of My Grandfather, Nuh (as), sought refuge and said, "I shall betake me to some mountain that will save me from the water" (Quran 11:43)

Allah (swt) sent a revelation to the mountain of Najaf, "O Najaf! Will you allow the son of Nuh (as) to seek refuge with you from Me?"

The mountain of Najaf instantly crumbled into pieces which scattered about the borders of Shaam."

Then Imam (asws) said, "Let's continue on."

We continued on our way until we arrived at Ghari. There the Imam (asws) stopped beside a grave and said salam upon all of the prophets beginning with Adam (as) and ending with RasoolAllah (saw). I said salam to them as well.

Then the Imam (asws) fell upon the grave and said salam to the one buried within. The voice of the Imam (asws) could be heard as He wept upon the grave. After some time had passed, the Imam (asws) stood and prayed four rakats of prayers. I prayed along with Him.

After we had finished praying, I asked Imam (asws), "O Son of RasoolAllah (saw)! Whose grave is this?"

Imam (asws) replied, "This is the grave of My Grandfather, Ali (asws) ibn Abi Talib (as)."

HADITH 8

Hasan ibn Jahim ibn Bukair narrates:

I reported to Abul Hasan (Imam Musa Kazim asws) about how Yahya ibn Musa annoys those who are going for the Ziarat of Ameerul Momineen (asws).

I explained how he goes to Thawiyyah for picnics. The grave of Ameerul Momineen (asws) is just beyond Thawiyyah. I said to the Imam (asws) that according to the narrations of Safwan al Jammal this is the place that Abu Abdullah (Imam Jafar Sadiq asws) described to him:

"When you arrive in Ghari behind Kufa, turn your back towards Ghari and go forward slightly to the right towards Najaf. When you come to the white colored gravel with the mountain road ahead of you, there you will find the grave of Ameerul Momineen".

I said to the Imam (asws), "I have gone to that place many times but some of our companions do not believe that Ameerul Momineen (asws) is buried there. Some believe that He is buried in Masjid al Kufa and some believe that He is buried in the palace of Kufa, but I always reply to them that Allah would not allow the grave of Ameerul Momineen (asws) to be in a palace because that is the dwellings of oppressors nor can it be in the Masjid because His children wanted His grave hidden. Which of us is correct?"

Imam (asws) replied, "You are because you have followed the words of Jafar (asws) ibn Muhammad (asws) (Imam Jafar Sadiq asws). O Abu Muhammad! None of Our companions say that which you say or believe in that which you believe."

I asked, "May my life be sacrificed upon You! Is this one of the blessings of Allah upon me?"

Imam (asws) replied, "Yes. Allah gives success to and secures whomsoever He wills. Therefore, praise Allah and say, "This is guidance from Allah.""

This hadith has also been narrated to me by Muhammad ibn Hasan and Muhammad ibn Ahmad ibn Hussain, both narrated from Hasan ibn Ali ibn Mahziyar who narrated from his father Ali who narrated from Hasan ibn Ali ibn Fadhal who narrated from Hasan ibn Jahim ibn Bukair who narrated from Abul Hasan (asws).

HADITH 9

Yunus ibn Zabiam narrates:

I was with Abu Abdullah (Imam Jafar Sadiq asws) when He was forcefully taken to Abu Jafar (Mansoor al Dawaniqi) in Hirah. One clear moonlit night, Imam (asws) looked at the sky and said:

"O Yunus! Do you see how beautiful these stars are? They are the protection of the inhabitants of the skies and We Ahlul Bayt (asws) are the protection of inhabitants of the earth."

Then Imam (asws) asked me to order the donkey and mule saddled. Once they had been, Imam (asws) asked me which I would prefer to ride. I thought the Imam (asws) would prefer to ride the mule because it was stronger than the donkey so I chose the donkey. However, the Imam (asws) asked that He be allowed to ride the donkey so I agreed. Once we were outside of Hirah, Imam (asws) asked me to lead the way and I did. He instructed me to turn right and left until we came to some red colored gravel. There Imam (asws) said, "This is the place."

Then the Imam (asws) went slightly towards the right where there was a well. Imam (asws) performed wudhu there and then went towards a mound and prayed beside it. He then fell upon it and wept. Afterwards He went to a smaller mound that was near the larger mound and repeated the same actions as He had done on the larger mound.

Then Imam (asws) said to me, "O Yunus! Do as I have done." I did as the Imam (asws) ordered me to.

Afterwards Imam (asws) asked me, "O Yunus! Do you know where we are?"

I replied, "No."

Imam (asws) said, "The first mound was the grave of Ameerul Momineen (asws) and the second is where the head of Hussain (asws) ibn Ali (asws) ibn Abi Talib (as) is buried. After the accursed Ubaidullah ibn Ziyad (may the curse of Allah be upon him) sent the head of Hussain (asws) to Shaam, it was sent back to Kufa. Ubaidullah (la) said, "Take the head out of Kufa so that it does not cause disunity amongst its people."

Allah placed the head next to Ameerul Momineen (asws). Now the head is with the body and the body is with the head."

HADITH 10

Abu Abdullah Imam Jafar Sadiq (asws) said:

"When I was in Hirah with Abul Abbas, at night I use to visit the grave of Ameerul Momineen (asws) which is situated to the right of Ghari of Noman in the direction of Najaf. I use to perform tahajjud prayers beside the grave and then return before fajr."

HADITH 11

Safwan ibn Miran narrates:

I asked Abu Abdullah (Imam Jafar Sadiq asws) about the location of the grave of Ameerul Momineen (asws). He said that it was situated in the land of hardened sands.

I went to where He had described and performed prayers there. The next year I returned to the Imam (asws) and informed Him that I had gone to the place He had described and prayed there. He told me that I had found the correct location. For the next 20 years, I would go to that place every year and pray next to it."

HADITH 12

Ahmad ibn Muhammad ibn Abu Nasir narrates:

I asked Imam Reza (asws) about the location of the grave of Ameerul Momineen (asws). He told me that it was in Ghari.

I replied, "May I be sacrificed upon You! Some people say that He is buried in Ruhbat."

Imam (asws) replied, "No. There are even some who say that He is buried in Masjid al Kufa."

Chapter 10

Reward for performing the Ziarat of Ameerul Momineen (asws)

HADITH 1

Abu Wahab al Basri narrates:

I entered Medina and went to Abu Abdullah (Imam Jafar Sadiq (asws) and said, "May I be sacrificed upon You! I have come to You but I have not yet performed the Ziarat of Ameerul Momineen (asws)."

Imam (asws) replied, "How awful! If you were not one of Our Shia, then I would not have even acknowledged you. Do you not wish to perform the Ziarat of the One whom Allah and His angels perform the Ziarat of and the One whose Ziarat the prophets and momineen perform?"

I said, "May I be sacrificed upon You! I did not know this."

Imam (asws) said, "Then know that the position of Ameerul Momineen (asws) with Allah is higher than all of the Imams (asws). "

HADITH 2

Mufaddhal ibn Umar narrates:

I went to Abu Abdullah (Imam Jafar Sadiq asws) and said, "I long for Ghari."

Imam (asws) asked, "Why do you long for it?"

I replied, "Because I love Ameerul Momineen (asws) and I love to perform His Ziarat."

Imam (asws) asked, "Do you know the merits of performing His Ziarat?"

I replied, "No, O Son (asws) of RasoolAllah (saw)! Please inform me."

Imam (asws) said, "When you desire to perform the Ziarat of Ameerul Momineen (asws) know that you will be performing the ziarat of the bones of Adam (as), the flesh of Nuh (as), and the body of Ali (asws) ibn Abi Talib (as)."

I asked, "Adam (as) descended in Sarandib in the middle of the day and it is believed his bones were next to Allah's Sacred House (Kaaba). How did his bones get to Kufa?"

Imam (asws) replied, "When Nuh (as) was in the Ark, Allah (swt) sent revelation to him to go to the Kaaba and circulate around it for seven days. Nuh (as) did as Allah ordered. Then he descended into the water from the Ark until the water was up to his knees. He then brought out of the water a coffin, which contained the bones of Adam (as), and he carried them onto the Ark. He then continued circulating around the Kaaba for as long as Allah willed. After he went to Kufa and stopped his ark inside of Masjid al Kufa. This is when Allah ordered the earth, "swallow down your water" (Quran 11:44). Then the earth swallowed its water beginning from Masjid al Kufa, which is also, where the flood began.

Those who were with Nuh (as) in the ark all went in separate directions. Nuh (as) carried the coffin and buried it in Ghari which is part of the mountain upon which Allah spoke to Musa (as), purified Isa (as), chose Ibrahim (as) as His friend and Muhammad (saw) as His Beloved. Allah chose that land as the dwelling place of the prophets.

I swear by Allah that from the time of His Purified Fathers, Adam (as) and Nuh (as), no one more honorable than Ameerul Momineen (asws) has lived there. Therefore, when you go to Najaf, perform the Ziarat of the bones of Adam (as), the flesh of Nuh (as) and the body of Ali (asws) ibn Abi Talib (as). By doing this, you will have performed the Ziarat of the first fathers of Muhammad (saw) who is the Seal of all Prophets and of Ali (asws) who is Syedul Wasieen (Master of all Successors).

The doors of jannah will be opened for those who perform the Ziarat of Ameerul Momineen (asws) so do not neglect performing this great act."

This hadith is also narrated by Muhammad ibn Abdullah ibn Jafar al Himyari who narrated from his father who narrated from Muhammad ibn Hussain ibn Abul Khattab who narrated from ibn Sinan who narrated from Mufaddhal ibn Umar who narrated from Abu Abdullah (Imam Jafar Sadiq asws).

HADITH 3

Abu Abdullah (Imam Jafar Sadiq asws) said:

"Hasan (asws) ibn Ali (asws) asked RasoolAllah (saw), "O Father (saw)! What is the reward for those who perform Your ziarat?"

RasoolAllah (saw) replied, "O My Son (asws)! On the day of judgment, it will be wajib (obligatory) upon Me before Allah to perform the Ziarat of those who performed My Ziarat, either during My life or after I leave this world, and those who performed the Ziarat of Your Father (asws). And I will absolve them of their sins."

Chapter II

How to Perform the Ziarat of Ameerul Momineen (asws) and Supplications to be Recited Near His Grave

HADITH 1

Imam Reza (asws) narrates from His Father Musa (asws) ibn Jafar (asws) (Imam Musa Kazim asws) who said His Father Imam Jafar Sadiq (asws) said:

"Ali (asws) ibn Hussain (asws), Zainul Abideen (asws), went to perform the Ziarat of the grave of Ameerul Momineen Ali (asws) ibn Abi Talib (as). He stood beside the grave and said:

السلام عليك يا أُميعر المؤمنينّ ورحمة الله وبركاته

Salam be upon You O Ameerul Momineen (asws) along with the blessings and mercy of Allah

السلام عليك يا أمين الله في أرضه وحجته علي عباده

Salam be upon You O Trustee of Allah in His earth and His Hujjat (proof) over His servants.

السلام عليك يا أمير المؤمنينّ

Salam be upon You O Ameerul Momineen (asws)

أشهد أنك جاهدت في الله حق جهاده وعملت بكتابه واتبعت سنن نبيه ﷺ حتى دعاك الله إلى جوارك
وقبضك إليه باختياره وألزم أعداءك الحجة في قتلهم اباك مع ما لك من الحجج البالغة على جميع خلقه

I testify that You strived truthfully in the way of Allah and Your actions are based upon His Book. You followed the sunnah of the Prophet (saw) until Allah called You to His side and raised You to Himself. He established a Hujjah (proof) for Your enemies even though they martyred You because You are the Hujjat (proof) of Allah over all of His creation

اللهم فاجعل نفسي مطمئنة بقدرك راضية بقضائك مولعة بذكرك ودعائك محية لصفوة أوليائك محبوبة في
أرضك وسمائك صابرة على نزول بلائك شاكرة لفواضل نعمائك

O Allah! Make me certain about that which You have ordained, pleased with all that You have decreed, desiring of Your Remembrance, prayerful for Your chosen Friends that are loved throughout Your earth and Your heavens, patient during tribulations, and thankful for Your bounteous blessings.

ذاكرة لسوابغ آلائك، مشتاقة إلى فرحة لقائك، متزودة التقوى ليوم جزائك، مستنة بسنن أوليائك، مفارقة لأخلاق
أعدائك، مشغولة عن الدنيا بحمدك وثنائك

Make me to remember Your endless bounties, long for the occasion of Your meeting, pious on the Day of Your Reward, a follower of the sunnah of Your Friends, to abandon the akhlaq (etiquette) of Your enemies, and immersed in this world with Your Praise and Glorification

Then He placed His cheek on the grave of Ameerul Momineen (asws) and said:

اللهم إن قلوب المخبتين إليك والهة وسبل الراغبين إليك شارعة وأعلام القاصدين إليك واضحة وأفئدة العارفين
منك فازعة وأصوات الداعين إليك صاعدة وأبواب الإجابة لهم مفتحة ودعوة من ناجاك مستجابة وتوبة من
أناب إليك مقبولة وعبرة من بكى من خوفك مرحومة والإعانة لمن استعان بك موجودة والإغاثة لمن استغاث
بك مبذولة وعداتك لعبدك منجزة وزلل من استقالك مقالة وأعمال العاملين لديك محفوظة وأرزاقك إلى
الخلائق من لدنك نازلة وعوائد المزيد لهم متواترة وذنوب المستغفرين مغفورة وحوائج خلقك عندك مفضية
وجوائز السائلين عندك موفورة وعوائد المزيد و اصلة وموائد المستطعمين معدة ومناهل الظمآء لديك مترعة

O Allah! The hearts of those who stand before You with humility are filled with an absolute belief. Those who desire nearness of You are aware of which path will lead them to You. Signs are made clear for those who seek Your marifat (recognition). The hearts of who know You are filled with fear of You. The gates through which You answer the people are open. The prayers of those who whisper to You are fulfilled. The repentance of those who return to You is accepted. The tears of those who weep in fear of You are dealt with mercifully. Assistance is available to those who seek it from You. Refuge is generously given to those seek it with You. You keep the promises made to Your servants. You reduce the sins of those who ask. You preserve the good deeds performed by the people for them. The rizq of Your creation descends upon them from You and is continuously increased by You. You forgive the sins of those who seek forgiveness and fulfill the needs of Your creation. The rewards for those who ask are available in multitudes with You and even greater rewards are bestowed upon Your creation by You. The tables of food are prepared for those who search for it and the fountains are filled for the thirsty.

اللهم فاستجب دعآئي واقبل ثنآئي وأعطني رجائي واجمع بيني وبين أو لياّئي بحق محمد ﷺ و عليّ و فاطمة ّ و الحسن ّ و الحسين ّ إنك ولي نعمآئي ومنتهى رجائي وغاية مناي في منقلبي ومثواي

O Allah! Answer my prayers, accept my praise, fulfill my hopes, and unite me with my friends for the sake of Muhammad (saw), Ali (asws), Fatimah (sa), Hasan (asws) and Hussain (asws). You are the Master of my blessings, my greatest desires, and my heartfelt hopes in my final resting place and last destination.

أنت إلهي و سيدي ومولاي اغفر لي ولأوليآئنا و كف عنا أعدآئنا واشغلهم عن أذانا وأظهر كلمة الحق واجعلها العليا وأدحض كلمة الباطل واجعلها السفلى إنك على كل شيء قدير

You are My God, My Lord and My Master. Forgive me and forgive our friends. Keep our enemies far from us and do not allow them to bring harm to us. Make clear the word of Haq (truth) and make it the highest word and make the word of batil (falsehood) be refuted and less than the word of Haq. You have power over all things.

HADITH 2

Muhammad ibn Hasan ibn Walid narrated in his book Kitab al Jami that:

Abul Hasan Imam Musa Kazim (asws) recited the following beside the grave of Ameerul Momineen (asws):

السلام عليك يا ولي الله

Salam be upon You, O Wali of Allah

أشهد أنك أول مظلوم وأول من غصب حقة ، صبرت واحتسبت حتى أتاك اليقين

I testify that You were the first oppressed one and the first one whose right was forcefully taken. You stayed patient awaiting that, which was certain to come to You

و أشهد أنك لقيت الله و أنت شهيد، عذب الله قاتلك بأنواع العذاب وجدد عليه العذاب،

And I testify that You went before Allah as shaheed (martyr). May Allah punish Your killer with ever-changing punishment. May He continuously renew the punishment of Your killer

جئتك عارفا بحقك ، مستبصراً بشأنك، معادياً لأعدائك و من ظلمك، ألفى على ذلك ربي إن شاء الله تعالى

I stand before You fully aware of Your right and Your status. I disassociate from Your enemies and those who oppressed You. InshaAllah I shall meet with my Lord while being in this state.

إن لي ذنوبا كثيرة فاشفع لي عند ربك يا مولاي، فإن لك عند الله مقاما معلوما، وإن لك عند الله جاها عظيما وشفاعة، وقد قال الله تعالى: و لا وشفعون إلا لمن ارتضى

My sins are numerous so intercede for me with Your Lord, O my Master, for You have an elevated position and status before Allah and You have the power to intercede for Allah says, *"they do not intercede except for him whom He approves"* (Quran 21:28)

Imam Musa Kazim (asws) would also recite the following next to the grave of Ameerul Momineen (asws):

الحمد لله الذي أكرمني بمعرفته ومعرفة رسوله ﷺ و من فرض الله علي طاعته، رحمة منه لي وتطوعا منه علي، ومن علي بالإيمان

Praise be to Allah who honored me by allowing me to know Him, to know His Messenger (saw), and those whose obedience Allah made wajib (obligatory) upon me, I turn towards Him through His mercy and through faith

الحمدلله الذي سيرني في بلاده وحملني على دوابه، وطوى لي البعيد، دفع عني المكروه حتى أدخلني حرم أخي رسوله ﷺ فأر انيه في عافية

Praise be to Allah who permitted me and provided for me a means of traveling through His land. He made that which was far be near and kept me safe until I entered sacred sanctuary of the Brother of His Messenger (saw) in well-being.

الحمد لله الذي جعلني من زوار قبر وصي رسوله ﷺ

Praise be to Allah who allowed me to be amongst those who perform Ziarat of the grave of the Wasi (successor) of His Messenger (saw)

الحمدلله الذي هدانا لهدا و ما كنا لنهدي لولا أن هدانا الله

Praise be to Allah who guided us and had it not been for His guidance then we would have remained amongst those who are lost

أشهد أن لا إله إلا الله وحده لا شريك له،

I testify that there is no god except Allah and He is One without any partners

وأشهد أن محمداً ﷺ عبده ورسوله جاء بالحق من عنده

I testify that Muhammad (saw) is His servant and messenger who came with Haq (truth) from Allah

وأشهد أن علياً عبد الله وأخو رسوله ﷺ

I testify that Ali (asws) is the servant of Allah and the brother of His Messenger (saw)

اللهم عبدك ورائرك يتقرب إليك بزيارة قبر أخي نبيك، و على كه مأتي حق لمن أتاه وزاره، وأنت خير مأتي و أكرم مزور، وأسألك

O'Allah! Your slave and visitor seeks Your nearness by performing the Ziarat of the grave of the Brother of Your Prophet (saw). Every host has a duty to those who visit. You are the best One to visit and the most

يا الله يا رحمن يا رحيم يا جواد يا واحد يا أحد يا فرد يا صمد

O'Allah! O' Rahman! O' Raheem! O' Jawad! O' Wahid! O' Ahad! O' Fard! O' Samid!

يا من لم يلد و لم يولد ولم يكن له كيفواً أحد

O' He who does not beget nor is begotten; for there is none like Him

أن تصلي على محمد ﷺ وآل محمدّ وأهل بيتة

I beseech You to send Your blessings upon Muhammad (saw) and Aal e Muhammad (asws) and His Ahlul Bayt (asws)

و أن تجعل تحقتك إباي من زيارتي في موقفي هذا فكاك رقبتي من النار و اجعلني ممن يسارع في الخيرات ويدعوك رهبا ورغبا، واجعلني لك من الخاشعين

Make my release from the Hellfire as my reward for performing the Ziarat of this spot. And make me amongst those who *"hasten to do good works"* (Quran 2:148), and among those who pray to You with longing and apprehension and among those who humble themselves before You.

اللهم إنك بشر تني على لسان محمد ﷺ فقلت: وبشر الذين آمنوا أن لهم قدم صدق عند ربهم

O'Allah! You have bestowed upon me good tidings through the tongue of Muhammad (saw) who said *"bring unto those who believe the good tidings that they have a sure footing with their Lord"* (Quran 10:2)

اللهم فإني بك مؤمن وبجميع أنبيائك موقن، فلا توقفني بعد معرفتهم موقفا تفضحني به على رووس الأشهاد، بل أوقفني معهم، وتوفني على التصديق بهم، فإنهم عبيدك و أنت خصصتهم بكر امتك وأمرتني باتباعهم

O' Allah! I am Your believer and am certain of all of Your Prophets. Since I have acknowledged Them, do not on the day of judgment cause me to stand and be exposed before the witnesses. Instead, allow me to beside them. Take my life while I believe in Them. For, They are Your Servants and You have bestowed honor upon Them and ordered me to follow Them.

Then come near to the grave and recite:

السلام من الله على محمد بن عبد الله ﷺ أمين الله على وحيه وعزائم أمره، ومعدن الوحي و التزيل، والخاتم لما سبق والفاتح لما استقبل، والمهيمن على ذلك كله، و الشاهد على خلقه، والسراج المنير،

Peace and blessings from Allah be upon Muhammad (saw) son of Abdullah (as), the Trustee of the revelation of Allah and His Will, The source of His Revelation and Inspiration, The last of that which has passed and the first of that which is to come, Master over the dominion, Witness upon the creation, and the shining light.

والسلام عليه ورحمة الله و بركاته

May the peace, blessings, and Mercy of Allah be upon Him

اللهم صل على محمد ﷺ و أهل بيتّ المظلومين أفضل و أكمل و أرفع وأشرف ما صليت على أحد من أنبيائك ورسلك و أصفيائك

O' Allah! Send upon Muhammad (saw) and His oppressed Ahlul Bayt (asws) the highest, most perfect and most exalted of any of the blessings which You have bestowed upon Your Prophets, Messengers, or Your Chosen.

اللهم صل على أمير المؤمنينّ، عبدك و خير خلقك بعد نبيك ﷺ وأخي رسولك و وصي رسولك الذي انتجبته من خلقك بعد نبيك،والدليل على من بعثته برسالاتك، و ديان الدين بعدلك، وفصل قضائك بين خلقك، و السلام عليه ورحمة الله وبركاته

O' Allah! Send Your blessings upon Ali Ameerul Momineen (asws), Your slave and the best of Your creation after Your Prophet (saw), the Brother of Your Prophet (saw) and the Wasi (inheritor) of Your Prophet (saw), the One whom You chose from Your creation after Your Prophet (saw), the Guide for those You sent with Your Message, the acknowledged ruler of the religion with Your justice, the Decisive Judgment upon Your creation. May Your Peace, Mercy, and Blessings be upon Him.

اللهم صل على الأئمة من ولده القوامين بأمرك من بعده، المطهرين الذين ارتضيتهم أنصاراً لدينك وحفظة لسرك، وشهداء على خلقك، وأعلاما لعبادك

O'Allah! Send Your blessings upon the Imams (asws) from His Sons (asws) who fulfill Your Affairs after Him, the Purified Ones with whom You are pleased as the supporters of Your religion, the maintainers of Your Secret, and as witnesses upon Your creation, and as flags of guidance for Your slaves.

Now recite durood as much as you can and then recite the following:

السلام على الأئمة المستودعين،

Peace be upon the entrusted Imams (asws),

السلام على خالصة الله من خلقه

Peace be upon the Pure Ones from the creation of Allah

السلام على الأئمة المتوسمين

Peace be upon the knowledgeable Imams (asws)

53

السلام على المؤمنين ، الذين قاموا بأمرك، و وازراو أولیآء الله، وخافوا بخوفهم

Peace be upon the momineen who fulfilled Your command and supported the Divine Authorities appointed by Allah, and who were fearful when They were fearful.

السلام على ملائكة الله المقربين

Peace be upon the Angels which are nearest to Allah

Then recite the following:

السلام عليك يا أمير المؤمنين ورحمة الله و بركاته

May the peace, blessings, and mercy of Allah be upon You, O' Ameerul Momineen (asws)!

السلام عليك يا حبيب الله

Peace be upon You, O' Beloved of Allah

السلام عليك يا صفة الله

Peace be upon You, O' Chosen of Allah

السلام عليك يا ولي الله

Peace be upon You, O' Wali of Allah

السلام عليك يا حجة الله

Peace be upon You, O' Hujjatul Allah (proof of Allah)

السلام عليك يا عمود الدين ووارث علم الأولين و الأخرين و الصراط المستقين

Peace be upon You, O' Pillar of the Religion and the Inheritor of the Knowledge from the first through the last, and Siratul Mustaqeem (the straight path).

أشهد أنك قد أقمت الصلاة، واتيت الزكاة، وأمرت بالمعروف، ونهيت عن المنكر، واتبعت الرسول ﷺ، وتلوت الكتاب حق تلاوته، وجاهدت في الله حق جهاده، و نصحت الله و لرسوله ﷺ، وجدت بنفسك صابراً محتسباً مجاهداً عن دعن الله، موقياً لرسول الله ﷺ، طالباً ما عند الله، راغباً و عد الله، و مضيت للذى كنت عليه شهيداً و شاهداً و مشهوداً

I testify that You established the prayers, gave zakat, enjoined the good and forbid the evil, followed the Messenger (saw), recited the Book as it should be recited, fought in the way of Allah as it should be, and were sincere with Allah and His Messenger (saw). For You sacrificed Yourself, fighting for the religion of Allah, protecting the Messenger (saw) of Allah, wishing for that which is with Allah and desiring only that which is promised by Allah. You left this way as You lived in this world, as a martyr who is a witness upon the creation and is witnessed to by Allah.

فجزاك الله عن رسوله ﷺ و عن الإسلام وأهله أفضل الجزاء

May Allah bestow upon You the best honor on behalf of His Messenger (saw), Islam and its nation.

لعن الله من قتلك، وُلعن الله من خالفك، ولعن الله من افترى عليك و ظلمك، و لعن الله من غصبك حقك، و من بلغه ذلك فرضى به، أنا إلى الله منهم براء

May the wrath of Allah be upon those who slay You, on those who were against You, on those who forged lies against You and oppressed You, on those who usurped Your right and upon those who were pleased upon hearing of the usurpation of Your right. I seek the nearness of Allah by disassociating myself from them.

لعن الله امة خالفتك، و امة جحدت ولايتك و امةتظاهرت عليك، وامة قتلتك، وامة حادت عنك و خذلتك، و الحمد لله الذى جعل النار مثواهم، و بئس الورد المورود، وبئس ورد الواردعن، و بئس درك المدرك

May the wrath of Allah be upon the nation who opposed You, who denied Your Wilayat, who rebelled against You, who slaughtered You and who deviated from You and disappointed You. Praise be to Allah who made Hell as their abode. What a vile destination it is and what a vile destination shall they enter! How lowly and abject is their place!

اللهم العن قتلة أنبيآئك و أوصيآء أنبيآئك بجميع لعناتك، وُأصلهم حر نارك، اللهم العن الجوابيت و الطواغيت و الفراعنة، و اللات و العزى و الجبت، وكل ند يدعى من دون الله، وكل مفتر على الله، اللهم العنهم و أشياعهم و أوليآئهم وأعوانهم و محبيهم لعناً كثيراً

O' Allah! Send Lanat upon those who slew Your Prophets (as) and those who slew the Successors (as) of Your Prophets (as) from all of Your abundant condemnations and burn them with Your blazing fires. O'Allah! Send Lanat upon the Jiabit, Taghut, and the pharaohs, and the Laat, the Uzza, and the Jibt, and every other object that is worshipped other than Allah. O' Allah! Incessantly send lanat upon them, those who follow and obey them, their friends, their supporters, and their lovers.

Then recite the following three times:

اللهم العن قتلة أمير المؤمنينّ،

O'Allah! Send Lanat upon the killers of Ameerul Momineen (asws)

اللهم العن قتلة الحسنّ و الحسينّ

O'Allah! Send Lanat the killers of Hasan (asws) and Hussain (asws)

اللهم عذ بهم عذاباً أليماً لا تعذبه أحداً من العالمين، وضاعف عليهم عذابك كما شاقوا و لاة أمرك، وأعد لهم عذاباً لم تحله من خلقك

O'Allah! Torment them with a chastisement that is so agonizing You would never punish anyone else with it. Increasingly multiply their punishment due to how they aggrieved Your Appointed Authorities. Prepare a punishment for them, which has never been afflicted upon any other of Your creation.

اللهم و أدخل على قتلة أنصار رسولك، و قتلة أنصار أمير المؤمنين، و على قتلة أنصار الحسن و على قتلة أنصار الحسينّ ، و قتلة من قتل في ولاية آل محمد أجمعين عذاباً مضاعفاً في أسفل درك من الجحيم لا تخفف عنهم من عذابها و هم فيه مبلسون ملعونون، ناكسوا رؤوسهم عند ربهم، قد عاينوا الندامة و الخزي الطويل بقتلهم عترة أنبيائك و رسلك و أتباعهم من عبادك الصالحين

O'Allah! Cast an ever increasing torment in the lowest levels of the Hellfire upon those who slaughtered the supporters of Your Rasool (saw), those who slaughtered the supporters of Ameerul Momineen (asws), those who slaughtered the supporters of Hasan (asws) and those who slaughtered the supporters of Hussain (asws) and those who slaughtered the supporters of the Wilayat of Aal e Muhammad (asws). And torment them with such a torment that will leave them hopeless and accursed with their heads bowed in disgrace before their Lord, seeing how their remorse and disgrace will last forever for having slaughtered the followers of the Progeny of Your Prophets, Messengers, and Righteous Slaves.

اللهم العنهم في مستسر السر وظاهر العلانية في أرضك وسمآئك

O'Allah! Send Lanat upon them in all times, openly and unseen, in Your earth and in Your heavens.

اللهم اجعل لي لسان صدق في أوليائك، وحبب إلي مشاهدهم حتى تلحقني بهم وتجعلني لهم تبعاً في الدنيا و الآخرة، يا أرحم الراحمين

O'Allah! Make my tongue truthful regarding Your Auwliya and make me love Their places until You cause me to join Them. And make me of those who follow Them in this life and in the Hereafter, O' the Most Merciful of the Merciful!

Then sit by His head and recite the following:

سلام الله و سلام ملائكته المقربين و المسلمين لك بقلوبهم، و الناطقين بفضلك، و الشاهدين على أنك صادق أمين صديق، عليك يا مولاي، السلام من الله عليك و على روحك و بدنك

May the salam of Allah and the salam of those angels nearest to Him be upon You, and the salam of those angels who submit to You with their hearts, who extol Your virtues, and testify to Your honesty, loyalty and integrity. May the salam of Allah be upon You, Your Ruh, and Your body.

أشهد أنك طهر طاهر مطهر

I testify that You are Tahir (Pure), Taheer (Purity), and Mutahir (Purifier).

و أسهد الك يا ولي الله و ولي رسوله ﷺ بالبلاغ و الأداء،

O'Wali of Allah and Wali of His Messenger (saw)! I testify You announced the decree of Allah and fulfilled Your duties.

و أشهد أنك جنب الله و أنك باب الله، و أنك وجه الله الذي منه يؤتى، و أنك خليل الله و أنك عبد الله، أخو رسوله

I testify You are Janibullah (side of Allah), You are Babullah (door of Allah), You are Wajullah (face of Allah) through which He is approached, You are Khaleelullah (friend of Allah), and You are Abdullah (slave of Allah) and the brother of RasoolAllah (saw).

و قد أتيتك و افداً لعظيم حالك و منزلتك عند الله و عند رسوله، أتيتك زائراً متقرباً إلى الله بزيارتك، طالباً كلاص نفسي، متعوذاً بك من نار استحقها مثلي بما جنيته على نفسي

I have come to visit You due to the greatness of Your position and status with Allah and His Messenger (saw). I have come to visit You in order to seek the nearness of Allah, to request salvation, and seeking refuge with You from the fires which the likes of me deserves for the crimes I have committed against myself.

أتيتك انقطاعاً إليك وإلى ولدك الخلف من بعدك على بركة الحق، فقلبي لك مسلم، وأمري لك متبع، و نصرتي لك معدة و أنا عبد الله و مولاك في طاعتك، والوافد إليك، ألتمس بذلك كمال المنزلة عند الله

I have come to You and to Your Son, the heir after You and Imam of the Time, with the blessing of Haq (truth) and with hope in no other. My heart is submissive to You, I follow Your commands, and I am prepared to support You. I have come as Your guest, seeking to perfect my status before Allah.

وأنت يا مولاي من أمر ني الله بطاعته، وحثني على بره، دلني على فضله، وهدني لحبه، ورغبني في الوفادة إلى طلب الحوائج عنده

O' my Moula! You are the one Allah has ordered me to obey and the one Allah has warned me to be loyal to and whose grace Allah has manifested for me. Allah has guided me towards loving You and given me the desire to visit You to ask for the fulfillment of my needs.

أنتم أهل بيت يسعد من تولاكم، ولايخيب من أتاكم، ولا يخسر من يهواكم، ولا يسعد من عاداكم، لا أجد أحداً أفزع إليه خيراً لى منكم، أنتم أهل بيت الرحمة، ودعائم الدين، وأركان الأرض، و الشجرة الطيبة

You are part of Ahlul Bayt (asws) whose lovers are blessed. Those who come to You will not be disappointed and those who desire You will not be lost. But those who oppose You will never obtain success. I cannot find any other more benevolent than You with whom to seek refuge. You are the merciful Ahlul Bayt, the pillars of the deen, the foundation of the earth, and Shajr e Tooba.

اللهم لا تخيب توجهي إليك برسولك و آل رسولك،

O'Allah! Do not hinder my approaching You through Your Rasool (saw) and Aal e Rasool (asws) (His Family).

اللهم أنت مننت علي بزيارة مولاي وولايته ومعرفته فاجعلني ممن تنصره وينتصر به، ومن علي بنصرك لدينك في الدنيا و الآخرة،

O'Allah! You bestowed Your favor upon me through the ziarat of my Moula, through His Wilayat, and His marifat (recognition). Therefore, make me among those whom You support and with those who will be victorious. Honor me by allowing me to support Your religion in this life and in the Hereafter.

اللهم أحيني على ما حيي عليه علي بن أبي طالبّ و أمتني على ما مات عليه علي بن أبي طالبّ

O'Allah! Make me live the way Ali (asws) ibn Abi Talib (as) lived and make me leave this world on the same path as the one Ali (asws) ibn Abi Talib (as) was on when He left this world.

HADITH 3

Imam al Hadi (asws) narrates:

Recite the following beside the grave of Ameerul Momineen (asws):

السلام عليك يا ولي الله أنت أول مظلوم وأول من غصب حقه، صبرت و احتسبت حتى أتك اليقين

Salam upon You, O' Waliullah! You are the first who was oppressed and the first one whose right was usurped. You remained patient, awaiting the rewards from Allah until that which was certain came to You.

و أشهد أنك لقيت الله و أنت شهيد، عذب الله قاتلك بأنواع العذاب، وجدد عليه العذاب

I testify You met Allah as a martyr. May Allah torment Your killer with endless kinds of torments and may Allah renew the torment of Your killer over and over.

جئتك عارفاً بحقك، مستبصراً بشأنك، موالياً لأوليآئك، معادياً لأعدائك و من ظلمك، ألقى على ذلك ربي إن شاء الله تعالى

I have come to You while being aware of Your right and blessed with the understanding of Your status. I love those who love You and I am hostile against Your enemies and those who oppressed You. InshaAllah I shall meet with My Lord in this very state.

يا ولي الله إن لي ذنوباً كثيرة فاشفع لي إلى ربك فإن لك عند الله مقاماً معلوماً، وإن لك عند الله جاهاً وشفاعة، و قال: (لا يشفعون إلا لمن ارتضى و هم من خشيته مشفقون) (٢١:٢٨)

O'Waliullah! My sins are great so intercede for me with Your Lord, for You have a known position and great status with Allah. You have the power to intercede before Allah. For He has said, *"and they offer no intercession except for those who are He has approved, and they stand in awe and reverence of His (Glory)."* (Quran 21:28)

Chapter 12

Bidding Farewell After the Ziarat of Ameerul Momineen (asws)

HADITH 1

Imam Musa Kazim (asws) narrates:

Recite the following when bidding farewell to the grave of Ameerul Momineen (asws):

السلام عليك وحمة الله وبركاته، أستودعك الله و أستر عيك، و أقرء عليك السلام، آمنا بالله وبالرسك وبما جائت به ودعت إليه ودلت عليه، فاكتبنا مع الشاهدين،

Salam to You and may the mercy and blessings of Allah be upon You. I entrust You with Allah and I ask Allah to protect You. I extend my salam to You. We believe in Allah, His messengers, all that which they brought with them and that to which they invited and guided the people. Include us among those who testify.

اللهم ال تجعله آخر العهد من زيارتي إتاه فإن توفيتني قبل ذلك، فإني أشهد في مماتي على ما شهدت عليه فى حياتي، أشهد أنكم الأئمة،

O' Allah! Do not let this be the last time I come for His Ziarat. If You take my life before I perform His Ziarat again, then I will testify after my death to that which I testified during my life. I testify that You are the Imams (and name the Imams (asws) one after another)

و أشهد أن من قتلهم و حاربهم مشركون، و من رد عليهم ورد علمهم في أسفل درك من الجحيم، و أشهد أن من حاربهم لنا أعداء و نحن منهم بر ءاء، و أنهم حزب الشيطان

And I testify those who killed and fought against Them were mushriks (polytheists). And those who opposed Their words and Their knowledge are in the lowest levels of Hell. I testify those who fought against Them are our enemies and we disassociate ourselves from them for they are the part of Shaitan

و على من قتلهم لعنة الله و الملائكة و الناس أجمعين، و مان شرك فيهم، و من سره قتلهم،

May the lanat of Allah, the lanat of the angels, and the lanat from all of the people be upon those who slaughtered Them, those who participated in Their slaughtering and those who were pleased with it.

اللهم إني أشألك بعد الصلاة و التسليم، أن تصلي على محمد و آل محمد، و لا تجعله آخر العهد من زيارته، فإن جعلته فاحشرني مع هئلاء المسمين الأئمة،

O' Allah! After the prayers and after saying salam to the Imams (asws), I ask You to send Your blessing on Muhammad (saw) and Aal e Muhammad (asws). Do not let this be the last time I come for His Ziarat and if it is then resurrect me with the mentioned Imams (asws).

اللهم و ذلل قلوبنا لهم بالطاعة و المناصحة و المحبة و حسن المؤازرة

O' Allah! Humble our hearts before Them through our obedience and sincerity to Them, our love for Them, and our support for Them.

Chapter 13

Merits of drinking the water of and performing ghusl in the River Furat

HADITH 1
Ameerul Momineen (asws) narrates:

"Water is Syedul Sharab (master of refreshment) in this world and in the hereafter. Four of the rivers in this world are from Jannah (paradise); the Euphrates, the Nile, the Sihan and the Jihan. The Euphrates is the water. The Nile is honey. The Sihan is nectar. The Jihan is milk."

HADITH 2
Abu Abdullah Imam Jafar Sadiq (asws) narrates:

"If the water of the Euphrates River is the first drink inside of the mouth of a newborn baby, then he will be amongst those who love Us, the Ahlul Bayt (asws)."

HADITH 3
Abu Jafar (Imam Muhammad Baqir asws) narrates:

"If the distance between Us and the Euphrates was this much, and He indicated a specific distance, then We would go to find cure with its water."

HADITH 4
Sulaiman ibn Haroon al Ajli narrates:

I heard Abu Abdullah (Imam Jafar Sadiq asws) say, "Those whose first drinks are with water from Euphrates River can never be anything except from amongst those who love Us, Ahlul Bayt (asws)."

Then the Imam (asws) asked me, "What is the distance between you and the Euphrates River?"

I replied to the Imam (asws) and then He said, "If I were next to it, then I would enter it at the two ends of every day."

HADITH 5
Abu Abdullah (Imam Jafar Sadiq asws) explained the meaning of the ayah, *"and We gave them a shelter on a lofty ground having meadows and springs"* (Quran 23:50)

Imam (asws) said, "Lofty ground refers to Najaf or Kufa and springs refers to the Euphrates River."

HADITH 6
Ameerul Momineen Ali (asws) narrates:

"The Euphrates River is Syedul Mai (master of the waters) in this world and in the hereafter."

HADITH 7
Imam Zainul Abideen (asws) narrates:

"Every night an angel descends and drops three drops of musk from the musk of Jannah (paradise) into the Euphrates River. There is no river anywhere in the east or the west that is more blessed than the Euphrates River."

HADITH 8
Abu Abdullah (Imam Jafar Sadiq asws) narrates:

"Every day some drops from Jannah (paradise) fall into the Euphrates River."

HADITH 9

Abdullah ibn Sulaiman narrates:

During the time of Abul Abbas, Abu Abdullah (Imam Jafar Sadiq asws) came to Kufa on His mount wearing His traveling clothes. He stopped at the bridge of Kufa and asked His servant for some water.

The servant took a vessel and filled it with water from the Euphrates River and then gave it to the Imam (asws). The Imam (asws) began to drink and as He drank some of the water spilled from the corners of His mouth onto His beard and clothes. Then the Imam (asws) asked for some more water. The servant filled the vessel again and gave it back to the Imam (asws). After Imam (asws) finished drinking the water, He praised Allah and said:

"What a blessed river this is! Every day seven drops from Jannah (paradise) fall into it. If people knew of the blessings of this river, they would build their tents on its banks. If it were not that which enters this river from the sinners, then every ill person who submerged himself in it would not leave without being cured."

HADITH 10

Abu Abdullah (Imam Jafar Sadiq asws) narrates:

"*The shores in the right side of the valley*" (Quran 28:30) mentioned by Allah in His Book is the Euphrates River. "*The blessed spot*" (Quran 28:30) is Karbala and "*the tree*" (Quran 28:30) is Muhammad (saw)."

HADITH 11

Abu Abdullah (Imam Jafar Sadiq asws) said:

"I cannot see any newborn whose first drink was water from the Euphrates River be anything but from amongst Our Shia."

HADITH 12

Imam Zainul Abideen (asws) narrates:

"Every night Allah sends an angel who drops 3 drops of musk from the musk of Jannah (paradise) into the Euphrates River. There is no river anywhere in the earth from the east to the west more blessed than the Euphrates."

HADITH 13

Abu Abdullah (Imam Jafar Sadiq asws) narrates:

"I cannot foresee any newborn whose first drink was water from the Euphrates River be anything but from those who love Us, Ahlul Bayt (asws)."

HADITH 14

Imam Jafar Sadiq (asws) narrated regarding the Euphrates River:

"It is from amongst the Shia of Ali (asws). No one's first drink is from it without him loving Us, Ahlul Bayt (asws)."

HADITH 15

Abu Abdullah (Imam Jafar Sadiq asws) narrates:

"If the water of the Euphrates River is the first drink that is given to a newborn baby, then he will be amongst those who love Us because the Euphrates is a momin (believer)."

HADITH 16

Abu Abdullah (Imam Jafar Sadiq asws) said:

"There are two rivers that are momin (believers) and two that are kafireen (disbelievers). The kafir (disbelieving) rivers are the Balkh and the Tigris Rivers. The two momin (believing) rivers are the Nile and the Euphrates. Therefore, make the first drink of your children be from the water of the Euphrates."

Chapter 14

The love of the Prophet (saw) for Imam Hasan (asws) and Imam Hussain (asws), and His order to love Them

HADITH 1

Ameerul Momineen Ali (asws) said:

"RasoolAllah (saw) use to say, "O Ali (asws)! These two Sons (referring to Imam Hasan (asws) and Imam Hussain (asws) have caused Me to forget the love of anything else except for Them. My Lord ordered Me to love Them and to love those who love Them."

HADITH 2

Imran ibn Hussain narrates:

RasoolAllah (saw) said to me, "O Imran! Everything has a place in the heart, but nothing can replace the love I have in My heart for these two Sons."

I said, "O RasoolAllah (saw)! You love Them this much?"

RasoolAllah (saw) replied, "That which is hidden from you is even greater than this. Allah has ordered Me to love Them."

HADITH 3

Abu Zarr al Ghifari narrates:

RasoolAllah (saw) ordered me to love Hasan (asws) and Hussain (asws). Therefore I love Them and love those who love Them because of the love of RasoolAllah (saw) for Them."

HADITH 4

Abu Zarr al Ghafari narrates:

I saw RasoolAllah (saw) kiss Hasan (asws) and Hussain (asws) and say:

"The fire will not touch the face of those who are sincere in their love for Hasan (asws) and Hussain (asws) and Their Offspring. Even if their sins are equal to the number of grains of sand, except for those who commit a sin which removes them from the faith."

HADITH 5

Abdullah ibn Masood narrates:

I heard RasoolAllah (saw) say, "Those who love Me must love these two Sons of Mine for Allah has ordered Me to love the two of Them."

HADITH 6

Imam Muhammad Baqir (asws) narrates:

RasoolAllah (saw) said, "Those who want to hold onto the *"firmest handle"* (Quran 2:256) of Allah, which is mentioned in His Book, should love Ali (asws) ibn Abi Talib (as), Hasan (asws), and Hussain (asws) for Allah loves Them from above the Arsh (throne)."

HADITH 7

Imam Jafar Sadiq (asws) narrates::

RasoolAllah (saw) said, "Those who hate Hasan (asws) and Hussain (asws) will appear on the Day of Judgment with the flesh torn from their faces and they will be excluded from My intercession."

HADITH 8

Imam Jafar Sadiq (asws) narrates:

RasoolAllah (saw) said, "Women (Syeda Khadija sa and Syeda Fatima sa) are Quraitul Aini (light of My eye) and My two flowers are Hasan (asws) and Hussain (asws)."

HADITH 9

Zadan w narrates:

I heard Ali (asws) ibn Abi Talib (as) say in Ruhbat, "Hasan (asws) and Hussain (asws) are the two flowers of RasoolAllah (saw)."

HADITH 10

RasoolAllah (saw) narrates:

"Hold onto this al Inza (title of Moula Ali asws). He is Siddiq e Akbar (most trustworthy) and He is the guide of those who follow Him. Those who proceed before Him have left the religion of Allah. Allah will destroy those who disappoint Him. Those who adhere to Him have adhered to *"rope of Allah"* (Quran 3:103)

Those who accept His Wilayat are guided by Allah and those who deny it are led astray.

Hasan (asws) and Hussain (asws) are the leaders of My ummah (nation), are from Ali (asws), and are My two Sons. The rightly guided Imams (asws) are from Their Offspring as is the Mahdi, al Qaim (atfs). Therefore, love Them and follow Them. Do not take Their enemies as friends and do not choose Their enemies as leaders over Them for if you do, then the wrath of the Lord will fall upon you and you will be disgraced in this world. *"He who lies fails miserably"* (Quran 20:61)

HADITH 11

RasoolAllah (saw) narrates:

"Hussain (asws) is from Me and I am from Hussain (asws). Allah loves those who love Hussain (asws). Hussain (asws) is My Son."

HADITH 12

Yahla al Amiri narrates:

I was traveling along with RasoolAllah (saw) to a place where He had been invited to eat food when we saw Hussain (asws) playing with some other children. RasoolAllah (saw) went ahead of us and opened His arms. Hussain (asws) was running around and RasoolAllah (saw) was chasing Him, making Him laugh, until RasoolAllah (saw) finally caught Hussain (asws).

Then RasoolAllah (saw) placed one hand under the chin of Hussain (asws) and the other behind His head and kissed Hussain (asws).

Then RasoolAllah (saw) said, "Hussain (asws) is from Me and I am from Hussain (asws). Those who love Allah love Hussain (asws). Hussain (asws) is a Son from My Sons."

HADITH 13

Imam Musa Kazim (asws) narrates:

"RasoolAllah (saw) held the hands of Hasan (asws) and Hussain (asws) and said:

Those who love these two boys and love Their Father (asws) and Mother (sa) will be with Me at My station on the Day of Judgment."

Chapter 15

Ziarat of Imam Hasan (asws) ibn Ali (asws) and the other
Imams (asws) in al Baqi

HADITH 1

Umar ibn Yazid Bayyah al Saburi narrates:

Muhammad ibn Ali (asws) ibn al Hanafiyah would go to the grave of Hasan (asws) ibn Ali
(asws) and recite:

السلام عليك يا بن أمير المؤمنينّ و ابن أول المسلمين، و كيف تكون كذلك، وأنت سليل الهدى وحلف
التقوى وخامس أهل الكساء

Salam be upon You, O Son of Ameerul Momineen (asws) and Son of the First Muslim,
how could You be anything other than this for You are descended from those who are
guided and You are foremost in piety. You are one of the five known as Ahlul Kisa (people of
the cloak).

غذتك يد الرحمة، وربيت في حجر الإسلام، ورضعت من ثدي الإيمان، فطيت حيا، وطبت ميتا، غير أن
النفس غير راضية بفراقك، ولا شاكة في حياتك برحمك الله

71

You were fed by the Hand of Mercy, raised in the lap of Islam, nurtured from the chest of faith. Blessed were You in Life and in Death, our souls are pained at being separated from You; however, there is no doubt that You are alive. May the mercy of Allah be upon You.

Then he would look at Hussain (asws) and say, "O Aba Abdullah (asws)! Salam be upon Abu Muhammad (asws) (Imam Hasan asws)!

HADITH 2

Masoom Imam (asws) narrates:

When you perform the Ziarat of the graves of the Imams (asws) in al Baqi, stand beside the graves while facing them and with your back towards qiblah. Then recite:

السلام عليكم أئمة الهدى

Salam be upon You, Imams of Guidance (asws)

السلام عليكم أهل البر والتقوى

Salam be upon You, People of Righteousness and Piety

السلام عليكم الحجج على أهل الدنيا

Salam be upon You, Hujjat (Proof) on the people of the world

السلام عليكم القوامون في البرية بالقسط

Salam be upon You, Just Guardians of the creations

السلام عليكم أهل الصفوة

Salam be upon the Chosen Family

السلام عليكم يا آل رسول الله ﷺ

Salam be upon You, O Family of RasoolAllah (saw)

السلام عليكم أهل النجوى

Salam be upon You, People of Devotion

أشهد أنكم قد بلغتم ونصحتم وصبرتم في ذات الله، وكذبتم، واسيء إليكم فغفرتم،

I testify that You conveyed the message of Allah and were patient in Allah, You were denied and abused but You forgave

وأشهد أنكم الأئمة الراشدون المهديون، وأن طاعتكم مفروضة، وأن قولكم الصدق، وأنكم دعوتم فلم تجابوا، وأمرتم فلم تطاعوا، و أنكم دعائم الدين، وأركان الأرض

I testify that You are the Rightly Guided Imams (asws) whose obedience is wajib (obligatory) and who speak only the truth. You called the people but Your call was ignored. You ordered the people but Your order was not obeyed. You are the Pillars of the Religion and the Foundations of the Earth.

لم تزالوا بعين الله، ينسخكم في أصلاب كل مطهر، وينقلكم من أرحام المطهرات، لم تدنسكم الجاهلية الجهلاء، ولم تشرك فيكم فتن الأهواء

Allah has always been with You. He took You from the loins of the Purified Fathers and placed You in the wombs of the Purified Mothers. The ignorance of the ignorant did not touch You and the desires of the flesh were not felt by You

طيتم وطاب منبتكم، من بكم علينا ديان الدين فجعلكم في بيوت أذن الله أن ترفع ويذكر فيها اسمه،

You are blessed and the places in which You were raised are also blessed. Dianul Deen blessed us through You by placing You *"in houses which Allah has permitted to be exalted and His name to be remembered therein"* (Quran 24:36)

وجعل صلواتنا عليكم رحمة لنا وكفارة لذنوبنا، إذ اختاركم الله لنا،

Allah has made our salawat upon You as a means of mercy for us and an expiation of our sins. Allah has chosen You for us.

وطيب خلقنا بما من علينا من ولايتكم، وكنا عنده مسمين بعلمكم، معترفين بتصديقنا إياكم،

And purified the creation by bestowing His blessings upon us through Your Wilayat. We possess knowledge of You and are counted amongst those who recognize Your Imamate.

و هذا مقام من أسرف وأخطأ واستكان وأقر بما جنى ورجى بمقامه الخلاص، وأن يستنقذه بكم مستنقذ الهلكى من الردى،

I am in the state of one who has been excessive and committed sins, but has renounced and admitted to his past actions and desires to be saved through his coming here. I am one who hopes the savior of those ruined will save him from chastisement through You

فكونوا لي شفعآء، فقد وفدت إليكم إذ رغب عنكم أهل الدنيا، واتخذوا آيات الله هزوا واستكبروا

Intercede for me for I have come to You while the People of the World have denied You, and have mocked and scorned the Ayatullahs (signs of Allah)

يا من هو قائم لا يسهو، ودائم لا يلهو، و محيط بكل شىء،

O He who oversees the affairs and is everlasting and never distraught and encompasses all things

لك المن بما وفقتني وعرفتني وعرفتني أئمتي، و بما أقمتني عليه، إذ صد عنه عبادك، وجهلوا معرفته، واستخفوا بحقه، ومالوا إلى سواه،

You have honored me by allowing me to know my Imams (asws) and by keeping me firm on Them while Your slaves have abandoned it, been ignorant in recognizing it, demeaned its right, and followed other paths

فكانت المنة منك علي أقو ام خصصتهم بما خصصتني به، فلك الحمد إذ كنت عندك في مقام منكوراً مكتوباً، فلا تحرمني ما رجوت، ولا تخيبني فيما دعوت في مقامي هذا، بحرمة محمد ﷺ و آله الطاهرين

You have chosen me, praise is for You for bestowing this position upon me. Do not deprive me of that which I long for and bless me through the honor of Muhammad (saw) and His Purified Family (asws)

Then pray for the fulfillment of your needs

HADITH 3

Imam Jafar Sadiq (asws) narrates:

"Recite whatever you like beside the grave of Ali (asws) ibn Hussain (asws) (Imam Sajjad)"

Chapter 16

Jibrael (as) reveals the Martyrdom of Hussain (asws) ibn Ali (asws)

HADITH 1

Imam Jafar Sadiq (asws) said:

"Fatima (sa) went to RasoolAllah (saw) and saw that His eyes were wet with tears. She asked Him, "What is troubling You?"

RasoolAllah (saw) replied, "Jibrael (as) has informed Me that My ummah (nation) will slaughter Hussain (asws)."

HADITH 2

Imam Muhammad Baqir (asws) narrates:

Ameerul Momineen (asws) narrates:

"RasoolAllah (saw) came to visit Us. Um Ayman had given to Us some milk, butter, and dates so We offered them to RasoolAllah (saw). After He had finished eating, He went to a corner of the house and began to pray. When He reached the last sajda, He began to weep immensely. Out of respect, We did not ask Him why He was crying.

Then Hussain (asws) went and sat upon His lap and said, "O Father (saw)! When You entered Our house, We felt such a happiness that We had never felt before, but now You have begun to weep and Your weeping has caused Us to be sorrowful. What has caused You to cry?"

RasoolAllah (saw) replied, "O My Son (asws)! Jibrael (as) just came to Me with the news of how You all will be martyred. The places in which You all will be martyred are very far from one another."

Hussain (asws) asked, "O Father (saw)! What is the reward for those who perform the Ziarat of Our graves even though They are far from each other?"

RasoolAllah (saw) replied, "O My Son (asws)! There will be some from My ummah (nation) who will perform Your Ziarat while seeking blessings. They will be counted amongst those whose Ziarat I will perform on the Day of Judgment. I will protect them from the intense fear of the Hour and forgive them of their sins. Allah will make their abode in Jannah (paradise)."

HADITH 3

Ali (asws) ibn Abi Talib (as) narrates:

"RasoolAllah (saw) visited Us one day. We offered Him a plate full of dates and a cup of milk and butter, which had been sent to Us from Um Ayman. After He ate, I rose and poured some water over His hands and I washed them. Then I wiped His face and beard with the water from His hands. Then He went to a corner of the house and began to pray. When He went into sajda, He began to weep. After weeping for a long time, He raised His head.

Then Hussain (asws) went and climbed on the lap of RasoolAllah (saw). Hussain (asws) placed RasoolAllah (saw)'s head on His chest and then laid His chin on top of the head of RasoolAllah (saw). Then He said, "O Father (saw)! What causes You to weep?"

RasoolAllah (saw) replied, "O My Son (asws)! When I saw You, Ahlul Bayt (asws), today I felt such a happiness that I had never felt before, but then Jibrael (as) came to Me and informed Me that each of You will be martyred and that Your graves will be far from each other. I praised Allah and asked Him to bless You all with the best."

Hussain (asws) asked, "O Father (saw)! Who will perform the Ziarat of Our graves and maintain their oaths with Them even though They are far from each other?"

RasoolAllah (saw) replied, "Those from My ummah (nation) who seek My pleasure and seek nearness to Me by performing Ziarat of Your graves. On the Day of Judgment, I will search for them and take them by the hand and save them from the hardships and tribulations of that day."

Chapter 17

Jibrael (as) shows RasoolAllah (saw) the land on which Imam Hussain (asws) will be Slaughtered

HADITH 1

Imam Jafar Sadiq (asws) said:

"Jibrael (as) came to RasoolAllah (saw) once while Hussain (asws) was playing in front of Him. Jibrael (as) told Him how His ummah (nation) would slaughter Hussain (asws) and RasoolAllah (saw) became ill at ease. Jibrael (as) then asked RasoolAllah (saw), "Should I not show to You the land upon which He will be killed?"

Then suddenly the land began to sink within the earth and the place where RasoolAllah (saw) was sitting and the land upon which Hussain (asws) would be slaughtered became as one. Then Jibrael (as) took some of its soil and then the earth returned to the way it had been originally within the blink of an eye.

RasoolAllah (saw) departed whilst saying, "Blessings upon You, O Clay! Blessings upon those who will be martyred along with You!"

Then Imam (asws) continued and said:

The companion of Sulaiman (as) also did this. He mentioned Ism e Azm (greatest name of Allah) and the earth between Sulaiman (as)'s bed and throne disappeared within the earth. The earth along with all of its movable and unmovable parts disappeared and Asif lifted the throne before the two became as one. Sulaiman (as) said, "It appears as if the throne came from under my bed."

Imam (asws) then added, "Then the earth returned to the way it had been originally in less than the blink of an eye."

HADITH 2

Imam Jafar Sadiq (asws) narrates:

"Jibrael (as) informed RasoolAllah (saw) about the martyrdom of Hussain (asws) in the house of Umm Salamah (sa). Hussain (asws) entered while Jibrael (as) was with RasoolAllah (saw). Jibrael (as) said to RasoolAllah (saw), "Your ummah (nation) will martyr Him."

RasoolAllah (saw) said, "Show Me the soil upon which His blood will be shed."

Jibrael (as) took a handful of that soil and it was red in color."

HADITH 3

Imam Jafar Sadiq (asws) said:

"Jibrael (as) informed RasoolAllah (saw) regarding the martyrdom of Hussain (asws) in the house of Umm Salamah (sa). Hussain (asws) entered while Jibrael (as) was with RasoolAllah (saw) and Jibrael (as) said to RasoolAllah (saw), "Your ummah will martyr Him."

RasoolAllah (saw) said, "Show Me the soil upon which His blood will be shed."

Jibrael (as) took a handful of that soil and it was red in color. Umm Salamah (sa) kept it with her until her death."

HADITH 4

Abdul Malik ibn Ayan narrates:

I heard Abu Abdullah (Imam Jafar Sadiq asws) say:

"Once when Jibrael (as) was with RasoolAllah (saw) in the house of Umm Salamah (sa), Hussain (asws) entered. Jibrael (as) said, "Your ummah will martyr this Son of Yours. Should I show You the soil upon which He will be martyred?"

RasoolAllah (saw) replied, "Yes."

Jibrael (as) extended his hand and took a handful of that soil and then showed it to RasoolAllah (saw)."

HADITH 5

Abu Baseer narrates:

I heard Abu Abdullah (Imam Jafar Sadiq asws) say:

"Once when Hussain (asws) ibn Ali (asws) was with RasoolAllah (saw), Jibrael (as) appeared and asked, "O Muhammad (saw)! Do You love Him?"

RasoolAllah (saw) replied, "Yes."

Jibrael (as) said, "Your ummah will slaughter Him." Then RasoolAllah (saw) became distressed so Jibrael (as) asked, "O RasoolAllah (saw)! Would You like for me to show You the land upon which He will be martyred?"

RasoolAllah (saw) said, "Yes."

Then the earth began to sink within itself and the spot where RasoolAllah (saw) was sitting and the land upon which Hussain (asws) would be martyred came next to each other just like this and the Imam (asws) placed His two index fingers together.

Then Imam (asws) continued:

"Jibrael (as) took some of the earth with his wing and gave it to RasoolAllah (saw). Then the land returned to the way it had been before in less than a blink of an eye.

Then RasoolAllah (saw) said, "Blessed is this soil and blessed are those who were martyred upon it."

HADITH 6

Imam Jafar Sadiq (asws) narrates:

"When Fatima (sa) appeared with Hussain (asws), Jibrael (as) came to RasoolAllah (saw) and said, "Your ummah (nation) will martyr Hussain (asws) after You. Should I show You some of His soil?"

Then Jibrael (as) hit the land of Karbala with his wing and took some of the soil and showed it to RasoolAllah (saw). Then Jibrael (as) said, "This is the soil upon which He will be martyred."

HADITH 7

ibne Abbas (as) narrates:

The angel who appeared to Muhammad (saw) to inform Him of the martyrdom of Hussain (asws) was Rooh al Ameen, Jibrael (as). He appeared before RasoolAllah (saw) with his wings spread while weeping and wailing. He was carrying some of the soil of Hussain (asws). A fragrance was coming from it just like that of musk.

RasoolAllah (saw) asked him, "Will a nation that slaughters My Son (asws) or the Son (asws) of My Daughter (sa) find success?"

Jibrael (as) replied, "Allah will inflict upon them disunity so their hearts will not be united with one another."

HADITH 8

Sulaiman narrates:

"Was there an angel in the heavens that did not come down to offer condolences to RasoolAllah (saw) regarding His Son, Hussain (asws), and to tell Him of the reward of Hussain (asws) with Allah? Or any who did not appear before RasoolAllah (saw) carrying some of the soil upon which Hussain (asws) fell, was slaughtered, and abandoned on?

RasoolAllah (saw) used to say, "O Allah! Abandon those who abandoned Hussain (asws), slaughter those who slaughtered Hussain (asws), slay those who slew Him and do not fulfill their requests."

Abdul Rahman said, "I swear by Allah that the accursed Yazid (la) was soon after taken from this world. He did not obtain any enjoyment or pleasure after the slaughtering of Hussain (asws). He died suddenly after spending the night drinking. In the morning, he was found dead and his body was deformed as if it had been covered with tar. Anyone who obeyed the order of Yazid (la) in the slaughtering of Hussain (asws) or anyone who participated in the fighting against Hussain (asws) went insane or became afflicted with leprosy, which they passed onto their descendants. May the lanat of Allah be upon them all!"

HADITH 9

Mualla ibn Khunais narrates:

One morning Fatima (sa) saw RasoolAllah (saw) weeping and upset. She asked Him, "What is troubling You, O RasoolAllah (saw)?"

But RasoolAllah (saw) refused to tell Her why He was upset.

Fatima (sa) said, "I will not be able to eat or drink until You tell Me."

Then RasoolAllah (saw) said, "Jibrael (as) brought to Me some of the soil upon which a Son who has not yet appeared will be slaughtered."

Then RasoolAllah (saw) continued and said, "His Noor has not yet appeared in this world but this is the soil of that place upon which He shall be martyred."

Chapter 18

Ayahs in Quran regarding the Martyrdom of Hussain (asws)
and the Avenging of His Blood

HADITH 1

Imam Jafar Sadiq (asws) said:

"And We had made known to the children of Israel in the Book: Ye will work corruption in the earth twice" (Quran 17:4)

The first "corruption" refers to the martyrdom of Ameerul Momineen (asws) and the second "corruption" refers to the martyrdom of Hasan (asws) ibn Ali (asws)."

"And you will be elated with a mighty arrogance" (Quran 17:4) refers to the martyrdom of Hussain (asws) ibn Ali (asws)."

"So when the promise for the first of the two came" (Quran 17:5) refers to when the avenger of the blood of Hussain (asws) will come."

"We sent over you Our servants, of mighty prowess, so they went to and fro among the houses" (Quran 17:5) refers to a group who will rise before the time of Qaim (atfs) and who will slaughter anyone who had participated in the shedding of the blood of the Family (asws) of Muhammad (saw).

"and it was a warning fulfilled" (Quran 17:5)

HADITH 2

Abu Baseer narrates:

Imam Muhammad Baqir (asws) recited this ayah, *"Most surely We help Our messengers, and those who believe, in this world's life and on the day when the witnesses shall stand"* (Quran 40:51)

Then Imam (asws) said, "Hussain (asws) ibn Ali (asws) is amongst those referred to in this ayah, but He has not yet been helped. I swear by Allah that the killers of Hussain (asws) may have been killed, but His blood has not yet been avenged."

HADITH 3

Imam Jafar Sadiq (asws) narrates regarding this ayah, *"And when the female infant buried alive is asked For what sin she was killed"* (Quran 81:8-9)

"It was revealed for Hussain (asws) ibn Ali (asws)."

HADITH 4

Abu Khalid al Kabuli narrates:

I heard Abu Jafar (Imam Muhammad Baqir asws) say regarding this ayah, *"Permission (to fight) is given to those upon whom war is made because they are oppressed, and most surely Allah is most powerful to assist them"* (Quran 22:39)

Imam (asws) said, "This ayah was revealed for Ali (asws), Hasan (asws), and Hussain (asws)."

HADITH 5

Muhammad ibn Sinan who narrated from another who said:

I asked Abu Abdullah (Imam Jafar Sadiq asws) regarding the meaning of the ayah, *"and whoever is slain unjustly, We have indeed given to his heir authority, so let him not exceed the just limits in slaying; surely he is aided"* (Quran 17:33)

Imam (asws) said, "This is about al Qaim (atfs) from the Family (asws) of Muhammad (saw). When He reappears, He will avenge the blood of Hussain (asws).

"so let him not exceed the just limits in slaying" (Quran 17:33) means that even if He slaughters every single person on this earth, He still will not have exceeded His limit. I swear by Allah that He will kill the descendants of the killers of Hussain (asws) for the deeds of their fathers."

HADITH 6

Imam Jafar Sadiq (asws) narrates:

"The ayah, *"then there should be no hostility except against the oppressors"* (Quran 2:193) refers to the children of the killers of Hussain (asws)."

HADITH 7

Imam Jafar Sadiq (asws) narrates:

"And We had made known to the children of Israel in the Book: Ye will work corruption in the earth twice" (Quran 17:4)

The first "corruption" refers to the martyrdom of Ameerul Momineen (asws) and the second "corruption" refers to the martyrdom of Hasan (asws) ibn Ali (asws)."

"And you will be elated with a mighty arrogance" (Quran 17:4) refers to the martyrdom of Hussain (asws)."

Chapter 19

The knowledge of the Prophets (as) regarding the Martyrdom of Hussain (asws) ibn Ali (asws)

HADITH 1

Imam Jafar Sadiq (asws) narrates:

"The Ismail mentioned in the ayah, *"And remember Ismail in the Book; surely he was truthful in his promise, and he was a messenger, a prophet"* (Quran 19:54) is not Ismail, son of Ibrahim (as). It is Ismail who was a prophet sent by Allah amongst His people, but his people captured him and skinned his scalp and face.

An angel from Allah (swt) came to him and said, "Allah has sent me to you. Order me to do upon this nation that which you desire."

Ismail (as) replied, "I follow the example of Hussain (asws) and that which will happen to Him."

HADITH 2

Imam Jafar Sadiq (asws) narrates:

"A prophet and messenger of Allah was seized by his nation. They removed the flesh from his face and the scalp from his head. A messenger from the Lord of the Worlds came to him and said, "Your Lord conveys His Salam upon you and says, "I see what they have done to you." He has ordered me to obey you and do whatever you order me to do upon this nation."

The prophet and messenger of Allah replied, "I follow the example of Hussain (asws)."

HADITH 3

Buraid ibn Muawiyah al Ijlee narrates:

I asked Abu Abdullah (Imam Jafar Sadiq asws), "O Son (asws) of RasoolAllah (saw)! Is the Ismail mentioned in this ayah, *"And remember Ismail in the Book; surely he was truthful in (his) promise, and he was a messenger, a prophet"* (Quran 19:54) Ismail the son of Ibrahim (as) for this is what the people believe?"

Imam (asws) replied, "Ismail (as) died before Ibrahim (as). Ibrahim (as) was the Hujjat (proof) of Allah and an owner of the Shariah (Islamic law). Then to whom was Ismail (as) sent?"

I asked, "May I be sacrificed upon You! Then to whom does this ayah refer?"

Imam (asws) replied, "It refers to Ismail (as), son of Prophet Hizqeel (as). Allah sent him to his nation but they denied him, killed him, and skinned his face. Then the wrath of Allah fell upon them and Allah sent Satateel, the Angel of Chastisement, to Ismail (as).

The angel said, "O Ismail (as)! I am Satateel, the Angel of Chastisement. The Lord of Glory has sent me to you to chastise your nation with numerous punishments, if you so desire."

Ismail (as) replied, "I do not desire this."

Allah sent a wahi (revelation) to him and said, "O Ismail (as)! Then what is it you desire?"

Ismail (as) replied, "O Lord! You have taken an oath of allegiance from the creation for Yourself through the Rubiat (lordship), for Muhammad (saw) through the Nabuwiat (prophet hood), and for His Successors (asws) through the Wilayat. You informed the best of Your creation about what the nation of Hussain (asws) ibn Ali (asws) would do after Him. You promised Hussain (asws) that You return Him to this world so that He may take vengeance upon those who martyred Him. O my Lord! I desire that You return me back to this world just as You will return Hussain (asws) back to this world so that I may seek vengeance against those who have done this to me."

Imam (asws) continued and said, "Allah promised Ismail (as) ibn Hizqeel (as) that He would return him therefore Ismail (as) will return to this world with Hussain (asws)."

HADITH. 4

Imam Jafar Sadiq (asws) narrates:

"The Ismail (as) mentioned by Allah in His Book, "*And remember Ismail in the Book; surely he was truthful in (his) promise, and he was a messenger, a prophet*" (Quran 19:54) was seized and his face and scalp were skinned.

Then an angel came to him and said, "Allah has sent me to you so that you may order me to do against this nation what you desire."

Ismail (as) replied, "I follow the example of Hussain (as)."

Chapter 20

The knowledge of the angels regarding
the martyrdom of Hussain (asws)

HADITH 1

Ibrahim ibn Shoaib al Maithami who narrates:

I heard Abu Abdullah (Imam Jafar Sadiq asws) say:

"When Hussain (asws) ibn Ali (asws) came into this world, Allah ordered Jibrael (as) to descend along with 1000 angels to congratulate RasoolAllah (saw) on behalf of Allah and on his (Jibrael as) own behalf. Along the way, Jibrael (as) descended upon an island in the sea where an angel named Fitrus lived. Fitrus was one of the carriers.

He had been negligent in obeying the order of Allah. His wings were broken and he was thrown onto this island. He worshipped Allah for six hundred years on that island before Hussain (asws) appeared in this world.

Fitrus asked Jibrael (as), "Where are you going?"

Jibrael (as) said, "Allah has bestowed a blessing upon Muhammad (saw) and I have been sent to congratulate Him on behalf of Allah and myself."

Fitrus said, "O Jibrael (as)! Take me with you so that Muhammad (saw) may intercede upon my behalf."

Jibrael (as) carried Fitrus. Upon arriving, Jibrael (as) congratulated Muhammad (saw) on behalf of Allah and from Himself. Then He informed Muhammad (saw) about Fitrus.

RasoolAllah (saw) told Jibrael (as) to bring Fitrus inside. When Fitrus was brought inside, he told RasoolAllah (saw) about his circumstances. RasoolAllah (saw) prayed for him and then said to him, "Rub your wings upon this newborn child and you shall be returned to your previous condition."

Fitrus rubbed his wings upon Hussain (asws) and immediately began ascending towards the heavens. As he was ascending, he said, "O RasoolAllah (saw)! Your ummah will slaughter Him. As my repayment to Him, I shall accompany anyone who performs His Ziarat and anyone who sends salam upon Him I shall bring their salam to Him and anyone who recites durood upon Him, I shall bring their blessings to Him."

Then Fitrus ascended to the heavens.

Chapter 21

Lanat of Allah (swt) and the Prophets upon the killers of Imam Hussain (asws)

HADITH 1

Imam Jafar Sadiq (asws) narrates:

"One day RasoolAllah (saw) was visiting in the house of Fatima (sa). Hussain (asws) was sitting on His lap. Suddenly RasoolAllah (saw) began to weep and fell into sajda.

Then He said:

"O Fatima (sa), daughter of Muhammad (saw), the Most High just appeared before Me in the most beautiful form in Your house and asked Me, "Do You love Hussain (asws)?"

I (RasoolAllah saw) replied, "Yes He is the light of My eyes, My flower, the fruit of My heart, and the skin between My two eyes."

Allah said, "O Muhammad (saw)—He placed His hand on the head of Hussain (asws)! You are blessed through this child upon whom I have bestowed My blessings, mercy, and pleasure. My curse, wrath, chastisement and punishment are upon those who slaughter Him, hold animosity towards Him, wage war against Him, and oppose Him. He is Syedul Shohadu (Master of the Martyrs) from the first to the last in this world and the hereafter."

HADITH 2

Khalid al Rabee who narrated from another who heard Kaaban say:

The first person to send lanat (curse) upon those who slaughtered Hussain (asws) ibn Ali (asws) was Ibrahim (as), Khaleelullah (Friend of Allah). He ordered his children to send lanat (curse) upon them and took an oath of allegiance from them regarding this. After Ibrahim (as), Musa (as) ibn Imran (as) sent lanat (curse) upon the killers of Hussain (asws) and ordered his nation to do so as well. Dawood (as) also sent lanat (curse) upon them and ordered Bani Israel to do so as well.

Then Isa (as) sent lanat upon them and he would continuously say to Bani Israel to "Send lanat upon the killers of Hussain (asws) and if you meet Hussain (asws), then you must support Him. Those martyred with Hussain (asws) are like those martyred with all of the prophets who faced their enemies and did not turn away."

It is as if I can see His burial place. Every prophet has visited Karbala. They have all stood upon that land and said, "You are a land full of blessings. the shining moon will be buried within you."

HADITH 3

Hisham ibn Sa'ad narrates:

Some sheikhs narrated that the angel who came to RasoolAllah (saw) and informed Him of the martyrdom of Hussain (asws) ibn Ali (asws) was the angel of the seas. An angel from the angels of Firdoos (highest point in Jannah) flew down to the ocean with his wings spread covering the entire ocean.

He cried out, "O inhabitants of the seas! Adorn yourselves with garments of grief for the son of RasoolAllah (saw) will be slaughtered."

Then he brought some of the soil of Hussain (asws) upon his wings to the heavens. There was not one angel who smelled its fragrance and did not become grieved by it. They all sent lanat (curses) upon the killers of Hussain (asws), their supporters, and their followers."

Chapter 22

Regarding the statement of RasoolAllah (saw) "My ummah will slaughter Hussain (asws)"

HADITH 1

Imam Jafar Sadiq (asws) narrates:

"One day Hussain (asws) ibn Ali (asws) was sat upon the lap of the Prophet (saw). RasoolAllah (saw) was playing with Him causing Hussain (asws) to laugh ayesha (la) said, "O RasoolAllah (saw)! How great is Your love for this boy?!"

RasoolAllah (saw) replied, "Woe be unto you (la)! How could I not love and adore Him when He is the fruit of My heart and the Light of My eyes?! My ummah will slaughter Him. Allah will write the reward for those who perform His Ziarat after His martyrdom equal to that of one Hajj performed by Me."

ayesha (la) said, "O RasoolAllah (saw)! A Hajj from one of Yours?"

RasoolAllah (saw) replied, "Yes or even two of My Hajj."

ayesha (la) said, "O RasoolAllah (saw)! Two hajj from Yours?"

RasoolAllah (saw) replied, "Yes or even four."

ayesha (la) continued asking RasoolAllah (saw) and the reward kept on increasing until it reached 90 of His Hajj as well as 90 of His Umrah."

HADITH 2

Imam Jafar Sadiq (asws) narrates:

"One day Fatima (sa) was holding Hussain (asws) when RasoolAllah (saw) took Him. He said to Hussain (asws), "Lanat (curse) of Allah be upon those who will slaughter You. Lanat (curse) of Allah be upon those who loot Your belongings. May Allah destroy those who help the ones who stood against You. May Allah judge between Me and those who supported those against You."

Fatima (sa) said, "O Father (saw)! What is this You are saying?"

RasoolAllah (saw) replied, "O My Daughter (sa)! I remembered the atrocities that will befall Him after Me and after You and how He will be harmed, oppressed, and betrayed. When this occurs, there will be a group who are like stars in the sky that will be go to their deaths.

RasoolAllah (saw) continued, "It is as if their camp is before Me, the spot where they will dismount from their animals and their soil."

Fatima (sa) asked, "O Father (saw)! Where is this place that You have described?"

RasoolAllah (saw) replied, "It is a land known as Karbala. It is the land of Karb (suffering) and Bala (anguish) for Us and for the ummah. The most corrupt ones from My ummah will rise against Them. Even if all of the inhabitants of the earths and heavens intercede for one from those who rise against Hussain (asws), their intercession will not be accepted and they will remain in Jahannum (hellfire) for all of eternity."

Fatima (sa) asked, "O Father (saw)! He will be martyred?"

RasoolAllah (saw) replied, "O' My Daughter (sa), yes! The heavens, the earths, the mountains, the angels, the beasts, and the whales will not cry on any who has ever been slaughtered or will be slaughtered the way they cry over this Hussain (asws).

A group of people who love Us will perform will go to Him. No one on earth knows Allah better than they and no one is more committed to Our rights than they are. They are the lights in the darkness of oppression. They are the intercessors and will join Me by My Pond on the day of judgment.

I will recognize them by their marks when I see them. On that day, the followers of every religion will look for their leaders and those who perform the ziarat of Hussain (asws) will look for no one other than Us. They are the pillars of the earth and the rains fall down through them."

HADITH 3

Imam Muhammad Baqir (asws) narrates:

RasoolAllah (saw) said:

"Those who want to live like Me, die like Me, enter the forever green Janah and hold onto the tree My Lord planted with His own Hand should follow Ali (asws) and the Successors after Him and should believe in Their attributes.

They are the guides whom Allah is pleased with. He has given My knowledge and understanding to Them. They are My descendants from My flesh and blood.

I complain to Allah about Their enemies from within My nation, about those who deny Their attributes, and those who abandon Me by oppressing Them.

I swear by Allah they will slaughter My Son (asws). May Allah remove them from My intercession."

HADITH 4

Imam Muhammad Baqir (asws) narrates:

RasoolAllah (saw) would pull Hussain (asws) close to Himself whenever Hussain (asws) would enter. Then He would say to Ameerul Momineen (asws) to hold Hussain (asws) and RasoolAllah (saw) would hug Him, kissing Him while weeping.

Hussain (asws) asked, "O Father (saw)! Why are You weeping?"

RasoolAllah (saw) replied, "I kissed those places of Your body that shall be struck with swords"

Hussain (asws), "O Father (saw)! Will I be killed?"

RasoolAllah (saw) replied, "Yes, I swear by Allah that You (asws), Your Father (asws), and Your Brother (asws) will be martyred."

Hussain (asws) asked, "Will the places of Our martyrdom be far from each other?"

RasoolAllah (saw) replied, "Yes, O My Son (asws)!"

Hussain (asws), "Who from Your ummah will perform Our Ziarat?"

RasoolAllah (saw) replied, "No one will perform the Ziarat of You (asws), Your Father (asws) or Your Brother (asws) except for the most trustworthy from My ummah."

HADITH 5

Umar ibn Hubairah narrates:

I saw RasoolAllah (saw). Hasan (asws) and Hussain (asws) were sitting upon His lap. He kept kissing Hasan (asws) and then Hussain (asws) and said to Hussain (asws), "Woe be unto those who will slaughter You."

HADITH 6

Imam Jafar Sadiq (asws) narrates:

"One day when RasoolAllah (saw) was visiting the house of Fatima (sa), Hussain was sitting upon His lap and suddenly RasoolAllah (saw) began to weep and fell into sajda.

Then He said:

"O Fatima (sa), daughter of Muhammad (saw), the Most High (العلي الأعلى) just appeared before Me in the most beautiful form in Your house and asked Me, "Do You love Hussain (asws)?"

I (RasoolAllah saw) replied, "Yes He is the light of My eyes, My flower, the fruit of My heart, and the skin between my two eyes."

Allah said, "O Muhammad (saw)—as He placed His hand on the head of Hussain (asws)! You are blessed through this child upon whom I have bestowed My blessings, mercy, and pleasure. My curse, wrath, chastisement and punishment are upon those who slaughter Him, who have animosity towards Him, wage war against Him, and oppose Him. He is Syedul Shohadu (Master of the Martyrs) from the first to the last in this world and the hereafter. He is the Master of the Youth of Paradise over the entire creation. His Father (asws) enjoys a station and rank that is greater than His.

Convey My Salam and inform Him of the good news that He is the banner of My guidance, light of the Auliya (friends), My caretaker and witness upon My creation, treasurer of My knowledge, and My Hujjat (proof) upon the people of the heavens and the earths, and over jinn and man."

HADITH 7

Imam Muhammad Baqir (asws) narrates:

RasoolAllah (saw) said:

"Those who want to live like Me, die like Me and enter My Jannah (paradise) that is forever green and whose trees were planted by My Lord with His Hand should follow Ali (asws), learn His virtues, and those of His Successors (asws) after Him, and disassociate from My enemies.

Allah has bestowed My knowledge and understanding upon Them. They are descended from My flesh and blood. I complain to My Lord about Their enemies from My ummah, about those who deny Their virtues and about those who abandon Me. I swear by Allah that they will slaughter My Son (asws). May Allah exclude them from My shifaat (intercession)."

Chapter 23

Sayings of Ameerul Momineen (asws) and Imam Hussain (asws) regarding Martyrdom of Hussain (asws)

HADITH 1

Abu Abdullah al Jadalee narrates:

I went to Ameerul Momineen (asws) and Hussain (asws) was beside Him. He touched the shoulder of Hussain (asws) and said, "He will be slaughtered and there will be none who aid Him."

I said, "O Ameerul Momineen (asws)! I swear by Allah if this occurs life will be intolerable."

Ameerul Momineen (asws) replied, "For certain, it shall occur."

HADITH 2

Imam Jafar Sadiq (asws) narrates:

"Ameerul Momineen Ali (asws) said to Hussain (asws), "O Abu Abdullah (asws)! It has been written that You are the chief example."

Hussain (asws) asked, "May I be sacrificed for You, What is My position?"

Ameerul Momineen (asws) replied, "You have the knowledge which others do not and those with knowledge benefit from their knowledge."

Then Ameerul Momineen (asws) said:

"O' My Son (asws)! Listen and be aware of this before it occurs to You. I swear by He who has My Life in His Hand that Bani Ummayyah will spill Your blood, but they will not be able to separate You from Your religion nor will they be able to make You forget to praise Your Lord."

Hussain (asws) replied, "I swear by He who has My Life in His Hand that this is sufficient for Me. I submit to that which has been revealed by Allah. I believe in the words of RasoolAllah (saw) and the words of My Father."

HADITH 3

Ameerul Momineen (asws) narrates:

"Hussain (asws) will be savagely slaughtered. I know the soil of the land upon which He will be slaughtered. It is the land close to the two rivers."

HADITH 4

Abu Saeed Aqeesa narrates:

Abdullah ibn Zubair met with Hussain (asws) ibn Ali (asws). They spoke privately for a very long time. Afterwards, Hussain (asws) came out and said to the people:

"He (Abdullah ibn Zubair) is advising Me to seek refuge within Masjidul Haram. I would rather be slaughtered farther than the distance of two outstretched arms from the Haram than to be slaughtered while I am as close to the Haram as the span of an outstretched palm. I prefer being martyred in Taf (Karbala) over being martyred in the Haram."

HADITH 5

Imam Jafar Sadiq (asws) narrates:

"Abdullah ibn Zubair told Hussain (asws) to seek refuge in Mecca but Hussain (asws) ibn Ali (asws) said, "We will not defile its sanctity and We will not allow its sanctity to be defiled by Our being slaughtered in it. I prefer being slaughtered upon a mound of red soil to being slaughtered in the Haram."

HADITH 6

Imam Muhammad Baqir (asws) narrates:

"Hussain (asws) left Mecca one day before the Day of Tarwiyah (8th Zil Hajj). As He was leaving, Abdullah ibn Zubair met with Him and said, "O Aba Abdullah (asws)! The time of Hajj is here and You are departing Mecca for Iraq?"

Hussain (asws) replied, "O son of Zubair! I prefer being buried by the banks of the Euphrates over being buried inside of the Kaaba."

HADITH 7

Imam Jafar Sadiq (asws) narrates:

"Hussain (asws) ibn Ali (asws) said to His companions on the day they were to be slaughtered, "I testify that permission for you to be slaughtered has been granted. Fear Allah and be patient."

HADITH 8

al Halabi narrates:

I heard Abu Abdullah (Imam Jafar Sadiq asws) say:

"Hussain (asws) led fajr prayers on the morning of Ashura for His companions and then turned towards them and said, "Allah has given permission for you to be slaughtered therefore remain patient."

HADITH 9

Hussain ibn Abul Alaa narrates someone said:

"I swear to He towards whom the Arsh (throne) ascended, that your father informed me of the companions of Hussain (asws) without adding one or missing one. This ummah (nation) will attack them just as Bani Israel transgressed on the Sabbath (Saturday). The Day of Ashura when Hussain (asws) was martyred was also a Saturday."

HADITH 10

Imam Jafar Sadiq (asws) narrates:

"Hussain (asws) led the fajr prayer for His companions on the day they were to be slaughtered and then said, "O people! I testify that permission has been given for you to be martyred. Fear Allah and remain steadfast.""

HADITH 11

Urwah ibn Zubair narrates:

On the day when Uthman exiled Abu Zarr (as) to Rabazat, the people said to him, "O Abu Zarr (as)! Be joyful for this hardship is small in the way of Allah."

Abu Zarr (as) replied, "How insignificant this is! How will you feel when Hussain (asws) ibn Ali (asws) is slaughtered in a most vicious way! I swear by Allah that there will be no slaughter in Islam greater than the slaughtering of Hussain (asws). Allah will unsheathe His sword upon this ummah (nation) and He will never sheathe it again. Allah will send One from the Progeny of Hussain (asws) who will seek revenge against the people.

I swear by Allah that if you knew about that which will overcome the inhabitants of the seas, mountains, hills, trees, and heavens due to the martyrdom of Hussain (asws) then you would weep so immensely that your soul would exit your bodies.

Seventy thousand angels will be astonished in each sky that the ruh of Hussain (asws) will pass through. They will all rise upon seeing Him and they will be shaking with awe for Him until the Day of Judgment.

Every cloud that moves, every clap of thunder and every strike of lightning sends lanat upon the killers of Hussain (asws). Every day the ruh of Hussain (asws) meets with RasoolAllah (saw)."

HADITH 12

Abd al Sameen narrates:

Ameerul Momineen (asws) was delivering a sermon to the people when He said, "Ask Me before you lose Me! I swear by Allah that I will answer you about anything you might ask regardless if it happened in the past or will happen in the future."

Sa'ad ibn Abu Waqqas stood and asked, "O Ameerul Momineen (asws)! Tell me the number of hairs that I have on my head and in my beard?"

Ameerul Momineen (asws) replied, "I swear by Allah that My Beloved, RasoolAllah (saw) told Me that you would ask Me this question. There is a shaitan attached to every strand of hair on your head and in your beard and in your house is a lamb that will slaughter My Son, Hussain (asws)."

Abd al Sameen added, "Umar ibn Sa'ad was a child then who was playing in front of his father, Sa'ad ibn Abu Waqqas."

HADITH 13

Imam Zainul Abideen (asws) narrates:

Hussain (asws) ibn Ali (asws) said:

"I swear by He who has the life of Hussain (asws) in His hand, that the Bani Ummayah will slaughter Me and will not be satisfied with their government until they slaughter Me. If they martyr Me, the people will never be able to pray in congregation nor will they ever be able to spend zakat in the way of Allah again."

HADITH 14

Imam Jafar Sadiq (asws) narrates:

"When Hussain (asws) ibn Ali (asws) passed Aqbatul Batn (a mountain on the road to Mecca) He said to His companions, "I do not see anything for Me except martyrdom."

The companions asked, "O Aba Abdullah (asws)! What makes You say this?"

Hussain (asws) replied, "I had a vision in a dream."

They asked, "What did You see?"

Hussain (asws) replied, "I saw numerous dogs biting Me and the fiercest one biting Me was a spotted dog."

HADITH 15

Imam Muhammad Baqir (asws) narrates:

"Hussain (asws) ibn Ali (asws) wrote a letter in Mecca to Muhammad ibn Ali (asws) that said:

"In the name of Allah, Most Gracious, Most Merciful, from Hussain (asws) ibn Ali (asws) to Muhammad ibn Ali (asws) and to those with him from amongst the Bani Hashim,

Those who follow Me will be martyred and those who remain behind will not find victory.

Wa Salam"

HADITH 16

Imam Muhammad Baqir (asws) narrates:

"Hussain (asws) ibn Ali (asws) wrote a letter from Karbala to Muhammad ibn Ali (asws) that said:

"In the name of Allah, Most Gracious, Most Merciful, from Hussain (asws) ibn Ali (asws) to Muhammad ibn Ali (asws) and to those with him from amongst the Bani Hashim:

It is as if this world never was and only the hereafter existed.

Wa Salam"

Chapter 24

Miraculous Signs of the Martyrdom of Hussain (asws)
that appeared in Various Places

HADITH 1

Imam Jafar Sadiq (asws) narrates:

"Hisham ibn Abdul Malik sent some soldiers to bring My Father (Imam Muhammad Baqir asws) to Shaam. When My Father (asws) entered, Hisham said, "O Abu Jafar (asws)! I have brought You here to ask a question that only can be asked by me. I do not believe that anyone knows of this nor is it possible that there is anyone even capable of answering it except for one man.""

My Father (Imam Muhammad Baqir asws) said, "You can ask Me anything that you wish. If I know, then I will surely answer, and if I do not know the answer, then I will say I do not for it is more gracious to tell the truth."

Hisham asked, "Tell me about the night Ali (asws) ibn Abi Talib (as) was martyred. How did those who were not present in the city hear of His martyrdom? What was the sign that appeared for the people of His martyrdom? If You know the answer, then tell me if this sign ever appeared for anyone other than Ali (asws)."

My Father (Imam Muhammad Baqir asws) said, "On the night Ameerul Momineen (asws) was martyred, there was no stone upon the earth that did not have fresh blood under it when it was moved until the fajr (morning). This also occurred on the night that Haroon (as), brother of Musa (as), was martyred. This also occurred on the night in which Yusha ibn Noon was martyred. This also occurred on the night that Isa (as) ibn Mariam (sa) ascended to the heavens. This also occurred on the night in which Shamoon ibn Hamoon al Safa was martyred. This also occurred on the night in which Ali (asws) ibn Abi Talib (as) was martyred. It also occurred on the night in which Hussain (asws) ibn Ali (asws) was martyred."

Then Imam Jafar Sadiq (asws) continued and said:

"Hisham's face changed color due to his anger and he was ready to attack My Father (asws). Then My Father (Imam Muhammad Baqir asws) said, "It is wajib (obligatory) upon the servants of Allah to obey their Imam and to be truthful with him. The reason I answered this question is because of My knowledge that I must say the truth."

Hisham said, "You may return to Your Family if You so desire."

As My Father (Imam Muhammad Baqir asws) was leaving, Hisham made Him promise not to narrate this hadith to anyone as long as Hisham was alive. My Father (asws) agreed."

HADITH 2

Abu Nasir narrates:

A man from Baytul Maqadis said, "I swear by Allah that the people of Baytul Maqadis (Jerusalem) and its surrounding areas heard of the martyrdom of Hussain (asws) ibn Ali (asws) on the eve of the day He was martyred."

I (Abu Nasir) asked, "How did you hear about it?"

He replied, "We could not move any rock, stone, or clump of mud without finding fresh, boiling blood under it and all of the walls turned red as blood. Blood rained from the skies for three days and at night, we heard a crier reciting:

"Does the ummah that slaughtered Hussain (asws) hope to receive the shifaat (intercession) of His Grandfather (saw) on the Day of Judgment? Allah forbids that you receive the intercession of Ahmad (saw) and Abu Turab (asws) (Moula Ali asws). You have slaughtered the best of those who ever did ride. You have slaughtered the best of all mankind from amongst the young and the old."

For three days, the sun was eclipsed and afterwards the sky was filled with uncountable stars. On the next day, we grieved over the martyrdom of Hussain (asws) and shortly thereafter, we were informed of the devastating news of the martyrdom of Hussain (asws).

HADITH 3

al Zuhri narrates:

When Hussain (asws) was martyred, there was no stone in Baytul Maqadis (Jerusalem) that could be moved without finding fresh blood under it."

Chapter 25

Narrations regarding the Killer of Hussain (asws) and the
Killer of Prophet Yahya(as)

HADITH 1

Imam Jafar Sadiq (asws) narrates:

"The killer of Yahya ibn Zakariya (as) was illegitimate and the killer of Hussain (asws) was also walad e zani (child born from adultery/illegitimate). The sky has never wept over anyone except for Them."

HADITH 2

Imam Muhammad Baqir (asws) narrates:

RasoolAllah (saw) said:

"There is a place in jahannum (hellfire) that no one will enter except for the killer of Hussain (asws) ibn Ali (asws) and the killer of Yahya ibn Zakariya (as)."

HADITH 3

Ismail ibn Jabeer narrates:

I heard Abu Abdullah Imam Jafar Sadiq (asws) say:

"I swear by Allah that the descendants of the killers of Hussain (asws) will be punished for the deeds of their fathers."

HADITH 4

Imam Jafar Sadiq (asws) narrates:

"The killer of Hussain (asws) was walad e zani (child born from adultery/illegitimate) and the killer of Yahya ibn Zakariya (as) was also walad e zani."

HADITH 5

Muthana narrates:

I heard Abu Jafar (Imam Muhammad Baqir asws) say:

"Allah has placed the killing of the Offspring of the Prophets (as) of the previous nations in the hands of the aulad e zani (illegitimate ones)."

HADITH 6

Imam Jafar Sadiq (asws) narrates:

"The killer of Hussain (asws) ibn Ali (asws) was walad e zani (illegitimate) and the killer of Yahya ibn Zakariya (as) was also walad e zani."

HADITH 7

Ismail ibn Abu Ziyad narrated from some scholars who said:

Abu Abdullah Imam Jafar Sadiq (asws) was asked, "Who stopped Firoan from killing Musa (as) as is mentioned in the ayah, *"Firoan said, "Let me kill Musa"* (Quran 40:26) ?"

Imam (asws) replied, "Because he was of legitimate birth. The Prophets (as) and Hujjah (proofs of Allah) are only killed by those who are aulad e zani (conceived illegitimately) and those whose mothers are adulteresses."

HADITH 8

Imam Jafar Sadiq (asws) narrates:

"The killer of Hussain (asws) ibn Ali (asws) was illegitimate."

HADITH 9

See hadith 10

HADITH 10

Imam Muhammad Baqir (asws) narrates:

"RasoolAllah (saw) said, "Only those who are illegitimate are the murderers of the prophets and the murderers of the progeny of the prophets".

HADITH 11

Ismail ibn Kuthair narrates:

I heard Abu Abdullah Imam Jafar Sadiq (asws) say:

"The killer of Hussain (asws) ibn Ali (asws) was a walad e zani and the killer of Yahya (as) ibn Zakariya (as) was walad e zani. The sky and earth did not weep over anyone like it did for Them."

Chapter 26

The Mourning of the Entire Creation over
Imam Hussain (asws)

HADITH 1

Imam Muhammad Baqir (asws) narrates::

"Mankind, jinn, birds, and animals all shed tears and mourned at the martyrdom of Hussain (asws) ibn Ali (asws)."

HADITH 2

Ameerul Momineen (asws) narrates:

"May My Mother (sa) and Father (as) be sacrificed for Hussain (asws), the one who shall be martyred on the outskirts of Kufa. I swear by Allah it is as if I can see the various wild animals mourning and weeping over His dead body throughout the night until dawn. When this occurs, beware of being negligent of His grave."

HADITH 3

Muhammad ibn Jafar al Qureshi al Razaz narrated from Muhammad ibn Hussain ibn Abul Khattab who narrated from Hasan ibn Ali ibn Abu Uthman who narrated from Abdul

Jabar al Nahawandi who narrated from Abu Saeed who narrated from Hussain ibn Thuwair ibn Abu Fakhitha, Yunus ibn Zabian, Abu Salamah al Sarraj, and Mufaddal ibn Umar who all said:

We heard Abu Abdullah Imam Jafar Sadiq (asws) say:

"When Abu Abdullah Hussain (asws) ibn Ali (asws) was martyred, the seven heavens, the seven earths, everything between them, everything within them, everything that orbits around them, Jannah, al Nar (hellfire) and everything which Our Lord has created from amongst that which is zahir (apparent) and that which is batin (hidden) mourned over Him."

HADITH 4

Mufaddal ibn Umar who all said:

We heard Abu Abdullah Imam Jafar Sadiq (asws) say:

"When Hussain (asws) ibn Ali (asws) was martyred, the entire creation of Allah mourned over Him except for the following three, Basra, Damascus, and the family of Uthman (la)."

HADITH 5

Hussain ibn Thuwair narrates:

Yunus ibn Zabian, Mufaddal ibn Umar, Abu Salamah al Sarraj and I were sitting with Abu Abdullah (Imam Jafar Sadiq asws). Yunus spoke to the Imam (asws) on our behalf due to him being the eldest from amongst us.

Imam (asws) said to us (this is taken from a longer hadith):

"When Abu Abdullah, Hussain (asws) ibn Ali (asws) was martyred, the seven heavens, the seven earths, all that is within them, all that is between them, everything in Jannah (paradise) and the Fire (of hell), everything which is zahir (apparent) and everything which is batin (hidden) mourned over Abu Abdullah (Imam Hussain asws) except for three."

I (Hussain ibn Thuwair) asked, "May I be sacrificed upon You! What are those three things?"

Imam (asws) relied, "Basra, Damascus, and the family of Uthman (la) ibn Affan."

HADITH 6

Imam Jafar Sadiq (asws) narrates:

"O Zurarah! The heavens wept blood for forty days over Hussain (asws), the earth wept by being covered in darkness for forty days, the sun wept by being eclipsed and turning red, the mountains were rent asunder and dispersed, the seas swelled and surged, and the angels wept for forty days over Him.

After Hussain (asws) was martyred, all of Our Women (sa) abandoned dying and adorning Their hair and applying kohl and oil until the head of ubaidullah (la) ibn ziyad(la) was brought to Us, but even after that We continued to mourn over Him.

Whenever My Grandfather (Imam Zainul Abideen asws) would remember Hussain (asws), He would weep so immensely that His beard would become wet from His tears and all those around Him would begin to weep.

The angels stationed by the grave of Hussain (asws) weep over Him so profusely that all of the angels in the heavens begin to weep at the sight of their tears. When the soul of Hussain (asws) departed, hellfire released such a mournful sigh that the earth was almost split in two. When the souls of ubaidullah (la) ibn ziyad (la) and yazid (la) ibn muawiyah (la) departed their bodies, hellfire roared so intensely that if Allah had not ordered it to be contained it would have burned everyone upon the earth. Hellfire became so violent due to its being restrained that more than once it almost broke free from its keepers' hold. Finally, Jibrael (as) went to it and hit it with his wings and only then did hellfire become calm. Hellfire mourns and weeps over Hussain (asws) and its fires burn brightly upon the killers of Hussain (asws). If it were not for the Hujjat (proofs) of Allah upon the earth, then hellfire would have destroyed the earth and all that is on it. For this reason, the earth shall quake increasingly as the Hour draws near.

There are no eyes and no tears more loved by Allah than those eyes that wept and those tears that were shed over Hussain (asws). Whosoever weeps over Hussain (asws) becomes associated with Fatima (sa), supports Her in Her grief and becomes associated with RasoolAllah (saw) and becomes a fulfiller of Our rights.

On the Day of Judgment, all will be resurrected weeping except for those who shed tears over My Grandfather, Imam Hussain (asws). Those who wept over Him will receive glad tidings when they are resurrected. Joy and happiness will emanate from their faces and they will feel comfort while others will feel fear.

Those who committed bad deeds will be punished while those who have wept over Hussain (asws) will be sitting with Him under the shade of the Arsh. They will be conversing with Hussain (asws) without any fear from the trials of the Day of Judgment. They will be told to enter Jannah but they will refuse. Instead preferring to sit with Hussain (asws) to listen to His words.

Then the hooris of Jannah will send after them and say "We and *the youths that never age*" (Quran 56:17) are waiting for you". However, they will not even turn their faces towards the hooris because the happiness and honor they feel while sitting in the presence of Hussain (asws).

On that day, some of their enemies will be pulled by their heads towards hellfire while others will cry out, *"Neither have any intercessors nor any true friend"* (Quran 26:100-101). The enemies will see the position of those who wept over Hussain (asws) but they will not be able to reach them or go near them.

The angels will bring messages to those who have cried over Hussain (asws) from their spouses and their servants, informing them of the blessings that have been prepared for them in Jannah.

But they will reply, "We shall come to you inshaAllah."

The angels will then inform their spouses of their reply. When their spouses hear of the way they have been honored and their nearness to Hussain (asws), their spouses will long for them even more.

Those who have wept over Hussain (asws) will continuously repeat, "Praise be to Allah who protected us from the great terror and the trials of the Day of Judgment and saved us from that which we fear."

Then saddled transports will be brought for them. They will ride to their places in Jannah while praising and glorifying Allah and sending blessings upon Muhammad (saw) and Aal e Muhammad (asws)."

HADITH 7

Abu Baseer narrates:

I was speaking with Abu Abdullah (Imam Jafar Sadiq asws) when His Son entered. The Imam (asws) welcomed Him, hugged Him, and kissed Him.

Then Imam (asws) said:

"May Allah degrade those who degraded You (children of Imam Hussain asws). May Allah punish those who oppressed You. May Allah disappoint those who abandoned You. May the lanat of Allah be upon those who slaughtered You. May Allah be Your friend, protector and supporter. The prophets, the truthful ones, the martyrs, the angels of the heavens, and Our women have been weeping for so long."

Then the Imam (asws) began to weep and said:

"O' Abu Baseer! When I look at the children of Hussain (asws), I am overcome with grief as I remember what was done to Them and to their Father (asws).

O' Abu Baseer ! Syeda Fatima (sa) grieves over Hussain (asws). When hellfire hears Her voice, it sights in such an intense way that if the keepers of Hellfire did not prepare to restrain it, then the Hellfire would burn all of the inhabitants of the earth with its fires and fumes. The keepers contain it and restrain it by holding its doors tightly closed for as long as Syeda Fatima (sa) weeps. They do this out of fear for the inhabitants of the earth. Yet Hellfire does not become calm until the voice of Syeda (sa) subsides.

The seas strain to split apart and collide when they hear the weeping of Syeda Fatima (sa). There is an angel responsible for every drop of water. When these angels hear the voice of Syeda (sa), they prevent every drop of water from boiling their wings. They keep the water from splitting out of fear for this world and everything in it, especially its inhabitants.

I (Abu Baseer) said, "May I be sacrificed upon You! This is such an egregious matter."

Imam (asws) replied, "That which you have not heard is even greater. O' Abu Baseer! Do you not want to be amongst those who support Syeda Fatima (sa)?"

When I heard this, I wept so greatly that I could no longer speak nor could the Imam (asws) speak due to His intense sorrow. Then the Imam (asws) moved towards His prayer mat and began supplicating to Allah. I left Him while He was in that state.

That night I was unable to eat or sleep. The next morning I was fasting and in great fear as I went to the Imam (asws). When I saw He was calm, I also became calm and praise Allah that no torment had befallen upon me."

Chapter 27

Mourning of the Angels over Imam Hussain (asws)

HADITH 1

Fudail ibn Yasar narrates Imam Jafar Sadiq (asws) said:

"What is wrong with you that you do not go to Him (perform the Ziarat of Imam Hussain asws)?! There are four thousand angels who weep by His grave and will do so until the Day of Judgment."

HADITH 2

Imam Jafar Sadiq (asws) narrates:

"On the day of Ashura four thousand angels came down to fight for Hussain (asws) ibn Ali (asws) led by an angel named Mansoor but He (Imam Hussain asws) did not grant them permission to fight. They returned to Allah to seek permission. When they returned back, Hussain (asws) had already been martyred."

HADITH 3

See hadith 1

HADITH 4

Imam Muhammad Baqir (asws) narrates:

"There are four thousand dishelved angels covered with dust who cry over Hussain (asws) and will do so until the Day of Judgment."

HADITH 5

Imam Jafar Sadiq (asws) narrates:

"Allah had dedicated seventy thousand angels to Hussain (asws). Each one is disheveled and cover with dust. They have sent blessings upon Hussain (asws) every day since the day He was martyred and will do so until that time which only Allah has knowledge of (reappearance of Imam e Zamana atfs)"

HADITH 6

See hadith 1

HADITH 7

Haroon ibn Kharija al Sarafi narrates:

Imam Jafar Sadiq (asws) said:

"Allah has dedicated four thousand dishelved angels covered with dust who cry over Hussain (asws) and will do so until the Day of Judgment."

HADITH 8

Fuzail ibn Yasir narrates:

Imam Muhammad Baqir (asws) or Imam Jafar Sadiq (asws) said:

"There are four thousand dishelved angels covered with dust who cry over Hussain (asws) and will do so until the Day of Judgment."

HADITH 9

Rib'ee narrates:

In Medina, I asked Imam Jafar Sadiq (asws), "Where are the graves of the martyrs?"

Imam (asws) replied, "Is not the best of martyrs (Imam Hussain asws) buried near you?! I swear by He who has My life in His Hand there are four thousand disheveled angels—covered with dust—that weep over Him and will do so until the Day of Judgment."

HADITH 10

Imam Muhammad Baqir (asws) narrates:

"There are four thousand disheveled angels covered with dust who cry over Hussain (asws) and will do so until the Day of Judgment. They receive everyone who performs the Ziarat of Hussain (asws). If the zuwar of Hussain (asws) become ill, the angels visit them and when they die, the angels attend their funerals."

HADITH 11

Imam Jafar Sadiq (asws) narrates:

"Allah had dedicated four thousand disheveled angels cover with dust to weep over the grave of Hussain (asws) daily from sunrise to midday. At midday these four thousand angels are replaced by another four thousand angels who weep over Him from midday to sunrise."

HADITH 12

Haroon ibn Kharijah narrates:

"One day while I was with Imam Jafar Sadiq (asws), a man asked the Imam (asws), "What is the reward for those who perform the Ziarat of the grave of Hussain (asws)?"

Imam (asws) replied, "When Hussain (asws) was martyred, everything mourned over Him including all of the various lands. Allah dedicated four thousand disheveled angels covered in dust to His grave and they mourn over Him. They will do so until the Day of Judgment."

HADITH 13

Muhammad ibn Marwan narrates:

I heard Imam Jafar Sadiq (asws) say:

"Perform the Ziarat of Hussain (asws) as often as possible, even if it is only once a year. Those who perform His Ziarat while believing in His rights and without denying His station, will have no reward other than Jannah. They will receive great sustenance and Allah will provide them with immediate relief.

Allah has dedicated four thousand angels to mourn at the grave of Hussain (asws) ibn Ali (asws). They accompany everyone who performs the Ziarat of Hussain (asws) as they return back to their families. If the zuwar become ill, these angels will visit him. When the zuwar die, these angels attend their funerals while seeking forgiveness for them and asking Allah to show mercy upon them."

HADITH 14

Bakr ibn Muhammad narrates:

Imam Jafar Sadiq (asws) said:

"Allah has dedicated seventy thousand disheveled angels covered with dust to the grave of Imam Hussain (asws). They mourn over Him and will do so until the Day of Judgment. They establish prayers by His grave. Each one of their prayers is equal to one thousand prayers from mankind and the reward of their salat will be written for those who go to the Ziarat of the grave of Imam Hussain (asws)."

HADITH 15

Malik al Johani narrates:

Imam Jafar Sadiq (asws) said:

"Allah has dedicated an angel known as Mansoor along with four thousand other angels, who mourn over Imam Hussain (asws). They pray for and seek the forgiveness of those who perform His Ziarat."

HADITH 16

Imam Jafar Sadiq (asws) narrates:

"When you perform the Ziarat of Aba Abdullah (Imam Hussain asws), you should maintain silence unless you are saying that which is good.

The angels of the night and of the day who are from among the Keepers and Guardians to the angels who are in Ha'yr (place of burial of Imam Hussain (asws) and the surrounding area) and shake hands with them. But the angels at Ha'yr do not speak for they are too overcome with grief.

The angels from amongst the Keepers wait for them until midday or at sunrise before speaking to them because the angels at Ha'yr refrain from speaking except during those times so their supplication and mourning does not become less. Then they ask regarding some of the affairs of the heavens.

The angels from amongst the Keepers do not distract the angels of Ha'yr between these two times. However they become distracted when those who are performing Ziarat speak."

I asked, "May I be sacrificed upon You! What do the angels ask each other and which group asks the other? Is it the angels from amongst the Keepers who ask or the angels at the Ha'yr who ask the angels from amongst the Keepers?"

Imam (asws) replied, "The angels at Ha'yr ask the angels from the Keepers because the angels at Ha'yr never move from their place while the angels from amongst the Keepers descend from the heavens and return back to them."

I asked, "What do the angels at Ha'yr ask the angels from the Keepers?"

Imam (asws) replied, "The angels from the Keepers pass by Ismael, the angel of air, in their ascent to the heavens. Sometimes they also reach him at the same time when the Prophet (saw), Syed Fatima (sa), Hasan (asws), and Hussain (asws) along with the Imams (asws) who have left this world are there with Ismael. The Ahlul Bayt (asws) ask the angels from the Keepers regarding some matters and also about those zuwar who are present in Ha'yr.

The Ahlul Bayt (asws) say to the angels from the Keepers, "Give those who have come to perform the Ziarat of Hussain (asws) glad tidings with your prayers."

The angels from the Keepers ask, "How should we give them glad tidings when they cannot hear us?"

Ahlul Bayt (asws) replies and says, "Congratulate them and pray for them on Our behalf. These are Our glad tiding to them. When they desire to leave, surround them and rub your wings on them so they become aware of your presence. We entrust them to He whose trust will never be lost."

Imam (asws) then continued and said:

"If the zuwar of Hussain (asws) and the people knew about the blessings regarding the Ziarat of Hussain (asws), they would have fought one another with swords and they would have sold their belongings in order to perform His Ziarat.

When Syeda Fatima (sa)—along with one thousand prophets, one thousand Siddiq (trustworthy), one thousand martyrs, and one million from amongst the highest ranking angels all of whom join Her in Her mourning over Hussain (asws)—looks upon those who perform the Ziarat of Hussain (asws), She (sa) releases a sigh in such a way that causes every angel in the heavens to join Her (sa) in Her (sa) sorrows.

Then RasoolAllah (saw) says, *"Allah shall bring His command to pass"* (Quran 65:3)."

Then Syeda Fatima (sa) looks at those who are present at the grave of Imam Hussain (asws) and asks Allah to shower them with His blessings.

Imam (asws) continued on and said, "Do not abstain from performing the Ziarat of Hussain (asws). The blessings for performing His Ziarat are too great to be counted."

HADITH 17

Hariz narrates:

"I said to Imam Jafar Sadiq (asws), "May I be sacrificed upon You! O' Ahlul Bayt (asws), how short Your lives are! And how close are Your deaths to one another even though the entire creation is in need of You?!"

Imam (asws) replied, "There is a sheet for each one of Us (Ahlul Bayt asws) which contains all that We need to do during Our time. Once every order on that sheet has been fulfilled, We know the time for Our departure from this world is near. RasoolAllah (saw) then comes to Us and informs Us that Our departure has come and informs Us of the rewards Allah has prepared for Us.

Hussain (asws) read the sheet entrusted to Him, which contained all that would happen and all that was yet come. However, when He rose to fight there were some things upon His sheet that had not yet been fulfilled. That which was not yet fulfilled was regarding the angels asking the permission of Allah to help Hussain (asws) and Allah granted permission to them. As they prepared themselves for battle, Hussain (asws) was martyred. And when the angels descended to the earth, they found Hussain's (asws) time had passed and He had been martyred.

Therefore, they turned to Allah and said, "O' Lord! You gave us permission to descend to the earth in support of Hussain (asws) but when we arrived You had already taken Him back to Yourself."

Allah replied to them, "Stay by His Grave until the day when you see Him rise again and on that day support Him. Until then mourn over Him and over being unable to support Him. You have been chosen for His support and to mourn over Him."

The angels were distressed and mourned at having lost their opportunity to support Hussain (asws). But when He rises, they will be amongst His supporters."

Chapter 28

Mourning of the Heavens and the Earth over the Martyrdom
of Imam Hussain (asws) and
Prophet Yahya (as)

HADITH 1

Hasan ibn Hakam al Nakhai narrates from someone who said:

"I heard Ameerul Momineen (asws) in Ruhbah reading this ayah, *"And neither heaven nor earth shed a tear over them: nor were they given a respite"* (Quran 44:29), when Hussain (asws) entered from one of the doors of the masjid.

Ameerul Momineen (asws) said, "As for Him (Hussain asws), He will be martyred and the heavens and the earth shall mourn over Him."

HADITH 2

Ibrahim al Nakhai narrates:

"Ameerul Momineen (asws) came out of the masjid and sat with His companions gathered around Him. Then Hussain (asws) came and stood in front of Ameerul Momineen (asws).

Ameerul Momineen (asws) placed His hand over the head of Hussain (asws) and said:

"O' My Son (asws)! Allah has debased some people in the Quran by saying *"And neither heaven nor earth shed a tear over them: nor were they given a respite"* (Quran 44:29), I swear by Allah they will martyr You after Me and the heavens and the earth will mourn over You."

HADITH 3

Imam Jafar Sadiq (asws) narrates:

"The heavens and the earth mourned over the martyrdom of Hussain (asws) until they turned red. They have never mourned over anyone except for Yahya ibn Zakariya (as) and Hussain (asws) ibn Ali (asws)."

HADITH 4

Abdullah ibn Hilal narrates:

"I heard Imam Jafar Sadiq (asws) say, "The heavens mourned over Hussain (asws) ibn Ali (asws) and Yahya ibn Zakariya (as). They have never mourned for anyone other than these two."

I asked, "How did the heavens mourn?"

Imam (asws) replied, "The heavens turned red for forty days like the sun at the time of sunrise and sunset."

I asked, "Is that how the heavens mourned?"

Imam (asws) replied, "Yes."

HADITH 5

Musheer al Qurashi narrates:

"My grandmother told me she was alive during the time of the martyrdom of Hussain (asws) ibn Ali (asws). She said, "The heavens turned red like blood for one year and nine months after the martyrdom of Hussain (asws), and the sun could not even be seen."

HADITH 6

Muhammad ibn Ali al Halabi narrates:

In the tafsir of this ayah, *"And neither heaven nor earth shed a tear over them: nor were they given a respite"* (Quran 44:29), Imam Jafar Sadiq (asws) said,

"The heavens never mourned over anyone after the martyrdom of Yahya ibn Zakariya (as) until the martyrdom of Hussain (asws). And when He (Imam Hussain asws) was martyred, the heavens mourned for Him."

HADITH 7

Imam Jafar Sadiq (asws) narrates:

"The heavens turned red for one year when Imam Hussain (asws) was martyred. The same occurred when Yahya ibn Zakariya (as) was martyred. The redness of the heavens is the way it mourns."

HADITH 8

Abdul Khaliq ibn Abd Rabbih narrates:

"I heard Aba Abdullah (Imam Jafar Sadiq asws) say:

"We have given the same name to none before (him)" (Quran 19:7).

Hussain (asws) ibn Ali (asws)'s name was not given to any before Him as Yahya ibn Zakariya (as)'s name was not given to any before him. And the heavens never mourned over anyone for forty days except for these two.

I asked, "How did the heavens mourn?"

Imam (asws) replied, "The heavens became red at the time of sunrise and sunset."

HADITH 9

Imam Muhammad Baqir (asws) narrates:

"The heavens never mourned over anyone after Yahya ibn Zakariya (as) until Hussain (asws) ibn Ali (asws) was martyred. When Hussain (asws) was martyred, the heavens mourned for forty days over Him."

HADITH 10

Imam Jafar Sadiq (asws) narrates:

"The heavens have never mourned over anyone other than Hussain (asws) ibn Ali (asws) and Yahya ibn Zakariya (as)."

HADITH 11

Muhammad ibn Salamah narrates from someone who narrates:

"When Hussain (asws) ibn Ali (asws) was martyred, red dust rained from the skies."

HADITH 12

Umar ibn Wahab narrates from his father who narrates:

Ali (asws) ibn Hussain (asws) (Imam Zainul Abideen asws) said:

"From the day of their creation, the heavens have never mourned over anyone except for Yahya ibn Zakariya (as) and Hussain (asws) ibn Ali (asws)."

I asked, "How did the heavens mourn?"

Imam (asws) replied, "If you would have faced the wind while holding a garment, you would have seen that which is similar to a red mist of blood on it."

HADITH 13

Hanan ibn Sadir narrates:

"I asked Aba Abdullah (Imam Jafar Sadiq asws), "What do you say about the Ziarat of the grave of Abi Abdullah al Hussain (asws)? Some people have informed us that it is equal to one Hajj and one Umrah."

Imam (asws) replied, "Do not be surprised by all of these rewards. Instead, perform His Ziarat and do not abandon Him, for He is the Syedul Shahadu (Master of the Martyrs) and He is the Master of the Youth of the Paradise. Yahya ibn Zakariya (as) is similar to Hussain (asws) in that the heavens and the earth mourned only over these two."

HADITH 14

Imam Jafar Sadiq (asws) narrates:

"The killer of Yahya ibn Zakariya (as) was walad e zani (conceived illegitimately) and the killer of Hussain (asws) was also walada e zani (illegitimately). The heavens have never mourned over anyone other than these two."

I asked, "How did the heavens mourn?"

Imam (asws) replied, "The heavens became red at the time of sunrise and sunset."

HADITH 15

Abdullah ibn Hilal narrates:

"I heard Imam Jafar Sadiq (asws) say:

"The heavens mourned only over Hussain (asws) ibn Ali (asws) and Yahya ibn Zakariya (as) and no other."

I asked, "How did the heavens mourn?"

Imam (asws) replied, "The heavens became red for forty days at the time of sunrise and sunset."

I asked, "Is that how the heavens mourn?"

Imam (asws) replied, "Yes."

HADITH 16

Khuhair ibn Shehab al Harithi narrates:

"One day while we were sitting with Ameerul Momineen (asws) in Ruhbah, Hussain (asws) entered. When Ameerul Momineen (asws) saw Him (Hussain asws), He (Ameerul Momineen asws) smiled broadly.

Then Ameerul Momineen (asws) said:

"Allah has mentioned some people in Quran by saying *"And neither heaven nor earth shed a tear over them: nor were they given a respite (again)."* (Quran 44:29. I swear by He who splits the grain and created the living beings that He (Hussain asws) will be martyred and the heavens and the earth will mourn over Him."

HADITH 17

Abu Salamah narrates:

Imam Jafar Sadiq (asws) said, "The skies have never mourned over anyone other than Yahya ibn Zakariya (as) and Hussain (asws)."

HADITH 18

Safwan al Jamal narrates:

"I asked Aba Abdullah (Imam Jafar Sadiq asws) on the way from Medina to Mecca, "O' Son of RasoolAllah (saw)! Why do I see You so saddened and serious?"

Imam (asws) replied, "If you could hear that which I hear you would have been distressed and unable to ask such a question."

I asked, "What do You hear?"

Imam (asws) replied, "The angels beseeching Allah (swt) to send His lanat upon the killers of Ameerul Momineen (asws) and the killers of Hussain (asws). And the lamentations of the jinn. And the immense anxiety and weeping of the angels who around Him (Imam Hussain asws). Therefore who is able to enjoy food or drink or sleep after hearing their voices?!"

HADITH 19

See Hadith 16

HADITH 20

Ibn Shehab al Zuhri narrates:

"When Hussain (asws) was martyred, the skies rained blood and no stoned was overturned in Baytul Maqdis (Jerusalem) without one finding fresh blood beneath it."

HADITH 21

Dawood ibn Farqad narrates:

"I heard Aba Abdullah (Imam Jafar Sadiq asws) say:

The killer of Hussain (asws) ibn Ali (asws) was walad e zani (illegitimate) and the killer of Yahya ibn Zakariya (as) was also walad e zani. When Hussain (asws) ibn Ali (asws) was martyred, the skies turned red for one year. The skies and the earth have only mourned by turning red over Hussain (asws) ibn Ali (asws) and Yahya ibn Zakariya (as)."

Chapter 29

The Grief of the Jinn over Imam Hussain (asws)

HADITH 1

Umm Salamah (sa) (Wife of RasoolAllah saw) narrates:

"Since the night RasoolAllah (saw) departed from this world, I have not heard the grieving of the Jinn until tonight. I believe I have been stricken with the martyrdom of my Son, Hussain (asws).

I heard a Jinni recite the following:

"O' my eyes! Shed plentiful tears.

Who will mourn over the martyrs?

Shed tears over a group who are being led towards their deaths by a tyrant who is from the progeny of a slave."

HADITH 2

Al Maythami narrates:

"Five men from Kufa wanted to go support Hussain (asws) ibn Ali (asws). On the way, they passed a village known as Shahi. There they met two men, one was elderly and the other a youth. The two men greeted them.

The elder man said, "I am a man from amongst the jinn and this is my nephew. We also wish to support the oppressed man (Imam Hussain asws) and I have an idea."

The five men asked, "What is your idea?"

He replied, "I will fly and bring some information regarding the situation so that when you go towards Him you will be aware of the situation."

The men replied, "This is an excellent idea." So he disappeared from their sight. After a day passed, they could not see him but they heard the man's voice reciting the following:

"I swear by Allah that I did not return until I saw Him in Taf with His cheeks covered with dust for He had been slaughtered.

He was surrounded by some men with blood gushing from their throats; they were shining like lamps whose light had been overcome by darkness.

I implored my ride to hurry so that I could meet them before they left this world to meet with the hooris.

Hussain (asws) was the light through which guidance was sought and Allah is my witness that I do not lie.

Now He sits in rooms beside RasoolAllah (saw), Batool (sa), and Tayyar (as)."

Upon hearing this recitation, one of the five men replied by reciting the following:

"Go back and stay by the grave upon which the rains of blessings are poured until the day of Judgment.

I shall follow the same path as you and shall drink from a cup that is filled with blessings.

And I follow the path of those who have freed themselves from everything and have abandoned their homes, their wealth, and their loved ones for the sake of Allah."

HADITH 3

Abu Ziyad al Qandi narrates:

"When Hussain (asws) was martyred, at dawn the masons who worked in Jabbana (an area in Kufa) would hear the grieving of the Jinn. They would hear the Jinn reciting the following:

RasoolAllah (saw) has rubbed His hands over the head of Hussain (asws), causing His cheeks to radiate with light. His Parents are from the best of the Quraesh and His Grandfather (saw) is the best of grandfathers."

HADITH 4

Walid ibn Ghassan narrates someone said to him:

The Jinn use to mourn over Hussain (asws) and recite the following:

"To whom do these houses in Taf belong, the houses which were built unwillingly?

These are the houses of Hussain (asws) and they exchange grief with each other over Hussain (asws)."

HADITH 5

Ali ibn Hazawar narrates:

"I hear Layla say she heard the mourning of Jinn over Hussain (asws) ibn Ali (asws). She heard them recite the following:

"O eyes! Shed plentiful tears over Hussain (asws) for the aggrieved one weep in agony.

O' eyes! Do now allow the people of Medina to distract you from the remembrance of Aal e Muhammad (asws) and mourning over Their sufferings.

Their bodies were left for three days on the desert where They were martyred among the beasts."

HADITH 6

Abdullah ibn Hasan al Kinanee narrates:

"The Jinn wept over Hussain (asws) ibn Ali (asws) and recited the following:

"How will you reply to the Prophet (saw) if He asks you:

O'people! You were the last of the nations. What did you do to My Family, My Brothers and those whom I honored? Why are They either captives or martyred covered in blood?"

HADITH 7

Imam Reza (asws) narrates:

"As Hussain (asws) was traveling towards Iraq, in the middle of the night He heard a man reciting the following:

"O' my camel! Do not be frightened by my reprimands and do not break before the rising of dawn. Carry me to the best of the riders on the best of journeys until you arrive at the most honorable of places.

Carry me to Hussain (asws) whose Grandfather (saw) is the most glorious grandfather and Hussain (asws) who is the most benevolent. Allah has chosen Him for the best of affairs. May He remain until the end of time!"

Imam Hussain (asws) replied by reciting the following:

"I shall go towards martyrdom and there is no shame for a man as long as His intentions are based upon Haq (truth) and He fights for Allah as a muslim. And as long as they support the righteous ones, fight against the offenders, and abandons the sinners. And if I live, I shall have no regrets. And if I am martyred, I shall not be blamed. Nothing is more humiliating than living under the abasement of the oppressors."

HADITH 8

Imam Muhammad Baqir (asws) narrates:

"When Hussain (asws) was about to leave Medina, the women of Bani Abdul Muttalib (as) gathered around Him and began to weep. Hussain (asws) stood up and began to walk between them, saying "I ask you by Allah not to be disobedient of Allah and His Messenger (saw) by revealing this openly."

The women replied, "Then when should we weep if we do not weep today? For today is like the day when RasoolAllah (saw), Ali (asws), and Syeda Fatima (sa) departed from this world.

O' the most beloved from amongst our loved ones who have left this world! We ask You by Allah to grant us permission in being Your ransom to keep the death away from You."

Then one of His aunts came forward while crying and saying:

"O' Hussain (asws)! I testify I hear the jinn mourning over You and reciting the following:

"The slain one from the Family of Hashim lowered the necks of Quraesh and disgraced them. He was the love of RasoolAllah (saw) and He (this is totally different from the Urdu check)

HADITH 9

Amr ibn Ikramah narrates:

"On the morning of the day after the martyrdom of Imam Hussain (asws), one of our servants told us that while in Medina he had heard a caller the night before recite the following:

"O those who unjustly martyred Hussain (asws)! Be ready for a severe chastisement and torturing! All of the inhabitants of the heavens, all of the prophets, and all of the angels send lanat on you! The son of Dawood (as), Musa (as), and by Isa (as). who brought the Injeel. have all sent their lanat upon you."

HADITH 10

Dawood al Raqi narrates:

My grandmother narrated to me that when Imam Hussain (asws) was martyred, the Jinn wept over Him and recited the following:

"O my eyes! Shed plentiful tears! Weep for the news of the martyrdom of Hussain (asws) was true!

Weep over the Son of Fatima (sa) who went to the banks of the Euphrates and never returned!"

The Jinn wept over Him with great agony when they heard the news of the martyrdom of Imam Hussain (asws) and His Companions. Such terrible news it was!

O' Hussain (asws)! I shall mourn over You morning and night, and I shall shed tears for You for as long as there is blood in my veins and as long as the trees bear fruit."

Chapter 30

Pigeons Send Lanat on the Killers of Imam Hussain (asws)

HADITH 1

Imam Jafar Sadiq (asws) narrates:

"Choose pigeons as the birds to keep in your houses for they send lanat upon the killers of Imam Hussain (asws)."

HADITH 2

Dawood ibn Farqad narrates:

"I was sitting in the house of Aba Abdullah (Imam Jafar Sadiq asws) when I saw a pigeon that had been cooing for a very long time.

Imam (asws) looked at me and asked, "O' Dawood! Do you know what this bird is saying?"

I replied, "May I be sacrificed upon You! No, I do not."

Imam (asws) said, "It is sending lanat upon the killers of Hussain (asws) ibn Ali (asws). Therefore choose pigeons as the birds to keep in your houses."

Chapter 31

The Mourning of the Owls over Imam Hussain (asws)

HADITH 1

Hussain ibn Abu Ghundar narrates:

Imam Jafar Sadiq (asws) asked, "Have you ever seen an owl during the day?"

The people replied, "No, it never appears in the day. It only comes out in the night."

Imam (asws) said, "The owls used to only live in developed structures but when Hussain (asws) was martyred, they refused to stay in developed structures and insisted upon only staying in abandoned wrecks as their homes.

The owls fast during the day and grieve until the night falls. At night they cry in grief over Hussain (asws) until the morning."

HADITH 2

Hussain ibn Ali ibn Sa'eed al Barbari (the custodian of the grave of Imam Reza (asws)) narrates from his father who narrates:

"I went to Imam Reza (asws) and He asked me, "What do the people say about the owls?"

I replied, "May I be sacrificed upon You! We have come to ask You regarding this."

Imam (asws) replied, "At the time of My Grandfather, RasoolAllah (saw), owls used to live in palaces, houses, and developed structures. When people would eat, the owls would fly and sit next to them. The people would throw food to the owls and give them water and then the owls would return to their dwellings.

After Hussain (asws) was martyred, the owls abandoned these dwellings for abandoned wrecks, mountains, and deserts. The owls said, "What an evil nation you are! You have martyred the Son of Your Prophet (saw)'s Daughter (sa)! We shall never feel safe with you again."

HADITH 3

Imam Jafar Sadiq (asws) narrates:

"Owls fast during the day and after they break their fast, they become overwhelmed with grief over Hussain (asws) ibn Ali (asws) until the morning."

HADITH 4

Yaqoob ibn Shoaib al Mathami narrates:

Imam Jafar Sadiq (asws) asked, "O' Yaqoob! Have you ever seen an owl during the day?"

I replied, "No."

Imam (asws) asked, "Do you know why?"

I replied, "No."

Imam (asws) said, "It is because during the day owls refrain from eating the sustenance which Allah has granted them. At night, after breaking their fast, they keep reciting with grief regarding Hussain (asws) ibn Ali (asws) until the morning."

Chapter 32

The Reward for Mourning over Imam Hussain (asws)

HADITH 1

Imam Muhammad Baqir (asws) narrates:

Imam Zainul Abideen (asws) use to say:

"Any believer who cries over Hussain (asws) ibn Ali (asws)—even if only a single tear runs down his cheek—will be rewarded by Allah for that tear. He will dwell in a beautiful abode in Jannah for ages and ages.

Any believer who cries over Us (asws)—even if only a single tear runs down his cheek due to anguish over the way in which Our enemies harmed Us in this world—will be rewarded by Allah for that tear. He will be made to dwell in a beautiful abode in Jannah."

And any believer who sheds even a single tear due to his suffering from the pain of being hurt in Our way will be kept away from the trials and tribulations of the Day of Judgment by Allah and he will be safe from the wrath of Allah and from the hellfire."

HADITH 2

Hasan ibn Ali ibn Abu Hamzah narrates from his father who narrates:

"I heard Aba Abdullah (Imam Jafar Sadiq asws) say:

"Crying and matam over any matter is makrooh for the slaves of Allah except the crying and matam over Hussain (asws) ibn Ali (asws). The one who cries and becomes restless over Hussain (asws) will be rewarded."

HADITH 3

Imam Jafar Sadiq (asws) narrates:

"Allah Himself will reward those who shed tears when Hussain (asws) is mentioned to them, even if their tears are as the wing of a fly. And Allah will not be pleased with any reward for them except the Jannah."

HADITH 4

Rabee ibn Munzir narrates from his father who narrates:

"I heard Ali (asws) ibn Hussain (asws) (Imam Zainul Abideen asws) say:

"One who cries over Us, even if they shed only a single tear, will be rewarded by Allah for that tear. He will be made to dwell in palaces in Jannah where he will remain for all of the ages."

HADITH 5

Abu Umarah al Munsheed narrates:

"If during the day, Hussain (asws) ibn Ali (asws) was mentioned in front of Aba Abdullah Jafar (asws) ibn Muhammad (asws) (Imam Jafar Sadiq asws) then He would not be seen smiling on that day until after the night fell."

HADITH 6

Abdul Malik Kirdin al Basri narrates:

"Abu Abdullah (Imam Jafar Sadiq asws) said to me, "O' Misma! You are from Iraq. Do you not visit the grave of Hussain (asws)?"

I replied, "No. I am well known amongst the people of Basra and there are some people there who are followers of the Caliph. We also have numerous enemies from amongst the tribes, nusab, and others. Therefore I do not feel safe for they may report me to the son of Sulaiman (the governor of Kufa) who would torture me as a deterrent for others who may be thinking of performing this act."

Imam (asws) asked, "Do you not remember what was done to Him (Hussain asws)?"

I replied, "Yes."

Imam (asws) asked, "Do you feel immense anguish?"

I replied, "Yes! I swear by Allah! I weep over what was done to Him (Hussain asws) so much that my family is able to see the affect it has on me. And I also abstain from eating and the affects of this also show on my face."

Imam (asws) said, "May the mercy of Allah be upon your tears! For you are counted amongst those who are restless and grief stricken for Us, those who are joyful for Our happiness and aggrieved over Our sorrows, and those who are fearful from Our fear and feel safe when We are safe.

And when you die, My Fathers (asws) will be there for you; giving you Their approval to Malik al Mowt (angel of death).

The glad tidings My Fathers (asws) will give you will be an even greater reward than this. For Malik al Mowt will be more kind and merciful to you than a loving mother is to her son."

Then the Imam (asws) began to weep and I wept with Him.

Then the Imam (asws) said, "Praise be to Allah who by His Mercy gave preference to Us and favored Us, the Ahlul Bayt (asws), above the rest of His creation. O' Misma! The earth and the heavens mourn over Us continuously, feeling compassion for Us ever since the day Ameerul Momineen (asws) departed this world. And the number of angels who mourn over Us is even greater than the mourning of the heavens and the earth. The tears of the angels have not stopped flowing since the day Our martyrdom began.

Allah will have mercy on those who cry out of compassion and sorrow over what was done to Us, even before the tears fall from their eyes. If one of the tears that runs down his cheeks were to fall into the hellfire, it would extinguish the burning heat of the fire in such a way there would be no heat left within it at all.

Those who hearts ache for Us will be pleased at seeing Us at the time of their deaths in such a way that the pleasure will remain in their hearts until they meet Us by the Pool on the Day of Judgment.

Al Kauthar will be delighted when one of Our lovers come to it and will serve him various kinds of food to such an extent the lover of Ahlul Bayt (asws) will never wish to leave from the side of al Kauthar.

O' Misma! Those who drink—even if it is but a single sip from al Kauthar—will never feel thirst again and will never again ask for another drink. It is as cold as camphor, as fragrant as musk, and as tasty as ginger. It is sweeter than honey, softer than butter, more pure than a tear and more aromatic than ambergris. It emerges from Tasneem and passes through the rivers of Jannah where it flows over a riverbed made of pearl and corundum. The number of jugs in it is greater than the number of stars in the sky and these jugs are made from gold, silver, and various kinds of gems.

Its (al Kauthar) fragrance can be smelled from a distance of one thousand years and such fantastic fragrances emanate from it onto the face of anyone who drinks from it until they say, "I long to remain here always. I do not need anything other than this. I do not wish to leave from this spot."

O' son of Kirdin! You will be amongst those whose thirst will be quenched by it and everyone whose eyes shed tears for Us will be blessed by looking at al Kauthar and will be given a drink from it.

The desires of those who love Us will be more than satisfied with an abounding pleasure and the ones who love Us greatly will find the water from the pool of al Kauthar to be more delicious than those whose love for Us is less.

Ameerul Momineen (asws) will be standing by the Pool of al Kauthar with a stick made from boxthorn. With it, He will destroy Our enemies in such a way that one from Our enemies will say "I testify there is no god except Allah and Muhammad (asws) is the messenger of Allah."

Ameerul Momineen (asws) will reply, "Go to your leader such and such and ask him to intercede for you."

The man will reply, "My leader, the one mentioned by you, has disassociated himself from me."

Ameerul Momineen (asws) will reply, "Go back and ask the one whom you used to love, follow, and preferred above the rest of creation to intercede for you since he was the best of creation in your eyes for only the best of the creation is able to intercede!"

The man will say, "I am dying from thirst."

Ameerul Momineen (asws) will reply, "May Allah increase your thirst and your desire for water."

I (Misma) asked, "May I be sacrificed upon You! How is this enemy even able to come close to the Pool of al Kauthar when others are not?"

Imam (asws) replied, "He refrained from hideous acts and refrained from the insulting of Us (Ahlul Bayt asws). When We were mentioned in his presence, he would avoid certain acts, which others were committing. But none of his abstaining was due to his following Us or loving Us. Rather it was due to his diligence in worship and performing religious acts. For he preferred being occupied by these things instead of speaking with others.

The heart of such a person is filled with hypocrisy and his religion is based upon the hatred of Us, following those who incite hatred against Us, believing in the two caliphs from the past, and giving preference to them above all others."

HADITH 7

Abdullah ibn Bukair al Arjani narrates:

"I accompanied Aba Abdullah Imam Jafar Sadiq (asws) from Medina to Mecca for Hajj. I asked Him, "O Son (asws) of RasoolAllah (saw)! If the grave of Hussain (asws) ibn Ali (asws) was to be exhumed, would anything be found within it?"

Imam replied, "O son of Bukair! Your questions are always of utmost greatness. Hussain (asws) along with His Father (asws), Mother (sa), and His Brother (asws) are with RasoolAllah (saw) in His House and They are rewarded and maintained the same way the Prophet (saw) is. For He looks at those who mourn over Him and seeks their forgiveness and asks His Father (asws) to seek forgiveness for them.

And He says to them, "O those who mourn over Me! If you knew about that which Allah has prepared for you, then your happiness would be greater than the feeling of sorrow which you feel over Me."

Imam (asws) continued and said, "Hussain (asws) seeks forgiveness for every sin and every mistake of those who mourn over Him."

HADITH 8

Imam Jafar Sadiq (asws) narrates:

"The sins of those who weep, even if they weep as little as that of the wing of the fly, when We are mentioned in front of them will be forgiven. Even if his sins are greater than the froth in the sea."

HADITH 9

Imam Muhammad Baqir (asws) narrates:

"Any believer who sheds tears over Hussain (asws)—even if it is no more than a single tear running down his cheek—will be rewarded by Allah for his tears. He will be made to dwell in palaces in Jannah for ages and ages."

HADITH 10

Imam Jafar Sadiq (asws) narrates:

"Allah forbade Hellfire from burning the faces of those who shed tears for Us whenever We are mentioned in their presence."

Chapter 33

The Reward for those who recite poetry about Hussain (asws) and not only cries himself but causes others to cry

HADITH 1

Abu Haroon al Makfoof narrates:

Imam Jafar Sadiq (asws) said to me, "O Abu Haroon! Recite for Me a poem regarding Hussain (asws)."

So I recited a poem for Him and He wept.

Then the Imam (asws) said, "Recite it the way you normally recite, with a grief stricken tone."

Then I recited the poem, which begins, "Pass by the grave of Hussain (asws) and say to His purified bones…"

Imam (asws) wept and asked me to recite more poetry for Him. I recite another poem for Him. The Imam (asws) again wept and I also heard the women weeping from behind the curtain.

When I finished, the Imam (asws) said to me, "O Abu Haroon! If a person cries while reciting poetry about Hussain (asws) and his recitation causes others to weep as well, Jannah will be written for him and for them. If a person cries while reciting poetry about Hussain (asws) and his recitation causes five other to cry, Jannah will be written for him and for them. If a person cries while reciting poetry about Hussain (asws) and causes even one other to weep as well, Jannah will be written for him and for the one who also cries.

Allah Himself rewards those who shed tears when Hussain (asws) is mentioned in their presence, even if their tears are like that of the wing of the fly. And Allah will not be pleased with any reward for them other than Jannah."

HADITH 2

Abu Umarah al Munsheed narrates:

Imam Jafar Sadiq (asws) said to me, "O Abu Umarah! Recite for Me a poem about Hussain (asws)."

I recited a poem for Him and He began to weep. Then I recited another poem and He wept even more. Then I recited another poem for Him and He wept even more than before. I swear by Allah that I kept reciting poetry for Him and He continued to weep. I also heard the weeping of others from inside the house as well.

Then the Imam (asws) said to me, "O Abu Umarah! Whoever recites poetry about Hussain (asws) and causes fifty people to weep will be rewarded with Jannah. Whoever recites poetry about Hussain (asws)and causes forty people to weep will be rewarded with Jannah. Whoever recites poetry about Hussain (asws) and causes thirty people to weep will be rewarded with Jannah. Whoever recites poetry about Hussain (asws) and causes twenty people to weep will be rewarded with Jannah. Whoever recites poetry about Hussain (asws) and causes ten people to weep will be rewarded with Jannah. Whoever recites poetry about Hussain (asws) and causes one person to weep will be rewarded with Jannah. Whoever recites poetry about Hussain (asws) and sheds tears while reciting will be rewarded with Jannah. Whoever recites poetry about Hussain (asws) and just tries to weep will be rewarded with Jannah."

HADITH 3

Abdullah ibn Ghalib narrates:

"I Went to Aba Abdullah (Imam Jafar Sadiq asws) and recited an exaltation about Hussain (asws) for Him. When I reached the verse, "What an atrocious calamity! Instead of scattering dust over Hussain (asws), He was trampled in the dust."

A weeping woman from behind the curtain screamed, "O Father!"

HADITH 4

Imam Jafar Sadiq (asws) narrates:

"If a person weeps while reciting even one verse of poetry regarding Hussain (asws) and makes ten people weep, then he and those who wept will be rewarded with Jannah. If a person weeps while reciting even one verse of poetry regarding Hussain (asws) and causes nine other people to weep, then he and those who wept will be rewarded with Jannah.."

Imam (asws) kept reducing the number and repeating the same reward until He said, "If a person weeps while reciting even one verse of poetry regarding Hussain (asws) or just tries to shed tears while reciting, then he will be rewarded with Jannah."

HADITH 5

Abu Haroon al Makfoof narrates:

"I went to Aba Abdullah Imam Jafar Sadiq (asws) and He asked me to recite for Him some poetry about Hussain (asws). I began to recite but He stopped me and said, "No. Recite the way you normally recite (with sorrowful inflections) exaltations at His grave."

Then I began to recite a poem, which begins with, "Pass by the grave of Hussain (asws) and say to His purified bones…"

The Imam (asws) began to weep so I stopped reciting. But the Imam (asws) said to me, "Pass over this line and continue."

After I had finished reciting the Imam (asws) said "Recite more."

So I began to recite this poem:

"O' Mariam (sa)! Begin the mourning over Your Master, Hussain (asws) and shed endless tears for Him."

When I read this verse, the Imam (asws) wept and the women of the house also wept and became restless. After the women had calmed, the Imam (asws) said to me, "O Abu Haroon! Whoever recites poetry about Hussain (asws) and causes ten people to weep will be rewarded with Jannah."

He continued on. Reducing the number each time by one until He said, "Whoever recites poetry about Hussain (asws) which causes one other person to weep will be rewarded with Jannah."

Then the Imam (asws) added, "Whoever remembers Hussain (asws) and sheds tears will be rewarded with Jannah."

HADITH 6

Imam Jafar Sadiq (asws) narrates:

"For every act there is a known reward except for the act of shedding tears over Us."

HADITH 7

Imam Jafar Sadiq (asws) narrates;

"If a person recites one verse of poetry about Hussain (asws) while weeping and causes ten others to also weep, then he and those who wept will be rewarded with Jannah. If a person recites one verse of poetry about Hussain (asws) while weeping and causes nine others to also weep, then he and those who wept will be rewarded with Jannah…"

Imam (asws) kept reducing the number and repeating the same reward until He said, "Whoever recites one verse of poetry about Hussain (asws) while weeping or just tries to shed tears will be rewarded with Jannah."

Chapter 34

The Reward for those who remember
Hussain (asws) while Drinking water
and Sending Lanat upon His killers

HADITH 1

Dawood al Raqee narrates:

"One day while sitting with Aba Abdullah (Imam Jafar Sadiq asws), He asked for some water. After He drank the water, His eyes were filled with tears and He began to cry.

Then the Imam (asws) said to me, "O Dawood! May the lanat of Allah be upon the killers of Hussain (asws). If a slave of Allah drinks water while remembering Hussain (asws) and sending lanat upon His killers, then Allah will record one hundred thousand good deeds for him and will increase his station by one hundred thousand ranks. It will be as if he had freed one hundred thousand slaves. On the Day of Judgment Allah will resurrect him with his heart filled with peace."

Chapter 35

The Mourning of Ali (asws) ibn Hussain (asws)
(Imam Zainul Abideen asws) on
Hussain (asws) ibn Ali (asws)

HADITH 1

Imam Jafar Sadiq (asws) narrates:

"Ali (asws) ibn Hussain (asws) (Imam Zainul Abideen asws) shed tears over His Father, Hussain (asws) ibn Ali (asws) for twenty or forty odd years. Whenever food was brought before Him, He would cry over Hussain (asws).

One day His servant said to Him, "May I be sacrificed upon You! O' Son (asws) of RasoolAllah (saw)! I am afraid You will depart from this world due to Your immense grief."

Imam (asws) replied, *"I only complain of my grief and sorrow to Allah, and I know from Allah what you do not know"* (Quran 12:86) whenever I remember the slaughtering of the Children (asws) of Fatima (sa), I am overcome by tears for Them."

HADITH 2

Ismael ibn Mansoor narrates from some companions who narrate:

"One day a servant of Ali (asws) ibn Hussain (asws) (Imam Zainul Abideen asws) observed Him crying while in sajda in His room. The servant said, "O' my Master! O' Ali (asws) ibn Hussain (asws)! Is it not yet time for Your grief to end?"

Imam (asws) raised His head and said, "Woe unto you! May your mother weep over you! I swear by Allah that Yaqoob complained to His Lord about that which was less harrowing than that which I have witnessed and He said, "Alas! My grief for Yusuf" (Quran 12:84). He had only lost one son and I saw My Father (asws) along with those from My Family slaughtered around Me."

The narrator adds:

"Ali (asws) ibn Hussain (asws) use to commiserate with the children of Aqeel. Some people asked Him, "Why do You have more sympathy for the children of Aqeel than for the children of Jafar?"

Imam (asws) replied, "I remember that day when they were with Aba Abdullah Hussain (asws) ibn Ali (asws) and I feel compassion for them."

Chapter 36

Hussain (asws) is "The Martyr of Tears"; No Momin Mentions Him without Shedding Tears

HADITH 1

Imam Jafar Sadiq (asws) narrates:

"Ameerul Momineen (asws) looked at Hussain (asws) and said, "O' ibrah (tear) of every believer!"

Hussain (asws) asked, "O' Father! Are You referring to Me?"

Ameerul Momineen (asws) replied, "O' My Son, Yes!"

HADITH 2

Abu Umarah al Munsheed narrates:

"Whenever Hussain (asws) was mentioned in the presence of Aba Abdullah Imam Jafar Sadiq (asws) during the day, He would not smile until after the night fall."

Imam (asws) use to say, "The tear of every momin is Hussain (asws)."

HADITH 3

Imam Jafar Sadiq (asws) narrates:

Hussain (asws) ibn Ali (asws) said, "I am the martyr of tears. No momin remembers Me without shedding tears."

HADITH 4

See hadith 3

HADITH 5

See hadith 3

HADITH 6

Haroon ibn Kharija narrates:

"We were with Aba Abdullah (Imam Jafar Sadiq asws) and we mentioned Hussain (asws)—may the lanat of Allah be upon His killers. Aba Abdullah (asws) began to weep and we wept with Him.

Then He raised His head and said, "Hussain (asws) said, "I am the martyr of tears. No believer remembers Me without shedding tears."

HADITH 7

Imam Jafar Sadiq (asws) narrates:

"Hussain (asws) said, "I am the martyr of tears. I will be martyred while suffering greatly. Whoever performs My Ziarat while also in great suffering is worthy of being returned to his family with his heart filled with pleasure by Allah."

Chapter 37

Imam Hussain (asws) is "Syedul Shohadah"
(The Master of Martyrs)

HADITH 1

Imam Jafar Sadiq (asws) narrates:

"Perform the Ziarat of Hussain (asws) and do not be averse to it. He is the Master of the Youths of Paradise from amongst the creation and He is Syedul Shohadah (master of martyrs)."

HADITH 2

Ribee ibn Abdullah narrates:

"While in Medina, I asked Aba Abdullah (Imam Jafar Sadiq asws), "Where are the graves of the martyrs (of Uhud)?"

Imam (asws) replied, "Is not the best of martyrs (Imam Hussain asws) near you? I swear by He who holds My life in His Hand there are four thousand disheveled angels around the grave of Hussain (asws) cover with dust and who cry over Him and will do so until the Day of Judgment."

HADITH 3

Um Sa'eed al Ahmasiya narrates:

"I was with Aba Abdullah (Imam Jafar Sadiq asws) when I sent someone to hire a donkey for me so that I could go to the graves of the martyrs (of Uhud).

Imam (asws) asked me, "What prevents you from performing the Ziarat of Syedul Shohadah (asws)?"

I asked, "Who is He?"

Imam (asws) replied, "Hussain (asws)."

I asked, "What is the reward for performing His Ziarat?"

Imam (asws) replied, "One purified hajj and umrah as well as this much reward."

Um Sa'eed added that the Imam (asws) extended His arms out and then closed Them three times to show the meaning of "this much reward".

HADITH 4

Um Sa'eed al Ahmasiya narrates:

"I went to Aba Abdullah Imam Jafar Sadiq (asws). While I was with Him, my bondmaid came to me and said, "I have prepared the mount for you."

Imam (asws) asked me. "O' Um Sa'eed! What is the mount for and where do you intend to go?"

I replied, "I want to perform the Ziarat of the graves of the martyrs (of Uhud)."

Imam (asws) said, "Postpone it for today. How strange are you people of Iraq. You perform the Ziarat of the martyrs of Uhud even though it is a long distance but you are negligent in performing the Ziarat of Syedul Shohadah (asws)!"

I asked, "Who is Syedul Shohadah (asws)?"

Imam (asws) replied, "Hussain (asws) ibn Ali (asws)."

I replied, "I do not perform Hi Ziarat because I am a woman."

Imam (asws) replied, "There is no wrong in women like you performing His Ziarat."

I asked, "What is the reward for performing His Ziarat?"

Imam (asws) replied, "The reward of one Hajj and one Umrah, Itikaf for two months in Masjid al Haram while fasting, and this much reward." Um Sa'eed added that the Imam (asws) extended His arms out and then closed Them three times in order to demonstrate "this much reward"."

HADITH 5

Um Sa'eed al Ahmasiya narrates:

"I entered Medina and hired a donkey to perform the ziarat of the graves of the martyrs (of Uhud). But then I thought I should begin by visiting with the Son (asws) of RasoolAllah (saw) (Imam Jafar Sadiq asws). So I went and visited the Imam (asws) and delayed the guide. After a time the guide raised his voiced in order to hurry me.

When the Imam (asws) heard him He asked me, "What is this regarding, o' Um Sa'eed?"

I replied, "May I be sacrificed upon You! I have hired a mount in order to perform ziarat of the graves of the martyrs (of Uhud)."

Imam (asws) asked, "Should I inform you about Syedul Shohadah (asws)?"

I replied, "Yes."

Imam (asws) said, "It is Hussain (asws) ibn Ali (asws)."

I asked, "Is He truly Syedul Shohadah?"

Imam (asws) replied, "Yes."

I asked, "What is the reward for those who perform His Ziarat?"

Imam (asws) replied, "The reward of Hajj and Umrah and this much reward."

HADITH 6

Um Sa'eed al Ahmasiya narrates:

"I entered Medina and hired a mount in order to perform the ziarat of the graves of the martyrs (of Uhud). But then I thought to myself no one is more worthy of being visited than Jafar (asws) ibn Muhammad (asws). So I went and visited the Imam (asws) delaying my guide for a bit.

After some time had passed, the guide raised his voice and said, "May Allah keep you well! You have delayed me."

Upon hearing the guide, the Imam (asws) said to me, "O Um Sa'eed! It seems as if someone wishes for you to hurry."

I replied, "May I be sacrificed upon You! I have rented a mount in order to perform the ziarat of the graves of the martyrs (of Uhud) but then I thought no one is more worthy of being visited than Jafar (asws) ibn Muhammad (asws)."

Imam (asws) asked, "What prevents you from performing the Ziarat of Syedul Shohadah (asws)?"

When I heard the Imam (asws) say this, I hoped He was going to reveal to me the location of the grave of Ali (asws) ibn Abi Talib (as) so I asked, "May I sacrifice my mother and father for You! Who is Syedul Shohadah?"

Imam (asws) replied, "Hussain (asws) Son of Fatima (sa). O' Um Sa'eed! Whosoever visits Him while having a longing for Him and having the marifat (recognition) of His status will earn the reward of a purified Hajj and Umrah and will gain this much reward."

HADITH 7

Imam Jafar Sadiq (asws) narrates:

"All the martyrs long to be with Hussain (asws) in order to be able to enter Jannah with Him."

Chapter 38

The Prophets (as) Perform the Ziarat of Imam Hussain (asws)

HADITH 1

Ishaq ibn Ammar narrates:

"I heard Aba Abdullah (Imam Jafar Sadiq asws) say:

"There is no prophet in the heavens or on the earth who does not ask Allah for permission to perform the Ziarat of Hussain (Asws). There is always an assembly of prophets descending from the heavens going for His Ziarat while another assembly is ascending back to the heavens."

HADITH 2

Hussain son of Abu Hamzah Thumali's daughter narrates:

"Towards the end of the reign of Bani Marwan, I went to the Ziarat of Hussain (asws) whilst trying to hide from the people of Shaam. When I arrived in Karbala, I hid in the suburbs of the village until midnight. After which I began to approach the grave of Hussain (asws). When I was near to the grave, someone came towards me and said, "Return for you have already been rewarded. You will not be able to go to Him now."

I immediately left out of fear. Then I waited for the dawn and once again began to approach the grave of Hussain (asws). When I was near to the grave, again the same person came to me and said, "O' man! You still may not go to Him."

So I asked, "May Allah keep you well! Why can I not go to Him? I have come from Kufa for His Ziarat. Do not prevent me from doing so. I fear the sun will rise and if the people of Shaam find me here, they will surely kill me."

He replied, "Then wait for awhile for Musa (as) ibn Imran (as) has asked Allah for permission to perform the Ziarat of the grave of Hussain (asws) and Allah has granted His request. Musa (as) descended from the heavens with seventy thousand angels and they have been here since the beginning of the night. They are waiting for dawn. At which time they'll ascend to the heavens."

I asked, "May Allah keep you well, who are you?"

He replied, "I am one of the angels ordered with the protection of the grave of Hussain (asws) and to seek the forgiveness of those who perform the Ziarat of His grave."

So I left whilst being in a grave state of confusion.

At dawn I returned back to the grave. This time I was not stopped. I went to the grave and bade Salam to Hussain (asws), sent lanat on His killers, prayed the fajr prayers and returned quickly due to my fear from the people of Shaam."

HADITH 3

Ibn Sinan narrates:

I heard Aba Abdullah (Imam Jafar Sadiq asws) say:

"The limits of the Haram of Hussain (asws) ibn Ali (asws) are twenty ells (approximately 45 inches) by twenty ells. This location is a garden from the gardens of Jannah. The ascent of the angels towards the heavens begins from here. Every high-ranking angel and every prophet who was chosen as a messenger asks Allah for permission to perform the Ziarat of Hussain (asws). There is an ever present crowd that is descending from the heavens to perform His Ziarat while another is ascending back to the heavens."

HADITH 4

Safwan al Jamat narrates:

When Aba Abdullah (Imam Jafar Sadiq asws) came to Hirah, He asked me, "Do you perform the Ziarat of Hussain (asws)?"

I replied, "May I be sacrificed upon You! Do you also perform His Ziarat?"

Imam (asws) replied, "How could I not perform His Ziarat when Allah Himself performs His Ziarat? Every Thursday night, Allah descends to Him with the angels, the prophets, the successors, and with Muhammad (saw), the Seal of the Prophets, and with Us, the Seal of the Successors."

I asked, "May I be sacrificed upon You! Then should we also perform His Ziarat on Thursday nights so that we could be included with those who accompany the Lord in performing His Ziarat?"

Imam (asws) replied, "Yes! O' Safwan! Remain committed to performing the Ziarat of Hussain (asws) every Thursday night so that it shall be recorded for you. What a privilege this is! What a privilege it is!"

Chapter 39

The Angels Perform the Ziarat of Imam Hussain (asws)

HADITH 1

Ishaq ibn Ammar narrates:

I heard Aba Abdullah (Imam Jafar Sadiq asws) say:

"There is no angel in the heavens or on the earth that does not ask Allah for permission to perform the Ziarat of the grave of Hussain (asws). There is a continuous assembly of angels descending to perform the Ziarat of Hussain (asws) whilst another is ascending back to the heavens."

HADITH 2

Dawood al Raqee narrates:

I heard Aba Abdullah (Imam Jafar Sadiq asws) say:

"Allah has not created any of the creation greater in number than the angels. Every evening seventy thousand angels descend from the heavens. They perform tawaf around Baytul Haram (Ka'bah) until the dawn. Afterwards they proceed to the grave of Ameerul Momineen (asws) and give their salam to Him. Then they head to the grave of Hussain (asws) and give their salam to Him. After which they ascend back to the heavens.

Then seventy thousand angels from amongst the day descend from the heavens. They also perform tawaf of Baytul Haram until the sunset. After they proceed to the grave of Ameerul Momineen (asws) and give their salam to Him. Then they proceed to the grave of Hussain (asws) and give their salam to Him. Then they ascend back to the heavens before the nightfall."

HADITH 3

Imam Jafar Sadiq (asws) narrates:

"The space between the grave of Hussain (asws) and the heavens is always filled with angels who are continuously ascending and descending for His Ziarat."

HADITH 4

Ibn Sinan narrates:

I heard Aba Abdullah (Imam Jafar Sadiq asws) say:

"The boundaries of the Haram of Hussain (asws) are twenty ells (approximately 45 inches) by twenty ells. This location is a garden from the gardens of Jannah. The miraj of the angels begins from here. Every high-ranking angel and prophet who was chosen as a messenger asks Allah (swt) for permission to perform the Ziarat of Hussain (asws). There is always an assembly descending from the heavens for His Ziarat and ascending back,"

HADITH 5

Ishaq ibn Ammar narrates:

I said to Aba Abdullah (Imam Jafar Sadiq asws), "May I be sacrificed upon You, O' Son (asws) of RasoolAllah (saw)! On the night of Arafah, I was in Hirah (the burial place of Imam Hussain asws and the surrounding area). I saw three to four thousand handsome and aromatic men wearing clothing of pure white who were praying all through the night. I wanted to go to the grave of Hussain (asws), kiss it, and perform prayer there. But I could not reach it due to the large crowd of these men. It was not until after the dawn before I could perform sajda. When I raised my head, I could no longer see any of them."

Imam (asws) asked me, "Do you know who they were?"

I replied, "May I be sacrificed upon You! No I do not."

Imam (asws) replied, "My Father (asws) narrated to Me from His Father (asws) who said, "Four thousand angels passed by Hussain (asws) and ascended to the heavens as He was being martyred. Allah revealed to them, "O ' assembly of angels! You passed by the Son of My Beloved and My Chosen from My creation, Muhammad (saw). He was being martyred and oppressed yet you did not help Him. Descend to the earth and weep by His grave while being disheveled and covered in dust until the Day of Judgment."

Imam (asws) continued, "Now they remain by His grave and will do so until the rising of the Hour."

HADITH 6
See hadith 5

Chapter 40

The Blessings of RasoolAllah (saw), Ameerul Momineen
(asws), Syeda Fatima (sa), and all of the Imams (asws)
for those Who Perform the Ziarat of Imam Hussain (asws)

HADITH 1

Muawiyah ibn Wahab narrates:

Aba Abdullah Imam Jafar Sadiq (asws) said to me:

"O' Muawiyah! Do not neglect going to the Ziarat of the grave of Hussain (asws) out of
fear. For he who abandons the Ziarat of Hussain (asws) will regret it so immensely that he
will wish His (Hussain asws) grave was near to him. Do you not want for Allah to see you
counted amongst those whom RasoolAllah (saw), Ameerul Momineen (asws), Syeda
Fatima (sa), and the Imams (asws) pray for?"

HADITH 2

Muawiyah ibn Wahab narrates:

I asked permission to enter and visit Aba Abdullah Imam Jafar Sadiq (asws). Once
permission was granted, I entered and found Him enveloped in prayer at His musalla
(place of prayer). I waited until He finished His prayers and then I heard Him recite the
following supplication:

"O' Allah! O' One who has chosen Us for honor, promised Us the power of shifaat (intercession), chosen Us as the successors, given Us knowledge of all that has occurred and all that will occur and made the hearts of some yearn for Us!

O' Allah! Forgive Me and My brothers who perform the Ziarat of My Father, Hussain (asws), and those who spend their wealth to travel, seeking Our pleasure and hoping for the reward that You have prepared for those associated with Us.

They go to the Ziarat of Hussain (asws) to make Your Prophet (saw) pleased, to obey Our commands, and to oppose Our enemies in order to gain Your pleasure. Therefore, reward them with Ridwan (greatest place in Jannah) on Our behalf, protect them day and night, compensate in the best way their families and their children who are left behind and befriend them, keep them away from the harm of every abusive tyrant and everyone who is weak or strong from Your creation, keep away from them the evil of every shaitan from amongst the men and the jinn, grant them the best of that which they have requested from You while they are away from their homes for their having chosen Us over their families, their children and their relatives.

O' Allah! Our enemies have chastised them for performing Our Ziarat yet that did not stop them from coming to Us and being against those who are against Us. Have mercy on those faces that have been changed by the sun. Have mercy on those cheeks that have rolled over the grave of Aba Abdullah al Hussain (asws). Have mercy on those eyes that have become impatient and anguished because of Us and have mercy on their outcries for Us.

O' Allah! I entrust those bodies and souls to You until the day of the great thirst when You will quench their thirst with the Pool of Kauthar."

Muawiyah ibn Wahab continued:

"Imam (asws) kept repeating this supplication while in sajda. When He finished, I said, "May I be sacrificed upon You! I think this supplication applies to even the people who do not know Allah (swt), the fire of hell will never touch them. I swear by Allah I wish I had gone for His Ziarat instead of going for Hajj."

Imam (asws) said, "You live so near to Him. What prevents you from performing His Ziarat? O' Muawiyah why are negligent in it?"

I replied, "May I be sacrificed upon You! I did not think it was of importance."

Imam (asws) said, "O' Muawiyah! The number of those in the heavens who pray for those who perform the Ziarat of Hussain (asws) is greater than those who pray for them on earth."

HADITH 3

Muawiyah ibn Wahab narrates:

Aba Abdullah Imam Jafar Sadiq (asws) said to me:

"O' Muawiyah! Do not neglect the Ziarat of Hussain (asws) due to fear. For he who abandons the Ziarat of Hussain (asws)—regardless of the reason—will regret so immensely that he will wish that His (Hussain asws) grave was near him. Do you not want Allah to see that you are amongst those whom RasoolAllah (saw), Ameerul Momineen (asws), Syeda Fatima (sa), and the Imams (asws) pray for?

Do you not yearn to be amongst those who return with forgiveness of their past sins and do you not yearn to return from His Ziarat with seventy years of sins forgiven for you? Do you not year to be amongst those who will not have any sins about which they will be questioned when they leave this life? Do you not yearn to be amongst those whose hands RasoolAllah (saw) will shake tomorrow on the Day of Judgment?"

HADITH 4

Imam Jafar Sadiq (asws) narrates;

"Syeda Fatima (sa), the Daughter of RasoolAllah (saw), visits those who perform the Ziarat of the grave of Her Son, Hussain (asws), and She seeks forgiveness for their sins."

Chapter 41

The Prayer of the Angels for Those Who Perform the Ziarat of Hussain (asws)

HADITH 1

Imam Jafar Sadiq (asws) narrates:

"There are four thousand disheveled angels covered with dust by the grave of Hussain (asws). They weep over Him and will continue to do so until the Day of Judgment. Their leader is an angel named Mansoor.

These angels receive all who come for the Ziarat of Hussain (asws) and the angels accompany them when they bid farewell to Hussain (asws). The angels visit them if they become ill and pray over them at their funerals and seek forgiveness for them after their death."

HADITH 2

Imam Jafar Sadiq (asws) narrates:

"Allah (swt) has devoted seventy thousand disheveled angels covered with dust to send blessings upon Hussain (asws) every day.

They prayer for those who perform His Ziarat by saying, "O' Lord! These are the zuwar (visitors) of Hussain (asws)! Do this or that for them and reward them with this or that."

HADITH 3

Imam Jafar Sadiq (asws):

"Do not neglect the Ziarat of Hussain (asws). Do you not desire to be amongst those the angels pray for?"

HADITH 4

See hadith 2

HADITH 5

Aban ibn Taghlib narrates Imam Jafar Sadiq (asws) said:

"It is as if I can see the Qaim (atfs) in Najaf next to Kufa wearing the armor of RasoolAllah (saw). He will shake the armor and then it will wrap itself around Him. Then He will cover it with a robe made of embroidery.

He will be riding a jet-black horse with a cluster of flowers upon its forehead. He will jump while riding the horse in such a way that the people in every land will be able to see Him as if He were in their own land.

Then He will unfold the flag of RasoolAllah (saw). The pole of the flag is from the pillars of the Arsh while the rest is from the victory of Allah. Allah will destroy whatever He points the flag towards. When He waves the flag, the heart of every momin (believer) will become like a strong piece of iron and each momin will be given the strength of forty men.

Every momin who has died will feel content in his grave. The momin who have died will begin visiting one another in their graves and will give glad tidings to one another regarding the rising of the Qaim (atfs).

Then thirteen thousand three hundred and thirteen angels will join the Qaim (atfs).

I (Aban ibn Taghlib) asked, "This many angels will join Him?"

Imam (asws) replied, "Yes. These are the angels who were with Nuh (as) in the Ark (Quran 11:36-48), with Ibrahim (as) when he was cast into the fire (Quran 21:51-70), with Musa (as) when he split the sea for Bani Israel (Quran 26:52-66), and were with Isa (as) when Allah ascended Him (Isa as) to Himself (Allah) (Quran 4:157-159).

Amongst these angels are the *"five thousands angels of terrific onslaught"* (Quran 3:125), and the *"one thousand angels who came rank upon rank"* (Quran 8:9) with RasoolAllah (saw), the three hundred and thirteen angels who fought at the battle of Badr, and the four thousand angels who descended to fight alongside Hussain (asws) but were not given permission to fight.

These four thousand remain by the grave of Hussain (asws) disheveled and covered in dust. They weep over Him and will continue to do so until the Day of Judgment. Their leader is an angel named Mansoor.

These angels receive whoever comes for the Ziarat of Hussain (asws) and the angels accompany the zuwar when they bid farewell to Hussain (asws). The angels visit them if the zuwar become ill, pray over them at their funerals when they die, and seek forgiveness for the zuwar after their death.

All of these angels wait upon the earth for the reappearance of Qaim (atfs)."

Chapter 42

The Rewards of the Prayers of the Angels
Will be bestowed upon those Who Perform the
Ziarat of Hussain (asws)

HADITH 1

Anbasa narrates:

I heard Imam Jafar Sadiq (asws) say:

"Allah has seventy thousand angels devoted to the grave of Hussain (asws) ibn Ali (asws) who worship Him (Allah) beside the grave of Hussain (asws). Each of their prayers is equal to one thousand prayers of a human being, and the reward for their prayers is recorded for those who perform the Ziarat of the grave of Hussain (asws) ibn Ali (asws).

May the lanat of Allah, the lanat of the angels, and the lanat of the people be upon those who slaughtered Hussain (asws) for all of eternity.

HADITH 2

See hadith 1

Chapter 43

The Ziarat of Hussain (asws) and the Ziarat of all the
Masoomeen (asws) is Wajib upon
Every Momin and Mominaat

HADITH 1

Imam Muhammad Baqir (asws) narrates:

"Order Our Shia to perform the Ziarat of the grave of Hussain (asws). Performing His Ziarat is wajib upon every momin who testifies that Hussain (asws) is an Imam divinely appointed by Allah (swt)."

HADITH 2

Al Washa narrates:

I heard Imam Reza (asws) say:

"There is a binding contract upon every Shia towards His Imam. The most perfect and beautiful way to fulfill this contact is by performing the Ziarat of the greave of that Imam.

On the Day of Judgment the Imams (asws) will intercede for those who performed Their Ziarat while having longed to perform ziarat and while believing in all they have been ordered to believe in."

HADITH 3

Um Sa'eed al Ahmasiya narrates:

Imam Jafar Sadiq (asws) asked me, "O' Um Sa'eed! Do you perform the Ziarat of the grave of Hussain (asws)?"

I replied, "Yes."

Imam (asws) replied, "Perform His Ziarat. For performing the ziarat of the grave of Hussain (asws) is wajib on both men and women."

HADITH 4

Abdul Rahman ibn Kuthair (servant of Imam Muhammad Baqir asws) narrates:

Imam Jafar Sadiq (asws) said:

"Even if you go for Hajj every year of your life but you do not perform the Ziarat of Hussain (asws) ibn Ali (asws) then you have abandoned one of your wajibats (obligations) towards Allah and His Messenger (saw).

Allah has made it wajib on the momin to fulfill the rights of Hussain (asws) and this Ziarat is wajib upon every Muslim".

Chapter 44

The Reward for those who perform the Ziarat of Hussain (asws) or Helps Others to Perform His Ziarat

HADITH 1

Imam Jafar Sadiq (asws) narrates:

I heard My Father, Imam Muhammad Baqir (asws), ask one of His servants who had just asked Him regarding the Ziarat of Hussain (asws), "To whose Ziarat are you going and whom do you seek to please by going to this Ziarat?"

The servant replied, "Allah swt."

My Father, Imam Muhammad Baqir (asws) said:

"Those who establish one salat behind the grave of Hussain (asws) seeking the nearness of Allah will meet Him on the Day of Judgment shining so brightly that the light emanating from them will cover everything that sees them.

Allah will honor those who perform the Ziarat of Hussain (asws) and will prevent the hellfire from touching them. They will not be prevented from coming to the Pool of al Kauthar and none shall precede them.

Ameerul Momineen (asws) will be standing by al Kauthar and He will shake their hands and quench their thirst with the water.

Then they will go to their abodes in Jannah accompanied by an angel appointed by Ameerul Momineen (asws). This angle will order Sirat (bridge over hellfire) to humble itself before them and will order Hell not to touch them with its blazing fires. They will pass over Sirat accompanied by the angel sent by Ameerul Momineen (asws)."

HADITH 2

Hisham ibn Salim narrates:

A man came to Aba Abdullah Imam Jafar Sadiq (asws) and asked, "O Son (asws) of RasoolAllah (saw)! Should one perform the Ziarat of Your Father, Hussain (asws)?"

Imam (asws) replied, "Yes, and establish prayer beside His grave. But one should not perform prayers in the front of the grave but should rather stand behind it while performing prayers."

The man asked, "What is the reward for those who perform His Ziarat?"

Imam (asws) replied, "Jannah, if they believe in His Imamate."

The man asked, "What about those who intentionally neglect performing His Ziarat?"

Imam (asws) replied, "They will regret on the Day of Regret."

The man asked, "What about those who stay a few days by His grave?"

Imam (asws) replied, "Every day will be equal to one thousand months of worship."

The man asked, "What about those who spend money while traveling to His Ziarat and who give sadqa (charity) near His grave?"

Imam (asws) replied, "Every dirham is equal to one thousand dirhams."

The man asked, "What about those who die on their way to Him?"

Imam (asws) replied, "The angels will bring embalmment and shrouds for them from Jannah and will accompany them in their funerals. After they are shrouded, the angels will perform prayers on them and shroud them again over their existing shrouds.

Then they will spread flowers under their bodies in their graves and will push the walls of their graves three miles in every direction.

Then a door from the doors of Jannah will be opened to their graves and its soothing fragrance will fill their graves until the rising of the Hour."

The man asked, "What about those who perform prayers next to Him?"

Imam (asws) replied, "Those who perform two rakats of prayer next to Him will not ask anything from Allah (swt) without Allah granting it."

The man asked, "What about those who perform ghusl with the water of the Euphrates and then go to Him?"

Imam (asws) replied, "If they perform ghusl with the water of the Euphrates with the niyyat (intention) of going to Him, their sins will fall of them and they will become sinless like the day their mothers gave birth to them."

The man asked, "What about those who make arrangements for others to go but do not go themselves due to fear of affliction?"

Imam (asws) replied, "Allah will recompense them for every dirham they have spent with rewards as great as the mountain of Uhud and will sustain them with multiple amounts. Also the afflictions which had been written for them will be pushed away and their wealth will be protected."

The man asked, "What about those who are killed next to Hussain (asws) and those captured by an oppressive authority and killed?"

Imam (asws) replied, "All of their sins will be forgiven with the first drop of their blood which is spilled. Then the angels will cleanse the clay from which they were created. The impurities that had originally been mixed within the clay from the disbelievers will be removed from their clay until it becomes as pure as the clay of the devoted prophets. Then their heart will be cleansed and their chest expanded and filled with iman (faith). They will meet Allah while being pure from every impurity that might have been mixed with the heart or the body.

They will be granted the power of intercession for their family members and for one thousand of their brothers in faith.

Jibrael (as) and Malik al Mowt (as) along with the other angels will perform prayers on them. Their shrouds and embalmment will be brought from Jannah. Their graves will be expanded. Lamps will be placed in their graves and a door from Jannah will be opened to their graves. After the angels will bring exquisite gifts from Jannah to them.

Eighteen days later, they will be moved to Hazbra Al Quds and they will remain there with the company of Auwliya Allah (friends of Allah) until the trumpet, which will leave nothing alive, sounds.

When the trumpet sounds for the second time, they will be resurrected from their graves, RasoolAllah (saw), Ameerul Momineen (asws), and the Imams (asws) will be amongst the first to shake their hands and will give them glad tidings and tell them to hold onto Them and follow Them to al Kauthar where they will be allowed to drink and give water to whomsoever they wish."

The man asked, "What about those who are imprisoned during Ziarat?"

Imam (asws) replied, "They will receive a different kind of reward for every day they were imprisoned until the Day of Judgment. And if they were also beaten while being imprisoned, they will be rewarded with one hoori for every time they were beaten. Every time they feel pain in their bodies, one million good deeds will be added to their deeds and one million bad deed will be removed from their deeds and one million ranks will be added to their status.

On the Day of Judgment, they will be speaking with RasoolAllah (saw) while others are going through the Hasab (accountability). The carriers of the Arsh will shake hands with them and they will be told to ask Allah for whatever they wish.

Those who beat them while imprisoned will be brought forth for judgment. But they will not be questioned regarding anything. Instead they will be held by their two upper arms and taken to an angel who will give them a drink from **Hameem** (*"a drink of boiling water"* Quran 6:70) and a drink from **Ghisleen** (*"filth,"* Quran 69:36). After this they will be placed over fires in Hell and told "Taste that which your hands brought forth by beating this man who was the guest of Allah and the guest of His Messenger (saw)."

Then those who were beaten will be brought to the door of Hellfire and will be told, "Look at those who beat you and look at what is happening to them. Are you satisfied with how you were avenged?"

Those who were beaten will say, "Praise be to Allah who achieved victory for us and for the Son (asws) of His Messenger (saw)."

HADITH 3

Abdullah ibn Bukair narrates:

Imam Jafar Sadiq (asws) said:

"O' son of Bukair! Allah has chosen six places on earth; Baytul Haram (Kaaba), Masjid al Haram, the graves of the prophets, the graves of the successors, the places of martyrdom of the Martyrs and the mosques in which the name of Allah is remembered.

O' son of Bukair! Do you know the reward for those who perform the Ziarat of the grave of Aba Abdullah al Hussain (asws), even though the jahil (ignorant) neglect it?"

Every morning, an angel beside the grave of Hussain (asws) calls out, "O those who seek blessings! Come to Allah's Chosen One (Imam Hussain asws) so that you may return with honor and will be protected from the regret!"

This call is heard by all of the inhabitants of the east and the west except for mankind and jinn.

Upon hearing this call, all of the angels on earth to the zuwar (visitors) of Hussain (asws) while they are asleep, sanctify Allah near them and ask Allah to be pleased with them (zuwar).

All of the angels in the skies who hear this call respond by glorifying Allah. The angels raise their voices and the inhabitants of the first sky are so loud the inhabitants of the seventh sky and the prophets can hear them and they (angels of the seventh sky and prophets) turn and ask Allah to send mercy and blessings on Hussain (asws) and pray for those who are performing His Ziarat."

Chapter 45

The Reward for those who perform the Ziarat of Imam Hussain (asws) during Times of Fear

HADITH 1

Zurarah narrates:

I asked Aba Jafar (Imam Muhammad Baqir asws), "What do You say about one who performs the Ziarat of Your Father (Imam Hussain asws) while being in a state of apprehension ?"

Imam (asws) replied, "On the Day of Great Terror Allah will keep him safe and the angels will receive him. They will give him glad tidings by saying "Do not be afraid or saddened. This is the day of your success."

HADITH 2

Ibn Bukair narrates:

I said to Aba Abdullah (Imam Jafar Sadiq asws), "I often travel to Arjan and my heart pulls me towards the Ziarat of the grave of Your Father (Imam Hussain asws). Yet when I go I feel fear; I dread the rulers, their governors, and their armed men until I return."

Imam (asws) replied, "O' son of Bukair! Do you not want Allah to see you in fear for Us? Do you not know that Allah will shelter under the shade of His Arsh those who are in fear because of Our fear and that Hussain (asws) will be speaking to them while under the Arsh? Do you not know that Allah will keep them safe from the terrors of the Day of Judgment? They will not be afraid while others will be terrified. And if they become frightened, the angels will calm them and soothe their hearts by giving them glad tidings."

HADITH 3

Muawiyah ibn Wahab narrates:

Aba Abdullah (Imam Jafar Sadiq asws) said:

"O' Muawiyah! Do not neglect performing the Ziarat of the grave of Hussain (asws) due to fear. He who abandons the Ziarat of Hussain (asws) for any reason will regret it so much that he will wish that His grave was next to him. Do you not desire for Allah to see you amongst those whom RasoolAllah (saw), Ameerul Momineen (asws), Syeda Fatima (sa), and the Imams (asws) pray for?

Do you not desire to be amongst those who return with forgiveness for their past sins and do you not desire to return from His Ziarat with seventy years of sins forgiven for you? Do you not desire to be amongst those who will not have any sins about which they will be questioned when they leave this life? Do you not desire to be amongst those whose hands RasoolAllah (saw) will shake tomorrow on the Day of Judgment?"

HADITH 4

Yunus ibn Zabian narrates:

I asked Aba Abdullah (Imam Jafar Sadiq asws), "May I be sacrificed upon You! How should one perform the Ziarat of the grave of Hussain (asws) in times which involve taqiyyah?"

Imam (asws) replied, "Perform a ghusl in the Euphrates and then wear your most purified clothes. Then pass by the grave and recite:

صلى الله عليك يا أبا عبدالله، صلى الله عليك يا أبا عبدالله، صلى الله عليك يا أبا عبدالله

May the blessings of Allah be upon You, O' Aba Abdullah (asws)! May the blessings of Allah be upon You, O' Aba Abdullah (asws)! May the blessings of Allah be upon You, O' Aba Abdullah (asws)!

Imam (asws) then said, "After doing this, your Ziarat is complete."

172

HADITH 5

Muhammad ibn Muslim narrates:

Abu Jafar Muhammad (asws) ibn Ali (asws) (Imam Muhammad Baqir asws) asked me, "Do you visit the grave of Hussain (asws)?"

I replied, "Yes. But I do so in fear and dread."

Imam (asws) replied, "The amount of reward for performing His Ziarat is based upon the amount of fear and apprehension involved. The greater the fear the greater the reward.

On the Day of Judgment when people are raised for the Lord of the Worlds, Allah will make peaceful the hearts of those who performed the Ziarat of Hussain (asws) while in fear.

Those who go for the Ziarat of Hussain (asws) while in fear will return forgiven. The angels say salam to them and RasoolAllah (saw) will perform their Ziarat and will pray for them.

They will return *"with Grace and bounty from Allah: no harm ever touched them: For they followed the good pleasure of Allah: And Allah is the Lord of infinite bounties"* (Quran 3:174).

Chapter 46

The Reward One will Receive for Every Dirham Spent While Performing Ziarat

HADITH 1

Imam Jafar Sadiq (asws) narrates:

"Those who perform the Ziarat of the grave of Aba Abdullah al Hussain (asws) have associated themselves with RasoolAllah (saw) and with Us (asws). It is haram to slander them and it is haram for Hellfire to touch their flesh.

Allah will compensate them for every dirham they spent whilst performing Ziarat with ten thousand cities. This will be recorded for them in the written book. Allah will look after all of their needs and all of that which they left behind will be protected. They will not ask Allah for anything without Allah granting it either immediately or in the future."

HADITH 2

Al Halabi narrates:

I asked Aba Abdullah Imam Jafar Sadiq (asws), "May I be sacrificed upon You! What do you say the one who has the ability to perform Ziarat but does not?"

Imam (asws) replied, "I say that he has refused to recognize RasoolAllah (saw) and has refused to recognize Us (asws). He has belittled a matter that is wajib upon him.

Allah will look after the needs of those who perform the Ziarat of Hussain (asws) and will take care of every matter that is important to them in this life. Performing the Ziarat of Hussain (asws) increases the rizq of the slaves of Allah and they will be compensated for the money they spent while in Ziarat.

Fifty years of sin will be forgiven for them and they will return to their families having every sin erased from their book of deeds. If they die during their Ziarat, the angels will descend and perform their ghusl. The doors of Jannah will be opened for them and its fragrance will surround them until the Day of Resurrection.

If they do not die while in Ziarat, the door from which rizq descends will be opened for them and they will be compensated with ten thousand dirhams for every dirham they spent while in Ziarat and this recompense will be kept safe for them.

When they are resurrected, they will be told, "You have ten thousand dirhams for every dirham you spent for Allah has postponed your recompense and kept it safe for you with Himself."

HADITH 3

Hisham ibn Saleem narrates:

A man came to Aba Abdullah Imam Jafar Sadiq (asws) and asked, "O' Son (asws) of RasoolAllah (saw)! Should a person perform the Ziarat of Your Father (asws)?"

Imam (asws) replied, "Yes. And they should perform salat beside His grave. But one should not pray in front of the grave. Instead one should stand behind it while performing salat."

The man asked, "What is the reward for those who perform His Ziarat?"

Imam (asws) replied, "Jannah, if they believe in His Imamate."

The man asked, "What about those who intentionally neglect performing His Ziarat?"

Imam (asws) replied, "They will regret on the Day of Regret."

The man asked, "What about those who remain for a few days at His grave?"

Imam (asws) replied, "Every day will be equal to one thousand months of ibadat (worship)."

The man asked, "What about those who spend money whilst traveling to His Ziarat and give sadqa near His grave?"

Imam (asws) replied, "Every dirham is equal to one thousand dirhams."

HADITH 4

Ibn Sinan narrates:

I said to Aba Abdullah Imam Jafar Sadiq (asws):

"May I be sacrificed upon You! Your Father (asws) use to say those who spend money going to Hajj will be recompensed with one thousand dirhams for every dirham they spent. Then what is the reward for those who spend money in order to travel to Your Father, Hussain (asws)?"

Imam (asws) replied, "O' ibn Sinan! For every dirham they spent, they will be recompensed with one thousand plus one thousand plus... dirhams (He repeated this ten times). Their status will be elevated to the same degree. They will benefit even more greatly from the pleasure of Allah and the prayers of Muhammad (saw), Ameerul Momineen (asws) and the Imams (asws)."

HADITH 5

Safwan al Jamal narrates:

I asked Aba Abdullah Imam Jafar Sadiq (asws):

"What is the reward for those who perform salat beside Him (Imam Hussain asws)?"

Imam (asws) replied, "Those who establish two rakat of prayer next to Him will not ask Allah for anything without Allah granting it."

I asked, "What about those who perform ghusl with the water of the Euphrates and then go to Him?"

Imam (asws) replied, "If they perform ghusl with the water of the Euphrates with the niyyat of going to Him, their sins will fall from them and they will become sinless like the day their mothers gave birth to them."

I asked, "What about those who make arrangements for others to go but do not go themselves due to being ill?"

Imam (asws) replied, "Allah will recompense them for every dirham they spent with rewards as great as the mountain of Uhud and will sustain them with ample amounts. The afflictions which had been written for them will be pushed away and their wealth will be protected."

Chapter 47

Things which are makrooh to be taken on the Ziarat of Hussain (asws) ibn Ali (asws)

HADITH 1

Imam Jafar Sadiq (asws) narrates:

"I have been told there are some who go for the Ziarat of Hussain (asws) whilst carrying different kinds of food with them, including akhbisah (a type of dessert made from mashed dates) and other similar desserts.

However, they would never have gone to the graves of their loved ones whilst carrying any of these things."

HADITH 2

Abul Mada narrates:

Aba Abdullah Imam Jafar Sadiq (asws) asked me, "Do you go to the grave of Aba Abdullah al Hussain (asws)?"

I replied, "Yes."

Imam (asws) said, "Do you take different kinds of food with you?"

I replied, "Yes."

Imam (asws) said, "If you were going to the graves of your own fathers and mothers, you would never do a thing such as this."

I asked, "Then what should we eat?"

Imam (asws) replied, "Bread and milk."

Abul Mada added, "Abdul Kareem ibn Amr al Khathami narrated the he said to Aba Abdullah Imam Jafar Sadiq (asws), "May I be sacrificed upon You! Some people perform the Ziarat of the grave of Hussain (asws) and take delicious foods with them."

Imam (asws) said, "If they were going to the graves of their own mothers and fathers, they would have never done a thing such as this."

HADITH 3

Imam Jafar Sadiq (asws) narrates:

"I have been informed some of the people who go for the Ziarat of Hussain (asws) ibn Ali (asws) are carrying with them various kinds of food including akhbisah and other similar desserts. Alas! they would never take such things with them to visit the graves of their loved ones."

HADITH 4

Imam Jafar Sadiq (asws) narrates:

"Performing the Ziarat of Imam Hussain (asws) is better than not performing it. But there are occasions when it is better to not perform His Ziarat than to perform it."

I exclaimed, "You broke my back!"

Imam (asws) replied, "By Allah! When you go to the graves of your fathers you are saddened and grief-stricken but when you go for the Ziarat of Hussain (asws) you carry various kinds of food with you. No! It is better for you to not go unless you go while being disheveled and covered with dust."

Chapter 48

The Way One Should Behave While Performing the Ziarat of Hussain (asws)

HADITH 1

Muhammad ibn Muslim narrates:

I asked Aba Abdullah Imam Jafar Sadiq (asws), "When we go for the Ziarat of Your Father Imam Hussain (asws), are we in Hajj?"

Imam (asws) replied, "Yes."

I asked, "Then does that which applies to those in Hajj apply to us?"

Imam (asws) asked, "To what are you referring?"

I replied, "The behavior of those at Hajj."

Imam (asws) said, "You should be a good companion to those who accompany you, speak less and say on that which is good, mention Allah to a great extent, wear purified clothes, perform ghusl before going to Ha'yr (the burial place of Imam Hussain asws and surrounding area), be humble, perform salat often, send blessings on Muhammad (saw) and Aal e Muhammad (asws), be honorable by not taking that which does not belong to you, refrain from looking at that which is haram, help your brothers in need and give them solace, and act in accordance with taqiyah which is a pillar of your religion.

You should abstain from that which is haram, from fighting, from swearing oaths, and from quarrels that lead to the swearing of oaths.

If you follow this which I have mentioned, your hajj and umrah will be complete. And by doing this you will earn the forgiveness, the mercy, and pleasure of Allah whose blessings you have sought by spending money during your journey, by being away from your family, and by having the desire to perform the Ziarat of Hussain (asws)."

HADITH 2

Mufaddal ibn Umar narrates:

Aba Abdullah Imam Jafar Sadiq (asws) said, "Performing Ziarat of Hussain (asws) is better than not performing it, but there are times when it is better for you that you do not perform the Ziarat than for you to perform it."

I said, "You broke my back!"

Imam (asws) said, "By Allah! You people go to the graves of your own fathers filled with sorrow and grief, but when you go for His Ziarat (Imam Hussain asws), you carry various kinds of foods with you. No! It is better for you to not go to Him unless you go disheveled and covered with dust."

HADITH 3

Imam Jafar Sadiq (asws) narrates:

"When you want to perform the Ziarat of Hussain (asws), do so while being sorrowful, heartbroken, grief-stricken, disheveled, covered with dust, hungry, and thirsty. For Hussain (asws) was martyred while being sorrowful, heartbroken, grief-stricken, disheveled, covered with dust, hungry and thirsty.

After you perform His Ziarat, ask Him for your needs and then leave. Do not settle in Karbala."

HADITH 4

See hadith 3

Chapter 49

The Reward for performing the Ziarat of Hussain (asws) on foot or by any means of transport

HADITH 1

Hussain ibn Thuwair ibn Abi Fakhitah narrates:

Aba Abdullah Imam Jafar Sadiq (asws) said to me:

"O' Hussain! Allah will record one good deed for those who their houses on foot in order to perform the Ziarat of the grave of Hussain (asws) ibn Ali (asws) and erase one bad deed from them for every step they take.

When they arrive at the Ha'yr (burial place of Imam Hussain (asws) and surrounding area), Allah will record them as amongst those who have achieved salvation and amongst those who are successful. After they complete the rituals of the Ziarat, Allah will record them amongst the victorious.

When they decide to return, an angel will come to them and say, "RasoolAllah (saw) sends His salam to you and says to inform you that all of your previous sins have been forgiven. Now continue with good deeds."

HADITH 2

Imam Jafar Sadiq (asws) narrates:

"When a man leaves his family to visit the grave of Hussain (asws), all of his sins will be forgiven when he takes the first step. And he will become more and more purified with every step.

Once he arrives at the grave of Hussain (asws), Allah will speak to him and say, "O My slave! Ask Me and I will grant it. Call Me for I will answer you. Request anything and I will fulfill it. Ask Me for any of your needs so that I may grant it.""

Imam (asws) added, "And he has earned this recompense by Allah for that which he has spent."

HADITH 3

Imam Jafar Sadiq (asws) narrates:

"Allah has devoted angels to the grave of Hussain (asws). When someone decides to go for the Ziarat of Hussain (asws), Allah will give his sins to these angels. The angels will erase his sins when he takes his first step and the angels will multiply his good deeds with every step he takes. His good deeds will keep increasing until he has earned Jannah.

Then the angels will surround him and bless him. They will call out to the angels in the heavens and say, "Bless the zuwar of the Beloved who is beloved of Allah (RasoolAllah saw)."

After the zuwar perform ghusl, Muhammad (saw) will call out to them and say, "O' guests of Allah! Be pleased for you shall join Me in Jannah."

Then Ameerul Momineen (asws) will call out to them and say, "I guarantee the fulfillment of your requests and to keep the afflictions away from you in this life and in the Hereafter."

Then RasoolAllah (saw) will join them on their right and left side until they return to their families."

HADITH 4

Abul Samit narrates:

I heard Aba Abdullah Imam Jafar Sadiq (asws) say:

"Allah records one thousand good deeds and erases one thousand bad deeds for every step taken by those on their way to Ziarat of the grave of Hussain (asws). He will also increase their rank one thousand times."

Then Imam (asws) added, "When you arrive at the River Furat, perform ghusl, carry your shoes, and walk barefoot like a humble slave. Once you arrive at the door of the Ha'yr, recite takbir (Allahu Akbar) four times. Then walk a little and repeat takbir four more times. Then go towards the side where His head is and repeat takbir four more times. Perform prayers beside His grave and ask Allah for your needs."

HADITH 5

Abdullah ibn Hilal narrates:

I asked Aba Abdullah Imam Jafar Sadiq (asws), "May I be sacrificed upon You! What is the least reward for those who perform Ziarat of the grave of Hussain (asws)?"

Imam (asws) replied, "O' Abdullah! The least reward for them is Allah will protect them and their families until they return to their families and on the Day of Judgment, Allah will be their protector."

HADITH 6

Ali ibn Maimoon al Sauigh narrates:

Aba Abdullah Imam Jafar Sadiq (asws) said to me, "O' Ali! Perform the Ziarat of Hussain (asws). Do not neglect it."

I asked, "What is the reward for one who performs His Ziarat?"

Imam (asws) replied, "Allah will record one good deed and erase one bad deed for every step taken on foot of those who perform the Ziarat of Hussain (asws). He will also add one rank to their ranks with each step taken.

Once the zawir arrives at the grave of Hussain (asws), Allah will devote to two angels to him who will only write the good that come from his mouth and will not write any of the bad things he may do or say.

When he leaves, they will bid him farewell and say, "O friend of Allah! You are forgiven. You are from the party of Allah, the party of His Messenger (saw) and the party of Aal e Muhammad (asws). We swear by Allah you will never see hellfire and it will never see you nor burn you."

HADITH 7

Sadir al Sairafee narrates:

We were with Abu Jafar Imam Muhammad Baqir (asws) when a young man mentioned the grave of Hussain (asws). Abu Jafar Imam Muhammad Baqir (asws) said to him,

"Allah will record one good deed and erase one bad deed for every step taken by those who are going to perform the Ziarat of the grave of Hussain (asws)."

HADITH 8

Imam Jafar Sadiq (asws) narrates:

"Those of Our Shia who perform the Ziarat of Hussain (asws) will not return without all of their sins having been forgiven. Allah will record one thousand good deeds and erase one thousand bad deeds for every step they take or their mount takes. He will also raise their rank one thousand times for every step."

HADITH 9

Abu Sa'eed al Qadi narrates:

I entered the chamber of Aba Abdullah Imam Jafar Sadiq (asws) and found Murazim with Him. I heard Aba Abdullah Imam Jafar Sadiq (asws) say:

"Allah will record the reward of freeing a slave from the children of Ismael (as) for each step taken by those who perform the Ziarat of the grave of Hussain (asws) on foot. For every time they raise their foot off the ground and then place it back down.

Regarding those who travel for Ziarat of Hussain (asws) by ship; if their ship sinks, a crier from the heavens will call out to them, "Be joyous and enjoy the pleasures of Jannah.""

HADITH 10

Abdullah ibn al Najjar narrates:

Aba Abdullah Imam Jafar Sadiq (asws) asked me, "Do you perform the Ziarat of Hussain (asws) by ship?"

I replied, "Yes."

Imam (asws) said, "Do you not know that if it should sink, a crier will call out to you "Be joyous and enjoy the pleasures of Jannah.""

Chapter 50

The Reward of Allah upon Those who perform the Ziarat of Hussain (asws)

HADITH 1

Abdullah al Tahan narrates:

I heard Aba Abdullah Imam Jafar Sadiq (asws) say;

"On the Day of Judgment, everyone will desire to be amongst those who had performed the Ziarat of Hussain (asws) because they will see the manner in which the zuwar of Hussain (asws) will be recognized and treated by Allah."

HADITH 2

Imam Jafar Sadiq (asws) narrates:

"Those who yearn to be sitting at the ma'idah (table spread) made of noor on the Day of Judgment should perform the Ziarat of Hussain (asws) ibn Ali (asws)."

HADITH 3

Mufaddal ibn Umar narrates:

Aba Abdullah Imam Jafar Sadiq (asws) said, "I swear by Allah it is as if I can see an assembly of angels around the momin (believers) beside the grave of Hussain (asws)."

I asked, "Do they appear for the momin?"

Imam (asws) replied, "I swear by Allah they are attached to the momin and the angels touch the faces of momin with their hands. Every morning and every night, Allah sends down food for the zuwar of Hussain (asws) from Jannah and the angels are their servants. If they ask Allah for anything, regardless if it is for this world or the Hereafter, Allah will grant it for them."

I said, "I swear by Allah this is a great honor."

Imam (asws) said, "O' Mufaddal! Should I tell you more?"

I replied, "Yes my Moula (asws)."

Imam (asws) said, "It is as if I can see a throne made of noor which has been erected. A dome made of red rubies and decorated with gems has been placed on its top and there are ninety thousand green domes surrounding it. It is as if I can see Hussain (asws) sitting on this throne and the momin are visiting Him and saying salam to Him.

Allah (swt) will say to them "O' My friends! Ask Me for you have been battered, humiliated, and oppressed for a long time. However today is the day that you will not ask Me for anything, whether it be for this world or the Hereafter, without it being granted."

Imam (asws) then added, "Their food and drink are in Jannah and I swear by Allah this is the blessing which will never end and its greatness is immeasurable."

Chapter 51

The Time spent whilst performing the Ziarat of Hussain (asws) is not counted as part of one's lifespan

HADITH 1

Imam Jafar Sadiq (asws) narrates:

"The days which one spends performing the Ziarat of Hussain (asws) are not counted as part of their lives; those days do not deduct from their appointed life span."

Chapter 52

Those Who Perform the Ziarat of Hussain (asws) will be the neighbor of RasoolAllah (saw), Ameerul Momineen (asws) and Syeda Fatima (sa) in Jannah

HADITH 1

Abu Usamah narrates:

I heard Aba Abdullah Imam Jafar Sadiq (asws) say:

"Those who wish to be raised near the station of their Prophet (saw), Ameerul Momineen (asws), and Syeda Fatima (sa) should not neglect performing the Ziarat of Hussain (asws) ibn Ali (asws)."

HADITH 2

Abu Baseer narrates:

I heard Aba Abdullah Imam Muhammad Baqir (asws) say, "Those who wish for their final abode to be Jannah should not neglect performing the Ziarat of the Oppressed One."

I asked, "Who is the Oppressed One?"

Imam (asws) replied, "Hussain (asws) ibn Ali (asws), the Man of Karbala. Allah will make those who perform His Ziarat while longing for Him and with love for RasoolAllah (saw), love for Syeda Fatima (sa), and love for Ameerul Momineen (asws) to sit at the Ma'ida (table spread) of Jannah. They will be dining with them while others are facing the Hasab (accountability)."

HADITH 3

Imam Jafar Sadiq (asws) narrates:

"Allah (swt) has devoted angels to the grave of Hussain (asws). When a person decides to perform the Ziarat of Hussain (asws) and after he performs ghusl, Muhammad (saw) will call out to them and say, "O' guests of Allah! Be pleased for you shall join Me in Jannah.""

Chapter 53

Those who perform the Ziarat of Hussain (asws) Will be amongst the first to enter Jannah

HADITH 1

Abdullah ibn Zurarah narrates:

I heard Aba Abdullah Imam Jafar Sadiq (asws) say, "On the Day of Judgment those who have performed the Ziarat of Hussain (asws) ibn Ali (asws) will be given preference over others."

I asked, "What kind of preference?"

Imam (asws) replied, "They will enter Jannah forty years before others do. They will enter Jannah whilst others will be waiting in the Desert of Judgment to face the Hasab (accountability)."

Chapter 54

The Reward for those who perform Ziarat of Hussain (asws) whilst having His Marifat

HADITH 1

Imam Musa Kazim (asws) narrates:

"Allah will forgive all of the past and future sins of those who perform the Ziarat of Hussain (asws) whilst having His marifat."

HADITH 2

Haroon ibn Kharijah narrates:

I said to Aba Abdullah Imam Jafar Sadiq (asws), "People narrate that those who perform the Ziarat of Hussain (asws) will receive the reward of performing a Hajj and Umrah."

Imam (asws) said, "I swear by Allah that those who perform His Ziarat whilst having His marifat will be forgiven for all of their past and future sins."

HADITH 3

Imam Musa Kazim (asws) narrates:

"The least reward for those who perform the Ziarat of Hussain (asws) by the shores of the River Furat whilst having His marifat and believing in His greatness and Wilayat is the forgiveness for all of their past and future sins."

HADITH 4

Imam Jafar Sadiq (asws) narrates:

"Allah will forgive all of the past and future sins for those who perform the Ziarat of the grave of Hussain (asws) whilst having His marifat."

HADITH 5

Muthana al Hanat narrates:

I heard Abul Hasan Imam Musa Kazim (asws) say,

"Allah will forgive the past and future sins for those who perform the Ziarat of the grave of Hussain (asws) whilst having His marifat."

HADITH 6

Hind al Hanat narrates:

I heard Aba Abdullah Imam Jafar Sadiq (asws) say,

"Allah will forgive the past and future sins of those who perform the Ziarat of Hussain (asws) whilst having His marifat and believing in His Imamate."

HADITH 7

Imam Jafar Sadiq (asws) narrates:

"Those who perform the Ziarat of the grave of Hussain (asws) whilst having His marifat will be forgiven for all of their past and future sins."

HADITH 8

Qaid al Hanat narrates:

I said to Abul Hasan Imam Musa Kazim (asws), "There are some who take people to mourn and food with them when they perform the Ziarat of the grave of Hussain (asws)."

Imam (asws) said, "I have heard of this. O' Qaid! Those who perform the Ziarat of the grave of Hussain (asws) whilst having His marifat will be forgiven for all of their past and future sins."

HADITH 9

See hadith 1

HADITH 10

Imam Zainul Abideen (asws) narrates:

I heard My Father say,

"Those who perform the Ziarat of the grave of Hussain (asws) whilst having His marifat will be forgiven for all of their past and future sins."

HADITH 11

See hadith 7

HADITH 12

See hadith 1

HADITH 13

See hadith 7

HADITH 14

Qaid narrates:

I went to Abd-e-Saleh Imam Musa Kazim (asws) and said,

"May I be sacrificed upon You! There are numerous peoples performing the Ziarat of Hussain (asws). Some who believe in the Wilayat of Ahlul Bayt (asws), some who deny it, and even women. It (Ziarat of Hussain asws) has become so popular that I no longer perform it out of fear of being known."

Imam (asws) did not immediately reply to me; remaining silent for a time.

Then Imam (asws) looked towards me and said, "O' Iraqi! Even if others are going, you should always go. Just do not make your identity known. I swear by Allah there is none who performs the Ziarat of Hussain (asws) whilst knowing His rights without Allah forgiving all of his past and future sins."

HADITH 15

See hadith 1

HADITH 16

Imam Jafar Sadiq (asws) narrates:

"Those who perform the Ziarat of the grave of Hussain (asws) whilst having His marifat are like those who have performed three Hajj's in the company of RasoolAllah (saw)."

HADITH 17

Muhammad ibn Abu Jareer al Qummi narrates:

I heard Abul Hasan Imam Reza (asws) say to my father,

"Those who perform the Ziarat of Hussain (asws) ibn Ali (asws) whilst having His marifat will be speaking with Allah on top of His Arsh on the day of judgment. *"Surely those who guard (against evil) shall be in gardens and rivers, In an Assembly of Truth, in the Presence of a Sovereign Omnipotent."* (Quran 54:54-55)

Chapter 55

Performing the Ziarat of Hussain (asws) Due to
One's Love for RasoolAllah (saw), Ameerul Momineen (asws),
and Syeda Fatima (sa)

HADITH 1

Imam Jafar Sadiq (asws) narrates:

"On the Day of Judgment a crier will call out, "Where are the zuwar (visitors) of Hussain (asws) ibn Ali (asws)?"

A number of people so great it can only be counted by Allah will stand. Allah will ask them, "What made you perform the Ziarat of the grave of Hussain (asws)?"

They will reply, "O Lord! Our love for RasoolAllah (saw), our love for Ameerul Momineen (asws), and our love for Syeda Fatima (sa) made us go to Him."

They will be told, "Here are Muhammad (saw), Ali (asws), Syeda Fatima (sa), Hasan (asws), and Hussain (asws). Join Them, for you will be with Them on Their station in Jannah. Now follow the flag of RasoolAllah (saw)."

Then they (the zuwar) will go to the flag of RasoolAllah (saw) which is carried by Ameerul Momineen (asws), and there they shall remain—surrounding it on all sides, under its shade, in front of it, to the left of it, to the right and behind it—until all of them enter Jannah."

HADITH 2

Abu Baseer narrates:

I heard Aba Abdullah Imam Jafar Sadiq (asws) say, "Those who desire for their final destination to be Jannah and those who wish for Jannah to be their final dwelling should not be negligent in performing the Ziarat of the Oppressed One."

I asked, "Who is the Oppressed One?"

Imam (asws) replied, "Hussain (asws) ibn Ali (asws), the Master of Karbala. Those who long for Him (Hussain asws) while having love for RasoolAllah (saw), love for Ameerul Momineen (asws), and love for Syeda Fatima (sa), Allah will make them to be seated at the Ma'ida (table spread) of Jannah. They will be eating with Them (RasoolAllah (saw), Ameerul Momineen (asws), and Syeda Fatima (sa)) while others are facing the Hasab (accountability) on the Day of Judgment."

HADITH 3

Imam Jafar Sadiq (asws) narrates:

"When Allah wills goodness for someone, He places the love of Hussain (asws) and the love of His Ziarat in his (the slave) heart. When Allah wills a punishment for someone, his heart is filled with the hatred of Hussain (asws) and the hatred of His Ziarat in the person's heart."

Chapter 56

The Reward for Those who have a strong desire to visit Imam Hussain (asws)

HADITH 1

Abu Usama Zaid al Shaham narrates:

I heard Aba Abdullah Imam Jafar Sadiq (asws) say,

"Allah will record those who perform the Ziarat of the grave of Hussain (asws) while having a strong desire to visit Imam Hussain (asws) in their heart amongst those who will be safe on the Day of Judgment. He will give them their book of deeds in their right hands and they will be under the flag of Hussain (asws) until they enter Jannah. Hussain (asws) will make them dwell at His station in Jannah. Allah is all Mighty and Wise."

HADITH 2

Abu Baseer narrates:

Imam Muhammad Baqir (asws) said:

"Those who desire their final destination and their final abode to be Jannah should not neglect performing the Ziarat of Sahib e Karbala (master of Karbala)."

I asked, "Who is Sahib e Karbala?"

Imam (asws) replied, "Hussain (asws) ibn Ali (asws), the Master of Karbala. Those who long for Him (Hussain asws) while having love for RasoolAllah (saw), love for Ameerul Momineen (asws), and love for Syeda Fatima (sa), Allah will make them to be seated at the Ma'ida (table spread) of Jannah. They will be eating with Them (RasoolAllah (saw), Ameerul Momineen (asws), and Syeda Fatima (sa)) while others are facing the Hasab (accountability) on the Day of Judgment."

HADITH 3

Muhammad ibn Muslim narrates:

Imam Muhammad Baqir (asws) said, "If people knew the reward for performing the Ziarat of the grave of Hussain (asws), their souls would leave their bodies out of remorse of not having performed Ziarat and they will die while longing for it."

I asked, "What is the reward for performing His Ziarat?"

Imam (asws) replied, "Allah will record for those who performing the Ziarat of Hussain (asws) while longing for Him the reward of one thousand accepted Hajj, one thousand accepted Umrah, one thousand martyrs from the martyrs of the battle of Badr, fasting of one thousand people, one thousand accepted sadqa (acts of charity) and the reward of freeing one thousand slaves in the way of Allah.

He will be protected for one year from every plague, the least evil of which is Shaitan. And Allah will devote an honorable angel who will protect him from the front, from behind, from the left side, from the right side, from above his head, and under his feet."

If he dies within that year, the angels of mercy will attend his ablution and shrouding. They will follow his funeral while seeking forgiveness for him.

His grave will be widened as far as he can see. Allah will keep him safe from the squeezing of the grave and remove his fear from the angels Munkar and Nakir. A door from his grave to Jannah will be opened.

On the Day of Judgment his book of deeds will be placed in his right hand, and he will be illuminated by a noor so bright it will brighten everywhere from the east to the west.

A crier will call out, "This is a person who performed the Ziarat of Hussain (asws) while longing for Him."

There will be none on the Day of Judgment who will not wish he had performed the Ziarat of Hussain (asws)."

HADITH 4

Muhammad ibn Muslim narrates:

I asked Aba Abdullah Imam Jafar Sadiq (asws), "What is the reward for those who perform the Ziarat of the grave of Hussain (asws)?"

Imam (asws) replied, "Those who perform the Ziarat of Hussain (asws) while having a longing for Hussain (asws) in their heart will be counted amongst Allah's most honorable slaves. On the Day of Judgment they will be under the flag of Hussain (asws) ibn Ali (asws) until Allah takes them to Jannah with Hussain (asws)."

HADITH 5

Zari al Muharibee narrates:

I complained to Aba Abdullah Imam Jafar Sadiq (asws) about the way my blood relatives treat me when I tell them about the reward for performing the Ziarat of the grave of Hussain (asws). I told how they call me a liar; accusing me of forging lies against Jafar (asws) ibn Muhammad (asws).

Imam (asws) replied, "O' Zari! Let the people do as they want! I swear by Allah that Allah glorifies those who perform the Ziarat of Hussain (asws) to the high-ranking angels and to the carriers of His Arsh who welcome those who arrive at the grave of Hussain (asws).

Allah says to them, "Do you not see the zuwar of the grave of Hussain (asws) who have come to Him while having a desire for Him and for Syeda Fatima (sa), the Daughter of RasoolAllah (saw)? I swear by My Glory, My Magnificence, and by My Greatness that I will decree for them to be honored. I will take them to My Jannah, the Jannah that I have prepared for My Auwliya (friends), prophets, and messengers.

O' My angels! These are the zuwar of Hussain (asws), who is the Beloved of Muhammad (saw), My Messenger and Muhammad (saw) is My Beloved. Those who love Me, love the one whom I love, and those who love the one whom I love also love the one beloved by Him (Imam Hussain asws).

Those who hate My Beloved, hate Me. It is My right to punish those who hate Me with My most intense chastisements, to burn them with the blazing flames of My fire, and to make Hell their final abode and their final destination where I will torment them with such an intense chastisement which I will not torment any other with."

Chapter 57

Performing Ziarat of Hussain (asws) with the
Niyyat of Receiving Thawab (reward)

HADITH 1

Imam Jafar Sadiq (asws) narrates:

"Those who perform the Ziarat of Hussain (asws) with the niyyat of receiving thawab from Allah and without the intention of showing off or being seen by others will have their sins purified the way the water purifies the clothes."

HADITH 2

Haroon ibn Kharijah narrates:

I asked Aba Abdullah Imam Jafar Sadiq (asws), "May I be sacrificed for You! What is the reward for those who perform the Ziarat of the grave of Hussain (asws) whilst having His marifat, seeking nearness to Allah and hoping for the blessings of the Akhira (hereafter)?"

Imam (asws) replied, "O Haroon! I swear by Allah that Allah will forgive all of the past and future sins of those who perform the Ziarat of the grave of Hussain (asws) whilst having His marifat seeking nearness to Allah, and hoping for the blessings of the Hereafter."

Then Imam (asws) added three times, "Did I not swear by Allah before you?"

HADITH 3

Abdullah ibn Mahmoon al Qaddah narrates:

I asked Aba Abdullah Imam Jafar Sadiq (asws), "What is the reward for those who perform the Ziarat of the grave of Hussain (asws) ibn Ali (asws) whilst knowing His rights and without being prideful or arrogant?"

Imam (asws) replied, "One thousand accepted Hajj and one thousand accepted Umrah will be recorded for them. And even if they are amongst the wretched, they will be recorded amongst the joyous and will be continuously encompassed in the mercy of Allah."

HADITH 4

Imam Jafar Sadiq (asws) narrates:

"Jibrael (as), Mikael (as) and Israfeel (as) will accompany those who perform the Ziarat of the grave of Hussain (asws) whilst seeking the nearness of Allah until they return to their homes."

HADITH 5

Abdullah ibn Musakan narrates:

I saw Aba Abdullah Imam Jafar Sadiq (asws) when a group of people from Kurasan came to visit Him. They asked Him about the rewards of performing the Ziarat of the grave of Hussain (asws).

Imam (asws) said, "My Father (asws) narrated to Me that My Grandfather (Imam Zainul Abideen asws) use to say,

"Allah will erase the sins of those who perform the Ziarat of Hussain (asws) with the intention of gaining the pleasure of Allah. They will be sinless like a newborn baby. Angels will accompany them on their way to Ziarat. The angels will spread their wings over them until they return to their families.

Angels will seek forgiveness for them from their Lord and cry out to them, "You have been blessed and blessed is the One whose Ziarat you have come to perform." The zuwar will be encompassed by the Mercy from the heavens and their families will be protected for them."

HADITH 6

Mu'ammar narrates:

I heard Zaid ibn Ali (asws) say, "Allah will forgive the sins of those who perform the Ziarat of the grave of Hussain (asws) ibn Ali (asws) whilst seeking nothing but the pleasure of Allah even if their sins are as great as the "scum check translation" found in the sea. Therefore you should perform Ziarat as much as you can so that Allah may forgive your sins."

HADITH 7

Imam Jafar Sadiq (asws) narrates:

"Those who perform the Ziarat of the grave of Hussain (asws) for the sake of Allah and in the way of Allah will be free from the hellfire by Allah. They will be kept safe by Him on the Day of the Great Terror.

They will not ask Allah for anything in this world or the hereafter that Allah will not grant for them."

Chapter 58

Ziarat of Hussain (asws) is the Best of All Deeds

HADITH 1

Salim ibn Mukram al Jamal narrates:

I asked Aba Abdullah Imam Jafar Sadiq (asws) regarding the Ziarat of the grave of Hussain (asws).

Imam (asws) replied, "It is the best of all deeds."

HADITH 2

See hadith 1

HADITH 3

See hadith 1

HADITH 4

Imam Jafar Sadiq (asws) narrates:

"Performing the Ziarat of the grave of Hussain (asws) is the most beloved of all deeds by Allah. And the action that Allah likes the most is when one momin helps another momin. And the nearest a slave can get to Allah is when he performs sajda while crying."

HADITH 5

See hadith 1

HADITH 6

See hadith 1

Chapter 59

Performing the Ziarat of Hussain (asws) is like performing Ziarat of Allah on His Arsh

HADITH 1

Zaid al Shaham narrates:

I asked Aba Abdullah Imam Jafar Sadiq (asws), "What is the reward for those who perform the Ziarat of the grave of Hussain (asws)?"

Imam (asws) replied, "They are like those who have performed Ziarat of Allah on His Arsh."

I asked, "What is the reward for those who perform the Ziarat of any of You (Imams asws)?"

Imam (asws) replied, "They are like those who have performed Ziarat of RasoolAllah (saw)."

HADITH 2

Imam Reza (asws) narrates:

"Those who perform the Ziarat of the grave of Aba Abdullah Imam Hussain (asws) by the shores of the River Furat are like those who have performed the Ziarat of Allah on His Arsh."

HADITH 3

Imam Jafar Sadiq (asws) narrates:

"Allah will record those who perform the Ziarat of the grave of Hussain (asws) whiling having His marifat (recognition) as amongst those who will be in Ala Illyyin (highest place in Jannah)."

HADITH 4

See hadith 3

HADITH 5

See hadith 3

HADITH 6

Haroon ibn Kharijah narrates:

I heard Aba Abdullah Imam Jafar Sadiq (asws) say,

"Allah will record those who perform the Ziarat of the grave of Hussain (asws) whiling having His marifat (recognition) as amongst those who will be in Ala Illyyin (highest place in Jannah)."

HADITH 7

Hussain ibn Muhammad al Qummi narrates:

Imam Reza (asws) said to me,

"Those who perform the Ziarat of the grave of My Father Imam Musa Kazim (asws) in Baghdad are like those who have performed the Ziarat of RasoolAllah (saw) and Ameerul Momineen (asws) except performing the Ziarat of RasoolAllah (saw) and Ameerul Momineen (asws) has its own unique attributes."

Then Imam (asws) added, "Those who perform the Ziarat of the grave of Aba Abdullah Imam Hussain (asws) by the banks of the River Furat are like those who have performed the Ziarat of Allah on His Kursi *(His Throne extends over the heavens and the earth)."* (Quran 2:255)

HADITH 8

See hadith 3

HADITH 9

See hadith 3

HADITH 10

See hadith 3

HADITH 11

Basheer al Dahan narrates:

Every year I use to go for Hajj, but one year I did not go. The next year after going for Hajj, I went to Aba Abdullah Imam Jafar Sadiq (asws).

Imam (asws) asked me, "O' Basheer! What prevented you from going to Hajj last year?"

I replied, "May I be sacrificed upon You! There were some who owed money to me. I was worried I would not collect it so I spent the day of Arafah next to the grave of Hussain (asws) instead."

Imam (asws) said, "Then you did miss any of the rewards given to those who were in Arafat. O' Basheer! Those who perform the Ziarat of the grave of Hussain (asws) while having His marifat are like those who have performed the Ziarat of Allah on His Arsh."

HADITH 12

See hadith 3

Chapter 60

Ziarat of Hussain (asws) and the Other Imams (asws) is equal to the Ziarat of RasoolAllah (saw)

HADITH 1

Imam Jafar Sadiq (asws) narrates:

"Those who want their time of death to be easy, those who want their fear for that which will come on the Day of Judgment to be reduced, and those who want to be able to look upon Allah on the Day of Judgment should perform the Ziarat of the grave of Hussain (asws) as much as possible. The Ziarat of Hussain (asws) is the Ziarat of RasoolAllah (saw)."

HADITH 2

Imam Jafar Sadiq (asws) narrates:

"The zawir (visitor) of Hussain (asws) ibn Ali (asws) is the zawir of RasoolAllah (saw)."

HADITH 3

Zaid al Shaham narrates:

I asked Aba Abdullah Imam Jafar Sadiq (asws), "What is the reward for those who perform the Ziarat of One of You (Imams asws)?"

Imam (asws) replied, "They are like those who performed the Ziarat of RasoolAllah (saw)."

HADITH 4

Zaid al Shaham narrates:

I asked Aba Abdullah Imam Jafar Sadiq (asws), "What is the reward for those who perform the Ziarat of RasoolAllah (saw) and Ameerul Momineen (asws)?"

Imam (asws) replied, "They become like those who have performed the Ziarat of Allah on His Arsh."

I asked, "What is the reward for those who perform the Ziarat of One of You (Imams asws)?"

Imam (asws) replied, "They become like those who have performed the Ziarat of RasoolAllah (saw)."

Chapter 61

The Ziarat of Hussain (asws) Prolongs One's Life and
Increases One's Rizq while Neglecting It Shortens
One's Life and Decreases One's Rizq

HADITH 1

Imam Muhammad Baqir (asws) narrates:

"Inform Our Shia to perform the Ziarat of the grave of Hussain (asws). Performing His
Ziarat increases rizq (sustenance), prolongs life, and keeps afflictions away. Performing His
Ziarat is wajib upon every momin who believes Hussain (asws) has been divinely appointed
by Allah as an Imam."

HADITH 2

Mansoor ibn Hazeem narrates:

We heard Imam Jafar Sadiq (asws) say,

"If one full year passes in which a person has not performed the Ziarat of Hussain (asws),
Allah reduces his life by one full year.

If I say to some of you that you will die a full thirty years before your written time of death
I will have said the truth because you have ignored performing the Ziarat of Hussain
(asws).

Therefore do not neglect performing His Ziarat for Allah will prolong the lives and increase the rizq of those who perform His Ziarat. But if you ignore performing His Ziarat then Allah will shorten your lives and decrease your rizq.

Encourage one another to perform the Ziarat of Hussain (asws) and do not neglect it. Hussain (asws) will testify on behalf of those who performed His Ziarat before Allah, RasoolAllah (saw), Syeda Fatima (sa), and Ameerul Momineen (asws)."

HADITH 3

Imam Jafar Sadiq (asws) narrates:

"Those who do not perform the Ziarat of the grave of Hussain (asws) will be deprived of numerous blessings and one year will be reduced from their lifespan."

HADITH 4

Muhammad ibn Marwan narrates:

I heard Aba Abdullah Imam Jafar Sadiq (asws) say,

"Perform the Ziarat of Hussain (asws) even if it is only once a year. Whosoever performs His Ziarat whilst having His marifat and without denying His status will be rewarded with Jannah, will have his rizq increased generously, and will be immediately joyful by that which Allah has brought for him."

HADITH 5

Abdul Malik al Khathami narrates:

Imam Jafar Sadiq (asws) said to me,

"O' Abdul Malik! Do not neglect performing the Ziarat of Hussain (asws) ibn Ali (asws) and order your friends to perform His Ziarat. By doing so (performing His Ziarat) Allah will prolong your life, increase your rizq, allow you a life full of bliss and let you die a joyous death. You will also be recorded amongst the joyous ones."

Chapter 62

Ziarat of Hussain (asws) Removes Sins

HADITH 1

Imam Jafar Sadiq (asws) narrates:

"The sins of those who perform the Ziarat of Hussain (asws) place their sins at the door of their house. When they leave, their sins are left behind them the way one leaves a bridge behind after crossing over it."

HADITH 2

Imam Jafar Sadiq (asws) narrates:

"When a man leaves his family to perform the Ziarat of the grave of Hussain, his sins will be forgiven with each step that he takes. As he travels, he will become more and more purified.

Once he arrives, Allah will secretly speak to him and say, "O' My slave! Ask Me for anything and I will grant it. Call upon Me for I will answer you. Request anything and I will fulfill it. Ask Me for any of your needs so I may grant it."

Imam (asws) added, "And he will be compensated by Allah for all which he spent during the Ziarat of Hussain (asws)."

HADITH 3

Imam Jafar Sadiq (asws) narrates:

"Allah has devoted some angels to the grave of Hussain (asws). When a person decides to perform the Ziarat of Hussain (asws), Allah will give his sins to these angels. The angels will erase his sins with each step he takes as well as multiply his good deeds. They will continue to do this until his reward will be Jannah.

Then the angels will surround him and bless him. They will cry out to the angels of the heavens and say, "Bless the zuwar of the Beloved of the Beloved of Allah (RasoolAllah saw)."

After the zuwar perform ghusl, Muhammad (saw) will cry out to them, "O' guests of Allah! Be joyous for you will join me in Jannah."

Then Ameerul Momineen (asws) will cry out to them, "I guarantee the fulfillment of your requests and to keep the afflictions away from you in this life and in the akhira (hereafter)."

Then RasoolAllah (saw), Ameerul Momineen (asws), and the angels will surround the zuwar. They will remain on their right and left sides until the zuwar return to their families."

HADITH 4

Imam Jafar Sadiq (asws) narrates:

"When you return from the grave of Hussain (asws), a crier will call out to you. If you could hear that call, you would remain next to the grave of Hussain (asws) for the rest of your life.

The crier will say, "Joy be for you, o' slave of Allah. You are victorious and are secured. Your past ins have been forgiven. Now go forward and continue with good deeds.""

HADITH 5

Imam Musa Kazim (asws) narrates:

"The least reward for those who perform the Ziarat of Hussain (asws) by the banks of the River Furat whilst having His marifat and believing in His Glory and Wilayat is their past and future sins will be forgiven."

HADITH 6

Those who wish to be honored by Allah and to be included in the shifaat (intercession) of Muhammad (saw) on the Day of Judgment should perform the Ziarat of Hussain (asws). Allah will honor those who do with the best of honors and rewards. He will not questions them regarding the sins they have committed during their lives even if their sins are greater in number than the grains of sand, the foam in the sea or the mountains of Tihama (Red Sea coastal plain of Arabia from the Gulf of Aqaba to the Bab el Mandeb Strait).

Hussain (asws) ibn Ali (asws) was oppressed and unjustly slaughtered while He, His Family, and His Companions were thirsty."

HADITH 7

Imam Musa Kazim (asws) narrates:

"When a person leaves his house to perform the Ziarat of Aba Abdullah Hussain (asws) ibn Ali (asws), Allah dedicates an angel to him who places his finger on the back of the zawir and will begin recording on his back every word that comes out of his mouth until he reaches the Ha'yr (burial place of Hussain (asws) and surrounding area).

After he leaves the Ha'yr, the angel will place his palm on the middle of his back and say, "All of your past sins have been forgiven. Continue on with good deeds."

HADITH 8

Abdullah ibn Muskan narrates:

I saw Aba Abdullah Imam Jafar Sadiq (asws) when a group of people from Khurasan came to visit Him. They asked Him regarding the Ziarat of the grave of Hussain (asws) and its rewards.

Imam (asws) said, "My Father (asws) narrated to Me from My Grandfather (Imam Zainul Abideen asws) who use to say,

"Allah will erase the sins of those who perform the Ziarat of Hussain (asws) for the sake of Allah. They will become sinless like a newborn baby. Angels will accompany them on their way to the Ziarat and will spread their wings over their heads until they return to their families.

Angels will seek forgiveness for them from their Lord and will cry out to them, "You have been blessed and Blessed is the One whose Ziarat you have come for." They will be covered by the mercy from the heavens and their families will be protected for them."

Chapter 63

The Ziarat of Hussain (asws) is equal to performing Umrah

HADITH 1

Ahmad ibn Muhammad ibn Abu Nasr narrates:

Some of our companions asked Abul Hasan Imam Reza (asws) regarding the reward for those who perform the Ziarat of the grave of Hussain (asws).

Imam (asws) replied, "It is equal to Umrah."

HADITH 2

Abi Sa'eed al Medaini narrates:

I went to Aba Abdullah Imam Jafar Sadiq (asws) and asked, "May I be sacrificed upon You! Should I perform the Ziarat of the grave of Hussain (asws)?"

Imam (asws) replied, "O' Abi Sa'eed! Yes! Perform the Ziarat of the grave of the Son (asws) of RasoolAllah (saw); the most blessed of the blessed ones, the most pure of the pure ones, and the most pious of the pious ones. If you perform His Ziarat, twenty-two umrah will be recorded for you."

HADITH 3

Muhammad ibn Sinan narrates:

I heard Imam Reza (asws) say, "Performing the Ziarat of the grave of Hussain (asws) is equal to performing a purified and accepted Umrah."

HADITH 4

Hasan ibn Jahm narrates:

I asked Abul Hasan Imam Reza (asws), "What do You say regarding the reward for performing the Ziarat of the grave of Hussain (asws)?"

Imam (asws) replied, "What are your thoughts about it?"

I said, "Some say it is equal to performing one Hajj while others say it is equal to performing one Umrah."

Imam (asws) said, "It is equal to performing an accepted Umrah."

HADITH 5

Abul Bilad narrates:

I asked Abul Hasan Imam Reza (asws) regarding the Ziarat of the grave of Hussain (asws).

Imam (asws) replied, "What are your thoughts on it?"

I replied, "We say it is equal to performing a Hajj and an Umrah."

Imam (asws) replied, "It is equal to performing one Umrah."

HADITH 6

Safwan ibn Yahya narrates:

I asked Imam Reza (asws), "What is the reward for performing the Ziarat of the grave of Hussain (asws)?"

Imam (asws) replied, "It is equal to performing one Umrah."

HADITH 7

Muhammad ibn Sinan narrates:

I heard Abul Hasan Imam Reza (asws) say,

"Performing the Ziarat of the grave of Hussain (asws) is equal to performing a purified and accepted Umrah."

HADITH 8

See hadith 6

HADITH 9

Imraki ibn Ali narrates from some of his companions who narrate from one of the Masoom Imams (asws) who said,

"Performing four Umrah is equal to performing one Hajj and performing the Ziarat of the grave of Hussain (asws) is equal to performing one Umrah."

HADITH 10

Abi Rabab narrates:

I asked Aba Abdullah Imam Jafar Sadiq (asws) regarding the Ziarat of the grave of Hussain (asws).

Imam (asws) replied, "It is equal to performing an Umrah and one is not permitted to stay away from performing it for more than four years."

Chapter 64

Ziarat of Hussain (asws) is equal to performing Hajj

HADITH 1

Imam Muhammad Baqir (asws) narrates:

"Performing the Ziarat of the grave of Hussain (asws), or the grave of RasoolAllah (saw), or the graves of the Martyrs of Uhud is equal to performing an accepted Hajj with RasoolAllah (saw)."

HADITH 2

Muhammad ibn Sinan narrates:

I heard Abul Hasan Imam Reza (asws) say,

"Allah will record an accepted Hajj for those who perform the Ziarat of the grave of Hussain (asws)."

HADITH 3

Abdullah ibn Ubayd al Anbari narrates:

I said to Aba Abdullah Imam Jafar Sadiq (asws), "May I be sacrificed upon You! I do not have the means to perform Hajj every year."

Imam (asws) replied, "If you ever want to go for Hajj but do not have the means, then perform the Ziarat of the grave of Hussain (asws). For it will be recorded as a Hajj for you. And if you ever wish to go for Umrah but do not have the means, then perform the Ziarat of the grave of Hussain (asws). For it will be recorded as an Umrah for you."

HADITH 4

Abdul Kareem ibn Hasan narrates:

I asked Aba Abdullah Imam Jafar Sadiq (asws), "What does it mean when it is said "performing the Ziarat of the grave of Hussain (asws) is equal to performing a Hajj and an Umrah"?"

Imam (asws) replied, "Hajj and Umrah can only be performed here in Mecca. However if one decides to go for Hajj but does not have the means and instead performs the Ziarat of Hussain (asws), then Allah will record a Hajj for him. Likewise if a person decides to perform Umrah but does not have the means so instead performs the Ziarat of Hussain (asws), then an Umrah will be recorded for him."

HADITH 5

Masoom Imam (asws) narrates:

"Performing the Ziarat of the grave of RasoolAllah (saw) or the graves of the martyrs of Uhud or the grave of Hussain (asws) is equal to performing Hajj with RasoolAllah (saw)."

HADITH 6

Imam Muhammad Baqir (asws) narrates:

"Performing the Ziarat of the grave of Hussain (asws) is equal to performing an accepted Hajj with RasoolAllah (saw)."

HADITH 7

Imam Jafar Sadiq (asws) narrates:

"Performing the Ziarat of the grave of RasoolAllah (saw), or the graves of the martyrs of Uhud or the grave of Hussain (asws) is equal to performing Hajj with RasoolAllah (saw)."

HADITH 8

Ibn Abi Yafoor narrates:

I heard Aba Abdullah Imam Jafar Sadiq (asws) say,

"If a person decides to perform Hajj but does not have the means to do so and instead performs the Ziarat of the grave of Hussain (asws) and spends the Day of Arafah beside His (Hussain asws) grave, then his Ziarat will be recorded as him having performed Hajj."

HADITH 9

Ibrahim ibn Uqbah narrates:

I wrote a letter to Abd-e-Saleh Imam Musa Kazim (asws) which said, "If our Master deems it appropriate, I would like to know about the greatest rewards for performing the Ziarat of Hussain (asws) and also if this reward is equal to the reward for performing Hajj for those who have missed performing Hajj."

Imam (asws) replied, "It is equal to Hajj for those who have missed performing Hajj."

Chapter 65

Performing the Ziarat of Hussain (asws) is Equal to Performing Hajj and Umrah

HADITH 1

Um Sa'eed al Ahmasiya narrates:

I asked Aba Abdullah Imam Jafar Sadiq (asws) about the reward for performing the Ziarat of the grave of Hussain (asws).

Imam (asws) replied, "It is equal to one Hajj and one Umrah and this much reward."

Um Sa'eed adds Imam (asws) stretched open His arms and closed them three times.

HADITH 2

Abdul Kareem ibn Hasan narrates:

I asked Aba Abdullah Imam Jafar Sadiq (asws), "What does it mean when it is said "performing the Ziarat of the grave of Aba Abdullah al Hussain (asws) is equal to performing Hajj and Umrah?"

Imam (asws) replied, "Hajj and Umrah can only be performed here in Mecca. But if a person decides to perform Hajj but does not have the means to do so and instead performs the Ziarat of Hussain (asws), then Allah will record a Hajj for him. Likewise if a person decides to perform Umrah but does not have the means to do so and instead performs the Ziarat of Hussain (asws), then Allah will record an Umrah for him."

HADITH 3

Haroon ibn Kharijah narrates:

I was with Aba Abdullah Imam Jafar Sadiq (asws) when a man asked Him, "What is the reward for those who perform the Ziarat of the grave of Hussain (asws)?"

Imam (asws) replied, "Allah had devoted four thousand disheveled angels to Hussain (asws) who are covered with dust and who mourn for Him and will continue to do so until the Day of Judgment."

I asked, "May my mother and father be sacrificed upon You! It is narrated from Your Father (asws) that performing the Ziarat of Hussain (asws) is equal to performing Hajj and Umrah."

Imam (asws) replied, "Yes. A Hajj and an Umrah, a Hajj and an Umrah…"

Haroon added, "Imam (asws) counted ten Hajj and ten Umrah."

HADITH 4

Abi Khadijah narrates:

A man asked Abu Jafar Imam Muhammad Baqir (asws) about performing the Ziarat of the grave of Hussain (asws).

Imam (asws) replied, "It is equal to one Hajj and one Umrah and this much (Imam (asws) stretched open His arms) rewards."

HADITH 5

Imam Jafar Sadiq (asws) narrates:

"The Ziarat of the grave of Hussain (asws) is equal to one Hajj. And after a person performs his wajib Hajj, then it is equal to one Hajj and one Umrah."

HADITH 6

Yunus narrates:

Imam Reza (asws) said,

"Those who perform the Ziarat of the grave of Hussain (asws) have performed Hajj and Umrah."

I asked, "Does it replace performing Hajjatul Islam?"

Imam (asws) replied, "No it is recorded as Hajj for those who do not have the means of performing Hajj.

Are you not aware that everyday seventy thousand angels make tawaf (circulate) of the Kaaba until nightfall. Then they ascend back to the heavens and another assembly of angels takes their place circulating the Kaaba until morning?

The Ziarat of Hussain (asws) is more glorified by Allah than the Kaaba. Seventy thousand disheveled angels, covered with dust, descend to His grave at the time of each prayer and they will not return to His grave until the Day of Judgment."

HADITH 7

Um Sa'eed al Ahmasiya narrates:

I asked Aba Abdullah Imam Jafar Sadiq (asws), "What do You say regarding the reward for the Ziarat of the grave of Hussain (asws)?"

Imam (asws) replied, "O' Um Sa'eed! We say it is equal to the reward of Hajj and Umrah, and there is this much reward in it." Um Sa'eed adds, "Imam (asws) stretched open His arms with His fingers bent."

HADITH 8

Fazail ibn Yasar narrates:

I heard Aba Abdullah Imam Jafar Sadiq (asws) say,

"Allah has devoted four thousand disheveled angels covered with dust to the grave of Hussain (asws) who mourn over Him and will do so until the Day of Judgment. Performing His Ziarat is equal to performing Hajj and Umrah and performing the ziarat of the graves of the martyrs of Uhud."

HADITH 9

Abul Nab Hussain ibn Atiyah Baya al Saburi narrates:

I heard Aba Abdullah Imam Jafar Sadiq (asws) say,

"Allah will record the reward of Hajj and Umrah for those who perform the Ziarat of the grave of Hussain (asws)."

HADITH 10

Imam Jafar Sadiq (asws) narrates:

"Allah will record the reward of Hajj and Umrah for those who perform the Ziarat of the grave of Hussain (asws)."

HADITH 11

See hadith 3

HADITH 12

Muhammad ibn Musadif narrates:

Malik al Jahani narrated to me from Imam Muhammad Baqir (asws) who said,

"Allah will record the performance of Hajj for those who perform the Ziarat of the grave of Hussain (asws) whilst having His marifat and they will remain protected until they return from His Ziarat."

Muhammad ibn Musadif adds, "Malik died in that year and I went for Hajj. After Hajj, I went to Aba Abdullah Imam Jafar Sadiq (asws) and said, "Malik narrated a hadith to me from Imam Muhammad Baqir (asws) regarding the Ziarat of the grave of Hussain (asws)."

Imam (asws) asked me regarding the hadith and I narrated the hadith to Him. Imam (asws) said, "Yes, o' Muhammad! Hajj and Umrah."

HADITH 13

Hussain ibn Mukhtar narrates:

I asked Aba Abdullah Imam Jafar Sadiq (asws) about the Ziarat of the grave of Hussain (asws).

Imam (asws) replied, "The reward for Hajj and Umrah is with it."

HADITH 14

Isa ibn Rasheed narrates:

I asked Aba Abdullah Imam Jafar Sadiq (asws), "May I be sacrificed upon You! What is the reward for those who perform the Ziarat of the grave of Hussain (asws) and pray two rakats next to His grave?"

Imam (asws) replied, "One Hajj and one Umrah will be recorded for them."

I asked, "May I be sacrificed upon You! Is it the same for those who perform the Ziarat of the grave of any Imam (asws) whose obedience Allah has made wajib?"

Imam (asws) replied, "It is the same for those who perform the Ziarat of the grave of any Imam (asws) whose obedience Allah made wajib."

HADITH 15

Yazid ibn Abdul Malik narrates:

I was with Aba Abdullah Imam Jafar Sadiq (asws) when a group of people riding on donkeys passed by.

Imam (asws) asked, "Where are they going?"

I replied, "To the graves of the martyrs of Uhud."

Imam (asws) asked, "What prevents them from performing the Ziarat of Shaheed Ghareeb (Imam Hussain asws)?"

One of the people from Iraq asked, "Is performing His Ziarat wajib (obligatory)?"

Imam (asws) replied, "(Does it say yes here) His Ziarat is greater than performing Hajj and Umrah and another Hajj and another Umrah and another Hajj and another Umrah and.."

Yazid ibn Abdul Malik adds, "Imam (asws) mentioned twenty accepted Hajj and Umrah. And I swear by Allah that I did not leave Imam (asws) until a man came to Him and said, "I have gone to Hajj nineteen times. Please pray for me so Allah blesses me with the twentieth time."

Imam (asws) asked, "Have you ever performed the Ziarat of the grave of Hussain (asws)?"

The man replied, "No.".

Imam (asws) said, "Performing His Ziarat is greater than twenty Hajj."

Chapter 66

Performing the Ziarat of Hussain (asws) is equal to performing Hajj numerous times

HADITH 1

Imam Jafar Sadiq (asws) narrates:

"The Ziarat of Hussain (asws) is equal to performing twenty Hajj and it is even greater than performing twenty Hajj."

HADITH 2

Abu Sa'eed al Medaini narrates:

I went to Aba Abdullah Imam Jafar Sadiq (asws) and asked, "May I be sacrificed upon You! Should I perform the Ziarat of the grave of Hussain (asws)?"

Imam (asws) replied, "O Abu Sa'eed! Perform the Ziarat of the grave of Hussain (asws), Son of RasoolAllah (saw), the most blessed of the blessed one, the most pure of the pure ones, and the most pious of the pious ones. If you perform His Ziarat, then Allah will record twenty-five Hajj for you."

HADITH 3

Shahab narrates:

Aba Abdullah Imam Jafar Sadiq (asws) asked me. "O' Shahab! How many times have you performed Hajj?"

I replied, "Nineteen times."

Imam (asws) said, "Complete the twentieth time so that these twenty hajj are recorded as the Ziarat of Hussain (asws) for you."

HADITH 4

Huzaifa ibn Mansoor narrates:

Aba Abdullah Imam Jafar Sadiq (asws) asked me, "How many times have you performed Hajj?"

I replied, "Nineteen times."

Imam (asws) replied, "If you perform hajj twenty-one times, then you will be like those who have performed the Ziarat of Hussain (asws)."

HADITH 5

Imam Jafar Sadiq (asws) narrates:

"Those who perform the Ziarat of the grave of Hussain (asws) while having His marifat are like those who have performed one hundred Hajj with RasoolAllah (saw)."

HADITH 6

Imam Jafar Sadiq (asws) narrates:

"Allah will record eighty accepted Hajj for those who perform the Ziarat of Hussain (asws)."

HADITH 7

Musa ibn Qasim narrates:

Aba Abdullah Imam Jafar Sadiq (asws) came to Iraq during the early days of the reign of Mansoor Abbas. When He stopped in Najaf, He said to me,

"O' Musa! Go and stand on the main route. Wait there until you see a man approaching from the direction of Qadisiya. When he comes near you, say, "There is a man from the Family of RasoolAllah (saw) waiting here. He asks for you to join Him." The man will follow you."

It was a very hot day. I went and stood on the path the Imam (asws) had told me to. I waited and was about to disobey the Imam (asws) by leaving when I saw something approaching from afar. It looked like a man riding on a camel so I kept looking until he came close to me. I said to him, "There is a man from the Family of RasoolAllah (saw) waiting here. He described you to me and asked me to invite you to join Him."

The man said for me to take him to the Imam (asws). When we arrived at the tents, he tied his camel near to them. The Imam (asws) called the man inside and he obeyed. I went and stood near the tent where I could hear them talking but could not see within.

Imam (asws) asked him, "Where are you coming from?"

The man replied, "From the furthest part of Yemen."

Imam (asws) asked, "Are you not from this place?" (Imam (asws) mentioned the name of his city.)

The man replied, "Yes I am."

Imam (asws) asked, "What brings you here?"

The man replied, "I have come to perform the Ziarat of Hussain (asws)."

Imam (asws) asked, "Have you come only for the Ziarat and having no requests?"

The man replied, "I have no requests and I only wish to pray next to Him, to perform His Ziarat, and then to return to my family."

Imam (asws) asked, "What do you believe to be the merits of His Ziarat?"

The man replied, "We believe we receive blessings for ourselves, our families, our children, our wealth, and our rizq. We also believe our requests are fulfilled through His Ziarat."

Imam (asws) asked, "O' brother of Yemen! Should I inform you about the other merits of His Ziarat?"

The man said, "Tell me more, O' Son (asws) of RasoolAllah (saw)."

Imam (asws) said, "The Ziarat of Hussain (asws) is equal to an accepted Hajj with RasoolAllah (saw)."

The man was shocked to hear this so the Imam (asws) added, "I swear by Allah. It is equal to two accepted Hajj with RasoolAllah (saw)."

The man was even more astonished and the Imam (asws) kept increasing the number until He mentioned thirty accepted Hajj with RasoolAllah (saw)."

HADITH 8

Yazid ibn Abdul Malik narrates:

I was with Aba Abdullah Imam Jafar Sadiq (asws) when a group of people riding on donkeys passed by. Imam (asws) asked me, "Where are they going?"

I replied, "To the graves of the martyrs of Uhud."

Imam (asws) asked, "What prevents them from performing the Ziarat of Shaheed Ghareeb (Imam Hussain asws)?"

One of the people from Iraq asked, "Is performing His Ziarat wajib?"

Imam (asws) replied, "His Ziarat is greater than performing Hajj and Umrah and another Hajj and another Umrah and another Hajj and another Umrah…"

Yazid ibn Malik adds, "Imam (asws) mentioned twenty accepted Hajj and Umrah. I swear by Allah that I did not leave until a man came to the Imam (asws) and said, "I have gone to Hajj nineteen times. Please pray for me so that Allah gives me the means to perform the twentieth time."

Imam (asws) asked, "Have you ever performed the Ziarat of Hussain (asws)?"

The man replied, "No."

Imam (asws) said, "Performing His Ziarat is greater than twenty Hajj."

HADITH 9

Masadah ibn Sadaqah narrates:

I asked Aba Abdullah Imam Jafar Sadiq (asws), "What is the reward for one who performs the Ziarat of the grave of Hussain (asws)?"

Imam (asws) replied, "Performing Hajj with RasoolAllah (saw) will be recorded for him."

I said, "May I be sacrificed upon You! Performing Hajj with RasoolAllah (saw)?"

Imam (asws) replied, "Yes and even two Hajj."

I said, "May I be sacrificed upon You! Two Hajj?"

Imam (asws) replied, "Yes and even three Hajj."

Imam (asws) kept increasing the number until He reached ten and then I said, "May I be sacrificed upon You! Ten Hajj with RasoolAllah (saw)?"

Imam (asws) replied, "Yes and even twenty Hajj."

I said, "May I be sacrificed upon You! Twenty Hajj?"

Imam (asws) kept increasing the number until He reached fifty and then He stopped.

HADITH 10

Abdullah ibn Maymoon al Qaddah narrates:

I asked Aba Abdullah Imam Jafar Sadiq (asws), "What is the reward for those who perform the Ziarat of the grave of Hussain (asws) whilst having His marifat and without being prideful or arrogant?"

Imam (asws) replied, "One thousand Hajj and one thousand Umrah will be recorded for them. Even if they are amongst the wretched one, they will be written as amongst the joyous ones and they will be continuously submerged in the mercy of Allah."

Chapter 67

Ziarat of Hussain (asws) is equal to freeing numerous slaves

HADITH 1

Imam Jafar Sadiq (asws) narrates:

"Allah will record the reward of freeing one thousand slaves for those who perform the Ziarat of the grave of Hussain (asws) whilst having His marifat. He will also earn the reward of offering one thousand saddled and bridles horses in the way of Allah (jihad)."

HADITH 2

Abu Sa'eed al Medaini narrates:

I asked Aba Abdullah Imam Jafar Sadiq (asws), "May I be sacrificed upon You! Should I go to the grave of the Son (asws) of RasoolAllah (saw) (Imam Hussain asws)?"

Imam (asws) replied, "O' Abu Sa'eed! Yes, you should go to the grave of the Son (asws) of RasoolAllah (saw), the most blessed of the blessed one, the most pure of the purified ones, and the most pious of the pious ones. If you perform His Ziarat, then Allah will recorded the reward of freeing twenty-five slaves for you."

Chapter 68

Those who perform the Ziarat of Hussain (asws) will be able to intercede for others on the Day of Judgment

HADITH 1

Imam Jafar Sadiq (asws) narrates:

"On the Day of Arafah, the Mercy of Allah will be revealed to those who perform the Ziarat of the grave of Hussain (asws) before those who were in Arafat. Allah will fulfill their (zuwar) needs, forgive their sins and accept their intercession.

Afterwards, He will attend to the people of Arafat and bless them in the same way."

HADITH 2

Saif al Tammar narrates:

I heard Aba Abdullah Imam Jafar Sadiq (asws) say,

"On the Day of Judgment a zawir (visitor) of Hussain (asws) will be able to intercede for one hundred people who were sinful in this life and upon whom hellfire is wajib."

HADITH 3

Safwan al Jamal narrates:

I asked Aba Abdullah Imam Jafar Sadiq (asws), "What is the reward for those who are martyred next to the grave of Hussain (asws) or those who are captured by an oppressive ruler and then martyred?"

Imam (asws) replied, "All of their sins will be forgiven with the first drop of their blood which is spelled. Then the angels will cleanse the clay from which they were created. The impurities that were mixed with their clay will be removed until it becomes as pure as the clay of the devoted prophets. Then their heart will be cleansed, broadened, and filled with iman (Faith). They will meet Allah whilst being pure from every impurity. They will be able to intercede for their family members and one thousand of their brothers in faith.

Jibrael (as) and Malik al Mowt (as) (Angel of Death) along with the angels will pray for them. Their shroud and embalmment will be brought for them from Jannah. Their graves will be expanded, filled with noor and a door opened from Jannah to their graves. The angels will bring gifts from Jannah to them.

Eighteen days later, they will be moved to the Sacred Sanctuary and will remain there in the company of Allah's Divine Authorities until the trumpet is sounded, leaving nothing alive.

When the trumpet is sounded for the second time, they will be resurrected from their graves and first to shake their hands will be RasoolAllah (saw), Ameerul Momineen (asws) and the Imams (asws). They (RasoolAllah (saw), Ameerul Momineen (asws) and Imams (asws)) will give glad tidings to the zawir and tell them to hold onto and follow Them to al Kauthar (pool in Jannah) where they will be allowed to drink and give water to whomever they wish."

HADITH 4

Sulaiman ibn Khalid narrates:

I heard Aba Abdullah Imam Jafar Sadiq (asws) say,

"Every day and night Allah looks upon the earth one hundred thousand times. With each look He forgives who He wills and punishes who He wills. Allah forgives those who perform the Ziarat of the grave of Hussain (asws), their family members, and those for whom the zuwar will intercede for on the Day of Judgment, even if they are among those upon whom hell if wajib."

I asked, "Even if they are amongst those upon whom hellfire is wajib?"

Imam (asws) replied, "Yes unless they are nasibi (one who hates Ahlul Bayt (asws) or encourages others to hate Ahlul Bayt (asws))."

HADITH 5

Imam Jafar Sadiq (asws) narrates:

"On the Day of Judgment, a crier will call out, "Where are the Shia of Aal e Muhammad (asws)?"

A group of people so large it can only be counted by Allah will rise and move aside."

Then a crier will call out, "Where are the zuwar of the grave of Hussain (asws)?"

A group of people will rise and they will be told, "Take the hand of whomsoever you wish and take them to Jannah with you."

They will take whomever they like to Jannah until others will become to call to them, "O so and so! Do you not remember me? I stood up for you once out of your respect."

The man will take him to Jannah without any interruption."

Chapter 69

Performing the Ziarat of Hussain (asws) removes one's
sufferings and all of one's requests will be fulfilled

HADITH 1

Imam Jafar Sadiq (asws) narrates:

"There is a grave near you to which no grief-stricken person goes without Allah removing his grief and fulfilling his requests."

HADITH 2

Abul Sabah al Kanani narrates:

I heard Aba Abdullah Imam Jafar Sadiq (asws) say,

"There is a grave near you to which no grief-stricken person goes without Allah removing his grief and fulfilling his requests. There are four thousand angels next to His grave who have been there since the day He left this world. They are disheveled, covered with dust and they mourn over Him and will do so until the Day of Judgment. These angels accompany those who perform the Ziarat of Hussain (asws) back to their dwellings. If the zuwar become ill, the angels visit them. When the zuwar die, the angels follow their dead bodies in their funerals."

HADITH 3

Ismael ibn Jabeer narrates:

I heard Aba Abdullah Imam Jafar Sadiq (asws) say,

"Hussain (asws) was slaughtered while being in a state of grief. This is why Allah removes the grief of those who perform His Ziarat."

HADITH 4

Imam Jafar Sadiq (asws) narrates:

"Allah offered Our Wilayat to the inhabitants of various lands but none accepted it immediately except the inhabitants of Kufa. There is a grave near Kufa which no grief-stricken person goes and prays four rakats of prayer without Allah removing his grief and fulfilling his requests."

HADITH 5

Imam Muhammad Baqir (asws) narrates:

"Hussain (asws), Sahib e Karbala (master of Karbala) was martyred while He was oppressed, afflicted, thirsty, and wronged.

It is only fitting that every grief-stricken person, every afflicted person, every sinful person, every discouraged person, every thirsty person, and every misfortunate person who performs the Ziarat of Hussain (asws), prays beside His grave, and seeks the nearness of Allah through Hussain (asws) will have his grief removed by Allah and Allah will fulfill his requests, forgive his sins, prolong his life and increase his rizq (sustenance). "Take warning, then, O ye with eyes (to see)!" (Quran 59:2)

HADITH 6

Imam Jafar Sadiq (asws) narrates:

"There is a grave on the outskirts of Kufa (the grave of Imam Hussain asws) where no grief-stricken person goes without Allah removing his grief."

HADITH 7

Imam Muhammad Baqir (asws) narrates:

"Our Wilayat was offered to the inhabitants of various lands but none accepted it without hesitation the way the inhabitants of Kufa did. This is because the grave of Ameerul Momineen (asws) is located within it.

There is another grave near to the grave of Ameerul Momineen (asws) (the grave of Imam Hussain asws) where none who goes there and prays 2 or 4 rakat beside it and then asks Allah for his needs without Allah granting their requests.

Indeed, one thousand angels encircle this grave daily."

HADITH 8

Ibn Abu Yafoor narrates:

I said to Aba Abdullah Imam Jafar Sadiq (asws), "My desire to see You is what allowed me to endure the difficulties of the journey towards You."

Imam (asws) replied, "Do not complain about this to your Lord. Why do you not go to the One who has more right upon you than Me?"

Hearing that there was someone whom I was more duty-bound than I was toward Him was more difficult for me to hear than when He told me "Do not complain about this to your Lord."

So I asked, "Towards whom am I more duty-bound than I am towards You?"

Imam (asws) replied, "Hussain (asws) ibn Ali (asws). Why do you not perform His Ziarat and beseech Allah whilst beside His grave regarding your needs?"

HADITH 9

Ishaq ibn Ziyad narrates:

A man came to Aba Abdullah Imam Jafar Sadiq (asws) and said, "I have sold all of my belongings and properties. I am thinking I shall move to Mecca."

Imam (asws) said, "Do do this for the people of Mecca openly disbelieve in Allah."

The man asked, "What about the city of RasoolAllah (saw) (Medina)?"

Imam (asws) replied, "The people there are even worse than the people of Mecca."

The man asked, "Then where should I move to?"

Imam (asws) replied, "Go to Kufa in Iraq, for the blessings of that land span twelve miles. There is a grave within it which is not visited by the grief-stricken without Allah removing his grief."

Chapter 70

The Reward for performing the Ziarat of Hussain (asws) on the Day of Arafah

HADITH 1

Basheer al Dahhan narrates:

I said to Aba Abdullah Imam Jafar Sadiq (asws), "Sometimes I do not have the opportunity to go for Hajj. Instead I spend the Day of Arafah beside the grave of Hussain (asws)."

Imam (asws) said, "Well done, o' Basheer! Allah will record twenty purified and accepted Hajj, twenty purified and accepted Umrah, and the reward of fighting in twenty battles with one of Allah's messengers or a Just Imam (asws) for that momin who performs the Ziarat of the grave of Hussain (asws) whilst having His marifat (recognition) on any day other than Eid.

Allah will record one hundred purified and accepted Hajj, one hundred purified and accepted Umrah, and the reward of fighting in one hundred battles with one of Allah's messengers or a Just Imam (asws) for that momin who performs the Ziarat of the grave of Hussain (asws) whilst having His marifat (recognition) on any day other than Eid.

Allah will record one thousand purified and accepted Hajj, one thousand purified and accepted Umrah, and the reward of fighting in one thousand battles with one of Allah's messengers or a Just Imam (asws) for that momin who performs the Ziarat of the grave of Hussain (asws) whilst having His marifat (recognition) on any day other than Eid."

I said, "But how is it possible to be anywhere better than Arafat on the Day of Arafah?"

Imam (asws) looked at me and said, "O' Basheer! When a momin performs the Ziarat of the grave of Hussain (asws) on the Day of Arafah—after having performed ghusl in the River Furat—Allah will record one complete Hajj with all of its rituals for every step he takes."

Basheer adds, "I believe Imam (asws) also mentioned Allah will register the reward of participating in a battle."

HADITH 2

Dawood al Raqee narrates:

I heard Aba Abdullah Imam Jafar Sadiq (asws) , Abul Hasan Imam Musa Kazim (asws), and Abul Hasan Imam Reza (asws) say,

"Allah will make those who performed the Ziarat of the grave of Hussain on the Day of Arafah to return with their hearts filled with ease."

HADITH 3

Ali ibn Asbat narrates from some companions who narrate:

Aba Abdullah Imam Jafar Sadiq (asws) said, "On the eve of Arafah, Allah (swt) looks at the zuwar (visitors) of the grave of Hussain (asws) first."

I asked, "Even before looking at the people who are in Arafat?"

Imam (asws) replied, "Yes."

I asked, "Why is that?"

Imam (asws) replied, "Because there those who are aulad e zani (children of adultery/ illegitimate) amongst those who are in Arafat but there are none who are aulad e zani amongst the zuwar of Hussain (asws)."

HADITH 4

Imam Jafar Sadiq (asws) narrates:

"On the Day of Arafah, Allah (swt) Allah reveals His mercy to the zuwar of the grave of Hussain (asws) before He does to the people who are in Arafat. He fulfills their needs, forgives their sins, and accepts their shifaat (intercession). Afterwards, He then attends to the people in Arafat and blesses them in the same way."

HADITH 5

Imam Jafar Sadiq (asws) narrates:

"Those who missed the opportunity to spend the Day of Arafah in Arafat and instead spent the day beside the grave of Hussain (asws) have indeed not missed it.

On the Day of Arafah, Allah (swt) begins with the people who are beside the grave of Hussain (asws) and showers them with blessings before the people who are in Arafat."

HADITH 6

Imam Jafar Sadiq (asws) narrates:

"Allah will record one thousand purified Hajj and one thousand accepted Umrah and will grant one thousand requests performing to this life and the Akhira (hereafter) for those who perform the Ziarat of Hussain (asws) on the night of the fifteenth of Shabaan, on the night of Fitr and on the night of Arafah all within the same year."

HADITH 7

Imam Jafar Sadiq (asws) narrates:

"On the Day of Arafah, Allah (swt) looks towards the visitors of the grave of Aba Abdullah al Hussain (asws) and says, "Go forward and only do good deeds for I have forgiven you." Then He looks towards the people in Arafat."

HADITH 8

Umar ibn Hasan al Arzami narrates:

I heard Aba Abdullah Imam Jafar Sadiq (asws) say,

"On the Day of Arafah, Allah looks towards the visitors of the grave of Hussain (asws) and says, "Return with your past sins forgiven." No sins will be recorded for them for up to seventy days after they return."

HADITH 9

Basheer al Dahhan narrates:

I heard Aba Abdullah Imam Jafar Sadiq (asws) speaking in Hirah to a group of Shia that was surrounding Him.

He turned His Face towards me and asked, "O' Basheer! Did you go for Hajj last year?"

I replied, "May I be sacrificed upon You! No, instead I spent the Day of Arafah beside the grave of Hussain (asws)."

Imam (asws) said, "O' Basheer! I swear by Allah that you did not miss anything from the blessings for those who were there in Mecca."

I said, "May I be sacrificed upon You! Explain this for me, for the blessings of being in Arafat are only available for those in Mecca."

Imam (asws) replied, "O' Basheer! Every time one of you raises a foot or places it down—after performing ghusl in the River Furat and begins walking toward the grave of Hussain (asws) and while having His marifat—Allah will record the reward of one hundred accepted Hajj and one hundred accepted Umrah and the reward of fighting in one hundred battles with one of Allah's messengers against His enemies and the enemies of His messenger.

O' Basheer! Listen carefully and inform only those whose hearts can bear this, "Those who perform the Ziarat of Hussain (asws) on the Day of Arafah are like those who perform the Ziarat of Allah on His Arsh."

HADITH 10

Imam Jafar Sadiq (asws) narrates:

"Allah will record the reward of performing one million Hajj with the Qa'im (atfs) and one million Umrah with RasoolAllah (saw), the freeing of one million slaves, and offering one million horses in the way of Allah (fighting in one million battles in the way of Allah) for those who perform the Ziarat of the grave of Hussain (asws) on the Day of Arafah.

Allah will refer to him as "My truthful slave who believed in My promise." And the angels will add the title of "sadiq" (trustworthy) to his name and will say, "Allah has purified him from atop His Arsh."

Imam (asws) added, "He will be referred to as "Karoob (guardian) on earth.""

HADITH 11

Basheer al Dahhan narrates:

Imam Jafar Sadiq (asws) said,

"Allah will record the reward of one thousand Hajj and one thousand Umrah and the reward of fighting one thousand times with one of Allah's messengers for those who perform the Ziarat of the grave of Hussain (asws) on the Day of Arafah whilst having His marifat. And Allah forgives those who perform His Ziarat on the first day of Rajab."

HADITH 12

Yasar narrates:

Imam Jafar Sadiq (asws) said:

"If an indebted, bankrupt person does not find the means to perform an obligatory Hajj then he should instead spend the Day of Arafah beside the grave of Hussain (asws). For this will suffice as having performed an obligatory Hajj.

Though be aware. This will only suffice as performing Hajj for the one who is indebted, bankrupt.

If a wealthy person has already performed his obligatory Hajj and then decides to go for an additional Hajj or Umrah but misses it because of some hindrance or because he was preoccupied with matters of this world, and instead performs the Ziarat of the grave of Hussain (asws) on the Day of Arafah, this will be as if he had performed the additional Hajj or Umrah and Allah will multiply the rewards of this act immensely for him"

I asked, "How many Hajj and how many Umrah will be recorded for him?"

Imam (asws) replied, "It cannot be counted."

I asked, "One hundred?"

Imam (asws) replied, "Who could count it?"

I asked, "One thousand?"

Imam (asws) replied, "And more."

Then Imam (asws) added, *"And if you would count Allah's favors, you will not be able to number them"* (Quran 16:18) *"Allah is All-Embracing, All-Knowing."* (Quran 2:115)

Chapter 71

The Reward for Performing the Ziarat of Hussain (asws) on the Day of Ashura

HADITH 1

Jabeer al Jufi narrates:

I went to Jafar ibn Muhammad (asws) (Imam Jafar Sadiq asws) on the day of Ashura and He said to me,

"The zuwar (visitors) of Hussain (asws) are the zuwar of Allah. It is the duty of the host to treat his visitors with respect. Those who spend the night of Ashura beside the grave of Hussain (asws) will meet Allah on the Day of Judgment stained with their blood as if they had been martyred alongside Him in the desert of Karbala. Those who perform the Ziarat of the grave of Hussain (asws) on the day of Ashura and spend the night beside His grave are like those who were martyred in front of Hussain (asws)."

HADITH 2

Imam Jafar Sadiq (asws) narrates:

"Jannah is wajib (obligatory) upon those who perform the Ziarat of Hussain (asws) on the day of Ashura."

HADITH 3

Imam Jafar Sadiq (asws) narrates:

"Those who possess the marifat of Hussain (asws) and perform the Ziarat of the grave of Hussain (asws) ibn Ali (asws) on the day of Ashura are like those who perform the Ziarat of Allah on His Arsh."

HADITH 4

Masoom Imam (asws) narrates:

"Those who perform the Ziarat of the grave of Hussain (asws) on the day of Ashura are like those whose blood was spilled before Hussain (asws)."

HADITH 5

Muhammad ibn Abu Sayar al Medaini narrates through his isnad:

"Those who distribute water to the people on the day of Ashura beside the grave of Hussain (asws) are like those who were with Hussain (asws) and distributed water to those in His camp."

HADITH 6

Imam Jafar Sadiq (asws) narrates:

"Allah will forgive the past and future sins of those who perform the Ziarat of Hussain (asws) on the night of the fifteenth of Shabaan.

Allah will record the reward of one thousand accepted Hajj and one thousand accepted Umrah for those who perform the Ziarat of Hussain (asws) on the day of Arafah.

Those who perform the Ziarat of Hussain (asws) on the day of Ashura are like those who have performed the Ziarat of Allah on His Arsh."

HADITH 7

Alqamah ibn Muhammad al Hadrami narrates:

Imam Muhammad Baqir (asws) narrates:

"Those who perform the Ziarat of Hussain (asws) on the tenth day of Muharram and spend the night beside Him, weeping over Him, will meet Allah (swt) with the reward of two million Hajj and two million Umrah and the reward of fighting in two million battles in the way of Allah. Also the reward of those who have performed Hajj and Umrah and have fought alongside RasoolAllah (saw) and the Righteous Imams (asws)."

I asked, "May I be sacrificed upon You! What about those who are in distant lands and far countries and cannot travel to Him on that day?"

Imam (asws) replied, "On the day of Ashura, in the middle of the day before noon, they should go to a desert or to an elevated part of their house and direct their salam to Hussain (asws) by pointing towards Him, send lanat upon His killers incessantly, and pray two rakats of salat. Then they should mourn and cry over Hussain (asws), inform those in their houses to mourn and cry over Hussain (asws); hold majlis (gatherings) in their houses and recite the masaib (tragedies) of Hussain (asws), becoming restless upon hearing the recitation of the masaib of Hussain (asws); greet one another in their houses while weeping; consoling one another over the tragedy of Hussain (asws).

If they do all of this, I guarantee Allah (swt) will record all of those rewards mentioned in performing His Ziarat on the day of Ashura for them."

I asked, "May I be sacrificed upon You! Will You guarantee and promise these rewards for those who do this?"

Imam (asws) replied, "I guarantee and promise these rewards for those who do this."

I asked, "How should they console one another?"

Imam (asws) replied, "They should say:

عظم الله اجورنا بمصابنا بالحسينّ ، و جعلنا وإباكم من الطالبين بثأره مع وليه الإمام المهدي من آل محمدّ

May Allah increase our rewards for being grief-stricken over the tragedy of Hussain (asws). May He make us and you amongst those who seek to avenge Him with His Heir, Imam al Mahdi (atfs) from Aal e Muhammad (asws).

Imam (asws) added, "If possible, do not attempt to fulfill your needs on this day. For it is an ominous day when needs are not fulfilled. And even if they are fulfilled, one will not be blessed with them nor will he find any success in them.

Do not buy or take anything to your house on this day. For those who do will not find any blessings in that which they take to their houses nor will they be blessed with their families.

Allah will record the reward of one million hajj, one million umrah, and one million battles fought in the way of Allah for those who follow these guidances and all of this will be recorded as if it was done with RasoolAllah (saw).

They will also earn the reward of having been afflicted with tragedies of all of the prophets, messengers, truthful ones, and the martyrs who died or were slain since the day Allah created this world until the rising of the Hour."

Salih ibn Uqbah al Juhani and Saif ibn Amirah narrated that Alqamah ibn Muhammad al Hadrami added,

I said to Abu Jafar Imam Muhammad Baqir (asws), "Teach me a supplication that I can recite on that day if I perform His Ziarat near His grave and a supplication that I can recite if I am not able to perform His Ziarat from near His grave and have to direct my salam to Him by pointing towards Him from afar on the roof of my house."

Imam (asws) said, "O' Alqamah! If you pray two rakats of salat after directing your salam to Him by pointing towards Him and then recite the following supplication while directing your salam to Him, then you will have supplicated to Allah in the way the angels supplicate to Him when they perform the Ziarat of Hussain (asws). Allah will record one million good deeds for you, erase one million bad deeds for you, and add one hundred million ranks to yours.

You will be considered amongst those who were martyred with Hussain (asws) ibn Ali (asws) and will share in their rank. You will not be known for anything except for being amongst the martyrs who were martyred along with Him and the reward of every prophet, every messenger, and every person who has performed the Ziarat of Hussain (asws) ibn Ali (asws) since the day He was martyred will be recorded for you."

Recite the following:

السلام عليك يا أبا عبدالله

Salam be upon You, O' Aba Abdullah.

السلام عليك يا بن رسول الله ﷺ

Salam be upon You O' Son of RasoolAllah (saw)

السلام عليك يا خيرة اله و ابن خيرته

Salam be upon You O' Khairutullah (choice of Allah) and ibn Khairat (son of the choice of Allah)

السلام عليك يا بن أمير المؤمنينّ و ابن سيد الوصيين

Salam be upon You O' Son of Ameerul Momineen (asws) and Son of Syedul Wasieen (Master of Successors)

السلام عليك يا ابن فظمةّ سيدةّ نساء العالمين

Salam be upon You O' Son of Fatima (sa) Syedatul Nisa al Alameen

السلام عليك يا ثار الله و ابن ثاره و الوتر الموتور

Salam be upon You O' Tharullah and the Son of HisThar wal Watir al Mutoor

السلام عليك و على الأرواح التي حلت بفنائك و أناخت برحلك، عليكم مني جميعاً سلام الله أبدا ما بقيت وبقي الليك و النهار

Salam be upon You and the souls who were martyred with You and were buried with You. I pray the salam of Allah be upon You for as long as I live and for as long as there is a night and a day

يا أبا عبد الله، لقد عظمت الرزية وجلت المصيبة بك علينا و على جميع أهل السماوات و الأرض

O' Aba Abdullah (asws)! The tragedy is very painful and is a great atrocity for us and for all the inhabitants of the heavens and the earth.

فلون الله امة أسست أساس الظلم و الجور عليكم أهل البيتّ

May the lanat of Allah be upon the party who laid the foundation of oppression and injustice against You, Ahlul Bayt (asws).

و لعن الله امة دفعتكم عن مقامكم، و أز التكم عن مر اتبكم التي رتبكم الله فيها

May the lanat of Allah be upon the nation who kept You away from Your station and usurped those positions that were granted to You by Allah.

و لعن الله امة قتلتكم، و لعن الله الممهدين لهم بالتمكين من قتالكم

May the lanat of Allah be upon the nation who slaughtered You and may the lanat of Allah be upon those who provided assistance so those who wanted to fight against You were able to.

برئت إلى الله و إليكم منهم و من أشياعهم و أتباعهم

I seek the nearness of Allah and to You by disassociating myself from them, from their followers, and from those who obey them.

يا أبا عبد الله،إني سلم لمن سالمكم و حرب لمن حاربكم إلى يوم القيامة

O' Aba Abdullah (asws)! I make peace with those who are at peace with You and I wage war against those who are at war against You until the day of Judgment.

فلعن الله آل زياد و آلمروان

May the lanat of Allah be upon the family of Ziyad and upon the family of Marwan

و لعن الله بني امية قاطبة

May the lanat of Allah be upon all of Bani Ummayah.

و لعن الله ابن مرجانة

May the lanat of Allah be upon the son of Marjanah

و لعن الله عمر بن سعد

May the lanat of Allah be upon Umar ibn Sa'ad

و لعن الله شمراً

May the lanat of Allah be upon Shimr

و لعن الله امة أسرجت و ألجمت و تهيأت لقتالك

May the lanat of Allah be upon the part that bridled and saddled the sumpters in preparation to fight against You.

يا أبا عبد الله، بأبي أنت و امي، لقد عظم مصابي بك، فأسأل الله الذي أكرم مقامك أن يكرمني بك ويرزقني طلب ثارك مع إمام منصور من آل محمدّ

O' Aba Abdullah (asws)! May I sacrifice my mother and father for You. The suffering I feel from knowing of Your tragedy brings immense pain upon me. Therefore I ask Allah who has blessed Your status to bless me through You by sustaining me so that I may seek Your revenge along with the supported Imam (atfs) from Aal e Muhammad (asws)

اللهم اجعلني وجيهاً عندك بالحسينّ في الدنيا و الآخرة

O' Allah Make me sincere in Your eyes through Hussain (asws) in this life and in the Akhira (hereafter)

يا سيدي يا أبا عبد الله، إني أتقرب إلى الله تعاليو إلى رسوله و إلى أمير المؤمنين و إلى فاطمة و إلى الحسن و إليك، صلى الله عليك و سلم و عليهم، بمو الاتك يا أبا عبد الله،

O' my Moula, O' Aba Abdullah (asws)! I seek nearness to Allah (swt) and to His Messenger (saw), to Ameerul Momineen (asws), Syeda Fatima (sa), Hasan (asws), and to You (asws) by my love for You, o' Aba Abdullah (asws)

وبالبراءة من أعدائك و ممن قاتلك و نصب لك الحرب، و من جميع أعدائكم، و بالبراءة أسس الجور و بنى عليه بنيانه، وأجرى ظلمه و جوره عليكم و على أشياعكم

And by disassociating myself from Your enemies, from those who fought against You and incited war against You, from those who laid the foundation of injustice and built the system of oppression against You and against Your Shia

برئت إلى الله و إليكم منهم، و أتقرب إلى الله ثم إليكم بموالاتكم و موالاة و ليكم، و البر اء ة من أعدائكم و من الناصبين لكم الحرب، و البراءة من أشياعهم و أتباعهم

I seek nearness to Allah through disassociating myself from them and I seek nearness to You by loving You and loving Your followers and by disassociating myself from Your enemies and from those who incite war against You and by disassociating myself from their followers and those who obey them.

إني سلم لمن سالمكم، و حرب لمن حاربكم، وولي لمن و الاكم، و عدو لمن عادكم

I make peace with those who make peace with You. I wage war against those who wage war against You. I make friends of those who are friends of You. I oppose those who oppose You.

فأسال الله الذي أكرمني بمعرفتكم و معرفة أوليائكم، ورزقني البراءة من أعدائكم، أن يجعلني معكم في الدنيا و الآخرة، و أن يثبت لي عندكم قدم صدق في الدنيا و الآخرة، و أسأله أن يبلغني المقام المحمود لكم عند الله، و أن يرزقني طلب ثاركم مع إمام مهدي ناطق لكم

I ask Allah—who glorified me through Your marifat (recognition) and the marifat of those with You; who provided my sustenance through my disassociation of Your enemies—to allow me to be with You in this life and in the hereafter. And to keep my foot steady on the path of truth in this life and in the hereafter. And I ask Allah to allow me to raise me near You and to maintain me through seeking Your revenge alongside Imam Mahdi (atfs).

و أسأل الله بحقكم و بالشأن الذي لكم عنده أن يعطيني بكم أفضل ما أعطى مصاباً بمصيبة

I ask Allah—through You and Your status before Him—to reward me the best reward He has ever given to those who felt sorrow and suffering upon knowing about Your tragedy

أقول: (إنا الله و إنا إليه راجعون)، يالها من مصيبة، ما أظمها و أعظم رزيتها في الإسلام و في جميع أهل السماوات و الأرض

I say, "*To Allah We belong, and to Him is our return*" (Quran 2:156). How great was Your affliction and how great of a hardship it was for Islam and for all of the inhabitants of the heavens and the earth

اللهم اجعلنى في مقامي هذا ممن تناله منك صلوات ورحمة و مغفرة

O' Allah! Make me to be in the place where those who receive Your blessings, Your mercy, and Your forgiveness will be

اللهم اجعل محياي محمد ﷺ و آل محمدّ و مماتي ممات محمد ﷺ و آل محمدّ

O'Allah! Make me to live my life the way Muhammad (saw) and Aal e Muhammad (asws) lived and cause me to leave this world the way Muhammad (saw) and Aal e Muhammad (asws) left this world

اللهم إن هذا يوم تنزلت فيه اللعنة على آل زياد و آل امية و ابن آكلة الأكباد، اللعين بن اللعين على لسان نبيك ﷺ ، فى كل معطن و موقف و قف فيه نبيك ﷺ

O' Allah! this is the day that the wrath descended upon the family of Ziyad (la), the family of Ummayah (la), and the son of the eater of livers (muawiyah son of hind la)—the accursed and son of the accursed—who were both damned by the tongue of the Prophet (saw) in every land and at every place the Prophet (saw) stopped

اللهم العن أبا سفيان و معاوية

O'Allah! Send Your lanat upon Abu Sufian (la), and Muawiyah (la).

و على يزيد بن معاوية، اللعنة أبد الآبدين

Send Your lanat upon Yazid (la), son of muawiyah (la) , for all of eternity

اللهم فضاعف عليهم اللعنة أبداً لقتلهم الحسينّ

O' Allah! Increase the chastisement upon them for slaughtering Hussain (asws)

اللهم إني أتقرب إليك في هذا اليوم في موقفي هذا و أيام حياتي، بالبراءة منهم و اللعنة عليهم و بالموالاة لنبيك محمد و أهل بيت نبيك صلى الله عليه و عليهم أجمعين

O'Allah! I seek nearness to You on this day and at this place and every day of my life by disassociating myself from them, by sending lanat upon them, and by following Your Prophet Muhammad (saw) and the Ahlul Bayt (asws) of Your Prophet (saw)—may the blessings of Allah be upon Them all

Then recite 100 times:

اللهم العن أعل ظلم حق محمد آل محمدّ ، و آخر تابعله على ذلك،

O'Allah! Send lanat upon the first oppressor who usurped the rights of Muhammad (saw) and Aal e Muhammad (asws) and upon every last person who followed him in this regard.

اللهم العن العصابة التي جاهدت الحسينّ و شايعت و بيعت أعداءه على قتله و قتل أنصاره،

O'Allah! Send lanat upon those who fought against Hussain (asws) and those who fought against the supporters of Hussain (asws)

251

اللهم العنهم جميعاً

O'Allah! Send lanat upon them all

Then recite 100 times:

السلام عليك يا أبا عبدالله و على الأرواح التي حلت بفنائك و أناخت برحلك، عليكم مني سلام الله أبداً ما بقيت و بقي الليل و النهار، ي لا جعله الله آخر العهد من زيارتكم

Salam be upon You, O'Aba Abdullah and upon the souls who dismounted beside You and remained with You. I pray the salam of Allah be upon You for as long as I live and for as long as there is a night and a day. May Allah not make this the last time I perform Your Ziarat.

السلام على الحسينّ و على علي بن الحسينّ و على أولاد الحسينّ و على أصحاب الحسينّ صلوات الله عليهم أجمعين

Salam be upon Hussain (asws), upon Ali (asws) ibn Hussain (asws), upon the children of Hussain (asws), and upon the companions of Hussain (asws)—may the blessings of Allah be upon them all

Then recite once:

اللهم خص أنت أول ظالم آل نبيك باللعن، ثم العن أعداء آل محمدّ من الأولين و الآخرعن

O'Allah! I ask that You especially send Your lanat upon the first oppressor who oppressed the Family of Your Prophet (saw) and then send lanat upon the enemies of Aal e Muhammad (asws) from the first to the last.

اللهم العن يزيد و أباه

O'Allah! Send lanat upon yazid (la) and his father (la).

و العن عبيد الله بن زياد، و آل مروان و بني امية قاطبة إلى يوم القيامة

Send lanat upon ubaidallah ibn ziyad (la) and upon the family of marwan (la) and all of the bani ummayyah (la) until the day of judgment

Then perform sujood and say:

اللهم لك الحمد حمد الشاكرين على مصابهم، الحمد الله على عظيم مصابي ورزيتي فيهم،

O'Allah! Praise be to You, the praise of those who are thankful during times of suffering. Praise be to Allah for the greatness of my grief over the sufferings and atrocities faced by Ahlul Bayt (asws)

اللهم ارزقنى شفاعة الحسينّ يوم الورود، ثبت لي قدم صدق عندك مع الحسينّ و أصحاب الحسينّ، الذين بذلوا مهجهم دون الحسينّ، صلوات الله عليم أجمعين

O'Allah! Maintain me with the intercession of Hussain (asws) on the day of judgment and keep my foot steady on the path of truth along with Hussain (asws) and the companions of Hussain (asws)—may the blessings of Allah be upon Them all

Alqamah added:

"Abu Jafar Imam Muhammad Baqir (asws) added, "O' Alqamah! If you can perform this Ziarat every day of your life, then do so. For if you do, then inshaAllah, you will have all of the rewards which I mentioned."

253

Chapter 72

The Reward for performing the Ziarat of Hussain (asws)
on the Fifteenth of Shabaan

HADITH 1

Imam Jafar Sadiq (asws) narrates:

"On the fifteenth of Shabaan, a crier calls out from the highest horizon, "O those who have come to the Ziarat of Hussain (asws)! Return forgiven and your rewards will be given to you by Allah, your Lord, and by Muhammad (saw), your Prophet.""

HADITH 2

Abu Hamzah narrates:

Imam Zainul Abideen (asws) said:

"Those who would like to shake hands with one hundred and twenty-four thousand prophets should perform the Ziarat of the grave of Aba Abdullah Imam Hussain (asws) ibn Ali (asws) on the fifteenth of Shabaan. The souls of the prophets including the five Ulul Azm Messengers, ask permission from Allah to perform His Ziarat on that day and they will be granted permission."

We asked, "Who are the five ulul azm?"

Imam (asws) replied, "Nuh (as), Ibrahim (as), Musa (as), Isa (as), and Muhammad (saw)."

We asked, "What does ulul azm mean?"

Imam (asws) replied, "They are the prophets who were sent to the east and the west of the earth and to all of jinn and mankind."

HADITH 3

See hadith 1

HADITH 4

Imam Jafar Sadiq (asws) narrates:

"The sins of those who perform the Ziarat of Aba Abdullah Imam Hussain (asws) on the fifteenth of Shabaan for three consecutive years without interruption will be forgiven."

HADITH 5

Imam Muhammad Baqir (asws) narrates:

"The sins of those who perform the Ziarat of Aba Abdullah Imam Hussain (asws) on the fifteenth of Shabaan for three consecutive years without interruption will be forgiven."

HADITH 6

Abdul Rahman ibn Hajjaj narrates from another named Hussain who narrates:

Imam Jafar Sadiq (asws) said:

"Allah will forgive all of the past and future sins of those who go to the Ziarat of the grave of Hussain (asws) on one of three nights."

I asked, "May I be sacrificed upon You! What are the three nights?"

Imam (asws) replied, "The night of Fitr (the eve of the last day of Ramazan), the night of Azha (the eve of the ninth day of Zil Hijjah) and the night of the fifteenth of Shabaan."

HADITH 7

Imam Jafar Sadiq (asws) narrates:

"Allah will record one thousand accepted hajj and one thousand accepted umrah and will grant one thousand requests related to this life and to the Akhira (hereafter) for those who perform the Ziarat of Hussain (asws) on the night of the fifteenth of Shabaan, on the night of Fitr, and on the night of Arafah all within the same year."

HADITH 8

Imam Jafar Sadiq (asws) narrates:

"Allah will devote two angels to those who spend the night of the fifteenth of Shabaan in Karbala and do the following:

Recite Sura Qul Huwa Allah one thousand times, seek forgiveness from Allah one thousand times, praise Allah one thousand times, and then pray four rakat of salat by reciting Ayatul Kursi one thousand times in each rakat.

The two angels will protect them from any harm and from the evil of every shaitan and every tyrant. They will record their good deeds and none of their bad deeds. The two angels will continuously seek forgiveness for them as long as they are with them."

HADITH 9

Imam Jafar Sadiq (asws) narrates:

"Allah will forgive all of the past and future sins of those who perform the Ziarat of the grave of Hussain (asws) on the fifteenth of Shabaan."

HADITH 10

Yunus ibn Yaqoob narrates:

Imam Jafar Sadiq (asws) said, "O Yunus! Allah will forgive all of the past and future sins of the momin who perform the Ziarat of Hussain (asws) on the night of the fifteenth of Shabaan and they will be told, "Go towards good deeds."

I said, "All of this will be recorded for those who perform the Ziarat of Hussain (asws) on the fifteenth of Shabaan?"

Imam (asws) replied, "O Yunus! If I were to tell people about that which will be given to those who perform the Ziarat of Hussain (asws) on this night, then they would travel on the backs of camels, with no saddles, in order to reach Him."

HADITH 11

Imam Jafar Sadiq (asws) narrates:

"Allah will forgive the past and future sins of those who perform the Ziarat of the grave of Hussain (asws) on the night of the fifteenth of Shabaan.

Allah will record the reward of one thousand accepted hajj and one thousand accepted umrah for those who perform the Ziarat of Hussain (asws) on the Day of Arafah. Those who perform the Ziarat of Hussain (asws) on the Day of Ashura are like those who have performed the Ziarat of Allah on the top of His Arsh."

Chapter 73

The Reward for performing the Ziarat of Hussain (asws) in the month of Rajab

HADITH 1

Ahmad ibn Muhammad ibn Abi Nasr al Bizanti narrates:

I asked Abul Hasan Imam Reza (asws), "In which month should we perform the Ziarat of Hussain (asws)?"

Imam (asws) replied, "On the fifteenth of Rajab and the fifteenth of Shabaan."

HADITH 2

Imam Jafar Sadiq (asws) narrates:

"Allah will record the reward of one thousand hajj and one thousand umrah and the reward of fighting one thousand times with one of the messengers of Allah for those who perform the Ziarat of Hussain (asws) on the Day of Arafah whilst having His marifat. Allah forgives those who perform His Ziarat on the first day of Rajab."

Chapter 74

The Reward for performing the Ziarat of Hussain (asws) on any day other than an Eid or the Day of Arafah

HADITH 1

Imam Jafar Sadiq (asws) narrates:

"Allah will record twenty accepted hajj and umrah and the reward of fighting in twenty battles with one of the messengers of Allah or with a Just Imam (asws) for any momin who performs the Ziarat of Hussain (asws) whilst having His marifat on any day other than an Eid or the Day of Arafah."

HADITH 2

Abdullah ibn Hilal narrates:

I asked Aba Abdullah Imam Jafar Sadiq (asws), "May I be sacrificed for You! What is the minimum reward for those who perform the Ziarat of Hussain (asws)?"

Imam (asws) replied, "O' Abdullah! The minimum reward for them is Allah will protect them and their possessions until they return to their families and on the Day of Judgment. Allah Himself will be their protector."

HADITH 3

Dawood ibn Abi Yazid narrates:

Imam Jafar Sadiq (asws) said, "Allah will surely forgive those who perform the Ziarat of the grave of Hussain (asws) every week. They will not leave this life with any sorrows and will dwell with Hussain (asws) ibn Ali (asws) in Jannah. O' Dawood! Who does not like to be the neighbor of Hussain (asws) in Jannah?"

I replied, "Only those who have not achieved salvation."

HADITH 4

Dawood ibn Farqad narrates:

I asked Aba Abdullah Imam Jafar Sadiq (asws), "What is the reward for those who perform the Ziarat of Hussain (asws) every month?"

Imam (asws) replied, "They will earn the reward of one hundred thousand martyrs like the martyrs of the battle of Badr."

HADITH 5

Imam Jafar Sadiq (asws) narrates:

"On the night of Qadr, *"wherein every wise affair is made distinct,"* (Quran 44:4), a crier will call out from inside the Arsh, "Allah has forgiven everyone who has performed the Ziarat of the grave of Hussain (asws) on this night."

HADITH 6

Basheer al Dahan narrates:

I said to Aba Abdullah Imam Jafar Sadiq (asws), "Sometimes I miss the chance to perform Hajj so I go and spend the Day of Arafah beside the grave of Hussain (asws) instead."

Imam (asws) said, "Well done, O' Basheer! Allah will record twenty accepted hajj and umrah and the reward of fighting in twenty battles with one of the messengers of Allah or with a Just Imam (asws) for any momin who performs the Ziarat of the grave of Hussain (asws) whilst having His marifat on any day other than an eid and the Day of Arafah."

Chapter 75

The Reward for performing ghusl with the water of the River Furat before performing the Ziarat of Hussain (asws)

HADITH 1

Imam Jafar Sadiq (asws) narrates:

"Those who perform ghusl with the water of the River Furat and then perform the Ziarat of the grave of Hussain (asws) become sinless like the day their mothers gave birth to them, even if they had committed major sins.

It is recommended that one performs ghusl before performing the Ziarat of the grave of Hussain (asws) and not when bidding farewell. Instead one should simply wipe his hands over the face when bidding the farewell."

HADITH 2

Imam Jafar Sadiq (asws) narrates:

"Woe unto you, o' Basheer! When a momin who has the marifat of Hussain (asws) performs the Ziarat of the grave of Hussain (asws) and performs ghusl with the water from the River Furat, an accepted hajj, umrah, and the reward of fighting in the way of Allah along with one of the messengers of Allah or with a Just Imam (asws) is recorded for him with every step that he takes."

HADITH 3

Basheer al Dahhan narrates:

I heard Aba Abdullah Imam Jafar Sadiq (asws) in Hirah speaking to a group of Shia gathered around Him. He turned His Face towards me and asked, "O' Basheer! Did you go for hajj last year?"

I replied, "May I be sacrificed upon You! No. Instead I spent the Day of Arafah beside the grave of Hussain (asws)."

Imam (asws) said, "O' Basheer! I swear by Allah you did not miss any of the blessings that were for those present in Mecca."

I said, "May I be sacrificed upon You! Explain this for me. Is not the blessing of being in Arafat only for those in Mecca?"

Imam (asws) replied, "O' Basheer! Every time one of you raises his foot or places it down while walking toward the grave of Hussain (asws) whilst having His marifat and after having performed ghusl in the water of the River Furat, Allah will give you the reward of one hundred accepted hajj and one hundred accepted umrah and the reward of fighting in one hundred battles with one of the messengers of Allah against His enemies and the enemies of the Messenger."

HADITH 4

Hisham ibn Saleem narrates:

A man came to Aba Abdullah Imam Jafar Sadiq (asws) and asked, "Should one perform the Ziarat of Your Father Imam Hussain (asws)?"

Imam (asws) replied, "Yes."

The man asked, "What is the reward for those who perform ghusl with the water of the River Furat and then go to Him (Hussain asws)?"

Imam (asws) replied, "If they perform ghusl with the water of the River Furat with the intention of visiting Him, then their sins will fall off of them and they will become sinless like the day their mothers gave birth to them."

HADITH 5

Ali ibn Jafar al Humani narrates:

I heard Ali (asws) ibn Muhammad al Askari (Imam Hadi asws) say, "Those who leave their homes in order to perform the Ziarat of Hussain (asws) and then go to the River Furat and perform ghusl with its water will be recorded by Allah as those who have achieved salvation. Once they say salam to Aba Abdullah Imam Hussain (asws) they will be recorded as victorious.

After they finish their prayers, an angel will come to them and say, "RasoolAllah (saw) conveys His salam to you and tells you that your sins have been forgiven and that you should return with good deeds."

HADITH 6

Ibrahim ibn Muhammad al Thaqafi narrates:

Aba Abdullah Imam Jafar Sadiq (asws) use to say the following when He performed the ghusl of Ziarat:

اللهم اجعله لي نوراً وطهوراً وحرزاً، و كافياً من كل داء وسقم، و من كل آفة و عاهة، وطهر به قلبي وجوارحي ولحمي ودمي، وشعري وبشري و مخي و عظامي و عصبى، و ما أقلت الأرض مني، فاجعله لي واهداً يوم القيامة، و يوم حاجتي و فقري و فاقتي

O' Allah! Make this ghusl as light, purification, and protection for me. And make it the prevention from every illness and disease and from every disability and injury. And purify my heart, my organs, my flesh, my blood, my hair, my skin, my brain, my bones, my nerves, and my mass with it. And make it my witness on the Day of Judgment; the day of my need, poverty, and destitution."

HADITH 7

Imam Jafar Sadiq (asws) narrates:

"Those who perform the Ziarat of Hussain (asws) ibn Ali (asws) and perform wudhu and ghusl with the water of the River Furat do not raise their foot or place it down without Allah recording a hajj and umrah for them."

HADITH 8

Imam Jafar Sadiq (asws) narrates:

"When you perform the Ziarat of the grave of Hussain (asws), go to the part of the River Furat closest to His grave and perform ghusl with its water."

HADITH 9

Imam Jafar Sadiq (asws) narrates:

"When a person travels towards the grave of Hussain (asws), while having His marifat, arrives at the River Furat and performs ghusl in it, he will be like one whose sins have fallen off of him as soon as he steps out of the water.

And Allah will record ten good deeds for him and erase ten of his bad deeds with every step that he takes as he walks towards the Ha'yr (burial place of Hussain (asws) and surrounding area)."

Chapter 76

Ghusl (in the River Furat) before performing the
Ziarat of Hussain (asws) is not wajib (obligatory)

HADITH 1

Hasan ibn Zibriqan al Tabari narrates to me through his Isnad from someone who said:

I said to Imam Sadiq (asws), "Sometimes when we perform the Ziarat of Hussain, it is difficult to perform ghusl (in the River Furat) because of the cold or due to other reasons."

Imam (asws) replied, "Many rewards will be recorded for those who go to the River Furat (Euphrates) and perform ghusl in it before performing the Ziarat of Hussain (asws); so many they are uncountable. And if they return anytime in the future to the place where they performed ghusl, and then perform wudhu, then the same rewards will be recorded for them."

Chapter 77

Angels welcome, bid farewell to, and ask forgiveness for the Zuwar (Visitors) of Imam Hussain (asws)

HADITH 1

Haroon ibn Kharijah narrates:

I heard Aba Abdullah Imam Sadiq (asws) say, "Allah has devoted four thousand disheveled angels covered with dust to the grave of Hussain (asws) who mourn over Him and will continue to do so until the Day of Judgment.

These angels accompany those who perform the Ziarat of Hussain (asws) whilst having His marifat until the zuwar (visitors) return back safely. If the zuwar become ill, then the angels will visit them every morning and evening. When the zuwar die, the angels will attend their funerals and seek forgiveness for them until the Day of Judgment.

HADITH 2

Imam Muhammad Baqir (asws) narrates:

"There are four thousand disheveled angels covered with dust who mourn over Hussain (asws) and will do so until the Day of Judgment.

These angels welcome everyone who performs the Ziarat of Hussain (asws), accompanies them as they return back from His Ziarat, visits the zuwar if they become ill, and attends the funerals of the zuwar when they die."

HADITH 3

Abul Saba al Kinanee narrates:

I heard Aba Abdullah Imam Jafar Sadiq (asws) say,

"There is a grave near you (the grave of Imam Hussain asws) which no mournful person goes without Allah removing his sorrows and fulfilling his requests. There are four thousand angels beside this grave who have been there since the day He departed this world. They are disheveled, covered with dust, and they mourn over Him and will do so until the Day of Judgment."

HADITH 4

Imam Jafar Sadiq (asws) narrates:

"When a man leaves his home in order to perform the Ziarat of Hussain (asws), seven hundred angels accompany him. They surround him from above his head, under his feet, to his right, to his left, and from behind him until he arrives safely.

After he performs the Ziarat of Hussain (asws), a crier will call out to the zawir, "You have been forgiven. Go forth and perform only good deeds."

These angels accompany him until he returns back to his home. When they arrive at his house, they will say to the zawir, "We leave you in the protection of Allah."

These angels will visit him repeatedly until he dies. After which, the angels will continue performing the Ziarat of the grave of Hussain (asws) every day, their reward will be recorded for that zawir."

HADITH 5

Muhammad al Halabi narrates:

I heard Aba Abdullah Imam Jafar Sadiq (asws) say,

"Allah has devoted four thousand disheveled, dust covered angels to the grave of Hussain (asws) who will remain there until the rising of the Hour. These angels accompany everyone who performs the Ziarat of Hussain (asws). The angels visit the zuwar if they fall ill, and attend their funerals when the zuwar die."

HADITH 6

Imam Jafar Sadiq (asws) narrates:

"Allah has devoted four thousand disheveled and dust covered angels to the grave of Hussain (asws). They mourn over Hussain (asws) from dawn until midday; when they ascend to the heavens. They are then replaced by another assembly of four thousand angels who mourn over Him until dawn.

These angels testify to the loyalty and sincerity of those who perform the Ziarat of Hussain (asws). The angels accompany the zuwar back to their families, the angels visit the zuwar when the zuwar fall ill, and the angels pray for the zuwar when the zuwar die."

HADITH 7

Imam Musa Kazim (asws) narrates:

"When a person leaves his home in order to perform the Ziarat of Aba Abdullah al Hussain (asws), Allah devotes an angel to him (the zawir) who will place his finger on the back of the zawir and will start writing on his back every word which comes from the mouth of the zawir until the zawir arrives at the Ha'yr.

After the zawir enters through the gate of the Ha'yr, the angel will place his palm on the middle of the back of the zawir and say, "All of your past sins have been forgiven. Go forth in goodness.""

HADITH 8

Haroon ibn Kharijah narrates:

I was with Aba Abdullah Imam Jafar Sadiq (asws) when a man asked Imam (asws), "What is the reward for those who perform the Ziarat of the grave of Hussain (asws)?"

Imam (asws) replied, "When Hussain (asws) was slaughtered, even the lands mourned Him. So Allah devoted four thousand disheveled angels covered with dust to mourn over Him and they will continue to do so until the Day of Judgment.

These angels accompany those who perform the Ziarat of Hussain (asws) with His marifat until the zawir (visitor) arrives safely at his destination. If the zawir becomes ill, the angels visit him every morning and evening. And when the zawir dies, these angels attend his funeral and seek forgiveness for the zawir until the Day of Judgment."

HADITH 9

Imam Jafar Sadiq (asws) narrates:

"Four thousand angels descended on the day of Ashura in order to fight alongside Hussain (asws) but they were not given permission by Imam Hussain (asws) to fight. So they ascended back to the heavens to seek permission from Allah. By the time they returned, Hussain (asws) had already been martyred. The angels remain disheveled and covered in dust beside Hussain (asws)'s grave, mourning over Him. They will continue to do so until the Day of Judgment.

Their leader is an angel named Mansoor. These angels welcome everyone who performs the Ziarat of Hussain (asws) and accompany the zuwar (visitors) as they bid farewell to Hussain (asws). The angels visit the zuwar if they become ill. The angels perform prayers for the zuwar at their funerals when the zuwar dies and the angels seek forgiveness for the zuwar after their death. All of these angels wait upon the earth for the reappearance of al Qaim (atfs)."

HADITH 10

Muhammad ibn Mudarib narrates Malik al Johani narrated:

Abu Jafar Imam Muhammad Baqir (asws) said:

"O' Malik! When Hussain (asws) left this world by the order of Allah, He (Allah) sent four thousand disheveled angels covered in dust to Hussain (asws). These angels mourn over Hussain (asws) and will continue to do so until the Day of Judgment. Allah will forgive all of the past and future sins and one hajj will be written for those who perform the Ziarat of Hussain (asws) whilst having His marifat. The zuwar will be protected until they return to their families."

Muhammad ibn Mudarib added, "After Abu Jafar Imam Muhammad Baqir (asws) left this world and Malik had died, I went to Aba Abdullah Imam Jafar Sadiq (asws) and narrated this hadith to Imam (asws). When I mentioned hajj will be written for those who perform the Ziarat of Hussain (asws), Imam (asws) said, "And an umrah as well, O' Muhammad!""

Chapter 78

The misfortune of those who neglect the Ziarat of Hussain (asws)

HADITH 1

Imam Muhammad Baqir (asws) narrates:

"Those from amongst Our Shia who do not perform the Ziarat of the grave of Hussain (asws) are lacking in iman (faith) and their deen (religion) is incomplete. And even if they enter Jannah, their position will be lower than that of the momin (true believers)."

HADITH 2

Imam Jafar Sadiq (asws) narrates:

"Those from amongst Our Shia who do not perform the Ziarat of the grave of Hussain (asws) are lacking in iman (faith) and their deen (religion) is incomplete. And even if they enter Jannah, their position will be lower than that of the momin (true believers)."

HADITH 3

Imam Jafar Sadiq (asws) narrates:

"Those who think they are amongst Our Shia but do not perform the Ziarat of the grave of Hussain (asws) before their death, are not from amongst Our Shia. And even if they are amongst those who enter Jannah, they will be regarded as mere visitors of Jannah."

HADITH 4

Abu Bakr al Hadrami narrates:

I heard Abu Jafar Imam Muhammad Baqir (asws) say,

"Those who want to know if they will be amongst the inhabitants of Jannah should introduce the love for Us to their hearts. If their hearts accept the love for Us, then they are momin. For those who love Us desire to perform the Ziarat of the grave of Hussain (asws).

Those who repeatedly perform the Ziarat of Hussain (asws) We recognize as lovers of Us, Ahlul Bayt (asws), and they will be counted amongst the inhabitants of Jannah whereas the iman (faith) of those who did not perform the Ziarat of Hussain (asws) is incomplete."

HADITH 5

Haroon ibn Kharijah narrates:

I asked Aba Abdullah Imam Jafar Sadiq (asws) about those who do not perform the Ziarat of the grave of Hussain (asws) ibn Ali (asws) without a just reason.

Imam (asws) replied, "Such a person will be amongst the inhabitants of Jahannum (hellfire)."

HADITH 6

Ali ibn Mamoon narrates:

I heard Aba Abdullah Imam Jafar Sadiq (asws) say:

"If any of you performs Hajj one thousand times but does not perform the Ziarat of the grave of Hussain (asws) ibn Ali (asws), then you have abandoned one of the rights Allah (swt) that are wajib upon you."

A person asked Imam (asws) the reason for this and Imam (asws) replied, "Fulfilling the rights of Hussain (asws) is wajib upon every muslim."

HADITH 7

Hisham ibn Salim narrates:

A man came to Aba Abdullah Imam Jafar Sadiq (asws) and asked, "Should a person perform the Ziarat of Your Father (Imam Hussain asws)?"

Imam (asws) replied, "Yes."

The man asked, "What is the reward for those who perform His Ziarat?"

Imam (asws) replied, "Jannah, if they are believers in His Imamate."

The man asked, "What about those who intentionally do not perform His Ziarat?"

Imam (asws) replied, "They will regret not doing so on the Day of Regret (Day of Judgment)."

Chapter 79

Ziarat to be recited at the Grave of Imam Hussain (asws)

HADITH 1

Imam Jafar Sadiq (asws) narrates:

Recite the following when you enter the Ha'yr:

اللهم إن هذا مقام كرمتني به و شرفتي به

O' Allah! You have honored and distinguished me by allowing me to be at this shrine.

اللهم فأعطني فيه رغبتي على حقيقة إيماني بک وبرسلك

O'Allah! Grant my requests due to my true faith in You and in Your Messengers

سلام الله عليك يا بن رسول الله ﷺ

Salam of Allah be upon You, O Son (asws) of RasoolAllah (saw).

و سلام ملائكته فيما تروح و تغتدي به الرائحات الطاهيرات الطيبات لك و عليك

And the salam and the pure and blessed greetings of the angels be upon You

273

و سلام على ملائكته الله المقربين

And salam be upon those angels nearest to Allah

و سلام على المسلمين لك بقلوبهم، الناطقين لك بفضلك بألسنتهم

And salam be upon those whose hearts are submissive before You and whose tongues recite Your attributes

أشهد أنك صادق صديق، صدقت فيما دعوت إليه، و دقت فيما أتيت به

I testify You are Sadiq al Sadeeq (the trustworthy of the trustworthy). You spoke the truth regarding that which You invited the people towards and in all that which You brought forth.

و أنك ثر الله في الأرض، من الدم الذي لا يدرك ثاره من الأرض إلا بأوليائك

For Allah is the avenger of Your blood on the earth, a blood which cannot be avenged on earth except through the hands of Your Auwliya.

اللهم حبب إلي مشاهدهم و شهادتهم حتى تلحقني بهم و تجعلني لهم فرطاً و تابعا! في الدنيا و الآخرة

O'Allah! Cause me to love visiting Their sites and to be martyred as They were martyred until you allow me to join Them and to be in Their service. Make amongst Their followers in this life and in the hereafter

Then walk a short distance, say Allahu Akbar seven times. Stand beside the grave and recite:

سبحان الذي سبح له الملك و الملكوت، و قدست بأسمئه جميع خلقه، و سبحان الله الملك القدوس، رب الملائكة و الروح

Glorified is He whom the physical world as well as the spiritual world glorifies and whose names are glorified by all of His creation. Glorified is Allah, al Malik, al Qadoos, Lord of the angels and of the ruh (spirits)

اللهم اكتبني في و فدك إلى خير بقاعك و خير خلقك

O'Allah! Record me as amongst Your visitors, who came to the best of Your places and to the best of Your creation

274

اللهم العن الجنت و الطاغوت، و العن أشياعهم و أتباعهم

O'Allah! Send Your lanat upon Jibt and Taghut and upon those who follow them and those who obey them

اللهم أشهدني مشاهد الخير كلها مع أهل بيتّ نبيك ﷺ

O'Allah! Allow me to behold all of the blessed stations in the company of the Ahlul Bayt (asws) of Your Prophet (saw)

اللهم توفني مسلماً، و اجعل لي قدم صدق مع الباقين الوارزين، الذين يرثون الفردوس هم فيها خالدون، من عبادك الصالحين

O'Allah! Make me die as a muslim and allow me to have a sure footing with the remaining inheritors from amongst Your righteous servants *"Who shall inherit the Paradise; they shall abide therein."* (Quran 23:11)

Then say Allahu Akbar five times, walk a short distance and recite:

اللهم إني بك مومن وبوعدك موقن

O' Allah! I believe in You and I am certain of Your promise.

اللهم اكتب لي إيماناً و ثبته في قلبي

O' Allah! Maintain me with iman (faith) and make it constant within my heart

اللهم اجعل ما أقول بلساني حقيقته في قلبي و شريعته في عملي

O' Allah! Make what I say with my tongue be a truth which I carry in my heart and a charter which I abide by through my actions

اللهم اجعلني له مع الحسينّ قدم ثبات، و أثبتني قيمن استشهد معه

O' Allah! Make me amongst those whose path is firm with Hussain (asws) and count me as amongst those who were martyred alongside Him

Then say Allahu Akbar three times, raise both of your hands and place them on the grave. And then recite:

أشهد أنك طهر طاهر من طهر طاهر

I testify that You are Tuhir (purity)and Tahir (purifier); the Son of Tuhir and Tahir

طهرت و طهرت بك البلاد، و طهرت أرض أنت بها، و طهر حرمك

You are purity and the lands become purified through You. The dust that You lie within is tahir and Your Haram is also tahir

أشهد أنك أمرت بالقسط و العدل، و دعوت إليهما

I testify You advised and invited the people towards justice and fairness

و أنك ثار الله في أرضه، حتى يستثير لك من جميع خلقه

Allah will avenge Your blood on the earth and His revenge will be taken from all of His creation

Then place both of your cheeks upon the grave. After sit down and glorify Allah. Supplicate to Him however you wish. Afterwards, place your hands beside His feet and recite:

صلوات الله على روحك و على بدنك، صدقت و أنت الصادق المصدق

May the blessings of Allah be upon Your soul and upon Your body. You always spoke truth for You are al Sadiq (trustworthy), al MuSadiq (the trustworthy one)

و قتل الله من قتلك بالأيدي و الألسن

May Allah kill anyone who participated in martyring You whether they participated by their hands or their tongues.

Then turn towards Ali (asws) ibn Hussain (asws); recite whatever you wish. After stand, turn towards the grave of the martyrs and recite:

السلام عليكم أيها الشهدآء

Salam be upon you, o' martyrs

أنتم لنا فرط و نحن لكم تبع، أبشروا بموعد الله الذي لا خلف له، الله مدرك لكم وتركم و مدرك بكم في الأرض عدوه، أنتم سادة الشهدآء في الدنيا و الآخرة

You are our leaders and we soon shall follow you. Be joyful regarding that unbroken promise of Allah. Allah will avenge your blood and will seek revenge from His enemies on the earth through you. You are the masters of the martyrs in this life and in the hereafter.

Then face the grave of Hussain (asws) and perform as many rakats of prayers as you wish. Then recite:

جئت و افداً إليك، و أتوسل إلى الله بك في جميع حوائجي من أمر دنياي و آختي، بك يتوسل المتوسلون إلى الله في حوائجهم، و بك يدرك عند الله أهل الترات طلبتهم

I have come to You as Your guest. I beseech Allah through You for all of my requests in this life and in the hereafter. Those who beseech Allah do so through You. Those who seek revenge will be avenged by Allah through You.

Then slowly and with calm recite Allahu Akbar eleven consecutive times. After walk a short distance, turn towards the Qiblah and recite:

الحمد لله الواحد المتوحد في الأمور كلها، خلق الخلق فلم يغب شيء من أمورهم عن علمه، فعلمه بقدرته

Praise be to Allah, al Wahid, who solely controls all of the affairs. He created the creation and none of their affairs is beyond His knowledge; for He knows everything through His power

ضمنت الأرض و من عليها دمن وثارك يا بن رسول الله، صلى الله عليك

The earth and those within it have guaranteed that Your blood will be avenged, O' Son of RasoolAllah (saw)! May the blessings of Allah be upon You

أشهد أن لك من الله ما و عدك من النصر و الفتح، و أن لك من الله الوعد الصادق في هلاك أعدائك، و تمام موعد الله إباك

I testify that Allah has promised to support You and to make You victorious. He (Allah) has promised to destroy Your enemies and Allah will fulfill His promise with You

أشهد أن من تبعك الصادقون، الذين قال الله تبارك و تعالى فيهم: (أولئك هم الصديقون و الشهدآء عند ربهم، لهم أجر هم ونير هم)

I testify that those who followed You are the Sadiqoon (truthful) whom Allah speaks about when He says, *"they are the truthful ones , and the witnesses (who testify), in the eyes of their Lord: They shall have their Reward and their Noor."* (Quran 57:19)

Then recite Allahu Akbar seven times, walk a short distance, then turn towards the grave again and recite:

الحمد الله الذي لم يتحذ و لداً و لم يكن له شريك في الملك، و خلق كل شيء فقديراً

Praise be to Allah who *"did not take to Himself a son, and Who has no associate in the kingdom, and Who created everything, then ordained for it a measure"* (Quran 25:2)

أشهد أنك دعوت إلى الله و إلى رسوله ﷺ ، و وفيت لله بعهده، وقمت لله بكلماته، و جاهدت في سبيل الله حتى أتاك اليقين

I testify You invited the people towards Allah and towards His Messenger (saw). And You fulfilled the promise of Allah. You rose with the words of Allah and fought in the way of Allah until that which was certain came to You

لعن الله امة قتلتك

May the lanat of Allah be upon the nation who slaughtered You

و لعن الله امة ظلمتك

May the lanat of Allah be upon the nation who oppressed You

و لعن الله امة خذلتك

May the lanat of Allah be upon the nation that abandoned You

و لعن الله امة خدعتك

And may the lanat of Allah be upon the nation that betrayed You

اللهم إني أشهدك بالولاية لمن و اليت ووالته رسلك، و أشهد بالبراءة ممن برئت منه وبرئت منه رسلك

O'Allah I take You as my witness that I love those whom You love and those whom Your messengers love. And I testify that I disassociate myself from those whom You and Your messengers have disassociated from

اللهم العن الذين كذبوا رسلك، وهدموا كعبتك، و حرفوا كتابك، و سفكوا دمآء أهل بيتّ نبعك، و أفسدوا في بلادك، و استذلوا عبادك

O' Allah! Send lanat upon those who opposed Your messengers, destroyed Your Kaaba, distorted Your Book, spilled the blood of the Ahlul Bayt (asws) of Your Prophet (saw), caused evil in Your land, and mocked Your servants

اللهم ضاعف عليهم العذاب فيما جرى من سبلك وبرك وبحرك

O'Allah! Continue to increase Your chastisement upon them for as long as there are travelers upon Your paths, Your lands, and Your seas

اللهم العنهم في مستسر السرائر و ظاهر العلانية في أرضك و سمائك

O'Allah! Send lanat upon them from everywhere and in every way

Imam (asws) added, "And every time you enter the Ha'yr say salam and place your hands upon the grave."

HADITH 2

Hussain ibn Thuwair ibn Abu Fakhitah narrates:

Yunus ibn Zabyan, Muffudal ibn Umar, Abu Salamah al Sarraj and I were sitting with Aba Abdullah Imam Jafar Sadiq (asws). Yunus, the eldest amongst us, spoke to Imam (asws) on our behalf. Yunus asked, "May I be sacrificed upon You! What should I say when I attend the gatherings of these people (Bani Abbas)?"

Imam (asws) replied, "When you attend their gatherings, glorify Us, and then say, "O' Allah! Grant us ease and pleasure". If you do this, then you will receive that which you wish for."

I (Hussain ibn Thuwair) asked, "May I be sacrificed upon You! I am always thinking of Hussain (asws). What should I say when I remember Him?"

279

Imam (asws) replied, "You should repeat three time, "Salam be upon You, O' Aba Abdullah (asws)!" For the salam reaches Hussain (asws) from afar and near.

When Aba Abdullah Imam Hussain (asws) departed this world, the seven heavens, the seven earths, all that is within them, all that is between them, everyone who moves within Jannah and Jahannum from amongst the creation of Our Lord, and all that which can be seen and that which cannot wept over Aba Abdullah Imam Hussain (asws) except for three things."

I asked, "May I be sacrificed upon You! What are those three things?"

Imam (asws) replied, "Basra, Damascus, and the family of Uthman."

I asked, "May I be sacrificed upon You! I wish to perform the Ziarat of Hussain (asws). How should I do this and what should I recite?"

Imam (asws) said, "When you perform the Ziarat of Aba Abdullah Imam Hussain (asws), perform ghusl on the banks of the River Furat (Euphrates) and wear your most purified (pak) clothes. Walk barefoot towards the grave for you are in one of the Harams of Allah and His Messenger (saw). You should continuously recite Takbir (Allahu Akbar) and Tahleel (la illah illa Allah). Continuously glorify Allah. Send blessings upon Muhammad (saw) and His Ahlul Bayt (asws) until you reach the door of the Ha'yr. Then you should recite:

السلام عليك يا حجة الله و ابن حجته

Salam be upon You, O' Hujjatullah (proof of Allah) and Son of Hujjatullah

السلام عليكم يا ملائكة الله وزوار قبر ابن نبي الله ﷺ

Salam be upon You, O' angels of Allah who are the visitors of the grave of the Son of the Prophet (saw) of Allah

Then take ten steps, stop and say Allahu Akbar thirty times. Then walk towards the grave from the direction of the head. Stand beside the grave with your face towards the face of Hussain (asws) and your back towards Qiblah and recite:

السلام عليك يا حجة الله و ابن حجته

Salam be upon You, O' Hujjatullah and Son of Hujjatullah

السلام عليك يا قتيل الله و ابن قتيله

Salam be upon You, O' Martyr of Allah and the Son of the Martyr of Allah

السلام عليك يا ثار الله و ابن ثاره

Salam be upon You, O' Tharullah and the Son of Tharullah

السلام عليك يا وتر الله الموتور في السماوات و الأرض

Salam be upon You O' the unavenged One of Allah in the heavens and the earth whose vengeance Allah has not yet taken

أشهد أن دمك سكن في الخلد، و اقشعرت له أظاة العرش، و بكى له جميع الخلائق

I testify that Your blood dwells in the eternal Jannah. Those who carry the Arsh tremble due to it and all of the creation mourns over it.

و بكت له السماوات السبع و الأرضون السبع و ما فيهن و ما بينهن، و من وتقلب في الجنة و النار من خلق ربنا، و ما يرى و ما لايرى

And the seven heavens, the seven earths, that which is on them and that which is between them, and all of the creation of our Lord which stirs within Jannah and Jahannum, that which can be seen and that which cannot cries over Your blood

أشهد أنك حجة الله و ابن حجته

I testify You are Hujjatullah and the Son of His Hujjat (proof).

و أشهد أنك قتيل الله و ابن قتيله

I testify You are the one who was slain in the way of Allah and the Son of the one who was slain in the way of Allah

و أشهد أنك ثار الله في الأرض و ابن ثاره

I testify You are Tharullah on the earth and the Son of Tharullah

و أشهد أنك وتر الله الموتور في السماوات و الأرض

I testify You are the unavenged of Allah in the heavens and the earth; the one whose vengeance has not yet been taken by Allah

و أشهد أنك قد بلغت ونصحت، ووفيت، وجاهدت في سبيل ربك، و مضيت على بصيرة للذي كنت عليه
شهيداً و مستشهداً و شهوداً

I testify You advised the people and proclaimed the message of Allah. You were devoted and faithful to Allah and fought in the way of Your Lord. I testify You left this world the same way as You lived in this world; as a martyr who desired martyrdom and as a witness over the creation of Allah and one who is witnessed to

أنا عبد الله ومولاك و في طاعتك، و الوافد إيك، ألتمس كمال المنزلة عند الله، وثبات القدم في الهجرة إليك،
و السبيل الذي لا يختلج دونك من الدخول في كفالتك التي امرت بها

I am the slave of Allah and Your servant. I have come to You as a guest to beg for You to protection my position before Allah and to keep my foot firmly following Your path and to beg to be on the path which will not prevent those who follow it from receiving a guarantee from You; the guarantee which Allah has ordered for those who follow You

من أراد الله بدء بكم، من أراد الله بدء بكم، من أراد الله بدء بكم

Those who seek Allah begin with You, those who seek Allah begin with You, those who week Allah begin with You

بكم يبين الله الكذب، و بكم يباعد الله الزمان الكلب، و بكم فتح الله و بكم يختم الله، و بكم يمحو الله ما
يشاء وبكم يثبت

Allah manifests the truth through You and He keeps afflictions away from us through You. Allah began with You and He shall end with You. Allah abolishes and upholds that which He pleases through You

و بكم يفك الذل من رقابنا، و بكم يدرك الله ترة كل ترة كل مؤمن يطلب، و بكم تنبت الأرض أشجارها، و
بكم تخرج الأشجار أثمارها، و بكم تنزل السماء قطرها ورزقها، و بكم يكشف الله الكرب، و بكم ينزل الله
الغيث، و بكم تسبح الله الأرض التي تحمل أبد انكم، و تستقر جبالها على مراسيها

Allah removes our shame through You and He shall avenge the unavenged blood of the momin through You. The trees in the earth grow and bear fruit through You. The skies rain and send down sustenance through You. Allah removes the sorrows through You and showers us with His mercy through You. The earth, which encompasses Your bodies, glorifies Allah through You. And it is through You the mountains are firmly fixed in the land.

إرادة الرب في مقادير اموره تهبط إليكم، و تصدر من بيوتكم، و الصادق عما فصل من أحكام العباد

The will of Allah regarding His destined affairs descends to You and issued to the creation from Your Houses just as the rulings of Allah over His slaves are issued from Your houses.

لعنت امة قتلتكم، و امة خالفتكم، و امة جحدت و لايتكم، و امة ظاهرت عليكم، و امة شهدت و لم تستشهد، الحمد الله الذي جعل النار مأواهم، وبئس ورد الواردين و بئس الورد الميرود،

Lanat be upon those who martyred You, those who opposed You, those who denied Your Divine Authority, those who supported one another against You, and those who were present when You were martyred but were not martyred with You. Praise be to Allah who made Hell their final destination. What a terrible abode hell is and what an evil dwelling their dwellings shall be.

الحمد لله رب العالمين

Praise be to Allah, the Lord of the Worlds

Then repeat the following:

صلى الله عليك يا ابا عبد اللّه، أنا إلى الله ممن خالفك بريء

May the blessings of Allah be upon You, o' Aba Abdullah. I seek nearness to Allah by disassociating myself from those who oppressed You

Then move towards His Son, Ali (asws), who is located beside the feet of Hussain (asws) and recite:

السلام عليك يا بن رسول الله ﷺ

Salam be upon You, O' Son of RasoolAllah (saw)

السلام عليك يا بن أمير المؤمنينّ

Salam be upon You O' Son of Ameerul Momineen (asws)

السلام عليك يا بن الحسانّ و الحسينّ

Salam be upon You O' Son of Hasan (asws) and Hussain (asws)

السلام عليك يا بن خديجة الكبرى و فاطمة الزهراء

Salam be upon You O' Son of Khadijah (sa) al Kubra and O' Son of Syeda Fatima Zahra (sa)

The recite the following three times:

صلى الله عليك، لعن الله من قتلك، أنا إلى الله منهم بريء

May the blessings of Allah be upon You, May the lanat of Allah be upon those who slaughtered You. I seek the nearness of Allah by disassociating myself from them

Then stand, point your hand towards the martyrs and recite the following three times:

السلام عليكم، فزتم و الله

Salam be upon You, I swear by Allah that You are victorious

Then recite:

فليت أني معكم فأفوز فوزاً عظيماً

I wish I was amongst you so that I could have achieved your great victory

Then go around the grave and stand behind the grave of Aba Abdullah Imam Hussain (asws). Pray six rakats of prayer while facing the grave. Once you have done all of this, your Ziarat will be complete. At that point, you can choose to remain or go; whichever you wish."

HADITH 3

Imam Jafar Sadiq (asws) narrates:

When you perform the Ziarat of the grave of Hussain (asws), first go to the River Furat and perform ghusl in the part which is opposite of the grave. Then walk towards Hussain (asws) with calm and reverence until you reach the Ha'yr. Enter from the door on the east side. Upon entering recite:

284

السلام على ملائكة الله المقربين، السلام على ملائكة الله المنزلين، السلام على ملائكة الله المردفين، السلام على ملائكة الله المسومين، السلام على ملائكة الله الذين هم في هذا الحائر بإذن الله مقيمون

Salam be upon the high-ranking angels of Allah. Salam be upon the descending angels of Allah. Salam be upon *"the angels, rank on rank"* (Quran 8:9). Salam be upon *"the havoc-making angels"* (Quran 3:125). Salam be upon the angels of Allah that reside inside this Ha'yr by the permission of Allah.

When you face the grave of Hussain (asws), recite:

السلام على رسول الله، صلى الله على محمد أمين الله على رسله و عزائم أمره، الخاتم لما سبق، و الفاتح لما استقبل، و المهيمن على ذلك كله، و السلام عليه و رحمة الله و بركاته

Salam be upon RasoolAllah (saw). May the blessings of Allah be upon Muhammad (saw), the trustee of Allah over His Messengers and the trustee over the amr (commands) of Allah, and the Seal of all of the Prophets Salam be upon Him and may the mercy and blessings of Allah be upon Him

Then recite:

السلام على أمير المؤمنين، عبدك و أخي رسولك الذي انتجبته بعلمك، و جعلته هادياً لمن شئت من خلقك، و الدليل على من بعثته برسالاتك، و ديان الدين بعدلك، فصل قضائك بين خلقك، و المهيمن على ذلك كله، و السلام عليه و رحمة الله و بركاته

Salam be upon Ameerul Momineen (asws), Your servant and the brother of Your Messenger (saw), the One whom You chose by Your knowledge and appointed as a guide for those amongst Your creation, the guide to whom You sent Your revelations, the undisputed ruler of the religion who rules with Your adl (justice), the One who judges between Your creation, Salam be upon Him and may the mercy and blessings of Allah be upon Him

اللهم صل على الحسن بن عليّ، عبدك و ابن رسولك الذي انتجبته بعلمك، و جعلته هادياً لمن شئت من خلقك، و الدليل على من بعثته برسالاتك، و ديان الدين بعدلك، و فصل قضائك بين خلقك، و المهيمن على ذلك كله، و السلام عليه و رحمة و بركاته

O'Allah! Send Your blessings upon Hasan (asws) ibn Ali (asws), Your servant and the Son of Your Messenger (saw), the One whom You chose by Your knowledge and appointed as a guide for those amongst Your creation, the guide to whom You sent Your revelations, the undisputed ruler of the religion who rules with Your adl (justice), the One who judges between Your creation, Salam be upon Him and may the mercy and blessings of Allah be upon Him

Then send salam upon Hussain (asws) and to the rest of the Imams (asws) in the same way as you sent salam and blessings upon Hasan (asws) ibn Ali (asws).

After you recite the salams, go beside the grave of Hussain (asws) and recite:

السلام عليك يا أبا عبد اللّة

Salam be upon You, O' Aba Abdullah!

السلام عليك يا بن رسول الله ﷺ

Salam be upon You, O' Son of RasoolAllah (saw)

صلى الله عليك يا أبا عبد الله، رحمك الله يا أبا عبد اللّة

May the blessings of Allah be upon You O' Aba Abdullah. May the blessings of Allah be upon You, O' Aba Abdullah!

أشهد أنك قد بلغت عن الله ما أمرك به، و لم تخش أحداً غيره، و جاهدت في سبيله، و عبدته صادقاً مخلصاً حتى أتاك اليقين

I testify that You made known all that which Allah ordered, and that You feared no one other than Allah. And You fought in His way and worshipped Him truthfully and sincerely until that which is certain came upon You (when You departed from this world).

أشهد أنكم كلمة التقوى، و باب الهدى، و العروة الوثقى، و الحجة على من يبقى و من تحت الثرى

I testify You, Imams (asws), are kalamatul taqwa *(words of piety* Quran 48:26), Babul Hadi (Door of Guidance), the firmest handle (Quran 2:256), and the Hujjat (proof) upon those who remain (alive) and those who are already beneath the ground (deceased)

أشهد أن ذلك لكم سابق فيما مضى، و ذلك لكم فاتح فيما بقي

I testify You have always held this status and it will always remain evident within You

أشهد أن أرواحكم و طينتكم طينة طيبة، طابت و طهرت هي بعضها من بعض مناً من الله و من رحمته

I testify Your souls and Your clay are blessed and pure by the mercy and favor of Allah

فاشهد الله و اشهدكم أني بكم مؤمن و بإيابكم موقن، و لكم تابع في ذات نفسي وشرائع ديني و خاتمة عملي و منقلبي و مثواي، فأسأل الله البر الرحيم أن يتمم لي ذلك

I take Allah and You as witnesses that I believe in You and I am certain of Your return. I follow You in my life and in the edicts of my religion. I follow You regarding the destiny of my deeds, my return to Allah, and my abode. And I ask Allah (swt) to fulfill this for me.

و أشهد أنكم قد بلغتم عن الله ما أمركم به، حتى لم تخشوا أحداً غيره، و جاهدتم في سبيله و عبدتموه حتى أتاكم اليقين

I testify that You made known all that which Allah ordered, and that You feared no one other than Allah. I testify You fought in His way and worshipped Him until that which is certain came upon You.

فلعن الله من قتلكم

May the lanat of Allah be upon those who slaughtered You

و لعن الله من أمر به

May the lanat of Allah be upon those who ordered those who slaughtered You

و لعن الله من بلغه ذلك فرضي به

May the lanat of Allah be upon those who heard about Your martyrdom and were pleased by it

أشهد أن الذين انتهكوا حرمتك و سفكوا دمك ملعونون على لسان النبي الامي

I testify those who violated Your holiness and spilled Your blood are accursed by the tongue of the Prophet of Mecca (saw)

Then recite:

اللهم العن الذين بدلوا نعمتك، و خلافوا ملتك، ورغبوا عن أمرك، و اتهموا رسولك، وصدوا عن سبيلك

O' Allah! Send Your lanat on those who denied Your blessings, went against Your nation, renounced Your orders, accused Your Messenger (saw) and deviated the people away from Your path

اللهم احش قبورهم ناراً، و أجو افهم ناراً، و احشرهم و أتباعهم إلى جهنم زرقاً

O' Allah! Fill their graves and their stomachs with fire and resurrect them and their followers, blind, in Hell

اللهم العنهم لعناً يلعنهم به كل ملك مقرب، و كل نبي مرسل، وكل عبد مؤمن امتحنت قله للإيمان

O' Allah! Send Your lanat upon them in such a way that every high-ranking angel, every prophet who was sent as a messenger, and every momin whose heart has been tested with faith will also send lanat upon them

اللهم العنهم في مستسر السر وظاهر العلانية

O' Allah! Send Your lanat upon them at every time, both openly and secretly

اللهم العن جوابيت هذه الامة و طواغيتها، و العن فرانتها

O' Allah! Send lanat upon all of the Jibt (idols), Taghut, and the pharaohs of this nation

و العن قتلة أمير المؤمنينّ

And send lanat upon the killers of Ameerul Momineen (asws)

و العن قتلة الحسنّ و الحسينّ ، و عذبهم عذاباً أليماً لا تعذب به أحداً من العالمين

And send lanat upon the killers of Hasan (asws) and Hussain (asws) and chastise them with a chastisement that is so immense You will never nor have never punished anyone from amongst the inhabitants of the worlds with a chastisement like it

اللهم اجعلنا ممن تنصره وتنتصر به، و تمن عليه بنصرك لدينك في الدنيا و الآخرة

O'Allah! Make us amongst those who receive Your support, those who support You, and those whom have gained Your favor by Your using them to support Your religion in this life and in the hereafter

Then sit beside His head (asws) and recite:

صلى الله عليك

May the blessings of Allah be upon You

أشهد أنك عبد الله و أمعنه، بلغت ناصحاً، و أديت أميناً و قتلت صديقاً، ومضيت على يقين

I testify that You are the servant of Allah and His trustee. You proclaimed the message of Allah with fidelity, fulfilled Your duties with devotion. You were the one with truth at the time of Your martyrdom and You left this world with absolute yaqeen (certainty)

لم تؤثر عمى على هدى، و لم تمل من حق إلى باطل

And that You did not give preference to ignorance over guidance and You never separated from haq to go towards falsehood

أشهد أنك قد أقمت الصلاة، و آتيت الزكاة، و أمرت بالمعروف، و نهيت عن المنكر، و اتبعت الرسول ﷺ ، و تلوت الكتاب حق تلاوته، و دعوت إلى سبيل ربك بالحكمة و المعوظة الحسنة،

I testify You performed salat, gave zakat, enjoined good, forbade evil, followed RasoolAllah (saw), recited the Book (of Allah) the way it was meant to be recited, and with wisdom and good counsel You called the people to the path of Your Lord

صلى الله عليك و سلم تسليماً كثيراً

May the everlasting, ever increasing blessings and salam of Allah be upon You

أشهد أنك كنت على بينة من ربك، قد بلغت ما امرت به، وقمت بحقه، وصدقت من قبلك، غير ق اهن و لا
موهن، صلى الله عليك و سلم تسليماً

I testify You had the understanding of Your Lord. You proclaimed that which You were
ordered to and fulfilled Your duty towards Allah. You believed in the truth of those who
came before You without hesitation. May the blessings and salam of Allah be upon You

فجزاك الله من صديق خيراً عن رعيتك

May Allah reward You with abundance on behalf of Your nation

أشهد أن الجهاد معك جهاد، و أن الحق معك و إليك، و أنت أهله و معدنه، و ميراث النبوة عندك و عند أهل
بيتكّ

I testify that Jihad is only jihad when it is with You, that You are haq and that haq leads to
You, that You are the people of haq and the source of haq (truth), and that the inheritance
of the Nabuwiat (prophet hood) is for You and for the Family of the Prophet (saw)

أشهد أنك صديق عند الله، و حجته على خلقه

I testify You are the most trustworthy before Allah and You are His Hujjat (proof) upon
His (Allah) creation

أشهد أن دعوتك حق، و كل داع منصوب غيرك فهو باطل مدحوض، و أشهد أن الله هو الحق المبين

I testify that Your cause is haq and that the cause of any other—appointed by the people—
is false and invalid and I testify Allah is haq al mabeen

Then move towards His feet, recite duas and pray for yourself. Afterwards, move towards
the head of Ali (asws) ibn Hussain (asws) and recite:

سلام الله و سلام ملائكته المقربين و أنبيائه المرسلين عليك يا مولاي و ابن مولاي ورحمة الله و بركاته

May the salam of Allah, His high-ranking angels and His prophets who were sent as
messengers be upon You, O' my Moula and Son of my Moula (asws), May the blessings
and mercy of Allah be upon You

صلى الله عليك و على أهل بيتك و عترة آبائك الأخعار الأبرار، الذين أذهب الله عنهم الرجس و طهر هم تطهيراً

May the blessings and mercy of Allah be upon You, Your Family and the Offspring of Your Righteous and Pious Forefathers (asws); those whom all impurities were kept away from Them by Allah

Then go to the graves of the martyrs and say salam to them by reciting:

السلام عليكم أيها الربانيون، أنتم لنا فرط وسلف، و نحن لكم أتباع و أنصار، أشهد أنكم أنصار الله كما قال الله تبارك و تعالي في كتابه: (و كأين من نبي قاتل معه ربيون كثير فما و هنوا لما أصابهم فو سبيل الله و ما ضعفوا و ما استكانوا)

Salam be upon you, o' godly men. You have preceded us. You are our leaders and we are your followers and supporters. I testify you supported Allah for Allah says in His book, *"How many of the prophets fought (in Allah's way), and with them (fought) Large bands of godly men? but they never lost heart if they met with disaster in Allah's way, nor did they weaken (in will) nor give in. And Allah Loves those who are firm and steadfast."* (Quran 3:146)

فما و هنتم و ما ضعفتم و ما استكنتم، حتى لقيتم الله على سبيل الحق و نصرة كلمة الله التامة

You never lost heart, were not weak, and did not back down before your enemies until you met Allah on the path of haq as the supporters of Kalamatullah (complete word of Allah, Imam Hussain asws)

صلى الله على أرواحكم و أبدانكم و سلم تسليماً، أبشروا بموعد الله الذي لا خلف له، لا يلخلف الميعاد، الله مدك لكم ثار ما و عدكم

May the blessings and salam of Allah be upon your souls and your bodies. Rejoice in the promise of Allah, which does not disappoint. *"for Allah never fails in His promise"* (Quran 3:9) and Allah will avenge you just as He promised.

أنتم سادة الشهداء في الدنيا و الآخرة، أنتم السابقون و المهاجرون و الأنصار، أشهد أنكم قد جاهدتم في سبيل الله، قتلتم على منهاج رسول الله ﷺ و ابن رسول الله ﷺ

You are the masters of the martyrs in this life and in the hereafter. You are the foremost, the Muhajirs, and the Ansars (Quran 9:100) and I testify you were martyred while following the traditions of RasoolAllah (saw) and the Son of RasoolAllah (saw)

الحمد الله الذي صدقكم و أراكم ما تحبون

Praise be to Allah who fulfilled His promise with you and showed you that which you love

Then bid farewell to Hussain (asws) and recite:

أتيتك يا حبيب رسول الله ﷺ و ابن رسيلة، و إني لك عارف، و بحقك مقر، و بفضلك مستبصر، و بضلالة من خلافك موقن، عارف بالهدى الذي أنت عليه، بأبي أنت و امي و نفسي

I have come to You O' Beloved of RasoolAllah (saw) and the Son of His Rasool (saw) while believing in Your. I testify to Your rights and I believe in Your greatness, am certain of the corruption in those who opposed You, and I believe in the path of guidance that You stand on. May my mother and father be sacrificed upon You

اللهم إني اصلي عليه كما صليت أنت عليه و رسلك و أمير المؤمنين صلاة متتابعة متواصلة مترادفة، يتبع بعضها بعضاً، لا انقطاع لها و لا أبد و لا أجل، في محضرنا هذا و إذا غبنا و شهدنا

O'Allah! I send blessings upon Hussain (asws) just as You, Your messengers, and Ameerul Momineen (asws) send blessings upon Him, blessings which are continuous, everlasting and every increasing, blessings which follow one after another with no interlude, blessings which have no end nor limit. Send these blessings upon Him while we are here and continue to send them once we depart until we come back for His Ziarat

و السلام عليه ع رحمة الله و بركاته

May the salam, mercy and blessings of Allah be upon Him (Hussain asws)

HADITH 4

Muawiyah ibn Ammar narrates:

I asked Aba Abdullah Imam Jafar Sadiq (asws), "What should I recite when I go to the Ziarat of the grave of Hussain (asws)?"

Imam (asws) replied, "Recite:

السلام عليك يا أبا ابد اللّه

Salam be upon You O' Aba Abdullah

صلى الله عليك يا أبا ابداللّه

May the blessings of Allah be upon You O' Aba Abdullah

رحمك الله يا أبا عبداللّة

May the mercy of Allah be upon You O' Aba Abdullah

لعن الله من قتلك،

May the lanat of Allah be upon those who martyred You

و لعن الله من شرك في دمك

May the lanat of Allah be upon those who participated in the spilling of Your blood

و لعن الله من بلغه ذلك فرضي به

May the lanat of Allah be upon those who heard of Your slaughter and were pleased by it

أنا إلى الله من ذلك بريء

I seek the nearness of Allah by disassociating myself from those who gain pleasure by the martyrdom of Hussain (asws)

HADITH 5

Jabir al Jufee narrates:

Aba Abdullah Imam Jafar Sadiq (asws) asked Mufaddal, "What is the distance between you and the grave of Hussain (asws)?"

Mufaddal replied, "May I sacrifice my mother and father upon You! A little more than a day."

Imam (asws) asked, "Do you perform His Ziarat?"

Mufaddal replied, "Yes."

Imam (asws) asked, "Would you like for Me to give you joyous news? Should I cause you great joy by telling you some of its rewards?"

Mufaddal replied, "May I sacrifice my soul upon You! Yes."

Imam (asws) replied, "When a man from amongst you beings preparing to perform His (Hussain asws) Ziarat, the inhabitants of the heavens give one another the good news about him (zawir). As soon as he departs from his home, either by foot or on sumpter, Allah devotes four thousand angels to him who send blessings upon him until the zawir arrives at the grave of Hussain (asws).

O' Mufaddal! When you perform the Ziarat of the grave of Hussain (asws) ibn Ali (asws), stand at the door of the Haram and recite these words; for if you do, you will receive an ever increasing share of the mercy of Allah with every word that you recite."

Mufaddal asked, "May I be sacrificed upon You! What should I recite?"

Imam (asws) replied:

السلام عليك يا وارث آدمّ صفوة الله

Salam be upon You O inheritor of Adam (as), Safwatullah (the chosen slave of Allah)

السلام عليك يا وارث نوحّ نبي الله

Salam be upon You O' inheritor of Nuh (as), Nabiullah (prophet of Allah)

السلام عليك يا وارث إبراهيمّ خليل الله

Salam be upon You O' inheritor of Ibrahim (as), Khaleelullah (friend of Allah)

السلام عليك يا وارث موسىّ كليم الله

Salam be upon You O' inheritor of Musa (as), Kaleemullah (the one who spoke with Allah)

السلام عليك يا وارث عيسىّ روح الله

Salam be upon You O' inheritor of Isa (as), Ruhullah (spirit of Allah)

السلام عليك يا وارث محمد ﷺ حبيب الله

Salam be upon You O' inheritor of Muhammad (saw), Habeebullah (beloved of Allah)

السلام عليك يا وارث عليّ وصي رسول الله ﷺ

Salam be upon You O' inheritor of Ali (asws), the Successor of RasoolAllah (saw)

السلام عليك يا وارث الحسنّ الرضي

Salam be upon You O' inheritor of Hasan (asws), al Razi

السلام عليك يا وارث فاطمةّ بنت رسول الله ﷺ

Salam be upon You O' inheritor of Fatima (sa), Daughter of RasoolAllah (saw)

السلام عليك أيها الصديق الشهيد

Salam be upon You, O' al Sadeeq al Shaheed (the truthful, the martyr)

السلام عليك أيها الوصي ال بار التقي

Salam be upon You O' al Wasi, al Bar, al Taqi

السلام عليك يا حجة الله و ابن حجته

Salam be upon You O'Hujjatullah (proof of Allah) and Son of His Hujjat (proof)

السلام على الأرواح التي حلت بفنائك و أناخت برحلك

Salam be upon the souls who dismounted beside You and remained in Your caravan

السلام على ملائكة الله المحدقين بك

Salam be upon the angels of Allah that surround You

أشهد أنك قد أقمت الصلاة، و آتيت الزكاة، و أمرت بالمعروف، و نهيت عن المنكر، و عبدت الله مخلصاً
حتى أتاك اليقين

I testify You performed salat, gave zakat, enjoined good, forbade evil, and worshipped Allah sincerely until that which is certain came to You

السلام عليك ورحمة الله و بركاته

Salam be upon You and may the mercy and blessings of Allah be upon You

Then walk towards the grave; with each step that you take, you will be granted the reward of those whose blood was spilled in the way of Allah. After you have said salam at the grave, place your hands upon it and recite:

السلام عليك يا حجة الله في سمائه وأرضه

Salam be upon You, O'Hujjatullah in His (Allah) heavens and earth

Then continue to pray for the reward of performing one thousand hajj and umrah, freeing one thousand slaves and fighting in the way of Allah one thousand times alongside a prophet who was sent as a messenger will be written for every rakat of prayer you perform beside the grave of Hussain (asws).

When you are ready to depart from the grave of Hussain (asws), a crier will call out something to you. If you could hear what was called out, then you would remain beside the grave of Hussain (asws) for the remainder of your life.

The crier calls out, "Happiness for you, O' slave of Allah! You are victorious and will be safe on the day of judgment. Your past sins have been forgiven so go forth and do good deeds."

None but Allah Himself takes the soul of one who dies, at night or in the day, while performing Ziarat or even if one dies within one year after having performed the Ziarat.

The angels accompany those who return from the Ziarat of Hussain (asws), seeking forgiveness for them and sending blessings upon them until the zawir arrives at his home.

Then the angels will say to Allah. "O Lord! This slave of Yours performed the Ziarat of the grave of the Son of Your Prophet (saw) and now has returned to him home. Now where should we go?"

The angels will hear a call from the heavens which says, "O My angels! Stay beside the door of the house of My slave, glorifying and praising Me, until he dies and then record these deeds amongst his good deeds."

The angels will remain beside his house, glorifying and praising Allah and they will register it among the zawir's good deeds until he dies. Then they will attend his funeral, perform his ghusl, shroud him and pray for him.

Then the angels will say, "O our Lord! You devoted us to the door of the house of Your slave and now he has died. Now where should we go?"

Allah will call out to them, "O My angels! Remain beside the grave of My slave, glorifying and praising Me, until the Day of Judgment and record these deeds amongst his good deeds."

HADITH 6

Ibrahim ibn Abul Bilad narrates:

I asked Abul Hasan Imam Musa Kazim (asws), "What is the reward for the Ziarat of the grave of Hussain (asws)?"

Imam (asws) asked, "What do you think?"

I replied, "Some of us believe it is equal to performing a hajj while others believe it is equal to performing an umrah."

Imam (asws) asked, "What do you recite when you perform His Ziarat?"

I replied, "I recite this:"

السلام عليك يا أبا عبد اللّه

Salam be upon You, O' Aba Abdullah

السلام عليك يا بن رسول الله ﷺ

Salam be upon You O Son of RasoolAllah (saw)

أشهد أنك قد أقمت الصلاة،و آتيت الزكاة، و أمرت بالمعروف، و نهيت عن المنكر، ودعوت إلى بسيل ربك بالحكمة و الموعظة الحسنة

I testify You performed the salat, paid zakat, enjoined good, forbade evil, and called the people to the path of Your Lord by wisdom and good counsel

و أشهد أن الذين سفكوا دمك و استحلوا حرمتك ملعونون معذبون على لسان داود و عيسى بن مريم، ذلك بما عصوا يعتدون

And I testify that those who spilled Your blood and violated Your holiness will be tormented and they will be *"cursed by the tongue of Dawood and Isa, son of Miriam; this was because they disobeyed and used to exceed the limit."* (Quran 5:78)

HADITH 7

Ibrahim ibn Abul Bilad narrates:

Abul Hasan Imam Musa Kazim (asws) asked me, "How do you say salam to Aba Abdullah Imam Hussain (asws)?"

I replied, "I recite:

السلام عليك يا أبا عبد اللّة

Salam be upon You, O' Aba Abdullah

السلام عليك يا بن رسول الله ﷺ

Salam be upon You O Son of RasoolAllah (saw)

أشهد أنك قد أقمت الصلاة،و آتيت الزكاة، و أمرت بالمعروف، و نهيت عن المنكر، ودعوت إلى بسيل ربك بالحكمة و الموعظة الحسنة

I testify You performed the salat, paid zakat, enjoined good, forbade evil, and called the people to the path of Your Lord by wisdom and good counsel

و أشهد أن الذين سفكوا دمك و استحلوا حرمتك ملعونون معذبون على لسان داود و عيسى بن مريم، ذلك بما عصوا يعتدون

And I testify that those who spilled Your blood and violated Your holiness will be tormented and they will be *"cursed by the tongue of Dawood and Isa, son of Miriam; this was because they disobeyed and used to exceed the limit."* (Quran 5:78)

Imam (asws) replied, "Yes, this ziarat is correct."

HADITH 8

Sulaiman ibn Hafs al Marwazi narrates:

Imam Ali Naqi (asws) said, "Recite the following beside the grave of Hussain (asws):

السلام عليك يا أبا عبد اللّة

Salam be upon You O Aba Abdullah

السلام عليك يا حجة الله في أرضه، و شاهده على خلقه

Salam be upon You O' Hujjatullah (proof of Allah) in His land and His witness over His (Allah) creation

السلام عليك يا بن رسول الله ﷺ

Salam be upon You O' Son of RasoolAllah (saw)

السلام عليك يا بن عليّ المرتضى

Salam be upon You O' Son of Ali (asws) al Murtaza

السلام عليك يا بن فاطمةّ الزهراء

Salam be upon You O' Son of Fatima (sa) al Zahra

أشهدّنك قد أقمت الصلاة، و آتيت الزكاة، و أمرت بالمعروف، و نهيت عن المنكر، و جاهدت فى سبيل الله حتى أتاك اليقين

I testify You performed salat, paid zakat, enjoined good, forbade evil, and fought in the way of Allah until that which was certain came to You

و صلى الله عليك حياً و ميتاً

May the blessing of Allah be upon You in Your Life and after You depart this world

Then place your right cheek upon the grave and recite:

أشهد أنك على بينة من ربك، جئتك مقرا باذنوب لتشفع لي عند ربك يا بن رسول الل ﷺ

I testify that You had the understanding of Your Lord. I have come to You admitting to my sins. Intercede for me with Your Lord. O' Son of RasoolAllah (saw)

Then mention each of the Imams (asws) by name and then say, "I testify They are Hujjatullah." Then recite:

اكتب لي عندك ميثاقا و عهداً أني أتيتك مجدداً الميثاق، فاشهد لي عند ربك، إنك أنت الشاهد

Be my witness with Your Lord and record my coming to You to renew my oath. For You are the witness."

HADITH 9

See hadith 8

HADITH 10

Imam Jafar Sadiq (asws) narrates:

"Recite the following when you go to the grave of Hussain (asws):

الحمد الله و صلى الله على محمد النبي ﷺ و آلة

Praise be to Allah and may the blessings of Allah be upon Muhammad (saw) the Prophet and His Family (asws)

و السلام عليهم و رحمة الله و بركاته

Salam be upon Him (saw) and His Family (asws). May the blessings of Allah be upon Them

Then recite the following three times:

صلى علله عليك يا أبا عبد اللّة

May the blessings of Allah be upon You O' Aba Abdullah (asws)

لعن الله من قتلك و من شارك في دمك و من بلغه ذلك فرضى به، أنا إلى الله منهم بريء

May the lanat of Allah be upon those who martyred You, those who participated in the spilling of Your blood, and those who heard about it and were pleased by it. I seek the nearness of Allah by disassociating myself from them"

HADITH 11

See hadith 10

HADITH 12

Imam Jafar Sadiq (asws) narrates:

"Recite the following when you perform the Ziarat of the grave of Hussain (asws):

السلام عليك يا بن رسول الله ﷺ

Salam be upon You O' Son of RasoolAllah (saw)

السلام عليك يا بن أمير المؤمنينّ

Salam be upon You O' Son of Ameerul Momineen (asws)

السلام عليك يا أبا عبد اللةّ

Salam be upon You O' Aba Abdullah (asws)

السلام عليك يا سيد شباب أهل الجنة و رحمة الله و بركاته

Salam be upon You O' Master of the Youths of Jannah and may the blessings and mercy of Allah be upon You

السلام عليك يا من رضه من رضا الرحمن، و سخطه من سخط الرحمن

Salam be upon You O' One whose pleasure comes from the pleasure of the Most Gracious (Allah) and whose displeasure comes from the displeasure of the Most Gracious (Allah)

السلام عليك يا أمين الله و حجته، و باب الله، و الدليل على الله، و الداعي إلى الله

Salam be upon You O' Ameenullah (Trustee of Allah), His Hujjat (proof), and Babullah (door of Allah) and Daleel (proof) of Allah and the Caller of Allah

301

أشهد أنك قد حللت حلال الله، و حرمت حرام الله، و أقمت الصلاة، و آتيت الزكاة، و أمرت بالمعروف، و نهيت عن المنكر، و دعوت إلى سبيل ربك بالحكمة و الموعظة الحسنة

I testify You declare halal what Allah has declared as halal and You declared as haram that which Allah declared haram. You performed salat, paid zakat, enjoined good, forbade evil, and called the people to the path of Your Lord through wisdom and guidance

و أشهد أنك و من قتل معك شهداء أحياء عند ربكم ترزقون

And I testify that You and those who were martyred alongside You are the martyrs who *"are alive (and) are provided sustenance from their Lord;"* (Quran 3:169)

و أشهد أن قاتليك في النار

And I testify that Your killers are in the hellfire

أدين الله بالبراآة ممن قاتلك و ممن قتلك و شايع عليك، و ممن جمع عليك، و ممن سمع صوتك و لم يجبك

I follow the religion of Allah by disassociating myself from those who fought against You, those who slaughtered You, those who were with them, those who gathered against You, and from those who heard Your voice calling for help and did not answer Your call. I wish I had been with You so that I could have gained this great victory."

HADITH 13

Imam Jafar Sadiq (asws) narrates:

"You may recite whatever you like beside the grave of Hussain (asws)."

HADITH 14

Abu Sa'eed al Medini narrates:

"I went to Aba Abdullah Imam Jafar Sadiq (asws), "May I be sacrificed upon You! Should I perform the Ziarat of the grave of Hussain (asws)?"

Imam (asws) replied, "Yes, o' Abu Sa'eed! Perform the Ziarat of the grave of Hussain (asws), the most blessed of the blessed ones, the most pure of the pure ones, and the most pious of the pious ones.

O'Abu Sa'eed! When you perform the Ziarat, recite one thousand times the tasbih of Ameerul Momineen (asws) beside the head of Imam Hussain (asws) and recite one thousand times the tasbih of Syeda Fatima (sa) beside the feet of Hussain (asws).

Then perform two rakats of prayer. Recite Sura Yaseen in the first rakat and Sura al Rahman in the second rakat. If you do this Allah will records its reward for you inshaAllah."

I said, "May I be sacrificed upon You! Teach me the tasbih of Ali (asws) and Fatima (sa)."

Imam (asws) replied, "O' Abu Sa'eed! The tasbih of Ali (asws) is:

سبحان الذي لا تنفد خزائنه

Glorified is He whose treasury is infinite.

سبحان الذي لا تبيد معالمه

Glorified is He whose signs do not perish

سبحان الذي لا يفنى ما عنده

Glorified is He whom whatever He has it will not finish

سبحان الذي لا يشرك أحداً في حكمه

Glorified is He who is alone in His command

سبحان الذي لا اضمحلال لفخره

Glorified is He whose glory does not disappear

سبحان الذي لا انقطاع لمدته

Glorified is He whose time does not end

سبحان الذي لا إله غيره

Glorified is He besides whom there is no god

The tasbih of Fatima (sa) is:

سبحان ذي الجلال الباذخ العظيم

Glorified is the Owner of Majesty, the Exalted, the Great

سبحان ذي العز الشامخ المنيف

Glorified is the owner of glory, the High, the Exalted

سبحان ذي الملك الفاخر القديم

Glorified is the owner of the kingdom, the Superior, the Everlasting

سبحان ذي المهجة و الجمال

Glorified is the Owner of Grace and Beauty

سبحان ذي تردى بالنور و الوقار

Glorified is He who is encompassed with Light and Dignity

سبحان من يرى أثر النمل في الصفا و وقع الطير في الهواء

Glorified is He who is aware of the needs of an ant on flat stones and the birds flying in the sky"

HADITH 15

Amir ibn Juza'ah narrates:

I heard Aba Abdullah Imam Jafar Sadiq (asws) say:

" When you go to the grave of Hussain (asws), recite;

السلام عليك يا بن رسول اللّٰه ﷺ

Salam be upon You, O' Son of RasoolAllah (saw)

السلام عليك يا بن أبا عبد الله ﷺ

Salam be upon You, O' Aba Abdullah

لعن الله من قتلك

May the lanat of Allah be upon those who martyred You

و لعن الله من بلغه ذلك فرضي به، أنا إلى الله منهم بريء

May the lanat of Allah be upon those who heard of Your martyrdom and were pleased by it. I seek the nearness of Allah by disassociating myself from them"

304

HADITH 16

Imam Jafar Sadiq (asws) narrates:

"When you perform the Ziarat of the grave of Hussain (asws), begin by praising Allah (swt) and sending blessing upon the Prophet (saw). Then recite:

سلام الله و سلام ملائكته فيما تروح و تغدو الزاكيات الطاهرات لك و عليك

Salam of Allah be upon You and salam of His angels be upon You along with the purified and blessed greetings which reach You at all times

و سلام الله و سلام ملائكته المقربين و المسلمين لك بقلوبهم، و الناطقين بفضلك و الشهداء على أنك صادق صديق، و نصحت فيما أتيت به، و نك ژار الله في الأرض، و الدم الذي لا يدرك ثاره أحد من أهل الأرض، و لا يدركه إلا الله وحده

Salam of Allah and of His high ranking angels be upon You as well as the salam of those whose hearts are submissive to You, those who speak of Your attributes, and those who testify that You are honest and truthful. That You were truthful about that which You invited the people towards. That You are the one whom Allah will avenge on earth and that Your blood can only be avenged by Allah and not by any from amongst the inhabitants of the earth

جئتك يا بن رسول اللّة و افداً إليك، و أتوسل إلى الله بك في جميع حوائجي من أمر دنياي و آخرتي، و بك يتوسل المتوسلون إلى الله في حوائجهم، و بك يدرك أهل الترات من عباد الله طلبتهم

I have to You, O' Son of RasoolAllah (saw) as Your guest. Asking Allah through You for all of my requests in this life and in the hereafter. Those who ask Allah, ask Him through You and those from amongst the slaves of Allah who seek vengeance will be avenged through You

Then take a few steps, face the grave with your back towards Qiblah and recite:

الحمد لله الواحد الأحد المتوحد بالأمور كلها، خالق الخالق فلم يعرب عنه شيء من أمرهم و عالم كل شيء بلا تعليم

Praise be to Allah, the One who is alone in overseeing all of the affairs, the Creator of the creation who is aware of all of the happenings of His creation, and the One who has the knowledge of all things

305

ضمن الأرض و من عليها دمك وثراك يا بن رسول الله ﷺ

The earth and everyone on it is responsible for Your blood and for avenging You, O' Son of RasoolAllah (saw)!

أشهد أن لك من الله ما و عدك من النصر و الفتح، و أن لك من الله الوعد الحق في هلاك عدوك و تمام موعده إياك

I testify that Allah will fulfill His promise of support and victory to You and I testify that Allah will fulfill His true promise to You and complete it by destroying Your enemies

أشهد أنه قاتل معك ربيون كثير كما قال الله تعالى (و كأين من نبي قاتل معه ربيون كثير فما و هنوا لما أصابهم)

I testify that countless godly men fought beside You as Allah (swt) says, *"And how many a prophet has fought with whom were many worshippers of the Lord; so they did not become weak-hearted on account of what befell them"* (Quran 3:146)

Then say Allahu Akbar seven times, take a few steps, turn towards the grave and recite:

الحمد الله الذي لم يتخذ صاحبة و لا و لداً، و لم يكن له شريك في الملك، خلق كل شيء فقدره تقديراً

Praise be to Allah who has not taken a wife nor son. Nor does He have any partner in the kingdom, the One who created everything and fixed for it a measure of time

أشهد أنك قد بلغت عن الله ما امرت به، ووفيت بعهد الله، و تمت بك كلماته

I testify You proclaimed to the people all that which Allah ordained for You to proclaim; that You fulfilled the oath of Allah and the words of Allah became complete through You

و جاهدت في سبيله حتى أتاك اليقين

and that You fought in the way of Allah until that which is certain came over You

لعن الله امة قتلتك، و امة خذلتك،

May the lanat of Allah be upon the nation that slaughtered You and upon the nation that abandoned You

306

و لعن الله امة خذات عنك

And may the lanat of Allah be upon the nation that caused others to abandon You

اللهم إني أشهد بالو لاية لمن و اليت و واالت رسلك

O' Allah! I testify that I love those whom You and Your messengers love.

أشهد بالبراءة ممن برئت منه و برئت منه رسلك

And I testify that I disassociate myself from those whom You and Your messengers disassociate Yourselves from

اللهم لعن الذين كذبوا رسولك، و هدموا كعبتك، و حرفوا كتابك، و سفكوا دماء أهل بيتَّ بنيك، و أفسدوا عبادك و استذلوهم

O' Allah! Send lanat on those who denied Your Messenger (saw), destroyed Your Kaaba, altered the meanings of Your Book, spilled the blood of the Family of Your Prophet (saw), and dishonored Your slaves

اللهم ضاعف لهم اللعنة فيما جرت به سنتك في برك وبحرك

O' Allah! Increase Your torment on them according to Your sunnah in Your lands and Your seas

اللهم العنهم فع سمائك و أرضك

O'Allah! Send lanat on them in Your heavens and in Your earth

اللهم و اجعل لي لسان صدق في أوليائك، و حبب إلي مشاهدهم حتى تلحقني بهم

O'Allah! Appoint for me a truthful tongue with Your Auwilaya and make me love Their shrines until You unite me with Them

و تجعلهم لي فرطاً، و تجعلني لهم تبعاً في الذنيا و الآخرة

Make Them my leaders and appoint me amongst Their followers in this life and in the hereafter

Then take a few steps, recite takbir (Allah Akbar) seven times, tahleel (la illaha illallah) seven times, praise Allah seven times, and glorify Allah seven times. Then answer the call of Hussain (asws) seven times by saying:

لبيك داعي الله

I am at Your service, O' Caller to Allah

Then recite:

إن كان لم يجبك بدني، فقد أجابك قلبي وشعري ورأيي و هواي على التسليم لخلف النبي المرسل، و السبط المنتجب، و الدليل العالم، و الأمين المستخزن، و الوصي المبلغ، و المظلوم المهتضم

Even though my body could not answer Your call, my heart, my hair, my skin, and my desire have replied to Your call and have submitted to the remainder of the Prophet (saw) who was sent as a messenger, the Chosen Grandson, the knowledgeable guide, the entrusted guardian, the successor who announced the message of Allah; the Oppressed One

جئت انقطاعاً إليك و إلى ولدك، و ولد ولدك الخلف من بعدك على بركة الحق

I have come solely to You, Your Son and to the Son of Your Son, the One who remains after You by the blessing of haq (Imam e Zamana atfs)

فقلبي لكم مسلم، و أمري لكم متبع، و نصرتي لكم معدة، حتى يحكم الله و هو خير الحاكمين لديني، و يبعثكم، فمعكم معكم لا مع عدوكم، إني من المؤمنين برجعتكم

My heart has submitted to You. I follow You in my affairs and my support is ready for You until Allah judges my religion. And He is the best of judges. And until Allah resurrects You, I shall be with You and only with You, and I shall not be with Your enemies. I believe in Your Rajat (resurrection at the end of time)

لا انكر لله قدرة، و لا اكذب له مشية، و لا أزعم أن ما شاء لا يكون

I do not deny the power of Allah, His Mashiyat (will), and I do not deny that once Allah has willed something, it will occur

Then walk towards the grave, stand beside it, and recite:

سبحان الله، يسبح لله ذي الملك و الملكوت و يقدس بأسمائه جميع خلقه

Glory be to Allah, all of the creation of Allah glorifies and honors Him and glorifies the names of Allah, the Owner of the Kingdom

سبحان الله الملك القدوس، ربنا و رب الملائكة و الروح

Glory be to Allah, al Malik, al Qadoos; our Lord and the Lord of the angles and the ruh

اللهم اجعلني في و فدك إلى خير بقاعك وخير خلقك

O' Allah! List me as one of Your guests from amongst the best of Your places and the best of Your creation

اللهم لعن الجبت و الطاغوت

O' Allah! Send lanat upon Jibt and Taghut

Then raise your hands, spread your arms out on the grave and recite:

أشهد أنك طهر طاهر من طهر طاهر

I testify that You are Tohir, Taheer from Tohir and Taheer

قد طهرت بك البلاد، و طهرت أرض أنت فيها

The lands have been purified through You and the land in which You are is purified through You

و أنك ثار الله في الأرض حتى يستثير لك من جميع خلقه

And You are Tharullah on the earth and will be so until Allah takes vengeance from all of His creation regarding You

Then place both of your cheeks and hands on the grave. Then sit beside His head and glorify Allah however you wish. Ask Allah and your needs will be fulfilled. Then go towards His feet, place your hands and cheeks beside His Feet and recite:

صلى الله عليك و على روحك و بدنك، فلقد صدقت و صبرت، و أنت الصادق المصدق قتل الله من قتلك بالأيدي و الألسن

May the blessings of Allah be upon You, Your Ruh, and Your Body. For You spoke with truth and remained patient. You are Siddiqi al Sadiq (trustworthy one) whose trustworthiness is substantiated by Allah. May Allah slaughter those who slaughtered You whether it be by their hands or their tongues

Then go to the grave of His Sons (asws) and praise Them however you like. Then ask Your Lord for your needs and wants. Then face the graves of the martyrs and while standing recite:

السلام عليك أيها الربانيون

Salam be upon you, O' those who precede us and those whom we follow

أنتم لنا فرط و نحن لكم تبع و أنصار، أبشروا بموعد الله الذي لا خلف له، و أن الله مدرك بكم تاركم، و أنتم سادة الشهداء في الدنيا و الآخرة

You went before us as our leaders while we remain back as those who follow and provide support. Rejoice in the promise of Allah that does not disappoint. Allah will avenge you for You are the master of martyrs in this life and in the hereafter.

Then stand behind the grave and perform as many rakats of prayer as you wish.

Imam (asws) added, "Every time you visit the Ha'yr, say salam and then walk to the grave. Place both your hands and cheeks on the grave. Do the same when you wish to leave. Perform pray in full form beside His grave for the entire time that you remain in Karbala.

When you are ready to depart from the Ha'yr, bid farewell to Hussain (asws) by saying:

سلام الله و سلام ملائكته المقربين و أنبيائه المرسلين و عباده الصالحين عليك يا بن رسول اللّه، و على روحك و بدنك و ذريتك، و من حضرك من أوليائك

Salam of Allah, His high ranking angels, His prophets who were sent as messengers, His righteous servants be upon You, O' Son of RasoolAllah (saw), and upon Your ruh, Your body, Your Progeny, and those from Your Auwilya who came to You

Repeat this entire Ziarat when you are ready to depart for your home just as you did when you first entered the Ha'yr. Once you arrive at your home, recite:

الحمد لله الذي سلمني و سلم مني

Praise be to Allah who kept me safe and accepted my salam from me

الحمد لله في الأمور كلها و على كل حال

Praise be to Allah in all of the affairs and in every state

الحمد لله رب العالمين

Praise to be Allah Lord of the worlds

Then say Allahu Akbar 21 times. Be sure to recite it slowly and calmly without being hurried. InshaAllah.

HADITH 17

Abu Nab Hussain ibn Atiyah Baya al Saburi narrates:

I heard Aba Abdullah Imam Jafar Sadiq (asws) say:

"For those who perform the Ziarat of the grave of Hussain (asws), Allah also records performing hajj and umrah for them."

I asked, "May I be sacrificed upon You! What should I recite when I perform His (Hussain asws) Ziarat?"

Imam (asws) said, "You should recite:"

السلام عليك يا أبا عبد الله

Salam be upon You O Aba Abdullah (asws)

السلام عليك يا بن رسول الله ﷺ

Salam be upon You O' Son of RasoolAllah (saw)

السلام عليك يوم ولدت و يوم تموت و يوم تبعث حياً

Salam be upon You on the day You entered this world, on the day You left this world, and on the day when You will be resurrected

أشهد أنك حي شهيد، ترزق عند ربك

I testify You are a martyr who is alive with and provided sustenance by Your Lord

و أتوالى وليك، و أبرء من عدوك

I love those who love You and I disassociate myself from Your enemies

و أشهد أن الذين قاتلوك و انتهكوا حرمتك ملعونون على لسان النبي الأمي، و أشهد أنك قدأقمت الصلاة، و آتيت الزكاة، و أمرت بالمعروف، و نهيت عن المنكر، و جاهدت في سبيل ربك بالحكمة و الموعظة الحسنة

I testify that those who fought against You and violated Your holiness are accursed by the tongue of the Prophet (saw) of Mecca. I testify You performed salat, paid zakat, enjoined good, forbade evil, and fought in the way of Allah with wisdom and guidance

أسال الله وليك و ولينا أن يجعل تحفتنا من زيارتك الصلاة على نبينا، و المغفرة الذنوبنا

I ask Allah who is our master and Your master, to send blessings on our Prophet (saw) and to forgive our sins as our reward for having performed Your Ziarat

إشفع لي يا بن رسول الله عند ربك

Intercede on my behalf, O' Son of RasoolAllah (saw), with Your Lord

HADITH 18

Abul Samit narrates:

I heard Aba Abdullah Imam Jafar Sadiq (asws) say:

"Allah will record one thousand good deeds and erase one thousand bad deeds for every step taken by those who perform the Ziarat of Hussain (asws) on foot. Allah will also increase the status of the zawir one thousand times for every step taken."

Imam (asws) added, "When you arrive at the River Furat, perform ghusl, carry your shoes, and walk barefoot like a humble slave. Once you arrive at the door of the Ha'yr say Allahu Akbar four times. Then perform prayer beside the grave of Hussain (asws) and ask Allah for your needs."

HADITH 19

Abu Baseer narrates:

I asked Aba Abdullah Imam Jafar Sadiq (asws), "How should I say salam to Hussain (asws) ibn Ali (asws)?"

Imam (asws) replied, "Recite:

السلام عليك يا أبا عبد اللّه

Salam be upon You O'Aba Abdullah (asws)

السلام عليك يا بن رسول الله ﷺ

Salam be upon You O' Son of RasoolAllah (saw)

لعن الله من قتلك

May the lanat of Allah be upon those who slaughtered You

و لعن الله من أعان عليك، و من بلغه ذلك فرضي به، أنا إلى الله منهم بريء

May the lanat of Allah be upon those who sided with Your enemies against You and upon those who heard about Your martyrdom and were pleased by it. I seek the nearness of Allah by disassociating myself from them

HADITH 20

See hadith 19

HADITH 21

Imam Jafar Sadiq (asws) narrates:

"When you decide to perform the Ziarat of the grave of Hussain (asws), fast Wednesday, Thursday, and Friday. When you are about to leave from your house, gather your family including your children and recite the dua of traveling.

Perform ghusl before you leave and recite the following while performing ghusl:

اللهم طهر ني و طهر قلبي، و اشرح لى صدري، و أجر على لساني ذكرك، و مدحتك و الثناء عليك، فإنه لا قوة إلا بك

O' Allah! Purify my heart and me. Expand my chest and allow my tongue to praise and glorify You. There is no power except You

و قد علمت أن قوام دعني التسليم لأمرك، و الإتباع لسنة نبيك، و الشهادة جميع أنبيائك و رسلك إلى جميع خلقك

I am fully aware that the foundation of my religion is obeying Your orders, following the sunnah of Your Prophet (saw), and testifying to the truth of all of Your prophets and Your messengers whom You sent to all of Your creation

اللهم اجعله نوراً و طهوراً و شفاء من كل داء و سقم و آفة و عهة، و من شر ما أخاف و أحذر

O' Allah! Make this ghusl a light and a means of purification for me. Make it a cure for my every illness, disease, plague, and disability. Make it a protection against the evil that terrifies and worries me

Then recite the following as you leave your house:

اللهم إني إليك و جهت و جهي، و إليك فوضت أمري، و إليك أسلمت نفسي، و إليك ألجأت ظهري، و عليك توكلت

O' Allah! I turn my face towards You, entrusted my affairs to You, submitted myself to You, protected my back with You, and I rely on You

لا ملجأ و لا منجا إلا إليك، تباركت و تعليت، عز جارك و جل ثناؤك

There is no refuge or shelter except with You. You are blessed and exalted. Great is Your protection and Exalted is Your Praise

Then recite:

بسم الله و بالله، و من الله إلى الله، و في سبيل الله، و على ملة رسول الله ﷺ ، على الله توكلت وإليه أنبت، فاطر السماوات السبع و الأرضين السبع، و رب العرش العظيم

In the name of Allah, by Allah, from Allah, to Allah, and in the way of Allah as one who is from the nation of RasoolAllah (saw). I rely on Allah and to Him I will return. He is the creator of the seven heavens and seven earths and the Lord of the Great Arsh

اللهم صل على محمد ﷺ و آل محمدّ ، و احفظني في سفري، و اخلفني في أهلي بأحسن الخلف

O' Allah! Send Your blessing on Muhammad (saw) and Aal e Muhammad (asws). Protect me during my journey and watch over my family in my absence

اللهم إليك توجهت و إليك خرجت و إليك و فدت، و لخيرك تعرضت، و بزيارة حبيب حبيبك تقربت

O' Allah! I have turned towards You. I travel to You. I come to You as Your guest. I have opened myself to Your blessings and I seek nearness to You through the Ziarat of the Beloved of Your Beloved

اللهم لا تمنعني خير ما عندك بشر ما عندي

O' Allah! Do not deprive me of the blessings that are with You because of the evil that I have within me.

اللهم اغفر لي ذنوبي، و كفر عني سيئاتي، و حط عني خطاياي، مني حسناتي

O' Allah! Forgive my sins, pardon my bad deeds, erase my errors, and accept my good deeds

Then recite three times:

اللهم اجعلني في درعك الحصينة التي تجعل فيها من تريد

O' Allah! Place me in Your protective shield where You place those whom You will.

اللهم إني أبرء إليك من الحول و القوة

O' Allah I disassociate myself from any will and power other than You

Then recite Fatihatul Kitab (Sura Fatiha), Muawwazatain (Sura 113-114), Qul Huwallahu Ahad (Sura 112), Inna Inzulnah (Sura 97), Ayatul Kursi (Quran :255-257), Sura Yaseen, and the end of Sura Hashr (Sura 59:21-24):

(لو أنزلنا هذا القرآن على جبل لرأيته خاشعاً متصدعاً من خشية الله و تلك الأمثال نضربها للناس لعلهم يتفكرون)(هو الله الذي لا إله هو عالم الغيب و الشهادة هو الرحمن الرحيم) (هو الله الذي لا إله إلا هو الملك

القدوس السلام المؤمن المهيمن العزيز الجبار المتكبر سبحان الله عمايشركون) (هو الله الخالق البارئ المصور له الأسماء الحسنى يسبح له ما في السموات و الأرض و هو العزيز الحكيم)

Had We sent down this Quran on a mountain, you would certainly have seen it falling down, splitting asunder because of the fear of Allah, and We set forth these parables to men that they may reflect. He is Allah besides Whom there is no god; the Knower of the unseen and the seen; He is the Beneficent, the Merciful. He is Allah, besides Whom there is no god; the King, the Holy, the Giver of peace, the Granter of security, Guardian over all, the Mighty, the Supreme, the Possessor of every greatness Glory be to Allah from what they set up (with Him). He is Allah the Creator, the Maker, the Fashioner; His are the most excellent names; whatever is in the heavens and the earth declares His glory; and He is the Mighty, the Wise.

Do not use scented oils or kohl until you reach the River Furat. Speak very little. Continuously glorify Allah and refrain from quarrelling or feeling joyful. Recite the following while you are walking/riding:

اللهم إني أعوذ بك من سطوات النكال، و عواقب الوبال، و فتنة الضلال، و من أن تلقاني بمكروه

O' Allah! I seek Your refuge from the punishments of the tyrants, from the evil outcomes, from the afflictions caused by deviation and from the disappointments You find within me

و أعوذ بك من الحبس و اللبس، و من و سوسة الشيطان، و طوارق السوء، و من شر كل ذي شر، و من شر شياطين الجن و الإنس، و من شر من ينصب لأولياء الله العداوة، و من أن يفرطوا علي و أن يطغوا

I seek Your refuge from imprisonment, from confusion, from the whispers of Shaitan, from terrible calamities, from the evil of the evil ones, from the evil of the demons amongst the jinn and mankind, and from the evil of those who incite hatred against the Wali of Allah and from their hostility and violence towards me

و أعوذ بك من شر عيون الظلمة، و من شر كل ذي شر، و شرك إبليس، و من يرد عن الخير بالسان و اليد

I seek Your refuge from the spies of the oppressors, from the evil of the evil ones, from the traps of Iblees, and from those who prevent others from seeking the blessings by their hands or tongues

If you are fearful, recite:

لا حول و لا قوة إلا بالله، به احتجبت و به اعتصمت

There is no will nor power except Allah. I seek refuge and protection with Him.

اللهم اعصمني من شر خلقك، فإنما أنا بك و أنا عبدك

O' Allah! Protect me from the evil of Your creation, for I am Your slave and I seek refuge with You

When you reach the River Furat, before crossing, recite:

اللهم أنت خير من و فد إليه الرجال، و أنت يا سيدي أكرم مأتي و أكرم مزور

O' Allah! You are the best to those who have traveled. And You, O' my Master, are the most honorable to those go to visit the most honorable one

و قد جعلت لكل زائر كرامة، و لكل و افد تحفة، و قد أتعتك زائراً قبر ابن نبيك صلواتك عليه، فاجعل تحفتك إباي فكاك رقبتي من النار

You have appointed a present for every zawir and a gift for every guest. I have come to You as a zawir of the grave of the Son of Your Prophet (saw). Make my releasement from the hellfire be Your gift to me

و تقبل مني عملي، و اشكر سعيي، و ارحم مسيري إليك بغير من مني، بل لك المن على إذ جعلت لي السبيل إلى زيارته، ع وعرفتني فضله، حفظتني حتى بلغتني قبر ابن و ليك

Accept my deed, acknowledge my efforts and have mercy on me as I have traveled to You even though I do not consider this to be a favor from me to You. Instead the favor is from You to me for making it possible for me to perform His Ziarat, for allowing me to know His attributes, and for protecting me until I arrived at the grave of the Son of Your Wali

و قد رجوتك فضل على محمد صلى الله عليه وآله و آل محمدّ، و لا تقطع رجائي، و قد أتيتك فلا تخيب أملي، و اجعل هذا كفارة لما كان قبله من ذنوبي، و اجعلني من أنصاره، يا أرحم الراحمين

I have asked for Your mercy so send Your blessing on Muhammad (saw) and Aal e Muhammad (asws). Do not deprive me of that which I have asked for. I have come to You; do not disappoint me. And make this Ziarat an atonement of my past sins and count me amongst His supporters, O' Most Merciful of the Merciful

Then cross the River Furat and recite:

اللهم صل على محمد و آل محمد، و اجعل سعيي مشكوراً و ذنبي مغفوراً و عملي مقبي لا، و ا غسلني من الخطايا و الذنوب، و طهر قلبي من كل آفة تمحق ديني أو تبطل عملي، يا أرحم الراحمين

O' Allah! Send Your blessing upon Muhammad (saw) and Aal e Muhammad (asws). Allow my efforts to be acknowledged, my sins to be forgiven, and my deeds to be accepted. Purify me from my past sins and purify my heart from any disease which destroys my religion and nullifies my deeds, O' Most merciful of the merciful

Then enter Karbala. Do not use any scented oils or kohl. Do not eat meat as long as you are there. Then come to the banks of the River Furat where it is closest to the grave of Hussain (asws), perform ghusl while being covered. Then recite the following as you perform ghusl:

اللهم طهرني و طهر لي قلبي، و اشرح لي صدري، و أجر على لساني محبتك و مدحتك و الثناء عليك، فإنه لا حول و لا قوة إلا بك

O' Allah! Purify me and my heart. Expand my chest. Cause my tongue to praise and glorify You and to speak only of Your love. For there is no will nor power except You

و قد علمت أن قوام ديني التسليم لأمرك، و الشهادة على جميع أنبيائك و رسلك بالألفة بينهم

I fully understand the foundation of my religion is submitting to Your orders and testifying all of Your prophets and Your messengers were unified in Their messages

أشهد أنهم أنبياؤك و رسلك إلى جميع خلقك

I testify They were all Your prophets and You messengers whom You sent upon Your creation

اللهم اجعله لي نوراً و طهوراً و حرزاً وشفاء من كل سقم و داء، و من كل آفة و عاهة، و من شر ما أخاف و أحذر

O' Allah! Make this ghusl a light and purification for me. Make it a means of cure for my every illness, disease, plague, and disability. Also make it a means of protection against the evil that causes me to worry and be fearful

اللهم طهر به قلبي و جوارحي، و عظامي و لحمي و دمي، و شعري و بشري، و مخي و عصبي، و ما ؤقلت الأرض مني، و اجعله لي شاهداً يعم فقري و فاقتي

O' Allah! Purify my heart, organs, bones, flesh, blood, hair, skin, brain, nerves, and body through this ghusl. Make it be my witness on the day of my poverty and need (day of judgment)

Then wear the most pure of your clothes and say Allahu Akbar thirty times. After recite:

الحمد لله الذي إليه قصدت فبلغني، و إلبه ّردت فقبلني و لم يقطع بي، و رحمته ابتغيت فسلمني

Praise be to Allah; whom I was searching for and He allowed me to find Him. The One I desired and He accepted me. The One who did not deprive me. The One whose mercy I longed for and the One who kept me safe

اللهم أنت حصني و كهفي و حرزي و رجئي و أملي، لا إله إلا أنت يا رب العالمين

O' Allah! You are my protective shelter. You are my refuge, my hope, my wish. There is no god except You O' Lord of the Worlds

As you begin walking towards the grave, recite the following:

اللهم إني أردتك فأردني، و إني أقبلت بوجهي إليك فلا تعرض بوجهك عني، فإن كنت علي ساخطاً فتب علي، و ارحم مسيري إلى ابن حبيبك، أبتغي بذلك رضاك عني فارض عني، و لا تخيبني يا أرحم الراحمين

O' Allah! I long for Your nearness. I want You to want that for me. I have turned my face towards You so do not turn Your face away from me. If you are unhappy with me, accept my repentance and have mercy on me due to my traveling to the Son of Your Beloved while wanting nothing except to gain Your pleasure. I ask for You to be pleased with me. Do not disappoint me O' Most Merciful of the Merciful

Walk barefoot calmly and with reverence whilst continuously reciting Allahu Akbar and La illaha illallah, and praising Allah and His Messenger (saw). And recite the following:4

الحمد لله الواحد المتوحد بالأمور كلها، خالق الخلق لم يعزب عنه شيء من امورهم، و عالم كل شيء بغير تعليم

Praise be to Allah, the One who manages all of the affairs alone. He is the creator of the creation and is aware of all that they do. For Allah has knowledge over every thing

صلوات الله و صلوات ملائكته المقربين و أنبيائه المرسلين و رسله أجمعين على محمد ﷺ و أهل بيتة الأوصياء

May the blessings of Allah, His high ranking angels and all of His prophets who were sent as messengers be upon Muhammad (saw) and Aal e Muhammad (asws) who are His successors

الحمد لله الذي أنعم علي و عرفني فضل محمد ﷺ و أهل بيتة

Praise be to Allah who bestowed His favor upon me by allowing me to understand the attributes of Muhammad (saw) and His Ahlul Bayt (asws)

Then walk a short distance; taking small steps. Once you arrive at the grave, face towards it and say Allah Akbar thirty times. Then recite:

لا إله إلا الله في علمه منتهى علمه، و لا إله إلا الله بعد علمه منتهى علمه، و لا إله إلا الله مع علمه منتهى علمه

La illaha illallah is with His (Allah) knowledge, La illaha illallaha is the peak of His knowledge, La illaha illallah is the culmination of His knowledge

و الحمد لله في علمه منتهى علمه، و الحمد لله بعد علمه منتهى علمه، و الحمد لله مع علمه منتهى علمه

Alhamdulillah is with His knowledge, Alhamdulillah is the peak of His knowledge, Alhamdulillah is the culmination of His knowledge

و سبحان الله في علمه منتهى علمه، و سبحان الله بعد علمه منتهى علمه، و سبحان الله مع علمه منتهى علمه، و الحمد لله بجميع محامده على جميع نعمه

And SubhanAllah is with His knowledge, SubhanAllah is the peak of His knowledge, SubhanAllah is the culmination of His knowledge

و لا إله إلا الله و الله أكبر و حق له ذلك، لا إله إلا الله الحليم الكريم، لا إله إلا الله العلي العظيم، لا إله إلا الله نور السماوات السبع، و نور الأرضين السبع، و نور العرش العظيم، و الحمد لله رب العالمين

All praise is for Allah, there is no god except Allah, and Allah is the greatest. There is no god except Allah and he is al Haleem al Kareem, There is no god except Allah and He is

Aliul Azeem, There is no god except Allah who is the noor of the seven heavens and the seven earths, and who is also the noor of Arshul Azeem, and all praise is for the Lord of the Worlds

السلام عليك يا حجة الله و ابن حجته

Salam be upon You, O' Hujjatullah and Son of His Hujjat

السلام عليك يا ملائكة الله و زوار قبر ابن نبي الله ﷺ

Salam be upon You, O' Angels of Allah and the zawir of the grave of the Son of the Prophet (saw) of Allah

Then take ten steps and say Allahu Akbar ten times and then while walking recite:

لا إله إلا الله تهليلا لا يحصيه غيره قبل كل و احد و بعد كل و احد و مع كل و احد و عدد كل و احد

La illaha illallah. This is a taleel that cannot be measured by anyone except Allah. A taleel which existed before anyone and which will exist after everyone. A taleel that exists with everyone and is equal to their number

و سبحان الله تسبيحاً لا يحصيه غيره قبل كل واحد و بعد كل و احد و مع كل و احد و عدد كل و احد

SubhanAllah. A tasbih that cannot be measured by anyone other than Allah. Which existed before anyone, and which will exist after everyone. A tasbih, which exists with everyone and is equal to their number

و سبحان الله و الحمد لله و لا إله إلا الله و الله أكبر، قبل كل و احد، و بعد كل و احد، و مع كل و احد، و عدد كل و احد أبداً أبداً أبداً

SubhanAllah and Alhamdulillah and La illaha illallah and Allahu Akbar was before anyone, will be after everyone. It is with everyone. Equal to their number for all of eternity

اللهم إني اشهدك و كفى بك شهيداً، فاشهد لي

O' Allah! I take You as my witness for You alone are sufficient as a witness. Be my witness that:

أني أشهد أنك حق و أن رسولك حق، و أن قولك حق، و أن قضاءك حق، و أن قدرك حق، و أن فعلك حق، و أن حشرك حق، و أن نارك حق، و أن جنتك حق

I testify to Your Haq (truth) and the Haq of Your Messenger (saw), the Haq of Your words, the Haq of Your Will, the Haq of Your decrees, the Haq of Your actions, the Haq of Your Resurrecting, the Haq of Your fire and the Haq of Your Jannah

و أنك مميت الأحياء و أنك محيي الموتى، و أنك باعث من في القبور، و أنك جامع الناس ليوم لاريب فيه، و أنك لا تخلف الميعاد

I testify that You take the life of those who are alive and give life to those who are deceased. You will resurrect those in their graves. You will gather the people for a Day about which there is no doubt and You do not break Your promises

السلام عليك يا حجة الله و ابن حجته

Salam be upon You O' Hujjatullah and the Son of His Hujjat

السلام عليك يا ملائكة الله و يا زوار قبر أبي عبد الله

Salam be upon You, O' Angels of Allah and the zuwar of the grave of Aba Abdullah (asws)

Then walk a short distance, taking small steps with calm reverence, and continuously recite tabkir and taleel while glorifying Allah and His Messenger (saw). Once you arrive at the eastern door, stand there and recite:

أشهد أن لا إله إلا الله وحده لا شريك له، و أشهد أن محمداً عبده و رسوله و أمين الله على خلقه، و أنه سيد الأولين و الآخرين، و أنه سيد الأنبياء و المرسلين

I testify there is no god except Allah. He is alone and has no partner. I testify Muhammad (saw) is His servant and messenger and that He (Muhammad saw) is the trustee of Allah over His (Allah) creation and that He (Muhammad saw) is the master over the first and the last and that He (Muhammad saw) is Syedul Nabieen wa Mursaleen (master of the prophets and messengers)

سلام على رسول الله ﷺ

Salam be upon RasoolAllah (saw)

الحمد لله الذي هدانا لهذا و ما كنا لنهتدي لو لا أن هدانا الله، لقد جاءت رسل ربنا بالحق

Praise be to Allah who guided us to this. For if it were not for the guidance of Allah we would never have been guided. The messengers of our Lord indeed came with haq

اللهم إني أشهد أن هذا قبر ابن حبيبك و صفوتك من خلقك، و أنه الفايز بكر امتك، أكرمته بكتابك، و خصصته و ائتمنته على و حيك، و أعطيته مواريث الأنبياء، و جعلته حجه على خلقك من الأصفياء

O' Allah! I testify this is the grave of the Son of Your Beloved (RasoolAllah saw) and Your Chosen One from amongst Your creation who achieved victory through Your honor. You honored Him (RasoolAllah saw) with Your Book, entrusted Him (RasoolAllah saw) with Your revelation, gave Him (Imam Hussain asws) the inheritance of the prophets, and appointed Him (Imam Hussain asws) as Your Hujjat from amongst the Chosen Ones over Your creation

فأعذر في الدعاء، و بذل مهجته فيك، ليستنقذ عبادك من الضلالة و الجهالة و العمى، و الشك و الإرتياب، إلى باب الهدى من الردى، و أنت ترى و لا ترى، و أنت بالمنظر الأعلى

He strived to call the people towards You. He gave the blood of His heart in Your way to save Your slaves from deviation, ignorance, blindness, doubt, and confusion. And to lead them to the door of guidance and away from destruction. You see all things but cannot be seen. You are at the highest place where You observe all things

حتى ثار عليه من خلقك من غرته الدنيا، ع باع الآخرة بالثمن الأوكس الأدنى، و أسخطك و أسخط رسولك، و أطاع من عبادك من أهل الشقاق و النفاق، و حملة الأوزار من استوجب النار

He guided the people towards You until some of Your creation—who were enamored by this world and sold their hereafter for the lowest price—rose against Him; angering You and Your Messenger (saw) by their obedience of the people of oppression and hypocrisy and those the hellfire is made wajib upon them from amongst Your slaves

لعن الله قاتلي ولد رسولك، وضاعف عليهم العذاب الأليم

May the lanat of Allah be upon the killers of the Son of Your Messenger (saw) and may their painful chastisement be continuously increased

Then move closer to the grave and recite:

السلام عليك يا وارث آدم صفوة الله

Salam be upon You O' inheritor of Adam (as), Safwatullah (the Chosen Servant of Allah)

السلام عليك يا وارث نوح نبي الله

Salam be upon You O' inheritor of Nuh (as), Nabiullah (prophet of Allah)

السلام عليك يا وارث إبراهيم خليل الله

Salam be upon You O' inheritor of Ibrahim (as), Khaleelullah (friend of Allah)

السلام عليك يا وارث موسى كليم الله

Salam be upon You O' inheritor of Musa (as), Kaleemullah (the One Allah spoke to)

السلام عليك يا وارث عيسى روح الله

Salam be upon You O' inheritor of Isa (as), Ruhullah (spirit of Allah)

السلام عليك يا وارث محمد ﷺ حبيب الله

Salam be upon You O' inheritor of Muhammad (saw), Habeebullah (Beloved of Allah)

السلام عليك يا وارث أمير المؤمنينّ علي بن أبي طالبّ وصي رسول الله ﷺ

Salam be upon You O' inheritor of Ameerul Momineen Ali (asws) ibn Abi Talib (as), the successor of RasoolAllah (saw)

السلام عليك يا وارث الحسنّ بن عليّ الزكي

Salam be upon You O' inheritor of Hasan (asws) ibn Ali (asws) al Zaki

السلام عليك يا وارث فاطمة الزهراءّ سعدة نساء العالمين الصديقة

Salam be upon You O' inheritor of Fatima (sa) al Zahra, Syedatul Nisa al Alameen, al Sadiqqi

السلام عليك أيها الصديق الشهيد

Salam be upon You, O' Sadiq (trustworthy) Shaheed (martyr)

السلام عليك أيها الوصي الرضي البار التقي

Salam be upon You, al Wasi, al Razi, al Bar, al Taqi

السلام عليك أيها الوفي النقي

Salam be upon You al Wafi, al Naqi

أشهد أنك قد أقمت الصلاة، آتيت الزكاة، و أمرت بالمعروف، و نهيت عن المنكر، و عبدت الله مخلصاً
حتى أتاك اليقين

I testify You performed salat, paid zakat, enjoined good, forbade evil and worshipped Allah sincerely until that which is certain came over You (when you departed this world)

السلام عليك يا أبا عبد الله ورحمة الله و بركاته

Salam be upon You O' Aba Abdullah and may the mercy and blessings of Allah be upon You

السلام عليك و على الأرواح التي حلت بفنئك و أناخت برحلك

Salam be upon You and to the souls who dismounted alongside You and remained in Your caravan

السلام على ملائكة الله المحدقين بك

Salam be upon the angels of Allah which surround You

السلام على ملائكة الله وزوار قبر ابن نبي الله ﷺ

Salam be upon the angels of Allah and the zuwar of the grave of the Son of the Prophet of Allah (saw)

Then enter the Ha'yr and as you enter, recite:

السلام على ملائكة الله المقربين

Salam be upon the high ranking angels of Allah

السلام على ملائكة الله المنزلين

May the salam of Allah be upon the angels that descend upon Your shrine

السلام على ملائكة الله المسومين

May the salam of Allah be upon the *"havoc-making angels"* (Quran 3:125)

السلام على ملائكة الله الذين هم مقيمون في هذا الحائر بإذن ربهم

Salam be upon the angels of Allah who reside within the Ha'yr by the permission of their Lord

السلام على ملائكة الله هم في هذا الحاير بعملون ولأمر الله مسلمون

Salam be upon the angels of Allah who work in this Ha'yr and submit to the orders of Allah

السلام عليك يا بن رسول الله ﷺ ، و ابن أمين الله، و ابن خالصة الله

Salam be upon You O' Son of RasoolAllah (saw), Son of Ameenullah (trustee of Allah) and Son of the Devoted Slave of Allah

السلام عليك يا أبا عبد اللّة

Salam be upon You O' Aba Abdullah

إنا الله و إنا إليه راجعون

For we belong to Allah and to Him we return

ما أعظم مصيبتك عند جدك رسول الله ﷺ

How immense Your suffering was to Your Grandfather, RasoolAllah (saw)

و ما أعظم مصيبتك عند من عرف الله عز وجل

And how immense was Your suffering for those who know Allah (swt)

و أجل مصيبتك عند الملا الأعلى و عند أنبياء الله و عند رسول اللة

And how immense was Your suffering for those assembled high above with the Prophets and Messengers of Allah

السلام مني إليك و التحية مع عظيم الرزية عليك

My salam be upon You during my time of sorrow over what happened to You

كنت نوراً في الأصلاب الشامخة، و نوراً في ظلمات الأرض، و نوراً في الهواء، و نوراً في السماوات العلى، كنت فيها نوراً ساطعاً لا يطفئ، و أنت الناطق بالهدى

You were a noor from Your Forefathers (asws), a light in the darkness of the earth, in the air, and in the heavens where Your light shines never to be extinguished. For You are the one speaker of guidance

Take a few steps and say Allahu Akbar seven times, taleel seven times, Alhamdulillah seven times and subhanAllah seven times.

Then answer the call of Hussain (asws) seven times by saying:

لبيك داعي الله

I am at Your service. O' Caller of Allah

Then recite:

إن كان لم يجبك بدني عند استغاثتك، و لساني عند استنصارك، فقد أجابك قلبي وسمعي و بصري، و رأي يو هواي، على التسليم لخلف النبي المرسل، و السبط المنتجب، و الدليل العالم، و الأمين المستخزن، و المؤدي المبلغ، و المظلوم المضطهد

327

Even though my body could not answer Your call for help and my tongue did not answer You when You asked for support; my heart, my ears, my eyes, my thoughts, and my desires have answered Your call and submitted to the Remainder of the Prophet (saw) who was sent as a messenger, the Chosen Grandson, the knowledgeable guide, the entrusted guardian, the one who fulfilled His duties and proclaimed the message of Allah, the Oppressed One

جئتك يا مولاي النقطاعاً إليك، و إلى جدك و أبيك، و ولدك الخلف من بعدك

O' my Moula! I have come only to You, Your Grandfather (saw), Your Father (asws), and to Your Son who remains after You (Imam e Zamana atfs)

فقلبي لكم مسلم، و رأيي لكم متبع، و نصرتي لكم معدة، حتى يحكم الله بدينه و يبعثكم

My heart has submitted to You, the Imams (asws). I follow You in my beliefs and my support is ready for You until the judgment of Allah comes upon His religion and until He resurrects You

و اشهد الله أنكم الحجة، و بكم ترجى الرحمة، فمعكم معكم لا مع عدوكم، إني بكم من المؤمنين، لا انكر لله قدرة، و لا اكذب منه بمشية

I take Allah as witness that You, the Imams (asws), are the Hujjat and that mercy can only come through You. I am with You and only with You. I am not with Your enemies. I am amongst those who believe in You. I do not deny the power of Allah nor do I deny His will.

Then walk towards the grave using small steps until you face the grave. Turn your back towards the Qiblah with your face towards His face and recite:

السلام عليك من الله

Salam from Allah be upon You

و السلام على محمد ﷺ أمين الله على رسله و عزائم أمره، الخاتم لما سبق، و الفاتح لما استقبل، و المهيمن على ذلك كله ر رحمة الله و بركاته

And Salam be upon Muhammad (saw), the trustee of Allah over His Messengers and over His decisive affairs, the last of that which came before the one who has yet to come and the absolute master over all. May the mercy and blessings of Allah be upon Him

و السلام عليك و تحياته

Salam be upon You and the salutations of Allah be upon You

اللهم صل على محمد و آل محمد صاحب ميثاقك، و خاتم رسلك، و سيد عبادك، و أمينك في بلادك، و خير بريتك، كما تلا تكابك و جاهد عدوك حتى أتاه اليقين

O' Allah! Send Your blessing upon Muhammad (saw) and Aal e Muhammad (asws), the owner of Your covenant, the last of Your messengers, the master of Your slaves, Your trustee in the lands, and the best of Your creation check translation

اللهم صل على أمير المؤمنين' عبدك و أخي رسولك، الذي انتجبته بعلمك، و جعلته هادياً لمن شئت من خلقك، و الدليل على من بعثت برسالاتك، و ديان الدين بعدلك، و فصل قضائك بين خلقك، و المهيمن على ذلك كله، و السلام عليه و رحمة الله و بركاته

O' Allah! Send Your blessing upon Ameerul Momineen (asws), who is Your servant and the brother of Your Messenger (saw); whom You chose as the trustee of Your knowledge and whom You appointed as a guide upon Your creation and a guide for those upon whom You sent Your message, who is the Hujjat (proof) upon the one You sent with the risalat (prophet hood), and He is the one who will act as judge on the Day of Judgment for He is the absolute master over all things

اللهم أتمم به كلماتك، و أنجز به، و عدك، و أهلك به عدوك، و اكتبنا في أوليائه و أحبائه

O' Allah! Complete Your words, fulfill Your promise, and destroy Your enemies through Him. Record us amongst His Auwilya and lovers

اللهم اجعلنا له شيعة و أنصاراً و أعواناً على طاعتك و طاعة رسولك، و ما و كلته به و استخلفته عليه، يا رب العالمين

O' Allah! Make us amongst His Shia, supporters, and helpers through Your obedience and the obedience of Your Messenger. Make us amongst His supporters in fulfilling that which You entrusted to Him and the affairs over which You gave Him authority, O' Lord of the Worlds

اللهم صل على فاطمةّ بنت نبيك،و زوجة وليك، و ام السبطين الحسنّ و الحسينّ ، الطاهرة المطهرة الصديقة الزكية، سيدة نساء أهل الجنة أجمعين، صلاة لا بقوى على إحصائها غيرك

O' Allah! Send Your blessing upon Fatima (sa), the Daughter of Your Prophet (saw), the wife of Your Wali, the Mother of Your two Grandsons, Hasan (asws) and Hussain (asws), al Taharat, al Mutahir, al Sadiq, al Zaki, Syedatul Nisa Ahlul Jannah, may the immeasurable blessings of Allah— that can only be counted by Allah— be upon You

اللهم صل على الحسنّ بن عليّ عبدك و ابن أخي رسولك، الذي انتجبته بعلم، و جعلته هادياً لمن شئت من خلقك، و الدليل على من بعثته برسالاتك، و ديان الدين بعدلك، و فصلقضائك بين خلقك، و المهيمن على ذلك كله، و السلام عليه و رحمة الله و بركاته

O' Allah! Send Your blessings upon Hasan (asws) ibn Ali (asws), who is Your servant and the brother of Your Messenger (saw); whom You chose as the trustee of Your knowledge and whom You appointed as a guide upon Your creation and a guide for those upon whom You sent Your message, who is the Hujjat (proof) upon the one You sent with the risalat (prophet hood), and He is the one who will act as judge on the Day of Judgment for He is the absolute master over all things. May the salam, mercy and blessings of Allah be upon Him

اللهم صلى على الحسينّ بن عليّ عبدك و ابن أخي رسولك، الذي انتجبيه بعلمك، و جعلته هادياً لمن شئت من خلقك، و الدليل على من بعثته برسالاتك، و ديان الدين بعدلك، و فصل قضائك بين خلقك، و المهيمن على ذلك كله، و السلام عليه و رحمة الله و بركاته

O' Allah! Send Your blessing upon Hussain (asws) ibn Ali (asws) who is Your servant and the brother of Your Messenger (saw); whom You chose as the trustee of Your knowledge and whom You appointed as a guide upon Your creation and a guide for those upon whom You sent Your message, who is the Hujjat (proof) upon the one You sent with the risalat (prophet hood), and He is the one who will act as judge on the Day of Judgment for He is the absolute master over all things. May the mercy, blessings, and salam of Allah be upon Him

Then send blessings on the rest of the Imams (asws) in the same way that you sent blessings on Hasan (asws) and Hussain (asws). Afterwards recite:

اللهم أتمم بهم كلماتك، و أنجز بهم و أهلك بهم عدوك و عدوهم من الجن و الإنس أجمعين

O' Allah! Complete Your words by Them, fulfill Your promise through Them, and destroy all of Your enemies and Their enemies from amongst the jinn and mankind through Them

اللهم اجز هم عنا خير ما جازيت نذيراً عن قومه

O' Allah! Reward Them on our behalf with a reward, which is greater than any reward You have ever given to a warner on behalf of His nation

اللهم اجعلنا لهم شيعة و أنصاراً و أعواناً، على طاعتك و طاعة رسولك

O' Allah! Make us amongst Their Shia, supporters, and helpers through Your obedience and the obedience of Your Messenger (saw)

اللهم اجعلنا ممن يتبع النور الذي انزل معهم، و أهينا محياهم، و أمتنا مماتهم، و أشهدنا مشاهدهم في الدنيا و الآخرة

O' Allah! Make us amongst those who follow the noor, which descended with Them. And make us live the way They lived and cause us to leave this world the way They left this world, and allow us to visit Their places in this world and in the hereafter

اللهم إن هذا مقام أكر متني به، و شرفتني به، و أعطيتني فيه رغبتي على حقيقة إيماني بك وبرسولك

O' Allah! You have honored and blessed me by allowing me to be here and You have granted that which I desired through my sincere belief in You and in Your messengers

Then move closer to the grave and recite:

السلام عليك يا بن رسول الله ﷺ

Salam be upon You, O' Son of RasoolAllah (saw)

و سلام الله و سلام ملائكته المقربين و أنبيائه المرسلين، كلما تروح الرائحات الطاهرات لك

And the salam of Allah, His high ranked angels, and His prophets who were sent as messengers be upon You along with the purified salutations that are sent to You at all times

و عليك سلام المؤمنين لك بقلوبهم، الناطقين لك بفضلك بألسنتهم

Salam be upon You from those whose hearts believe in You and whose tongues speak Your virtues

أشهد أنك صادق صديق فيما دعوت إليه و صدقت فيما أتيت به، و أنك ثار الله في الأرض

I testify You are Sadiq (trustworthy). You were truthful in that which You called the people towards and You were truthful about that which You brought forth. For Allah will avenge You on the earth

اللهم أسخلني في أوليائك، و حبب إلي شهادتهم و مشاهدهم في الدنيا و الآخرة، إنك على كل شيء قدير

O' Allah! Include me amongst the followers of Your Divinely Appointed Authorities. And make me desire to be martyred the way They were martyred and allow me to visit Their shrines in this life and in the hereafter. For You have power over all things.

Then recite:

السلام عليك يا أبا عبد اللّة، رحمك الله يا أبا عبد اللّة، صلى الله عليك يا أبا عبد اللّة

Salam be upon You O' Aba Abdullah. May the mercy of Allah be upon You O' Aba Abdullah May the blessings of Allah be upon You O' Aba Abdullah

السلام عليك يا إمام الهدى

Salam be upon You O Imam al Hadi (Imam of Guidance)

السلام عليك يا علم التقى

Salam be upon You, O' Alam al Taqi (Flag of Piety)

السلام عليك يا حجة الله على أهل الدنيا

Salam be upon You, O' Hujjatullah (Proof of Allah) over the people of the world

السلام عليك يا حجة الله و ابن حجته

Salam be upon You, O' Hujjatullah and the Son of His Hujjat

السلام عليك يا بن نبي الله ﷺ

Salam be upon You O' Son of RasoolAllah (saw)

السلام عليك يا ثار الله و ابن ثاره

Salam be upon You, O' Tharullah and Son of His Thar

السلام عليك يا وتر الله و ابن وتره

Salam be upon You, O' the Unavenged One of Allah and O' Son of the Unavenged One of Allah

أشهد أنك قتلك مظلوماً و أن قاتلك في النار، و أشهد أنك جاهدت في سبيل الله حق جهاده، لم تأخذك في الله لومة لائم، و أنك عبدته حتى أتاك اليقين

I testify You were martyred unjustly and that Your killer is in hell. I testify You fought in the way of Allah the way Allah should be fought for. You were not affected by the denials of any denier and You worshipped Allah until that which is certain came to You

أشهد أنكم كلمة التقوى، و باب الهدى، و الحجة على خلقه، أشهد أن ذلك لكم سابق فيما مضى، و فاتح فيما بقي

I testify that You, the Imams (asws), are Kalamat al Taqwa (words of piety), Babul Hadi (doors of guidance), and Hujjat (proof) upon the creation of Allah. I testify that You have always held these status and they will remain apparent in You

و أشهد أن أرواحكم و طينتكم طينة طيبة، طابت و طهرت بعضها من الله و مان رحمته

I testify that Your souls and Your clay are from purified clay. They purified and blessed one another through Allah and His mercy

و أشهد الله تبارك و تعالى و كفى به شهيداً، و اشهدكم أني بكم مؤمن و لكم تابع في ذات نفسي، و شرايع ديني و خواتيم عملي و منقلبي و مثواي

I take Allah as witness for He is sufficient as a witness and I take You, the Imams (asws), as witnesses that I believe in You and follow You in my affairs, in the rulings of my religion, in my deeds, and in my destination in the hereafter

فأسال الله البر الرحيم أن يتمم ذلك لي

I ask Allah, al Bar, al Raheem, to fulfill this for me

أشهد أنكم قد بلغتم ونصحتم، و صبرتم و قتلتم، ع غصبتم و اسيء إليكم فصبرتم

I testify that You, the Imams (asws), proclaimed and advised the people on the message of Allah. You remained patient. You were martyred. Your rights were usurped. You were abused and yet You remained patient

لعن الله امة خالفتكم، و امة جحدت و لايتكم، و امة تظاهرت عليكم، و امة شهدت و لم تستشهد

May the lanat of Allah be upon the nation who opposed You, upon the nation who denied Your wilayat, upon the nation who supported those against You, and upon the nation who witnessed Your martyrdom but did not fight alongside You

الحمد لله الذي جعل النار مثواهم، و بس الورد المورود، و بس الرفد المرفود

Praise be to Allah who made hell their final destination. What a terrible destination hell is and what a terrible punishment their chastisement is!

Then recite:

صلى الله عليك يا أبا عبدالله، صلى الله عليك يا أبا عبدالله، صلى الله عليك يا أبا عبدالله، و على روحك و بدنك

May the blessings of Allah be upon You, O' Aba Abdullah. May the blessings of Allah be upon You, O' Aba Abdullah. May the blessings of Allah be upon You, O' Aba Abdullah, and upon Your ruh and Your body

لعن الله قاتليك

May the lanat of Allah be upon those who martyred You

و لعن الله سالبيك

May the lanat of Allah be upon those who looted Your dead body

لعن الله خاذليك

May the lanat of Allah be upon those who disappointed You

و لعن الله من شايع على قتلك، و مان أمر بقتلك، و شارك في دمك، و لعن الله من بلغه ذلك فرضي به أو سلم إليه

May the lanat of Allah be upon those who followed the orders to martyr You and upon those who ordered the people to martyr You and those who participated in the spilling of Your blood May the lanat of Allah be upon those who heard of Your martyrdom and were pleased with by it or made peace with it

أنا أبرء إلى الله من ولايتهم، و أتولى الله و رسوله ﷺ و آل رسوله

I seek the nearness of Allah by disassociating myself from following them (enemies of Ahlul Bayt asws) and by following Allah, His Messenger (saw), and the Family of His Messenger (saw)

و أشهد أن الذين انتهكوا حرمتك و سفكوا دمك ملعونون، ولى لسان النبي الامي

I testify that those who violated Your holiness and spilled Your blood are accursed by the tongue of the Prophet (saw) of Mecca

اللهم العن الذين كذبوا رسلك، و سفكوا دماء أهل بيتّ نبيك صلواتك عليهم

O' Allah! Send lanat upon those who denied Your messengers and spilled the blood of the Ahlul Bayt (asws) of Your Prophet (saw). May the blessings of Allah be upon Them

اللهم العن قتله أمير المؤمنينّ ، ضاعف عليهم العذاب الأليم

O' Allah! Send lanat upon the killers of Ameerul Momineen (asws) and continuously increase the chastisement on them

اللهم العن قتله الحسينّ بن عليّ ، ق قتله أنصار الحسينّ بن عليّ، و أصلهم حر نارك، و أذقهم بأسك، و ضاعف عليهم العذاب الأليم، و العنهم لعناً و بيلاً

O' Allah! Send lanat upon the killers of Hussain (asws) ibn Ali (asws) and the killers of the supporters of Hussain (asws) ibn Ali (asws). Burn them with Your fire. Make them taste Your wrath, increase the chastisement on them and send a severe lanat upon them

اللهم احلك بهم نقمتك، وآتهم من حيث لا يحتسبون، و خذهم من حيث لا يشعرون، و عذبهم عذاباً نكراً

O' Allah! Cause Your wrath to fall upon them, attack them when they do not expect it, seize them when they are unaware, and punish them with a intense punishment

و العن أعداء نبيك و أعداء آل نبيك لعناً و بيلاً

And send lanat upon the enemies of Your Prophet (saw) and the enemies of the Family of Your Prophet (saw) with a severe lanat

اللهم لعن الجبت و الطاغوت و الفراعنة، إنك على كل شيء قدير

O' Allah! Send lanat upon Jibt, Taghut, and the pharaohs. For You have power over all things

Then recite:

بأبي أنت و امي يا أبا عبد اللّة، إليك كانت رحلتي مع بعد شقتي، و لك فاضت عبرتي، و عليك كان أسفي و نحيبي، و صراخي و زفرتي و شهيقي

May I sacrifice my father and mother upon You, O' Aba Abdullah! I have traveled to You even though my home is far. I have shed tears over You. My sorrow, my grief, my sorrow and my sobbing is over You

و إليك كان مجيئي، و بك أستتر من عظيم جرمي، أتيتك زائراً و افداً قد أوقرت ظهري

I came to You and I use You to hide from my sins. I have come to You as a zawir and a guest whose back has become heavy from the weight of my sins

بأبي أنت و امي يا سعدي، بكيتك يا خيرة الله و ابن خيرته، و حق لي أن أبكيك، و قد بكتك السماوات و الأرضون، و الجبال والبحار

May I sacrifice my mother and my father upon You, O' my Master. I have wept over You, O' Khairatullah (best of the creation of Allah) and Son of Khairatullah. I should be grieving over You because the heavens, the earths, the mountains, and the seas grieve over You

فما عذري إن لم أبكم، و قد بكاك حبيب ربي، و بكتك الأئمةّ ، و بكاك من دون سدرة المنتهى

What can be my excuse for not weeping over You while the Beloved of My Lord (RasoolAllah saw) and the Imams (asws) mourn over You and everyone below Sidratul Muntaha to the earth mourn sincerely over You?

Then touch the grave and recite:

السلام عليك يا أبا عبدالله ّ يا حسينّ بن عليّ يا بن رسول الله ﷺ

Salam be upon You, O' Aba Abdullah, O' Hussain (asws) ibn Ali (asws), O' Son of RasoolAllah (saw)

السلام عليك يا حجة الله و ابن حجته

Salam be upon You O' Hujjatullah and the Son of His Hujjat

أشهد أنك عبد الله و أمينه، بلغت ناصحاً و أديت أميناً، و قلت صادقاً و قتلك صديقاً، فمضيت شهيداً و مضيت على يقين، لم تؤثر عمى على هدى، و لم تملمن حق إلى باطل، و لم تجب إلا الله وحده

I testify that You are the servant of Allah and His trustee. You proclaimed the message of Allah with sincerity and fulfilled Your duties faithfully. You spoke the truth. You were martyred as al Sadiq (most trustworthy). You left this world with certainty as a martyr. You did not prefer the blindness of ignorance over guidance. You did not lean towards falsehood and away from Haq. You did not answer the call of anyone except Allah alone

و أشهد أنك كنت على بينة من ربك، بلغت ما امرت به، و قمت بحقه، و صدقت من كان قلك غير و اهن و لا ميهن، فصلى الله عليك و سلم تسليماً

I testify You had understanding of Your Lord. You proclaimed that which You were ordered to. You fulfilled Your duties towards Him. You believed in the haq of those appointed by Allah who preceded You without weakness. May the salam and blessings of Allah be upon You

جزاك الله من صديق خيراً، أشهد أن ال جهاد معك جهاد

337

May Allah reward You with the most truthful and best of rewards. I testify that jihad is only jihad if it is with You

و أن الحق معك و إليك، و أنت أهله و معدنه، و ميراث النبوة عندك و عند أهل بيتكّ

And I testify that haq is with You and leads You. For You are the source of haq and from amongst its people. I testify that the inheritance of the nabuwiyat is for You and Your Ahlul Bayt (asws)

و أشهد أنك قد بلغت و نصحت و وتيت و جاهدت في سبيل الله بالحكمة و الموعظة الحسنة

I testify that You proclaimed the message of Allah. That You advised the people and remained loyal to Allah. You fought in the way of Allah with wisdom and good counsel

و مضيت الذي كنت عليه شهيداً و مستشهداً، فصلى الله عليك و سلم تسليما

You were martyred the way You lived—as a martyr who desired martyrdom and witnessed by Allah. May the blessings and salam of Allah be upon You

أشهد أنك طهر طاهر مطهر، من طهر طاهر مطهر

I testify that You are Tuhir (purity), and Tahir (pure)and that You are the Son of Tuhir, Tahir, and Mutahir

طهرت و طهرت أرض أنت بها، و طهر حرمك

You are pure, the land in which You are is pure and Your haram is pure

و أشهد أنك أمرت بالقسط و العدل، و دعوت إليهما، و أشهد أن امة قتلتك أشرار خلق الله و كفرته

I testify that You enjoined equality and justice and called the people towards it. And I testify that the nation who killed You is the most evil and the most disbelieving creation of Allah

و إني أستشفع بك إلى الله ربك و ربي من جميع ذنيبي، و أتوجه بك إلى الله في جميع حوائجي و رغبتي، في أمر آخرتي و دنياي

I ask Allah who is Your Lord and my Lord for intercession through You for all of my sins. I turn to Allah through You for all of my wants and needs which pertains to matters of the hereafter and this life

Then place your right cheek on the grave and recite:

اللهم إني أسألك بحق هذا القبر و من فيه، و بحق هذه القبور و من أسكنتها، أن تكتب اسمي عندك في وُسمائهم حتى توردني مواردهم، و تصدرني مصادر هم، إتك على كل شيء قدير

O' Allah! I ask You through the right of this grave and He who is buried within it. I ask You through the right of these graves and those whom You have made to dwell within them, to record my name with You amongst Their names so that You take me to where

They are and cause me to reach where they have reached. For You are powerful over all things.

Then recite:

رب أفحتني ذنوبي و قطعت مقالتي، فلا حجة لي و لا عذر لي

O' Lord! My sins have left no excuse for me and have left me silent and now I have no excuse

فأنا المقر بذنبي، الأسير ببليتي، المرتهن بعملي، المتجلد في خطيئتي، المتحير عن قصدي، المنقطع بي

I admit my sins and I am the prisoner of the afflictions I inflicted upon myself. I am held hostage by my actions, compelled by my sins, confused about my destination, and unsure of how to reach it

قد أوقفت نفسي يا رب موقف الأشقياء المذنبين، المجترئين عليك، المستخفين بوعيدك

O' Lord! I have placed myself alongside the wretched, disgraced and sinful ones who insulted You and underestimated Your promise of punishment

يا سبحانك، أي جرأة اجترءت عليك، و أي تغرير غررت بنفسي، و أي سكرة أوبقتني، و أي غفلة أعطبتني، ما كان أقبح سوء نظري، و أوحش فعلي

You are glorified. How could I ever challenge You? And with what temptations have I deceived myself? What intoxicants have impaired me? What negligence has overcome me? How terrible my thoughts are and how inhumane are my actions.

يا سيدي فارحم كبوتي لحر و جهي و زلة قدمي و تعفيري في التراب خدي و ندامتي على مافرط مني

O' my Master! Have mercy on me as I fall down upon my face for all that I have done, for the slipping of my foot, for placing my cheek on dust and for regretting my sins

و أقلني عثرتي، و ارحم صراخي و اقبل معذرتي، و عد بحلمك على جهلي، و بإحسانك على خطيئاتي، و بعفوك علي، رب أشكو إليك قساوة قلبي، و ضعف عملي، فامنح بمسألتي

Remove my sins and have mercy upon my wailing and my tears. Accept my apology, through Your patience and compassion overlook my ignorance and sins and turn towards me with Your forgiveness. O' Lord I complain to You of the cruelty of my heart and the weakness of my deeds; therefore fulfill my requests

فأنا المقر بذنبي، المعترف بخطيئتي، و هذه يدي و ناصيتي، أستكين لك بالقود من نفسي، فاقبل توبتي، و نفس كربتي

I am the one who testified regarding his sins and admitted his errors. This is my hand. This is my forehead. I have surrendered myself, shackled, before You. Therefore accept my repentance and relieve my suffering

و ارحم خشوعي و خضوعي و انقطاعي إليك سيدي و أسفي على ما كان مني و تضرعي و تعفيري في تراب قبر ابن نبيك بين يديك

Have mercy on my meekness, my submission, and my devotion to You. And have mercy on my sorrow over the things I have done. Have mercy on me for asking You and for covering my face—as I stand before You—with the dust of the grave of the Son of Your Prophet (saw)

فأنت رجائي و ظهري و عدتي و معتمدي، لا إله إلا أنت

You are my hope, my support, and my means. I rely only on You. For there is no god except You.

Then say Allahu Akbar thirty-five times. After raise your hands and recite:

إليك يا رب صمدت من أرضي، و إلى ابن نبيك قطعت البلاد رجاء للمغفرة

O' Lord! I have departed my homeland in order to come to You. I have traveled across the countries towards the Son of Your Prophet (saw) all the while seeking Your forgiveness

فكن لي يا ولي الله سكناً و شفيعاً، و كن بي رحيماً، و كن لي منجأً يوم لا تنفع الشفاعة عنده إلا لمن ارضى، يوم لاتنفع شفاعة الشافعين، و يوم يقول أهل الضلالة ما لنا من شافعين و لا صديق حميم

O' Wali of Allah, be the cause of my peace, be my intercessor and be merciful to me. Act as my salvation on the day when *"no intercession except for those He approves"* (Quran 21:28) will be of any help for him and on the day when those who have gone astray will say *"Now we have no intercessors, nor any true loving friend"* (Quran 26:100-101)

فكن يومئذ في مقامي بين يدي ربي لي منقذاً، فقد عظم جرمي إذا ارتعدت فرائصي، و اخذ بسمعي، و أنا منكس رأسي بما قدمت من سوء عملي و أنا عار كما و لدتني امي و ربي يسألني

Be my salvation on that day. The day when I will stand before my Lord with crimes so great I will tremble with fear and the sound of which will deafen me. I will stand there bare as the day my mother gave birth to me, my head lowered from the weight of the evil deeds I have brought forth as my Lord questions me.

فكن لي يومئذ شافعاً و منقذاً، فقد أعددتك ليوم حاجتي و يوم فقري و فاقتي

Be my salvation and intercessor on that day. For You are that which I prepared for the day of my need , the day of my poverty, and the day of my destitution

Then place your left cheek on the grave and recite:

اللهم ارحم تضر عي في تراب قبر انب قبر نبيك ﷺ فإني معضع رحمة يا رب

O' Allah! Have mercy on me for I beg You while standing on the dust of the grave of the Son of Your Prophet (saw). For I am in that place where Your mercy can be expected, O' Lord

Then recite:

بأبي أنت و امي يا بن رسول الله ﷺ

May I sacrifice my mother and my father upon You, O' Son of RasoolAllah (saw)

إني أبرء إلى الله من قاتلك و من سالبك، يا ليتني كنت معك فأفوز فوزاً عظيماً، و أبذل مهجتي فيك، و أقيك بنفسي، و كنت فيمن أقام بين يديك حتى يسفك دمي معك، فأظف معك بالسعادة و الفوز بالجنة

I seek the nearness of Allah by disassociating myself from Your killers and from those who looted Your body. I wish I had been with You so that I would also have been victorious. Giving the blood of my life for You; protecting You. I wish I had been amongst those who stood before You so that my blood could have been spilled with You and I could have earned the everlasting happiness with You in jannah

Then recite:

لعان الله من رماك

May the lanat of Allah be upon he who threw an arrow at You

لعن الله من طعنك

May the lanat of Allah be upon he who stabbed You

لعن الله من اجتز رأسك

May the lanat of Allah be upon he who beheaded You

لعن الله من حمل رأسك

May the lanat of Allah be upon he who carried Your head

لعن الله من نكت بقضيبه بين ثناياك

May the lanat of Allah be upon he who hit Your teeth with his staff

لعن الله من أبكى نساءك

May the lanat of Allah be upon he who made Your women cry

لعن الله من أيتم أولادك

May the lanat of Allah be upon he who made Your children orphans

لعن الله من أعان عليك

May the lanat of Allah be upon he who helped Your enemies against You

لعن الله من سار إليك

May the lanat of Allah be upon he who traveled to join those against You

لعن الله من منعك من ماء الفرات

May the lanat of Allah be upon he who forbade You from drinking the water of the River Furat

لعن الله من غشك و خلاك

May the lanat of Allah be upon he who cheated and abandoned You

لعن الله من سمع صوتك فلم يجبك

May the lanat of Allah be upon he who heard Your voice but did not answer Your call

لعن الله ابن آكلة الأكباد

May the lanat of Allah be upon the son of the liver eater (muawiyah la)

لعن الله من ابنه و أعوانه و أتباعه و أنصاره و ابن سمية

May the lanat of Allah be upon his son (yazid la) and the son of sumayyah (ubaidullah ibn ziyad la) and upon his supporters, helpers, and followers

و لعن الله جميع قاتليك و قاتلي أبيك و من أعان على قتلكم

May the lanat of Allah be upon all of Your killers and the killers of Your Father and those who helped them to martyr You

و حشا الله أجو افهم و بطونهم وقبورهم ناراً، و عذبهم عذاباً أليماً

May Allah fill their intestines, stomachs, and graves with fire and punish them with a most grievous chastisement

Then recite the tasbih of Ameerul Momineen (asws) one thousand times beside His head. Or you can also move towards His feet and perform supplications in the way We mentioned to you. Then after the supplication, you can move back to His head and recite the tasbih. The tasbih should be recited after performing the prayer of Ziarat and that prayer is as follows:

سبحان من لا تبيد معالمه

Glorified is He whose signs do not perish

سبحان من لا تنقص خزائنه

Glorified is He whose treasury is infinite.

سبحان من لا انقطاع لمدته

Glorified is He whose time does not end

سبحان من لا ينفد ما عنده

Glorified is He whom whatever He has it will not finish

سبحان من لا اضمحلال لفخره

Glorified is He whose glory does not disappear

سبحان من لا يشاور أحداً في أمره

Glorified is He who is alone in His command

سبحان من لا إله غيره

Glorified is He besides whom there is no god

Then move beside His feet, place Your hand on the grave, and recite:

صلى الله عليك يا أبا عبدالله، صلى الله عليك يا أبا عبدالله، صلى الله يا أبا عبدالله

May the blessings of Allah be upon You O' Aba Abdullah! May the blessings of Allah be upon You O' Aba Abdullah! May the blessings of Allah be upon You O' Aba Abdullah!

صبرت و أنت الصادق، قتل الله من قتلم بالأيدي و الألسن

You remained patient. You are al Sadiq. May Allah slaughter those who slaughtered You whether they did so by their tongue or their hands

Then recite:

اللهم رب الأرباب، صريح الأخيار، إني عذت معاذاً، ففك رقبتي من النار

O' Allah! Lord of the Lords! Rescuer of the Righteous Ones! I sincerely seek refuge with You. Therefore release me from the hellfire

جئتك يا بن رسول الله ﷺ و افداً إليك ، توسل إلى الله في جميع حوائجي من أمر آخرتي و دنياي، و بك يتوسل إلى الله في جميع جوائجهم، و بك يدرك أهل الثواب من عباد الله طليبتهم

O' Son of RasoolAllah (saw)! I have come to You as Your guest, in order to ask Allah regarding all of my needs in this world and in the hereafter. For those who ask Allah, do so through You. It is through You the slaves of Allah are rewarded and their requests are fulfilled

أسال وليك و ولينا أن يجعل حظي من زيارتك الصلاة على محمد ﷺ و آلة، و المغفرة الذنوبي

As my reward for performing Your Ziarat, I ask He—who has more authority upon You and us—to send His blessing upon Muhammad (saw) and His Family (asws) and to forgive my sins.

اللهم اجعلنا ممن تنصره وتنتصر به لدينك في الدنيا و الآخرة

O' Allah! Cause us to be amongst those whom You support and those whom You use to support Your religion in this life and in the hereafter

Then place Your cheeks upon the grave and recite:

اللهم رب الحسينّ اشف صدر الحسينّ

O' Allah! Lord of Hussain (asws), heal the chest of Hussain (asws)

اللهم رب الحسينّ اطلب بدم الحسينّ

O' Allah! Lord of Hussain (asws), avenge the blood of Hussain (asws)

اللهم رب الحيسينّ انتقم ممن خلاف الحسينّ

O' Allah! Lord of Hussain (asws) seek vengeance from those who oppose Hussain (asws)

اللهم رب الحسينّ انتقم ممن فرح بقتل الحسينّ

O' Allah! Lord of Hussain (asws) seek vengeance from those who were joyful regarding the martyrdom of Hussain (asws)

Continuously ask Allah to send lanat upon the killers of Hussain (asws) and the killers of Ameerul Momineen (asws). Then recite the tasbih of Syeda Fatima (sa) one thousand times beside His feet. If you cannot recite one thousand times, then recite it one hundred times.

The tasbih of Syeda Fatima (sa) is:

سبحان ذي العز الشامخ المنيف

Glorified is the owner of glory, the High, the Exalted

سبحان ذي الجلال و الإكرام الفاخر العظيم

Glorified is the owner of majesty and honor, the Superior, the Great

سبحان ذي الملك الفاخر القديم

Glorified is the owner of the kingdom, the Superior, the Everlasting

سبحان ذي الملك الفاخر العظيم

Glorified is the owner of the kingdom, the Superior, the Great

سبحان من لبس العز و الجمال

Glorified is He who is encompassed with Grace and Beauty

سبحان من تردى بالنور والوقار

Glorified is He who is encompassed with Light and Dignity

سبحان من يرى أثر النمل في الصفا، و خفقان الطير في الهواء

Glorified is He who is aware of the needs of an ant on flat stones and the birds flying in the sky

سبحان من هو هكذا و لا هكذا غيره

Glorified is He who possesses these attributes, which are not possessed by any other than Him

Then go to the grave of Ali (asws) ibn Hussain (asws)—located at the feet of Hussain (asws)— and recite:

السلام عليك يا بن رسول الله ﷺ و بركاته

Salam be upon You, O' Son of RasoolAllah (saw), the mercy and blessings of Allah be upon You

و ابن خليفة رسول الله ﷺ ، و ابن نبت رسول الله ﷺ ، و رحمة الله و بركاته مضاعفة، كلما طلعت شمس أو غربت

And Son of the Caliph of RasoolAllah (saw) and Son of the Daughter of RasoolAllah (saw). May the ever-increasing blessings and mercy of Allah be upon You for as long as the sun rises and sets

السلام عليك و على روحك و بدنك، بأبي أنت و امي من مذبوح و مقتول من غير جرم

Salam be upon You, Your ruh, and Your body. May I sacrifice my mother and father upon You O' martyred one who was martyred without having committed any crime

بأبي أنت و امي دمك المرتقى به إلى حبيب الله

May I sacrifice my mother and father upon You, O' One whose blood was taken up to the Beloved of Allah (RasoolAllah saw)

بأبي أنت و امي من مقدم بين يدي أبيك يحتسبك و يبكي عليك، محترقاً عليك قلبه، يرفع دمك بكفه إلى أعنان السماء لا ترجع منه قطرة، و لا تسكن عليك من أبيك زفرة، و دعك للفراق

May I sacrifice my mother and father upon You! You stood before Your Father who wept but remained patient, knowing the rewards from Allah for His (Imam Hussain asws) having lost You (Hz Ali Asghar asws). His heart ached over You and He raised Your blood with His hands to the heavens and not a single drop from Your blood returned to the earth. Your Father's sorrow over You did not stop after He bid farewell to You

فمكانكما عند الله مع آبائك الماضين، و مع امهاتك في الجنان منعمين، أبرء إلى الله ممن قتلك و ذبحك

The status the Two of You (Hz Ali Asghar (asws) and Imam Hussain (asws)) have before Allah is with Your Forefathers and Your Mothers who are blessed in the heavens. I seek the nearness of Allah by disassociating myself from those who martyred You and oppressed You

Then fall upon the grave, place your hands upon it and recite:

سلام الله و سلام ملائكته المقربين، و أنبيائه المرسلين و عباده الصالحين عليك يا مولاي و ابن مولاي، و رحمة الله و بركاته

Salam of Allah, His high-ranking angels, His prophets who came as messengers, and His righteous slaves be upon You, O' my Moula and the Son of My Moula (asws)—may the mercy and blessings of Allah be upon You

صلى الله عليك و على عترتك و أهل بيتك و آبائك، و أبنائك و امهاتك الأخيار الأبرار الذين أذهب الله عنهم الرجس و طهر هم تطهيراً

May the blessings of Allah be upon You, upon Your pious Ahlul Bayt (asws), Your Family, Your Fathers, Your Children, and Your Mothers; whom Allah kept all impurities and uncleanliness from Them

السلام عليك يا بن رسول الله ﷺ و ابن أمير المؤمنينّ و ابن الحسينّ بن عليّ، و رحمة الله و بركاته

Salam be upon You O' Son of RasoolAllah (saw), Son of Ameerul Momineen (asws), and Son of Hussain (asws) ibn Ali (asws)—may the blessings and mercy of Allah be upon You

لعن الله قاتلك

May the lanat of Allah be upon Your killers

و لعن الله من استخف بحقكم و قتلكم

May the lanat of Allah be upon those who belittled Your rights and martyred You

لعن الله من بقي منهم و من مضى

May the lanat of Allah be upon those who have already died and on those who are still living

نفسي فداؤكم و لمضجعكم

May I be sacrificed upon You and Your graves

صلى الله عليكم و سلم تسليماً كثيراً

May the ever-increasing blessings and salam of Allah be upon You

Then place your cheek on the grave and recite:

صلى الله عليك يا أبا الحسنّ، صلى الله عليك يا أبا الحسنّ، صلى الله عليك يا أبا الحسنّ، بأبي أنت و امي

May the blessings of Allah be upon You, O' Abul Hasan (asws). May the blessings of Allah be upon You O' Abul Hasan (asws) May the blessings of Allah be upon You O' Abul Hasan (asws) May my mother and father be sacrificed upon You

أسأل الله وليك وولي أن يجعل حظي من زيارتك عتق رقبتي من النار

I have come to Your Ziarat as Your guest while seeking refuge with You for the sins I committed against myself and the sins which I carry upon my back

أسال الله و ليك و وليي أن يجعل حظي من زيارتك عتق رقبتي من النار

As my reward for performing Your Ziarat, I ask Allah—who has more authority over You and me— to release me from the fire of hell

349

Then pray for whatever you want and go around the grave until you come to His head. Perform two rakats of prayer beside His head. In the first rakat, recite Sura al Hamd and Sura Yaseen. In the second rakat recite Sura al Hamd and Sura al Rahman. You may perform salat behind the grave, but it is better to perform salat beside His head. After you finish these two rakats, you may pray as much as you wish. But you must perform these two rakats of prayer of Ziarat beside each grave. Once you have finished performing prayers, raise your hands and recite:

اللهم إنا أتيناه مؤمنين به، مسلمين له، معتصمين بحبله، عارفين بحقه، مقرين بفضله، مستبصرين بضلالة من خالفه، عارفين بالهدى هو عليه

O' Allah! We have come to Him (Hussain asws) while believing in Him, submitting to Him, clinging to His rope, understanding His rights, and proclaiming His attributes. We are aware of the deviation of those who opposed Him, and we are aware of the path of guidance on which He stood

اللهم إني اشهدك و اشهد من حضر من ملائكتك، أني بهم مؤمن، و أني بمن قتلهم كافر

O' Allah! I take You as witness and I take those angels of Yours who were present here as witnesses that I believe in Them (Imams asws) and I disassociate myself from those who martyred Them

اللهم اجعل لما أقول بلساني حقيقة في قلبي، و شريعة في عملي

O' Allah! Make the words I speak with my tongue be a truth that lives in my heart and a guidance in my actions

اللهم اجعلني ممن له مع الحسينِّ بن عليّ قدم ثابت، و أُثبتني فيمن استشهد معه

O' Allah! Cause me to be amongst those who have their foot steady on the path of Hussain (asws) ibn Ali (asws) and record me amongst those who were martyred with Him

اللهم العن الذين بدلوا بعمتك كفراً

O' Allah! Send lanat on those who denied Your blessings through kufar

سبحانك يا حليم عما يعمل الظالمون في الأرض، تباركت و تعاليت يا عظيم، ترى عظيم الجرم من عبادك فلا تعجل عليهم، تعاليت يا كريم

You are glorified, O' Forbearing One. You are blessed and exalted. You see the great crimes of Your slaves but do not hurry to punish them O' Greatest One. You are exalted O' Generous

أنت شاهد غير غائب، و عالم بما اتي إلى أهل صفوتك و أحبائك من الأمر الذي لا تحمله سماء و لا أرض

You are witness and present over all things. You know all that was done against Your Chosen Ones and Your Loved Ones even those things the heavens and earth cannot bear

و لو شئت لا نتقمت منهم و لكنك ذو أناة و قد أمهلت الذين اجترؤوا عليك و على سولك ﷺ و حبيبك

Had You willed, You could have avenged Them already. Yet You are patient and have given respite to those who dared You and dared Your Messenger (saw) and Your Beloved

فأسكنتهم أرضك، و غذوتهم بنعمتك، إلى أجل هم بالغوه، و وقت هم صائرون إليه، ليستكملوا العمل الذي قدرت، و الأجل الذي أجلت

You allowed them to dwell within Your earth. You fed them from Your blessings until the appointed time, which will come upon them. Toward that appointed time they continue moving; all the while continuing to perform evil deeds until that time you have appointed for them

لتخلدهم في محط و وثاق و نار جهنم، و حميم و غساق، و الضريع و الأحراق، و الأغلال و الأوثاق، و غسلين و زقوم و صديد، مع طول المقام في أيام لظى، و في سقر التي لا تبقي و لا تذر وفي الحميم و الجحيم

When that time comes, You will make them dwell eternally in devastation and shackled in the fire of hell, in **HAMEEM** (*boiling fluid Quran 38:57*) and **GHASSAQ** (*a fluid intensely dark, murky and cold Quran 38:57*), tortured by burning thorns, chained and manacled in **GHISLEEN** (*"filth" Quran 69:36*),, **ZAQOOM** (*Quran 37:62-66*), and **SADEED** (*festering water Quran 14:16*). They shall last eternally in the time of burning in the fire of **SAQAR** (*Quran 74:26-30*) which *"leaves naught nor does it spare aught"* (Quran 74:28) and they will last eternally in **HAMEEM** and hellfire

Then fall upon the grave and recite:

351

يا سيدي أتيتك زائراً موقراً من الذنوب، أتقرب إلى ربي بوفودي إليك، و بكائي عليك، و عويلي و حسرتي و أسفي و بكائي

O' my Master! I have come to Your Ziarat while carrying my sins and seeking nearness to my Lord by coming to You, mourning, grieving, and weeping over You

و ما أخاف على نفسي رجاء أن تكون لي حجاباً و سنداً و كهفاً و حرزاً و شافعاً و وقاية من النار غداً

And carrying that about which I fear (my sins) and hoping You will keep me away from the hellfire and that You will be my support, my cave, my protector, and my intercessor and that You will shield me from the fire of tomorrow (day of judgment)

و أنا من مواليكم الذين اعادي عدوكم و اوالي و ليكم، على ذلك أحيا و على ذلك أموت، و عليه ابعث إن شاء الله تعالى

I am one of Your followers. I disassociate myself from Your enemies and I love Your friends. InshaAllah I will live, die and be resurrected while maintaining this belief

و قد أشخصت بدني، و ودعت أهلي، و بعدت شقتي، و اؤمل فى قربكم النجاة، و أرجو في أيامكم الكرة، و أطمع في النظر إليكم و إلى مكانكم غداً في جنات ربي مع آبائكم الماضين

I have bid farewell to my family and traveled to You. I am far from my home; hoping to find salvation by being near You. I hope to return and I hope to look upon You and Your station in the heavens of my Lord, tomorrow along with Your Forefathers (asws)

Then recite:

يا أبا عبد الله يا حسينّ بن رسول الله، جئتك مستشفعاً بك إلى الله

O' Aba Abdullah! O' Hussain (asws), Son of RasoolAllah (saw)! I come to You seeking Your intercession with Allah

اللهم إني أستشفع إليك بولد حبيبك، و بالملائكة الذين يضجون عليه وييكون و يصرخون، لا يفترون و لا يسأمون، و هم من خشيتك مشفقون و من عذابك حذرون، لا تغيرهم الأيام و لا يهرمون

O' Allah! I seek the intercession of the Son of Your Beloved (saw) with You (Allah). And I seek the intercession of the angels who weep, cry, and wail over Him. The angels who do not slacken, who are never bored, who remain alert at all times and who are cautious of Your punishment and who do not change with time nor grow old

في نواحي الحير يشهقون، و سيدهم يرى ما يصنعون، و ما فيه يتقلبون، قد انهملت منهم العيون فلا ترقأ، اشتد منهم الحزن بحرقة لا تطفأ

They weep in the corners of the Ha'yr and their Master can see what they do and how restless they are Their eyes never stop shedding tears and their agony continues to increase and are never pacified

Then raise your hands and recite:

اللهم إني أسألك مسألة المسكين المستكين، العليل الذليل الذي لم يرد بمسألته غيرك، فإن لم تدركه رحمتك عطب

O' Allah! I beg You as a poor, humble, weak, and humiliated slave; who does not make a request to any except You. If Your mercy does not save, then we shall be destroyed

أسألك أن تداركني بلطف منك، و أنت الذي لا تخيب سائلك، و تعطي المغفرة و تغفر الذنوب

I ask You to save me by Your kindness. For You are the One who does not disappoint those who ask Him. You give pardon and forgive sins

فلا أكون يا سيدي أنا أهون خلقك عليك، و لا أكون أهون من و فد إليك بابن حبيبك

O' my Master! Do not make me the lowest from amongst Your slaves. Do not make me the lowest amongst those who came to You through the Son of Your Beloved (saw).

فإني أملت و رجوت و طمعت و زرت و اغتربت، رجاء لك أن تكافيني إذ أخرجتني من رحلي فأذنت لي بالمسير إلى هذا المكان رحمة منك، و تفضلا منك، يا رحمن يا رحيم

I have hoped, begged and sought Your mercy. I have abandoned my homeland and come to His Ziarat; hoping You will reward me now that You have allowed me to travel here and have allowed me to come to this place with Your mercy and Your grace, O' Rahman O' Raheem

Then strive hard in asking Allah as much as you can and increasingly pray InshaAllah. After, exit the roofed chamber and go beside the graves of the martyr. Point towards them and recite:

السلام عليكم و رحمة الله و بركاته

Salam be upon You and may the mercy and blessings of Allah be upon You

السلام عليكم يا أهل ديار المؤمنينّ

Salam be upon You, O' inhabitants of the graves from amongst the inhabitants of the land of the momineen

السلام عليكم بما صبرتم فنعم عقبى الدار

"Peace be on you for being patient, how excellent, is then, the issue of the abode." (Quran 13:24)

السلام عليكم يا أولياء الله

Salam be upon You, O' Auwilyahullah (friends of Allah)

السلام عليكم يا أنصار الله رسوله، و أنصار أمير المؤمنينّ، و أنصار ابن رسوله، و أنصار دينه

Salam be upon You O' Ansarullah (supporters of Allah), O' Ansar e RasoolAllah (saw), O' Ansar e Ameerul Momineen (asws), O' Ansar e Son of His Messenger (saw), and O' Ansar e His Deen

أشهد أنكم أنصار الله كما قال الله عز وجل (و كأين من نبي قاتل معه ربيون كثير فما و هنوا لما أصابهم في سبيل الله و ما ضعفوا و ما استكانوا)

I testify You are ansarullah for Allah (swt) said, *"And how many a prophet has fought with whom were many worshippers of the Lord; so they did not become weak-hearted on account of what befell them in Allah's way, nor did they weaken, nor did they abase themselves; and Allah loves the patient."* (Quran 3:146)

فما ضعفتم و ما استكنتم، حتى لقيتم الله على سبيل الحق

You were not weakened nor did You humble Yourselves before Your enemies until You met Allah on the path of haq

صلى الله عليكم و على أرواحكم و أبدانكم و أجسادكم

May the blessings of Allah be upon You, Your ruh, and Your bodies

أبشروا بموعد الله الذي لا خلف له و لا تبديل، إن الله لا يخلف و عده، و الله مدرك بكم ثار ما و عدكم

Rejoice in the promise of Allah which does not change nor disappoint, *"for Allah never fails in His promise"* (Quran 3:9) and Allah will avenge You as He promised

أنتم خاصة الله، اختصكم الله لأبي عبد اللّه، أنتم الشهداء و أنتم السعداء سعدتم عند الله، و فزتم بالدرجات من جنات لا يطعن أهلها و لا يهرمون و رضوا بالمقام في دار السلام مع من نصرتم

You are the Chosen Ones of Allah and He chose You for Aba Abdullah (asws). You are the martyrs and are the victorious ones. You achieved victory with Allah and earned the highest ranks in the heavens, where its inhabitants do not age, do not grow old, and are pleased with their positions in the land of peace (jannah) along with the One you supported

جزاكم الله خيراً من أعوان، جزاء من صبر مع رسول الله ﷺ

May Allah reward You with the best of rewards for the supporters, the reward of those who remained patient while supporting RasoolAllah (saw)

أنجز الله ما و عدكم من الكرامة في جواره و داره مع النبيين و المرسلين ﷺ، و أمير المؤمنينّ و قائد الغر المحجلينّ

May Allah fulfill His promise of honoring You by making You neighbors with RasoolAllah (saw) and allowing You to dwell with Him at His station along with the prophets and messengers and Ameerul Momineen (asws), the leader of those with bright shining foreheads

أسأل الله الذي حملني إليكم حتى أراني مصارِ عكم أن يرينيكم على الحوض رواء مرويين، و يريني أعداءكم في أسفل درك من الجحيم، فإنهم قتلوكم ظلماً و أرادوا إماتة الحق، و سلبوكم لابن مسية و ابن آكلة الأكباد

I ask Allah—who brought me to You and allowed me to see Your place of martyrdom—to allow me to see You by the Pool of Kauthar where Your thirst is quenched and allow me to see Your enemies in the lowest places in hell. For they martyred You unjustly. They wanted to kill haq by martyring You. They looted You for the son of sumayyah (ubaidullah ibn ziyad la) and the son of the liver eater (muawiyah la)

فأسال الله أن يرينيهم ظمآء مظمئين، مسلسلين مغللين، يساقون إلى الجحيم

I ask Allah to allow me to see them thirsty, chained, and shackled as they are pulled towards the hellfire

السلام عليكم يا أنصار الله و أنصار ابن رسوله ﷺ مني ما بقيت و بقي الليل و النهار

Salam be upon You O' Ansarullah and Ansar e Son of His Rasool (saw) for as long as I live and for as long as there is night and day

و السلام عليك دائماً إذا فنيت و بليت

Salam be upon You after I am dead and perished. Salam be upon You for all eternity

لهفي عليكم أي مصيبة أصابت كل مولى المحمد ﷺ و آل محمدّ

I mourn over You. What a tragedy that befell every follower of Muhammad (saw) and Aal e Muhammad (asws)

لقد عظمت و خصت و جلت و عمت مصيبتكم

Your tragedy is great, unique, and unbearable. It encompasses all things

أنا بكم لجزع، و أنا بكم لموجع محزون، و أنا بكم لمصاب ملهوف

I have become restless over You. I am in pain and grief-stricken. I am afflicted by and distraught over Your tragedy

هنيئاً لكم ما اعطيتم، و هنيئاً لكم ما به حييتم

Enjoy the rewards that are given to You and enjoy that which Allah has greeted You with

356

فلقد بكتكم الملائكة و حفتكم و سكنت معسكركم و حلت مصار عكم و قدست و صفت بأجنحتها عليكم

The angels wept over You, surrounded You, dwelled in Your camp, and they have remained there beside Your graves. They glorify You and have placed their wings over You

ليس لها عنكم فراق إلى يوم التلاق، و يوم المحشر و يوم المنشر طافت عليكم رحمة من الله، و بلغتم بها شرف الدنيا و الآخرة

They will never leave You until the Day of Meeting (day of judgment). And on the Day of Resurrection and the Day of Publishing, You will be surrounded by the mercy of Allah; that You earned by the greatest honor in this life and in the hereafter

أتيتكم شوقاً، وزرتكم خوفاً، أسال الله أن يرينيكم على الحوض و في الجنان مع الأنبياء و المرسلين، و الشهداء و الصالحين، و حسن أولئك رفيقاً

I came to You while longing for You and visited You while in fear. I ask Allah to allow me to see You by al Kauthar and in the heavens along with the prophets, messengers, *"martyrs and the good, and a goodly company are they!"* (Quran 4:69)

Then circle around the Ha'yr while reciting:

يا من إليه و فدت، و إليه خرجت، و به استجرت، و إليه قصدت، و إليه بابن نبيه تقربت، صلى على محمدﷺ و آل محمدٌ، و من علي بالجنة، و فك رقبتي من النار

O' One to whom I have come and the One whom I have traveled to, the One whom I have sought refuge, the One whom I chose as my destination and the One to whom I sought nearness through the Son of His Messenger (saw). Send Your blessings upon Muhammad (saw) and Aal e Muhammad (asws) and bestow Your favor on me by taking me to Jannah and releasing me from the hellfire

اللهم ارحم غربتي وبعد داري، و ارحم مسيري إليك و إلى ابن حبيبك ﷺ

O' Allah! Have mercy on my loneliness and on being so far from my homeland. And have mercy on me for having traveled to You and to the Son of Your Beloved (saw)

و اقلبني مفالحاً منجحاً قد قبلت معذرتي و خضوعي و خشوعي عند إمامي و سيدي و مولاي

Allow me to return with success and victory; after having accepted my apology, my humbleness, and my humility before my Imam (asws), my Master, and my Moula.

و ارحم صرختي و بكائي و همي و جزعي و خشوعي و جزني، و ما قد باشر قلبي من الجزع عليه

Have mercy on my wailing, my tears, my grief, my sorrow, my humility, and the restlessness of my heart over Him

فبنعمتك علي و بلطفك لي خرجت إليه، و بتقويتك إباي، و صرفك المحذور عني، و كلائتك بالليل و النهار لي، و بحفظك و كر امتك إباي

I came to Him through Your blessings and kindness to me; through the strength which You gave me, through You averting harm from me, through Your keeping me safe at night and day, and through You protecting me and honoring me

و كل بحر قطعته، و كل و اد و فلاة سلكتها، و كل منزل نزلته، فأنت حملتني في البر و البحر، و أنت الذي بلغتني و وفقتني و كفيتني

Any sea that I have crossed, any desert I have passed, and any place where I have stayed during my journey was due to You allowing me to travel across the lands and seas. You are the one who allowed me to succeed in arriving here and kept me safe

و بفضل منك و و قاية بلغت، و كانت المنة لك علي في ذلك كله، و أثري مكتوب عندك و اسمي و شخصي

I arrived here by Your grace and protection. You bestowed Your favors upon me in every part of my journey. My footprints, my name and my journey are recorded with You

فلك الحمد على ما أبليتني و اصطنعت عندي

Praise be to You for testing me and for bestowing Your favors upon me

اللهم فارحم فرقي منك، و مقامي بين يديك و تملقي، و اقبل مني توسلي إليك بابن حبيبك، و صفوتك و خيرتك من خلقك، و توجهي إليك

O' Allah! Have mercy on my fear of You and have mercy on me for standing before You and praising You. Accept my asking and turning to You through the Son of Your Beloved (saw), Your Chosen One, and the Best of Your Creation

و أقلني عثرتي و اقبل عظيم ما سلف مني، و لا يمنعك ما تعلم مني من العيوب و الذنوب و الإوراف على نفسي

Forgive my mistakes and the great sins I committed. Do not allow Your knowledge of my fault and sins—that I committed against myself—to prevent You from forgiving me.

و إن كنت لي ماقتاً فارض عني، و إن كنت علي ساخطاً فتب علي، إنك على كل شيء قدير

If You had detested me before, then now be pleased with me. And if You were displeased with me before, then now accept my repentance. For You have power over all things.

اللهم اغفر لي و لوالدي و ارحمهما كما ربياني صغيراً، و اجزهما عني خيراً

O' Allah! Forgive me and forgive my parents and *"Have mercy on them both as they did care for me when I was little."* (Quran 17:24) and reward them with blessings on my behalf

اللهم اجز هما بالإحسان إحساناً و بالسيئات غفراناً

O' Allah! Reward them with good for their good deeds and forgive their evil deeds.

اللهم أدخلهما الجنة برحمتك، و حرم وجوههما عن عذابك، و برد عليهما مضاجعههما، و افسح لهما في قبريهما، و عرفنيهما في مستقر من رحمتك و جوار حبيبك محمدﷺ

O' Allah! Allow them to enter Jannah through Your mercy and make it haram for their faces to be punished, make cool their resting place, widen their graves, and introduce me to them in the dwellings of Your mercy and in the neighborhood of Your Beloved, Muhammad (saw)

Chapter 80

How to perform prayers beside the grave of Hussain (asws)

HADITH 1

Imam Jafar Sadiq (asws) narrates:

"Prayers should be performed near the head of the grave of Hussain (asws)."

HADITH 2

Imam Jafar Sadiq (asws) narrates:

"After saying salam to the martyrs, return back to the grave of Hussain (asws), face towards the grave and pray as many prayers as possible."

HADITH 4

Ubaidullah ibn Ali al Halabee narrates:

I said to Aba Abdullah Imam Jafar Sadiq (asws), "When we perform the Ziarat of the grave of Hussain (asws), how should we perform prayers next to Him?"

Imam (asws) replied, "Stand behind the grave near His shoulders and then send salawat on the Prophet (saw) and send salawat on Hussain (asws)."

Hadith 5

Hisham ibn Saleem narrates:

A man came to Aba Abdullah Imam Jafar Sadiq (asws) and asked, "O Son (asws) of RasoolAllah (saw)! Should a person perform the Ziarat of Your Father (Imam Hussain asws)?"

Imam (asws) replied, "Yes and perform salat next to His grave. However, one should not stand in front of the grave. Instead stand behind it while performing salat."

Chapter 81

Mustahab Prayers One should perform at the Ha'yr

HADITH 1

Ali ibn Abu Hamzah narrates:

I asked Abdul Saleh Imam Musa Kazim (asws) about performing the Ziarat of the grave of Hussain (asws) ibn Ali (asws).

Imam (asws) replied, "You should not abandon it."

I asked, "What about performing mustahab (recommended) salat there if I will not be remaining there for ten nights?"

Imam (asws) replied, "You may perform as many mustahab prayers as you like in Masjid al Haram, in Masjid al Nabwi and next to the grave of Hussain (asws)."

I asked, "Can I perform mustahab prayers next to the grave of Hussain (asws) during the day?"

Imam (asws) replied, "Yes."

HADITH 2

Ibn Abu Umair narrates:

I asked Abul Hasan Imam Musa Kazmi (asws) regarding performing mustahab prayers next to the grave of Hussain (asws), in Mecca, and in Medina if I will not be remaining there for ten nights."

Imam (asws) replied, "Yes. Perform as many mustahab prayers as you can. For there is great blessing in it."

HADITH 3

Ishaq ibn Ammar narrates:

I asked Abul Hasan Imam Musa Kazim (asws) if a person who is staying for less than ten nights can perform nafillah prayers beside the grave of Hussain (asws), at various other holy sites of RasoolAllah (saw), and in the two Harams.

Imam (asws) replied, "Yes. Perform as many nafillah prayers as you can for it is a blessing."

HADITH 4

Ishaq ibn Ammar narrates:

I asked Abul Hasan Imam Musa Kazim (asws), "May I be sacrificed upon You! Can I perform mustahab prayers in the two Harams and next to the grave of Hussain (asws) if I am a traveler?"

Imam (asws) replied, "Yes, as much as you are able."

HADITH 5

Ali ibn Abu Hamzah narrates:

I asked Abu Ibrahim Imam Musa Kazim (asws) if a traveler can perform mustahab prayers beside the grave of Hussain (asws), in the various holy sites of the Prophet (saw), and in the two Harams.

Imam (asws) replied, "Yes. Perform as many mustahab prayers as you are able."

Chapter 82

Reciting Prayer in Full Beside the Grave of Hussain (asws)

HADITH 1

Abu Shebee narrates:

I asked Aba Abdullah Imam Jafar Sadiq (asws), "Should I perform the Ziarat of the grave of Hussain (asws)?"

Imam (asws) replied, "Perform the Ziarat of check meaning and perform full prayers beside His grave."

I asked, "Perform salat in full beside Him?"

Imam (asws) replied, "Yes, perform full salat."

I said, "But some of our companions narrates prayers should be shortened."

Imam (asws) replied, "Only the weak do this."

HADITH 2

Imam Jafar Sadiq (asws) narrates:

"You can perform wajib prayers without shortening them in three locations: in Masjid al Haram, in Masjid al Nabwi, and beside the grave of Hussain (asws)."

HADITH 3

Imam Jafar Sadiq (asws) narrates:

"You can perform prayers without shortening them in four locations: in Masjid al Haram, in Masjid al Nabwi, in Masjid al Kufa, and the Ha'yr (grave of Hussain asws)."

HADITH 4

See hadith 3

HADITH 5

Imam Jafar Sadiq (asws) narrates:

"May the blessings of Allah be upon Masjid al Haram, Masjid al Nabwi, haram of Ameerul Momineen (asws) (Masjidul Kufa), and in the Haram of Hussain (asws)."

HADITH 6

Ziad al Kandi narrates:

Abul Hasan Imam Musa Kazim (asws) said to me, "I love for you that which I love for Myself and I dislike for you that which I dislike for Myself. Perform prayers in their full rakat in the two Harams, in Masjid al Kufa, and beside the grave of Hussain (asws)."

HADITH 7

Amr ibn Marzooq narrates:

I asked Abul Hasan Imam Musa Kazim (asws) about performing prayers in the two Harams, in Masjid al Kufa, and beside the grave of Hussain (asws).

Imam (asws) replied, "At these locations you should perform prayers fully."

HADITH 8

Hudaifah ibn Mansoor narrates:

A man heard Aba Abdullah Imam Jafar Sadiq (asws) say,

"Prayers should be performed fully at Masjid al Haram, Masjid al Nabwi, Masjid al Kufa, and in the Haram of Hussain (asws)."

HADITH 9

Qaid al Hannat narrates:

I asked Abul Hasan Imam Musa Kazim (asws) regarding performing prayer at the two Harams.

Imam (asws) replied, "Perform your prayers fully even if you are passing through Mecca or Medina."

HADITH 10

Imran narrates:

I asked Abul Hasan Imam Musa Kazim (asws), "Should I shorten my prayers when I am in Masjid al Haram?"

Imam (asws) replied, "You can choose to pray shortened prayers but it is better if you pray fully. For doing good deeds is always a blessing."

Chapter 83

Wajib Prayers offered at the Haram of Imam Hussain (asws) is equal to Hajj and Mustahab prayers are equal to Umrah

HADITH 1

Ibn Abi Umair narrates from someone who said:

Imam Muhammad Baqir (asws) said to a man:

"In times of need, what prevents you from going to the grave of Hussain (asws) praying four rakat and then asking from Allah for your needs? Performing a wajib prayer beside His grave is equal to performing a Hajj and performing a mustahab (recommended) prayer beside His grave is equal to performing an umrah."

HADITH 2

Jabeer al Jufee narrates:

Imam Jafar Sadiq (asws) said to Mufaddal:

"...then continue performing prayers, for every rakat of prayer you pray beside the grave of Hussain (asws), you shall have the reward of performing one thousand hajj and one thousand umrah, the reward of freeing one thousand slaves, and fighting in the way of Allah one thousand times with one of the messengers of Allah."

HADITH 3

Abi Ali al Harranee narrates:

I asked Aba Abdullah Imam Jafar Sadiq (asws), "What is the reward for those who perform the Ziarat of the grave of Hussain (asws)?"

Imam (asws) replied, "Allah will record the reward of performing a Hajj and an umrah for those who go to the grave of Hussain (asws), perform His Ziarat, and pray two or four rakat of prayer."

I asked, "May I be sacrificed upon You! Is this reward the same for those who perform the Ziarat of the grave of other Imams (asws) whose obedience is wajib (obligatory)?"

Imam (asws) replied, "The reward is the same for anyone who performs the Ziarat of the graves of the other Imams (asws) whose obedience is wajib."

HADITH 4

Shoaib al Aqraquf narrates:

I asked Aba Abdullah Imam Jafar Sadiq (asws), "May I be sacrificed upon You! What is the reward for those who perform the Ziarat of the grave of Hussain (asws)?"

Imam (asws) replied, "O'Shoaib! There is not one who prays beside Him without Allah accepting his prayer and there is no request asked beside Him without Allah fulfilling it immediately or in the near future."

I said, "May I be sacrificed upon You! Please tell me more."

Imam (asws) replied, "O' Shoaib! The least amongst that which is granted to a zawir (visitor) of Hussain (asws) ibn Ali (asws) will be granted is being told, "O' slave of Allah! Your past sins have been forgiven. Now go forth and begin again with only good deeds."

Chapter 84

Bidding Farewell to the Grave of Imam Hussain (asws)

HADITH 1

Imam Jafar Sadiq (asws) narrates:

"Recite the following when you bid farewell to Hussain (asws) ibn Ali (asws):

السلام عليك و رحمة الله و بركاته

May the mercy, blessings, and salam of Allah be upon You.

أستودعك الله و أقرء عليك السلام، آمنا بالله و بالرسولﷺ و بما جئت به و دلك عليه، و اتبعنا الرسولﷺ، فاكتبنا مع الشاهدين

I bid You farewell and I send my salam upon You. For I believe in Allah, in RasoolAllah (saw), in that which You brought and in that which You guided the people towards. We have followed the Messenger (saw), therefore record us as amongst those who testify.

اللهم لا تجعله آخر العهد منا و منه

O' Allah! Do not make this our last time in visiting Him nor the last time He invites us towards His Ziarat.

اللهم إنا نسألك أن تنفعنا بحبه

O' Allah! We ask You to make us beneficent in His love.

اللهم ابعثه مقاماً محموداً تنصر به دينك و تقتل به عدوك و تبير به من نصب حرباً لآل محمد ﷺ ، فإنك و عدته ذلك و أنت لا تخلف الميعاد، و السلام عليك و رحمة الله و بركاته

O' Allah! Resurrect Him (Imam Hussain asws) in that appraised position where You support Your religion through Him, slay Your enemies through Him and destroy those who wage war against Aal e Muhammad (asws) through Him. For You have promised this to Him and You do not break Your promises. May the mercy, blessings, and salam of Allah be upon You.

اشهد أنك شهداء نجباء، جاهدتم في سبيل الله و قتلتم على منهاج رسول الله صلى الله عليه و آله و سلم تسليماً

I testify You (companions of Hussain asws) are the noblest of martyrs. You fought in the way of Allah and were martyred while following the path of RasoolAllah (saw)

أنتم السابقون و المهاجرون و الأنصار، أشهد أنكم أنصار الله و أنصار رسوله ﷺ

You (companions of Imam Hussain asws) are al sabaqoon *(the foremost)*, al muhijaroon *(those who left their homes)*, and al Ansar *(the supporters)* (Quran 9:100)

أشهد أنكم أنصار الله و أنصار رسوله ﷺ

I testify that You are the Ansar (supporters) of Allah and the Ansar (supporters) of His Rasool (saw)

فالحمد لله الذي صدقكم و عده و أراكم ما تحبون، و صلى الله على محمد ﷺ و آل محمدّ ورحمة الله

Praise be to Allah who fulfilled His promise to You and showed You that which You love. May the mercy and blessings of Allah be upon Muhammad (saw) and Aal e Muhammad (asws)

اللهم لا تشغلني في الدنيا عن ذكر نعمتك، لا بإكث تلهيني عجائب بهجتها، و تفتنني زهرات زينتها، و لا بإقلال يضر بعملي كده، و يملأ صدري همه، أعطني من ذلك غنى عن شرا خلقك، و بلاغاً أنال به رضاك، يا أرحم الراحمين

O' Allah! Do not make it so I am distracted by this world and therefore neglectful in thanking You for Your blessings. Do not give me numerous adornments of this world so that I do not become awestruck by its shiny adornments and lost in its fleeting happiness. Do not give me so little that I become unable to perform good deeds due to my worry for having to work so hard in this world. Give me enough so that I do not need to seek assistance from the oppressive and evil tyrants.

و صلى الله على رسوله محمد ﷺ بن عبد اللّہ، و على أهل بيته الطيبين الأخيار، و رحمة الله و بركاته

May the blessings and mercy of Allah be upon His Rasool Muhammad (saw) ibn Abdullah (as) and upon His Righteous and Blessed Ahlul Bayt (asws)

HADITH 2

When you decide to bid farewell after having performed the Ziarat of Hussain (asws), recite as many Ziarats as you can.

Ensure you perform ghusl before bidding farewell and performing the final farewell Ziarat (any ziarat of your choosing). After you have finished reciting the farewell Ziarat, turn your face towards His, touch the grave and recite the following:

السلام عليك يا ولي الله

Salam to You, O' Wali of Allah

السلام عليك يا أبا عبد اللّہ

Salam to You, O' Aba Abdullah (asws)

أنت لي جنة من العذاب، و هذا أوان انصر افي عنك، غير راغب عنك، و لا مستبدل بك سواك، و لا مؤثر عليك غيرك، و لا زاهد في قربك

You are My protection from the chastisement in the Hereafter. Even though the time has come for me to depart, I do so without abandoning You nor shall I replace You with one other than You, nor will I give preference to any above You. My longing to be near You has not diminished.

و قد جست بنفسي للحدثان، و تركت الأهل والأوطان، فكن لي يوم حاجتي و فقري و فاقتي، و يوم لا يغني عني و الدي و لا ولدي، لاحميمي و لا رفيقي و لا قريبي

During my travels I faced dangers and hardships all while leaving my family behind. I beseech You to be there for me on the day of my need, on the day of my poverty; the day when my parents, my children, my close friends, my companions, and my kin will be of no help to me (Day of Judgment)

أسأل الله الذي قدر و خلق أن ينفس بك كربي، و أسأل الله الذي قدر علي فراق مكانك أن لا يجعله آخر العهد مني و من رجعتي

I beseech Allah to remove my anguish through You and I ask Allah to not make this Ziarat my last Ziarat of You and to allow me to return to You again

و أسأل الله الذي أبكى عليك عيني أن يجعله سنداً لي، و أسأل الله الذي نقلني إليك من رحلي و أهلي أن يجعله ذخراً لي

I beseech Allah who caused my eyes to weep over You to make my tears as a means of support on the Day of Judgment. And I beseech Allah who provided my means of travel to You to record this Ziarat for me.

و أسأل الله الذي أراني مكانك و هداني للتسليم عليك و لزيارتي إباك، أن يوردني حوضكم و يرزقني مرافقتكم في الجنان مع آبائك الصالحين صلي الله عليهم أجمعين

I beseech Allah who made me aware of Your Station and guided me towards Your Salam and the performing of Your Ziarat, to appoint for me a place at Your Pool (al Kauthar) and to comfort me in the Heavens by allowing me a place near to You and Your Righteous Fathers (asws)

السلام عليك يا صفوة الله و ابن صفوته

Salam be upon You O' Safwatullah (the Chosen of Allah) wa ibn Safwat (and Son of the Chosen One)

السلام على رسول الله محمد ﷺ بن عبد اللّه، حبيب الله و صفوته، أمينه و رسوله، و سيد النبيين

Salam be upon RasoolAllah, Muhammad (saw) ibn Abdullah (as), Habeebullah (beloved of Allah), His Chosen One (safwat), His Trustee, His Messenger, and Syedul Nabieen (master of the prophets).

السلام على أمير المؤمنينّ، و وصي رسول رب العالمين، و قائد الغر المحجلين

Salam be upon Ameerul Momineen (asws), Wasi ul Rasool Rabbil Alameen (successor of the Messenger of the Lord of the Worlds), and the Leader of those with shining faces on the day of judgment

السلام على الأئمة الراشدين و المهديين

Salam be upon the Divinely Guided Imams

السلام على من في الحائر منكم و رحمة الله و بركاته

Salam be upon those who are at the Ha'yr (burial place and its surrounding areas of Imam Hussain asws). May the blessings and mercy of Allah be upon You

السلام على ملائكة الله الباقين المسبحين المقيمين، الذين هم بأمر ربهم قائمون

Salam be upon the Angels of Allah who reside there glorifying Allah and fulfilling the obligations of their Lord

السلام علينا و على عباد الله الصالحين، و الحمد لله رب العالمين

Salam be upon us and upon the righteous slaves of Allah. Alhamdulillah rabbil alameen (praise is for Allah, the Lord of the Worlds)

سلام الله و سلام ملائكته المقربين، و أنبيائه المرسلين و عباده الصالحين، على يا بن رسول الله، و على روحك و بدنك، و على ذريتك و على من حضرك من أوليئك

May the salam of Allah, the salam of the angels nearest to Allah, the salam of His prophets who were sent as messengers, and the salam of His Righteous Slaves be upon You, O' Son of RasoolAllah (saw). May their salam be upon Your Ruh (spirit), Your body, Your Progeny (asws), and upon those of Your Auwliya who were with You.

أستودعك الله و أسترعيك و أقرء عليك السلام، آمنا بالله و برسوله و بما جاء به من عند الله، اللهم اكتبنا مع الشاهدين

I bid farewell to You and leave You in the care of Allah. I send my salam upon You. We believe in Allah, in His Messenger, and in the message that He brought from Allah. O' Allah! Record us amongst those who have testified to this!

اللهم صل على محمد ﷺ و آل محمدّ، و لا تجعله آخر العهد من زيارتى إبن سولك، و ارزقني زيارته أبداً ما أبقيتني

O' Allah! Send Your blessings on Muhammad (saw) wa Aal e Muhammad (asws). Do not make this the last time I come to the Ziarat of the Son (asws) of Your Messenger (saw). Provide me with sustenance so that I may perform His Ziarat again and again; for as long as You give me life

اللهم و انفعني بحبه يا رب العالمين

O' Allah! Assist me through His Love, O Rabbil Alameen (Lord of the Worlds)

اللهم ابعثه مقاماً محموداً، إنك على كل شيء قدير

O' Allah! Resurrect me in a Praised Station alongside Him. For You have dominion over all things.

اللهم إني أسالك بعد الصلاة و التسليم، أن تصلى على محمد و آل محمدّ، و أن لا تجعله آخر العهد من زيارتي إباه، فإن جعلته يا رب فاحشرني معه و مع آبائه و أوليائه، و إن أبقيتني يا رب فارزقني العود إليه ثم العود إليه بعد العود برحمتك يا أرحم الراحمين

O' Allah! Now that I have performed prayers and said my Salam to Them (asws), I ask You to send Your blessings upon Muhammad (saw) wa Aal e Muhammad (asws); and I implore You to not make this the last time I perform His Ziarat.

اللهم اجعل لي لسان صدق في أوليائك، و جبب إلي مشاهدهم

O'Rab (Lord)! If You do make this my last Ziarat, then resurrect me alongside Him, His Fathers, and His true followers. But if you prolong my life, then I ask You to provide me, through Your mercy, with rizq (sustenance) so that I may perform His Ziarat again and again, O' Most Merciful of the Merciful

اللهم اجعل لي لسان صدق في أوليائك، و حبب إلي مشاهدهم

O' Allah! Make me be a truthful tongue from amongst Your Auwliya (friends) and make me love their station

اللهم صل على محمد ﷺ و آل محمدّ

O' Allah! Send Your blessings upon Muhammad (saw) wa Aal e Muhammad (asws).

و لا تشغلني عن ذكرك بإكثار علي من الدنيا تلهيني عجائب بهجتها و تفتنني زهرات زينتها، و لا بإقلال يضر بعملي كده و يملأ صدري همه، و أعطني بذلك غنى عن شرار خلقك و بلاغاً أنال به رضاك يا رحمن

Keep me from being preoccupied with the trappings of this world so that I do not become negligent in Your remembrance. And do not provide me with so much that I become enamored with this world and its shining adornments. But do not provide me with so little that I am unable to perform numerous good deeds due to my worrying and having to strive in this world for sustenance. Give me just enough so that I do not have to ask anything from the evil ones of this world but enough so that I am able to obtain Your Pleasure, O' Most Merciful!

و السلام عليكم يا ملائكة الله و زوار قبر أبي عبد اللةّ

Salam be upon You, O' Angels of Allah and the zuwwar (visitors) of the grave of Aba Abdullah (asws).

Now place your right and left cheek on the grave. Continue to pray and ask for the fulfillment of your needs. As you exit the Ha'yr, do not turn your back on the grave.

Chapter 85

Ziarat of Hz Abbas (as)

HADITH 1

Abu Hamza Thumali narrates Imam Jafar Sadiq (asws) said:

"When you wish to perform the Ziarat of the grave of Abbas (as) ibn Ali (asws), which lies on the banks of the River Furat, near the Ha'yr, stand at the door of Saqifa and recite the following:

سلام الله و سلام ملائكته المقربين و أنبيائه المرسلين و عباده الصالحين و جميع الشهداء و الصديقين، و الزاكيات الطيبات فيما يغتدي و تروح عليك يا بن أمير المؤمنينّ

May the salam of Allah, the salam of the angels nearest to Allah, the salam of His prophets who were sent as messengers, the salam of His Righteous Slaves, the salam of all of the martyrs and truthful ones, and all of the pure and blessed salams be upon You at all times, O' Son of Ameerul Momineen (asws)

أشهد لك بالتسليم و التصديق و الوفاء و النصيحة، لخلف النبي المسل و السبط المنتجب، و الدليل العالم و الوصي المبلغ، و المظلوم المهتضم

I testify with full submission, devotion and loyalty to You that You are the Khalif al Nabi (caliph of the Prophet), the Chosen Grandson, Proof of His Knowledge, and the Successor of the Prophet (saw), and You were mazloom (oppressed).

فجزاك الله عن رسوله ﷺ و عن أمير المؤمنينّ و عن الحسنّ و الحسينّ صلوات الله عليهم، أفضل الجزاء بما صبرت و احتسبت و أعنت، فنعم عقبى الدار

May the reward of Allah on behalf of His Messenger, Ameerul Momineen (asws), Hasan (asws), and Hussain (asws) with the best of rewards. For even though You suffered in this world, You remained patient in expectation of the rewards from Allah. How excellent is Your station!

لعن الله من قتلك

May the lanat of Allah be upon those who slaughtered You.

و لعن الله من جهل حقك و استخف بحرمتك

May the lanat of Allah be upon those who ignored Your rights and violated Your holiness

و لعن الله من حال بينك و بين ماء الفرات

May the lanat of Allah be upon those who stood between You and the water of the River Furat

أشهد أنك قتلت مظلوماً، و أن الله منجز لكم ما و عدكم

I testify You were brutally slain and without doubt Allah will fulfill His Promise with You

جئتك يا بن أمير المؤمنينّ و افداً إليكم، و قلبي مسلم لكم، و أنا لكم تابع و نصرتي لكم معدة، حتى يحكم الله و هو خير الحاكمين

I have come to You, O Son of Ameerul Momineen (asws), as Your guest whose heart is in submission to You. I shall follow and support You until the judgment of Allah falls upon me for He is the best of judges.

فمعكم معكم لا مع عدوكم

I side with You and only You. I shall never side with Your enemies.

إني بكم و بإيابكم من المؤمنين، و بمن خالفكم و قتكلم من الكافرين

I believe in You and in Your return. And I reject those who opposed and those who martyred You are from the kafireen

قتل الله امة قتلتكم بالأيدي و الألس

May Allah destroy the nation that slaughtered You; whether it be by their hands or their tongue

Then enter, fall upon the grave and recite:

السلام عليك أيها العبد الصالح المطيع الله و لرسوله ﷺ و لأمير المؤمنينّ و الحسنّ و الحسينّ

May my Salam be upon You, O' righteous and obedient slave of Allah, and upon His Messenger (saw), and upon Ameerul Momineen (asws), and upon Hasan (asws) and Hussain (asws)

السلام عليك و رحمة الله و بركاته و رضوانه، و على روحك و بدنك

May my salam be upon You and may the mercy, blessings, and pleasure of Allah be upon You, Your Ruh (spirit), and Your body

أشهد و أشهد الله أنك مضيت على ما مضى عليه البدريون المجاهدون في سبيل الله، المناصحون له في جهاد أعدائه، المبالغون في نصرة أوليائه، الذابون عن أحبائه

I testify and make Allah as my witness that You left this world on the same path as the martyrs of the Battle of Badr, who fought in the way of Allah. I testify that You remained loyal to Him (Allah) as You battled against His enemies, and that You struggled in support of His Auwliya (nearest friends), and that You are Their (Auwliya) protector against those who lower their status and the friends of those who lower their status.

378

فجزاك الله أفضل الجزاء، و أكثر الجزاء، و أوفر الجزاء، و أوفى جزاء أحد ممن و فى ببيعته، واستجاب له دعوته، وأطاع ولاة أمره

May Allah rewards You with the best of rewards; an ever increasing reward; a reward that is above all the other rewards He has granted to those who remained loyal to Their oath, who answered His call, and obeyed those who were Divinely Appointed by Him (Imams asws).

و أشهد أنك قد بالغت في النصيحة و أعطيت غاية المجهود، وبعثك الله في الزهدآء، و جعل روحك مع أرواح الزهدآء، و أعطاك من جنانه أفسحها منزلا، و أفضلها غرفاً، و رفع ذكرك في عليين، و حشرك مع النبيين و الصديقين و الشهدآء والصالحين، و حسن أوليك رفيقاً

I testify You faced struggles due to Your loyalty and placed all of Your efforts in the way of Allah. Thus, Allah resurrected You amongst the martyrs, joined Your Ruh with the Ruh of the Aleen (those who have a very high status in Jannah) and gave to You from the most expansive and glorious of His dwellings in His Heavens; and elevated Your Remembrance to the highest of places and raised You in the company of *"the prophets and the truthful and the martyrs and the righteous, and what an excellent company are they!"* (Quran 4:69)

أشهد أنك لم تهن و لم تنكل و أنك مضيت على بصيرة من أمرك، مقتدياً بالصالحين و متبعاً للنبيين

I testify that You never disgraced anyone nor were You unjust to anyone. You remained in the company of only the pious people and the prophets.

فجمع الله بيننا و بينك، و بين رسوله و أوليائه في منازل المخبتين، فإنه أرحم الراحمين

May Allah unite us with You, with His Messenger (saw), and His Auwliya; for He is the Most Merciful of the Merciful.

Chapter 86

Bidding Farewell at the Grave of Abbas (as) ibn Ali (asws)

HADITH 1

Abu Hamza Thumali narrates Imam Jafar Sadiq (asws) said:

"When you wish to bid farewell to Abbas (as), go to His grave and recite:

أستودعك الله و أسترعيك و أقرء عليك السلام، آمنا بالله وبرسوله ﷺ و بكتابه و بما جاء به من عند الله

I bid farewell to You. I leave You in the care of Allah and send my salam upon You. Protect us through Allah, His Rasool (saw), His Book, and through that which was brought by Allah

اللهم اكتبنا مع الشاهدين

O' Allah! Record us as amongst those who were witnesses

اللهم لا تجعله آخر العهد من زيارة قبر ابن أخي نبيك، و ارزقتي زيرته أبداً ما أبقيتني، و ا حشرني معه و ما آبائه في الجنان، اللهم و عرف بيني و بينه رسولك و أوليائك

O' Allah! Do not let this be the last time I perform the Ziarat of the Grave of the Son (as) of Your Prophet (saw)'s Brother (asws). Provide me with sustenance so that I may perform

His Ziarat for as long as I am alive. Resurrect me with Him (as) and with His Fathers (asws) in the Heavens. O' Allah! Enlighten me through Him, Your Rasool (saw) and through Your Auwliya (chosen ones)

اللهم صلى على محمد ﷺ و آل محمدٌ، و توفني على الإيمان بك و التصديق برسولك و الولاية لعلي بن أبي طالب و الأئمة من ولدةٌ، و البراءة من عدوهم، فإني قد رضيت بذلك يارب

O'Allah! Send Your blessings upon Muhammad (saw) wa Aal e Muhammad (asws) and cause me to die while believing in You, in Your Rasool (saw), in the wilayat of Ali (asws) ibn Abi Talib (as) and the Imams (asws) from His Sons; and while at the same time disassociating myself from Their enemies. For I am pleased by this, O' Lord.

Now pray for yourself, your parents, the momin (true believers) and the muslims and afterwards recite whatever supplications you prefer.

Chapter 87

Bidding Farewell at the graves of the Martyrs from
the companions of Hussain (asws)

HADITH 1

Abu Hamza Thumali narrates Imam Jafar Sadiq (asws) said:

Recite the following:

اللهم لا تجعله آخر العهد من زيارتي إباهم، و أشركني معهم و أدخلني في صالح ما أعطيتهم على نصرهم ابن
بنت نبيك، و حجتك على خلقك، وجهادهم معه في سبيلك

O'Allah! Do not let this be the last time I perform Their Ziarat. Make me a partner with
them, and include me in the blessings that You have bestowed upon Them for supporting
the Son (asws) of Your Prophet (saw)'s Daughter (sa), and for supporting Your Hujjat
(proof) upon Your Creation, and for fighting alongside Him in Your way.

اللهم اجمعنا و إباهم في جنتك مع الشهداء و الصالحين، و حسن أولئك رفيقاً

O'Allah! Join us with Them (martyrs and righteous ones) in Your Jannah. How exemplary
these companions are!

382

أستودعكم الله و أقرء عليكم السلام

I bid farewell to You and send my salam upon You

اللهم ارزقني العود إليهم، و احشرني معهم يا أرحم الراحمين

O'Allah! Provide me with sustenance so I may return to Them and resurrect me alongside Them, O' Most Merciful of the Merciful

Chapter 88

The Virtues of Karbala and Performing the
Ziarat of Hussain (asws)

HADITH 1

Zaidah narrates:

Imam Zainul Abideen Ali (asws) ibn Hussain (asws) said to me, "O Zaidah! I have been made aware that you perform the Ziarat of the grave of Aba Abdullah al Hussain (asws) on occasion."

I replied, "Yes that is true."

Imam (asws) asked, "Why do you do this even though you are held in high honor by your governor? A man who does not look kindly upon those who love Us or those who give preference to Us over others, or those who mention Our attributes, or those who fulfill any of his obligations towards Us?"

I (Zaidah) replied, "I swear by Allah that I do not do this for the sake of anyone other than Allah and His Rasool (saw). I do not worry about the anger of anyone who becomes angry over my performing this act. I am ready to face any and all afflictions that may befall me when I perform His Ziarat."

Imam (asws) asked, "I ask you by Allah, is what you've just said the absolute truth?"

I replied, "I swear by Allah it is the truth."

Imam (asws) asked me this same question three times and I repeated my answer three times.

Then Imam (asws) said, "Be joyous. Then be more joyous. And then even more joyous, for I shall narrate to you a hadith which is from the most noble of hadiths that are kept safe with Me."

Imam (asws) continued and said, "After the atrocities in Taf (Karbala)—which ended in the martyrdom of My Father Hussain (asws), the martyrdom of His Children who accompanied Him, the martyrdom of His Brothers, and the martyrdom of His other Family members—His women and children who remained alive were taken captive and were forced to ride on camels without any saddle towards Kufa.

As We were about to leave Karbala, I began to look over Their unburied bodies. It was extremely difficult for Me to see Them in such a state. I became upset and felt as if My Ruh was about to leave My body. In that moment, My Aunt Zainab al Kubra (sa), the great Daughter of Ameerul Momineen Ali (asws) ibn Abi Talib (as), looked upon Me and saw My immense anguish. She asked Me, "O' My Son! Why do I see You disturbed by the sight of death?"

Imam (asws) replied, "How can I not be distressed after seeing the martyrdom of My Master (asws), My Brothers (as), My Uncles (as), My Cousins (as), and the rest of My Family? Especially when Their bodies are strewn about covered with blood and dust, looted and unshrouded. There is none who looks upon Them or goes near Them as if They were from the family of Daylam and Khazar (as if They are not the Sons of RasoolAllah (saw) but instead from any ordinary families)."

Syeda Zainab (sa) replied, "Do not allow that which You have witnessed to cause You distress. I swear by Allah that RasoolAllah (saw) confided in Your Grandfather, Ameerul Momineen (asws), Your Father Hussain (asws), and Your Uncle Hasan (asws), that Allah has taken an oath from a certain group from amongst this nation whose presence is unknown to the tyrants from this ummah, but whose identity is well known in the heavens. This group will collect the eviscerated bodies and they will bury Them.

Then they will designate a marker here at the grave of Your Father (asws), the Master of Martyrs. Regardless of how much time passes, the signs of this marker will never vanish nor will its remnants ever be erased.

The leaders of Kufa and the followers of deviation will strive to eradicate and destroy it but it will continue to be exalted and ever apparent."

Imam (asws) asked, "What is this oath and incident You spoke of?"

Syeda Zainab (sa) replied, "Um Ayman narrated to Me, "One day RasoolAllah (saw) went to the House of Fatima (sa). Syeda Fatima (sa) had prepared some harira (traditional Arab stew) for Him, and Ali (asws) brought a dish filled with dates. I (Um Ayman) went with two goblets for them. One filled with milk and another with butter.

RasoolAllah (saw), Ali, Fatima (sa), Hasan (asws), and Hussain (asws) ate from the harira and after They drank from the milk. Then They ate the dates and the butter.

Then RasoolAllah (saw) washed His hands as Ali (asws) poured water over them. RasoolAllah (saw) then wiped His hands over His face and looked upon Ali (asws), Fatima (sa), Hasan (asws), and Hussain (asws) in such a way His happiness could be clearly seen upon His face.

RasoolAllah (saw) then turned His face towards the heavens for quite some time. After He turned His face towards Qiblah, raised His hands and began to pray. Then He fell into sajood (prostration) and began to weep for a very long time. His voice began to rise from His lamentations and He began shedding tears.

After some time has passed, He raised His head from sajood. He looked upon the ground as tears fell from His eyes like a fountain.

Syeda Fatima (sa), Ali (asws), Hasan (asws), Hussain (asws) and I (Um Ayman) were aggrieved to see RasoolAllah (saw) in such a state but We could not bring ourselves to ask Him for the cause of His distress.

After a length of time has passed, Ali (asws) and Syeda Fatima (sa) asked, "O' RasoolAllah (saw)! What causes You to weep so? May Allah remove Your distress and never cause You to cry! Our hearts are filled with pain at seeing You in such an agitated state."

RasoolAllah (saw) replied, "O' My Brother! Today after looking upon You, I felt such a joy that I had never felt before. And as I looked upon You, I praised Allah for giving to Me such a great blessing in You.

Then Jibrael (as) appeared before Me and said, "O' Muhammad (saw)! Allah (swt) is aware of Your feelings and knows the pleasure You gain by looking at Your Brother (asws), Your Daughter (sa), and Your two Grandsons (asws). Allah has completed His blessing upon You and has decreed to place Them (asws), Their progenies, Their muhib (lovers), and Their Shia (followers) with You in Jannah. They shall not be separated from You. They will be honored as You shall be and blessed until You are satisfied with Their blessings. And the blessings shall be even more than that.

However, in this world, They will face great tribulations and hardships. They will be harmed by the very people who claim to be followers of Your religion and people who claim to be a part of Your ummah (nation), but who in reality they have disassociated themselves from Allah and from You.

Your Ahlul Bayt (asws) will be martyred in the harshest of ways. And Their places of martyrdom will be great distances from one another. This has been decreed by Allah. Therefore You should accept this and be satisfied with it."

Then RasoolAllah (saw) replied, "I am in agreement with all that Allah has ordained for Us and am (like) all that He has ordained for Us."

Then Jibrael (as) said, "O' Muhammad (saw)! Your Brother (asws) will be oppressed after You. His rights will be usurped by Your ummah (nation) and He will face numerous hardships from Your enemies. Then He will be martyred by the most vile and wretched of the created beings; the equals of *those who slew the she-camel* (Quran 7:77).

He (Ali asws) will be martyred in the city to which He migrated. A city that shall become the center of His Shia and the Shia of His Children. A city wherein they shall face many immense difficulties.

And this Grandson of Yours (RasoolAllah (saw) pointed towards Imam Hussain (asws)) along with a group from Your Progeny, Your Family Members, and the best of those from amongst Your ummah will be martyred on the banks of the River Furat in a land called Karbala; a land which shall be the cause of much anguish (Karb) and afflictions (bala) on Your enemies and the enemies of Your Progeny (asws) on the day when anguish is endless and regrets are everlasting (Judgment Day).

Karbala, the place where Your Grandson (asws) and His Family shall be martyred, is the most blessed and the most sacred land on the earth. It is one of the valleys of Jannah.

There shall be earthquakes in all parts of the earth, and the mountains will tremble, the waves in the oceans will collide, and the heavens and their inhabitants will become distressed on the day when the accursed armies from the people of disbelief will surround and martyr Your Grandson (asws) and His Family.

O' Muhammad (saw)! Everything that was created by Allah will seek His permission to help those of Your Family against Their enemies. They will seek the permission of Allah to take the revenge of Your Family who are Hujjatullah (Proof of Allah) upon the creations of the earth and the heavens.

There will be none from the creation that will not seek the permission of Allah to come to the support of Your oppressed Family who are Hujjatullah (Proofs of Allah) upon the creation after You.

Then Allah will declare to the heavens, the earth, the mountains, the oceans, and all of the inhabitants therein, "I am Allah, al Qadeer (All Powerful, All Capable) from whom none can escape and the one from whom none can hide from My decrees. I am the most powerful of His (Imam Hussain asws) avengers. I swear by My Glory and My Magnificence that I will afflict those who oppressed My Rasool (saw), My Chosen One, those who disgraced Him, those who martyred His Ahlul Bayt (asws), those who abandoned His orders, and those who oppressed His Ahlul Bayt (asws) with such afflictions and chastisements the likes of which have never been placed upon anyone else in all of the worlds."

Upon hearing that, everything within the heavens and the earths will cry out; sending lanat those who oppressed, martyred, and disgraced Your Ahlul Bayt (asws).

And when Hussain (asws) and His Companions shall arrive at the place of Their martyrdom, Allah (swt) Himself will take Their Ruh and the angels from the Seventh Heaven will descend to earth carrying garments and perfumes from Jannah along with vessels made of rubies and emeralds filled with the Water of Life (the water from which Khizr drank). The angels will form ranks and begin performing prayers.

Then Allah will appoint some people from amongst Your ummah who are unknown to the kafireen (disbelievers)—people who were not a part of the spilling of the martyrs' blood either with their intentions, their tongues, or their actions. They will bury the bodies of the martyrs and place a marker on the grave of the Master of Martyrs (Imam Hussain asws) in that land. That marker will become the standard for those who follow haq and a means of salvation for the momineen (true believers).

Afterwards, every day and every night, one hundred thousand angels from every sky will descend and surround the grave of Hussain (asws). They will send blessings upon Him, circulate around His grave, glorify Allah beside His grave, and seek forgiveness from Allah for those who perform His Ziarat. They will record the names of those from amongst Your ummah who seek the nearness of Allah (swt) by performing His Ziarat and will record the names of their fathers, their tribes, and homelands. Then these angels will place a mark upon the faces of the zuwwar (visitors) made of the noor from the Arsh (throne) of Allah which reads, "This is the Zawir (visitor) of the Grave of the Master of the Martyrs and Son of the Seal of the Prophets."

On the Day of Judgment, the noor from this marking will illuminate their faces in such a way that it will blind all who look upon it. The Zuwwar will be known from this noor."

Jibrael (as) continued and said, "O' Muhammad (saw)! It is as if I can see You standing between Mikael (as) and Myself as Ali (asws) stands before Us. There will be countless numbers of angels with Us, and We will be separating those who have this mark on their faces from the creation so they shall be saved from the tribulations and hardships of the hazab (Accounting).

O' Muhammad (saw)! This is the decree of Allah. It is His gift for those who performed the Ziarat of Your Grave, the Grave of Your Brother (asws), or the Graves of Your Two Grandsons (asws) whilst seeking nothing except the pleasure of Allah.

There are some accursed people who have incurred the wrath of Allah that shall attempt to destroy all traces of this grave. However, Allah (swt) shall never allow this to happen."

Then RasoolAllah (saw) said, "This is the cause of My sorrow."

Syeda Zainab (asws) continued and said, "After ibn Muljam (la) struck My Father (asws) I saw the signs of death upon Him (Ameerul Momineen asws).

I said to Him, "O' Father! Um Ayman narrated this hadith regarding the martyrdom of Hussain (asws) to Me, but I would like to hear it from You."

Ameerul Momineen (asws) replied, "O' Daughter (sa)! The hadith is as Um Ayman narrated it to You. It is as if I can see You and the rest of the women of Your Family as captives in this city. When the time comes, My Daughter (sa), You must remain patient when faced with all of the sufferings.

I swear to You by He who split the grain and created the creation, on that day there will be no friends of Allah on earth other than You, Your Muhib (lovers), and Your Shia (followers). When RasoolAllah (saw) narrated this hadith to Us, He said, "Iblees (la), along with his shaitan (la), will fly around the earth on that day joyful,

He will call out to them and say, "O' Shaitan (la)! We have achieved our goal with the children of Adam (as). We have attained our goal for their destruction. And we have caused them to be the inherit ants of hellfire, except for those who remain committed (Imam Hussain (asws) and His Companions).

Now focus all of your energies on creating doubts and inciting hatred amongst the people against Them (Ahlul Bayt (asws)). Lure the people away from Them (Ahlul Bayt asws) and away from Their (Ahlul Bayt asws) followers so that you may strengthen the deviation and kufr (disbelief) amongst the people."

Ameerul Momineen (asws) added, "Even though Iblees (la) is but a liar, he has spoken the truth about the people. For no good deed will be of any benefit to those who oppose You and excepting major sins, no bad deed will harm a person who loves and follows You."

Zaidah added, "After Ali (asws) ibn Hussain (asws) narrated the above hadith to me, He (Imam Zainul Abideen asws) added, "Even if you were to ride your camel for one full year in order to come to hear this hadith, it would still not be enough."

HADITH 2

Imam Jafar Sadiq (asws) narrates:

"The land of Kaaba once said, "Who is there that is like me? For Allah built His House upon Me. People travel from far away to visit Me. And I have been chosen by Allah as His Haram and as His sanctuary."

Allah replied to it and said, "Refrain from speaking. I swear by My Glory and My Magnificence that your honor compared to the honor that I bestowed upon the land of Karbala is like the drop of water upon a needle that was dipped into the sea. If it were not for the dust of Karbala, I would not have honored You. If it were not for that which is buried within the land of Karbala, I would not have created You nor would I have created the House about which you have boasted. Now compose yourself and be humble in front of the land of Karbala. Do not be proud or arrogant in front of it or I shall throw you into the fires of Hell."

HADITH 3

Imam Muhammad Baqir (asws) narrates:

"Allah (swt) created, blessed, and made pure the land of Karbala twenty-four thousand years before He created the Kaaba. It was blessed and purified before the creation of any created being and will remain this way until Allah ascends it unto the Heavens and appoints it as the best of lands in Jannah. It will become the best dwelling in Jannah and Allah will make it as the dwelling of His Auwliya (chosen ones)."

HADITH 4

Imam Zainul Abideen Ali (asws) ibn Hussain (asws) narrates:

"Allah chose the land of Karbala as a safe and blessed Haram twenty-four thousand years before He created the land of the Kaaba and chose it (land of Kaaba) as a Haram. When Allah (swt) shall make the earth quake on the Day of Judgment, Karbala and all of its dust will ascend while being shining and pure. It will be placed amongst the best of the gardens and dwellings in Jannah. None except the Prophets and the Messengers from the Ulul 'Azm shall dwell within it.

It will shine amongst the gardens of Jannah like a star shines amongst the stars for the people of the earth. Its radiate light will be so great it will blur the vision of all of the inhabitants of Jannah.

The land of Karbala will cry out and say, "I am the purified and blessed land of Allah which held the body of the Master of the Martyrs and the Master of the Youth of Paradise.""

HADITH 5

Imam Muhammad Baqir (asws) narrates:

Ghadiriyah (another name for Karbala) is the land on which Allah spoke to Musa (as) ibn Imran (as) and the land on which He confided in Nuh (as). It is the most honorable land with Allah and if it had not existed, there would be no place for Allah to entrust with the bodies of His Hujjat (proofs) and His Prophets. Therefore, you should perform the Ziarat of Our graves in Ghadiriyyah."

HADITH 6

Imam Jafar Sadiq (asws) narrates:

"Ghadiriyyah is from the plains of Baytul Maqaddis."

HADITH 7

Imam Jafar Sadiq (asws) narrates from His Fathers (asws) who narrate from Ameerul Momineen (asws) who narrates from RasoolAllah (saw) who said:

"My Son (asws) will be buried in a land called Karbala. It is the land which contained the Dome of Islam where Allah saved the momin who believed in Nuh (as) at the time of the flood."

HADITH 8

Imam Muhammad Baqir (asws) narrates:

"Whoever spends the night of Arafah in Karbala and remains there until Eidul Adha will be protected by Allah from corruption throughout the year."

HADITH 9

Ibn Yahya narrates from his father who narrates:

Imam Jafar Sadiq (asws) narrates:

"Perform the Ziarat of Karbala. Do not neglect it for the Best of the Sons of the Prophets is buried within it. The angels performed the Ziarat of Karbala one thousand years before My Grandfather, Hussain (asws), became an inhabitant within it. Not one night passes where Jibrael (as) and Mikael (as) do not perform His Ziarat. O'Yahya! Seek to journey to that land."

HADITH 10

Imam Jafar Sadiq (asws) narrates:

"Ameerul Momineen (asws) and some of His companions passed by Karbala. When He (Ameerul Momineen asws) passed by it, His eyes were filled with tears and He said:

"This is where They will descend from their mounts. This is where They will unpack. This is where Their blood will be spilled. Blessed are you, o' clay of Karbala, for the blood of the Greatest Essence will be shed upon you."

HADITH 11

Imam Jafar Sadiq (asws) narrates:

Ameerul Momineen Ali (asws) ibn Abi Talib (as) was traveling with some companions. They were nearing to Karbala, when Ameerul Momineen (asws) rode ahead of the others. When He reached the place of the martyrdom of the martyrs of Karbala, He said, "Two hundred prophets, two hundred successors, and two hundred of the grandsons of the prophets have died here. All of them and all of their followers are martyrs.

Then Ameerul Momineen (asws) rode around the area, and said, "This is where they will descend from Their mounts. And this is where the martyrs will be slaughtered. No one previous has preceded them in status and no one to come will ever attain their station."

HADITH 12

Imam Muhammad Baqir (asws) narrates:

"Allah (swt) blessed and purified Karbala twenty-four thousand years before He created the Kaaba. Karbala was blessed and purified before the creation of any of the created beings. Allah will make it the best of lands in Jannah."

HADITH 13

See hadith 12

HADITH 14

Safwan al Jammal narrates:

I heard Aba Abdullah Imam Jafar Sadiq (asws) say, "Allah (swt) has elevated some lands and some bodies of water about others. Some of these lands and waters bragged to the others. Some transgressed and were punished for not being humble before Allah.

Therefore, Allah empowered the mushriks (polytheists) over the land of the Kaaba and made the water of Zamzam become salty.

However, the land of Karbala and the water of the River Furat were the first land and water that glorified Allah.

Therefore Allah blessed them and said to the land of Karbala, "Convey to them that which Allah has honored you with. For the lands and waters have shown off to one another."

The land of Karbala said, "I am the sacred and blessed land of Allah. The ability to cure has been placed within my soil and in my water. Even so I am not a braggart. Instead I am humbled and subdue before He who has blessed me. I do not boast to those who are beneath me. Instead I am thankful to Allah."

Afterwards, Allah honored the land of Karbala, increased His blessings upon it for its humbleness and rewarded it with Hussain (asws) and His Companions.

Then Imam (asws) added, "Allah elevates those who humble themselves before Him and degrades those who are arrogant."

Chapter 89

The Greatness of the Ha'yr (burial place) of Hussain (asws)

HADITH 1

Ishaq ibn Ammar narrates:

I heard Aba Abdullah Imam Jafar Sadiq (asws) say, "The location of the grave of Hussain (asws) ibn Ali (asws) has been a garden from the gardens of Jannah since the day He departed this world."

HADITH 2

Imam Jafar Sadiq (asws) narrates:

"The sacred boundaries of the grave of Hussain (asws) are one parasang (approximately four miles) by one parasang from each of its four corners."

HADITH 3

Ishaq ibn Ammar narrates:

I heard Aba Abdullah Imam Jafar Sadiq (asws) say, "There is a known boundary for the location of the grave f Hussain (asws) ibn Ali (asws) and whoever knows it and seeks refuge while in it will be protected. "

I said, "May I be sacrificed upon You! Describe its boundary for me."

Imam (asws) replied, "According to the current location of His grave, measure twenty-five ells (approximately 18 inches) from the direction of His feet, twenty-five ells from the direction of His face, twenty-five ells from the direction of His back, and twenty-five ells from the direction of His head.

The location of the grave of Hussain (asws) has been a garden from the gardens of Jannah since the day He (Hussain asws) left this world, and the deeds of the zuwwar (Visitors) ascend to the heavens from its location. There is neither a prophet nor any angel in the heavens that does not seek the permission of Allah to perform the Ziarat of the grave of Hussain (asws). There is always a continuous assembly descending to perform His Ziarat and an assembly ascending back to the heavens."

Chapter 90

Most Beloved Place for Dua (supplication) is Shrine of Imam Hussain (asws)

HADITH 1

Abi Hashim al Jafari narrates:

When Abul Hasan Imam Ali Naqi (asws) was ill, He sent for me and Muhammad ibn Hamzah.

Muhammad ibn Hamza arrived before I did. When I arrived, he (Muhammad ibn Hamza) informed me that the Imam (asws) had repeatedly said, "Send someone to the Ha'yr on My behalf."

I (Abi Hashim al Jafari) said to Muhammad ibn Hamzah, "Why did you not offer to go to the Ha'yr on His behalf?"

I (Abi Hashim al Jafari) then went to the Imam (asws) and said, "May I be sacrificed upon You! I will go to the Ha'yr on Your behalf."

Imam (asws) replied, "Make your plans carefully, for Muhammad will not keep this matter hidden from Zaid ibn Ali and I do not wish for him to find out."

I (Abi Hashim al Jafari) mentioned this to Ali ibn Bilal. Upon hearing this Ali ibn Bilal asked, "Why would the Imam (asws) want to send someone to the Ha'yr when He is the Ha'yr?"

I (Abi Hashim al Jafari) returned to Askar (Samarra) and went to visit with the Imam (asws). When I was about to leave Imam (asws) asked me to stay. After some time had passed, I informed the Imam (asws) about that which Bilal had said.

Imam (asws) replied, and said, "Why did you not reply to him and say, "RasoolAllah (saw) used to circulate around the Kaaba and kiss the Hajar al Aswad even though the sacredness of RasoolAllah (saw) is greater. Even a momin is greater in sacredness than the House of Allah.

Allah, also, ordered RasoolAllah (saw) to go to Arafat and remain there while RasoolAllah (saw) is more sacred than Arafat. The reason Allah ordered RasoolAllah (saw) to perform these actions is because Allah prefers duas (supplications) be made in those places. And I (Imam asws) love to have someone pray for Me in those places, which Allah prefers. And the Ha'yr is one of those places."

HADITH 2

Abi Hashim al Jafari narrates:

Muhammad ibn Hamzah and I (Abi Hashim al Jafari) went to visit Imam Ali Naqi (asws) during a time when the Imam (asws) was ill. The Imam (asws) said to us, "Take some of My money and send some people to the Ha'yr on My behalf."

After we left the Imam (asws), Muhammad ibn Hamzah said, "The Imam (asws) wants us to send someone to the Ha'yr while He is as sacred as the One in the Ha'yr (Imam Hussain asws)."

When I returned to the Imam (asws), I (Abi Hashim al Jafari) mentioned to Him what Muhammad ibn Hamzah had said.

The Imam (asws) replied, "There are certain places Allah loves to be worshipped at and the Ha'yr of Hussain (asws) is one of those places."

HADITH 3

See hadith 1

Chapter 91

The Clay of the Grave of Hussain (asws) is Khak e Shifa (a means of curing ailments)

HADITH 1

Ibn Abu Yafoor narrates:

I asked Aba Abdullah Imam Jafar Sadiq (asws), "Why is it that some find benefit from the clay of the grave of Hussain (asws) while others do not?"

Imam (asws) replied, "I swear by Allah, whom there is no god but Him, that anyone who uses it while believing he will receive benefit from Allah will receive the benefit from Allah."

HADITH 2

Some companions narrated:

A woman gave me some yarn and asked me to give it to the keepers of the Kaaba to use it to make the cover of the Kaaba.

When we arrived in Medina, I went to Abu Jafar Imam Muhammad Baqir (asws) and said, "May I be sacrificed upon You! A woman gave me some yarn and asked me to give it to the keepers of the Kaaba. So that they may use it to make the cover of the Kaaba, However I am hesitant to give to those people because they are not trustworthy."

Imam (asws) said, "Sell it and buy some honey and saffron from the money. Mix some rain water with the honey and saffron, and mix that with the clay of the grave of Hussain (asws). Distribute it amongst the Shia so they may cure their ill with it."

HADITH 3

Imam Jafar Sadiq (asws) narrates:

"The clay of the grave of Hussain (asws) is the cure for every disease."

HADITH 4

See hadith 3

HADITH 5

Imam Jafar Sadiq (asws) narrates:

"The clay of the grave of Hussain (asws) is a cure for every disease even if the clay is collected from the distance of one mile away from the Grave."

HADITH 6

Imam Jafar Sadiq (asws) narrates:

"Allah will cure anyone who has an illness if he starts using the clay of the grave of Hussain (asws) as a means of treatment except for the death."

HADITH 7

Muhammad ibn Muslim narrates

Once, when I (Muhammad ibn Muslim) was ill, I went to Medina and some people informed Imam Muhammad Baqir (asws) of my illness. Imam (asws) sent a boy to me with a drink that was covered by a cloth. The boy gave me the drink and said, "Drink! The Imam (asws) has ordered me to not return until you have drunk it."

I drank the drink immediately. It smelled of musk and was cold but very tasty. After I finished drinking the drink, the boy said to me, "Your Master (Imam Baqir asws) has ordered you to come to meet Him as soon as you have finished drinking."

I was hesitant to obey this command because of the weakness I had felt prior to drinking this drink which caused me to be unable to stand, but as soon as the drink entered my body, I felt my strength returning and the pain I felt was eased. I then went to the Imam (asws) and asked His permission to enter.

Imam (asws) replied, "O' healthy one! Enter."

I entered while tears fell down my face. I said salam to the Imam (asws) and kissed His hand and head.

Imam (asws) asked, "O' Muhammad! Why are you crying?"

I (Muhammad ibn Muslim) replied, "May I be sacrificed upon You! I cry because of the ache I feel in my heart due to living so far from You and for not having the ability to be able to live near You so that I may look upon You often."

Imam (asws) replied, "Regarding your lack of means, this is the will of Allah that afflictions and tribulations fall quickly upon all of Our friends and those who love Us.

Regarding the heartache, the momin are heartbroken in this life; having to live among the deviated creation until they leave this world by the mercy of Allah.

Regarding the distance you live from Us, you should find solace by remembering Aba Abdullah Imam Hussain (asws) who is in a land beside the River Furat, which is even farther from Us.

Regarding your love for Us and your desire to look upon Us, Allah knows what is in your heart and He will reward you for it accordingly."

Then Imam (asws) asked, "Do you visit the grave of Hussain (asws)?"

I replied, "Yes, but I am in a state of great fear and apprehension when I do."

Imam (asws) replied, "The more danger you face, the greater the reward will be. The reward will be equal to the amount of fear in your heart. Those who visit the grave of Hussain (asws) while fearing for their life will return being forgiven. The angels say salam to them. RasoolAllah (saw) sees them and their actions and He will pray for them. Allah will make them feel safe on the day when people will be raised before the Lord of the Worlds. *they returned with grace and favor from Allah, and no harm touched them. They followed the good pleasure of Allah,*" (Quran 3:174)

Then Imam (asws) asked, "How did you find the drink?"

I replied, "I testify that You (Imam asws) are from the Family of Mercy and You are the successor of the successors. When the boy brought the drink You had sent for me, I could not even stand as my legs were too weak. I had lost all faith that I would regain my health. After I drank the drink that he brought for me, I smelt a smell the likes of which I had never smelt before and tasted a coolness the likes of which I had never tasted before. I have never tasted a drink sweeter than the one You sent for me. After I finished drinking it, the boy said to me, "The Imam (asws) ordered me to inform you to meet with Him as soon as you finish the drink."

Even though I knew my condition was extremely poor, I thought to myself that I would come to you even if it meant my death. But as soon as I began coming towards You, I felt the strength returning to my body and the pain began to ease. All praise be to Allah who created You, a Mercy upon the Shia and upon me."

Imam (asws) said, "O' Muhammad! That which you drank contained the clay of the grave of Hussain (asws). It is the best of cures. Do not replace it with anything else. We give this to Our children and women. We find the all of the blessings within it."

I asked, "May I be sacrificed upon You! Should we take some of this clay in order to cure our ailments?"

Imam (asws) replied, "Often people take the clay with them when they leave the Ha'yr. But sometimes they pass by a jinn or animal which is ill or they may pass by some other being which is ill or diseased, and as they pass this ill being, the ill one smells the clay. And by doing so the ill being benefits from this and the blessing within the clay disappears. But the clay, which We use, is not like this.

However, what I just mentioned to you is the reason why not everyone who touches the clay of the grave of Hussain (asws) or not everyone who drinks from water that was mixed with the clay is cured immediately. For the clay is like the Hajar al Aswad. Originally it was as clear as the purest corundum, but as time passed and the ill, the kafireen and the pagans continuously touched it in order to cure their ailments, it (Hajar al Aswad) turned black."

I (Muhammad ibn Muslim) asked, "May I be sacrificed upon You! What is wrong with the manner in which I take the clay?"

Imam (asws) replied, "You show it to others and do as they do. You disrespect its sanctity by placing it in your saddlebag or in things that will tarnish it. Thereby causing it to lose the benefit you seek to receive from it."

I replied, "May I be sacrificed upon You! All which You is true."

Imam (asws) then said, "Most who take the clay from the grave of Hussain (asws) do not know the way in which it should be taken. This is why its benefit does not remain in the hands of the people."

I asked, "May I be sacrificed upon You! How should I take the clay so that I take it in the same manner as You?"

Imam (asws) replied, "Would you like for Me to give you some?"

I replied, "Yes."

Imam (asws) asked, "What will you do with it?"

I replied, "I will take it with me."

Imam (asws) asked, "Where will you carry it?"

I replied, "In my clothes."

Imam (asws) replied, "Then you are repeating your old ways. Drink from the water here which contains the clay. Do not carry it with you for its benefit will not remain if you leave with it."

Afterwards Imam (asws) had me (Muhammad ibn Muslim) to drink twice from the water. I felt no signs of the illness from which I had originally been suffering from so I left."

HADITH 8

Imam Jafar Sadiq (asws) narrates:

If a momin who suffers from an illness but the momin believes in the (rights check translation) of Aba Abdullah Imam Hussain (asws) and believes in His purity and His Divine Authority, if that momin takes as little as a touch of a fingertip from the clay of the grave of Hussain (asws), the momin will be cured by it."

Chapter 92

The Clay from the Grave of Hussain (asws)
is Khak e Shifa (cure) and a means of protection

HADITH 1

A companion narrates:

Imam Reza (asws) sent me (the companion) some clothes which had been wrapped in a bundle. In the middle of the wrapped clothing was some clay. I asked the person who had brought the clothes about the clay.

The person who brought the clothes said, "It is the clay of the grave of Hussain (asws). The Imam (asws) does not send clothes or any other thing to anyone without placing some of the clay within it and saying "It (clay) is a means of protection by the permission of Allah."

HADITH 2

Hussain ibn Abul Ala narrates:

I heard Aba Abdullah Imam Jafar Sadiq (asws) say, "Make the first thing a newborn tastes be the clay from the grave of Hussain (asws). For the clay is a means of protection."

HADITH 3

Abul Yasa narrates:

I heard a man ask Aba Abdullah Imam Jafar Sadiq (asws), "Can I keep some of the clay from the grave of Hussain (asws) with me so that I may seek blessings from it?"

Imam (asws) replied, "There is nothing wrong with that."

HADITH 4

Muhammad ibn Ziyad narrates from his aunt who narrates:

I heard Aba Abdullah Imam Jafar Sadiq (asws) say, "The clay of the burial place of Hussain (asws) is the cure for every disease and a protection from every worry."

HADITH 5

See hadith 4

HADITH 6

See chapter 91 hadith 8

Chapter 93

How and from where the clay of the grave of Hussain (asws) should be taken

HADITH 1

Yunus ibn Rafee narrates:

Imam Jafar Sadiq (asws) said, "There is a red dust near the Head of Hussain (asws) ibn Ali (asws) which is the cure for every disease except death."

After hearing this hadith, we went to the grave of Hussain (asws) and began digging in the area next to the Head of the Grave. After digging an ell (approximately 18 inches), about one dirham (approximately 3 grams) of red dust which had the appearance of sand began flowing down from the direction of the Head of Imam Hussain (asws).

We took it to Kufa, mixed it with water, and then distributed it amongst the people as a means of curing their ailments."

HADITH 2

Imam Jafar Sadiq (asws) narrates:

"The clay of the grave of Hussain (asws) can be collected up to a distance of seventy fathoms (one fathom is approximately 1.8 meters) from the Grave."

HADITH 3

Abdullah ibn Sinan narrates:

Imam Jafar Sadiq (asws) said,

"When any of you holds the clay of the grave of Hussain (asws), you should recite:

اللهم إني أسالك بحق الملك الذي تناوله، و الرسول الذي بوأه، و الوصي الذي ضمن فيه، أن تجعله شفاء من كل دآء

O' Allah! I ask You through the angel who chose it, the Messenger who appointed it and the Successor who is lying with it to make this clay the cure for every disease (here you should mention the name of the particular disease)

HADITH 4

Imam Muhammad Baqir (asws) narrates:

"When you take the clay from the Grave of Hussain (asws) you should say:

اللهم بحق هذه التربة، و بحق الملك الموكل بها و الملك الذي كربها، و بحق الوصي هو فيها صل على محمد ﷺ و آل محمدّ، و اجعل هذا الطين شفاء من داء و أماناً من كل خوف

O' Allah! I ask You through the right of this dust, through the right of the angel who is devoted to it and the angel who collected it and brought it (Jibrael as) and through the right of the Successor who lies within it to send Your blessing on Muhammad (saw) wa Aal e Muhammad (asws) and to make this clay a cure for my every ailment and a means of protection against my every fear.

"If you do this, then the clay will be a cure for you from every ailment and a protection from every worry."

HADITH 5

Abu Hamzah Thumali narrates:

I was in Mecca when I said to Aba Abdullah Imam Jafar Sadiq (asws), "May I be sacrificed upon You! I have seen some of our companions take the clay from the Ha'yr (burial place of Imam Hussain asws) in order to use it as a means of curing an ailment. Doe the clay truly contain a cure the way they say it does?"

Imam (asws) replied, "Yes. Even if it is collected at a distance of four miles away from the Ha'yr, there is still a means of cure within it. The same applies to the grave of My

Grandfather, RasoolAllah (saw). As well as the graves of Hasan (asws), Ali (asws) ibn Hussain (asws) (Imam Zainul Abideen asws), and Abu Jafar Imam Muhammad Baqir (asws).

Imam (asws) continued, "Partake of the clay of the grave of Hussain (asws) for within it is a cure for every ailment and a shield against every worry. There is no comparison to it (clay) except for supplicating.

Unfortunately, the vessels in which it is kept and the manner in which the people use it removes the benefits from it. Those who have no doubt will find benefit from it, and by the permission of Allah, it will serve to suffice them and they will not be in need of any other cure.

Another way, which causes the clay to lose its benefit, is when the shaitans and kafir jinns pass by it. For there is no being that passes near it that does not smell its fragrance. These shaitans and kafir jinns brush against it out of envy causing its fragrance to disappear.

The shaitans and kafir jinns assemble themselves outside of the Ha'yr; waiting for any person to collect some of the clay and bring it with them outside of the Ha'yr. They do this because they are prevented from entering the Ha'yr by the angels that surround it. So they wait for the people to collect it so that they may be able to remove the benefit from the clay.

If a person was able to carry the clay properly so that the benefit remains intact, and then used that clay to treat a patient, his ailment would be cured immediately.

Whenever you take from this clay, be sure to keep it hidden and to continuously mention the name of Allah."

Imam (asws) then said, "I am aware there are some who degrade the clay immensely by carrying it in the feedbag or saddlebags of their camel, mules or donkeys. Some also carry it in their own food containers while others place it in the handkerchiefs they use to wipe their hands with after eating.

How can a person who dishonors the clay in this way think he can find a cure within it? The uncertainty which resides in the hearts of those who belittle the sanctity of the clay is what causes the clay to lose its benefit for them and others."

HADITH 6

Imam Jafar Sadiq (asws) narrates:

"The clay of the grave of Hussain (asws) can be collected within a radius of seventy fathoms (approximately 128 meters) by seventy fathoms from the actual grave."

HADITH 7

Ali ibn Muhammad narrates a Masoom Imam (asws) said:

"In order to seal the benefit within the clay of the grave of Hussain (asws), one should recite Sura Inna Anzalnah (Quran Sura 97 Al Qadr) on it."

HADITH 8

Masoom Imam (asws) narrates:

When one takes the clay of the grave of Hussain (asws), he should recite the following:

اللهم بحق هذه التربة الطاهرة، و بحق البقعة الطينة، و بحق الوصي الذي تواريه، و بحق جده و أبيه، و امه و أخيه، و الملائكة الذين يحفون به، و الملائكة العكوف على قبر و ليك، ينتظرون نصره صلى الله عليهم أجمعين، اجعل لي فيه شفاء من كل داء، و أماناً من كل خوف، و غنى من كل فقر، و عزاً من كل ذل، و أوسع به علي في رزقي، و أصح به جسمي

O'Allah! I beseech You through the right of this purified dust, and through the right of this blessed spot, and through the right of the Successor who is buried within it and through the right of His Grandfather (saw), His Father (asws), His Mother (sa), His Brother (asws), the angels who surround Him, and those angels which dedicated themselves to wait until the reappearance of Imam e Zamana (Atfs), to place within the clay a means of cure for my every ailment and a means of protection for me from every worry. To make it a source of wealth in my time of need and a mark of honor in my time of disgrace, increase my rizq and maintain my health through it.

HADITH 9

Imam Jafar Sadiq (asws) narrates:

"The sacred boundaries of the grave of Hussain (asws) are one parasang (approximately four miles) by one parasang by one parasang by one parasang."

HADITH 10

A companion narrates:

I said to Aba Abdullah Imam Jafar Sadiq (asws), "I am a man with many illnesses. There is no medicine which I have not tried."

Imam (asws) said, "Why have you not used the dust from the grave of Hussain (asws)? For within it lies a means of cure for every disease and a means of protection from every worry.

When you take from it, you should say:

اللهم إني أسألك بحق هذه الطينة، و بحق الملك الذي أخذها، و بحق النبي الذي قبضها، و بحق الوصي الذي حل فيها، صل على محمد ﷺ و أهل بيته، و اجعل لي فيها شفاء من كل داء، و أماناً من كل خوف

O'Allah! I beseech You through the right of this clay, through the right of the Angel who collected it (Jibrael as), through the right of the Prophet (saw) who held it, and through the right of the Successor who is lying within it to send Your blessing upon Muhammad (saw) wa Aal e Muhammad (asws) and to make this clay as a means of cure against every illness and a means of protection against my every fear."

Then Imam (asws) added, "The angel who collected it is Jibrael (as). He (Jibrael as) presented it to RasoolAllah (saw) and said, "This is the dust of this Son (asws) of Yours. Your ummah (nation) will martyr Him (Hussain asws) after You (RasoolAllah saw)."

The Prophet who held it is Muhammad (saw) and the successor lying within it is Hussain (asws) ibn Ali (asws), the Master of Martyrs."

I (narrator) said, "I understand that it is a cure for my every illness but how is it a means of protection against my worries?"

Imam (asws) replied, "If you are worried due to a tyrant or oppressor, do not leave your house unless you are carrying some of it with you. When you take from it, you should say:

اللهم إن هذه طينة قبر الحسينّ وليك و ابن وليك، اتخذتها حرزاً لما أخاف و لما لا أخاف

O'Allah! This is the clay of the grave of Hussain (asws), Your Wali and the Son (asws) of Your Wali (asws). I carry it with me as a means of protection against that which worries me and that which does not.

Imam (asws) added, "It is possible a misfortune you do not fear may befall you."

I took the clay as He (Imam asws) ordered and I swear by Allah I became healthy. It also served as a means of protection against those things which caused me to worry and that which I was unaware of just as the Imam (asws) said it would. Praise be to Allah I have not met any misfortunes since I began carrying this clay."

HADITH 11

Muhammad ibn Ishaq al Qazwini narrates:

I took some of the clay, which is close to the head of the grave of Hussain (asws) ibn Ali (asws). It was a red colored clay. I took it to Imam Reza (asws).

Imam (asws) held it in His hand, inhaled its fragrance, and then began to weep.

Then the Imam (asws) said, "This is the dust of the grave of My Grandfather (Hussain asws)."

HADITH 12

Abu Hamzah Thumali narrates Imam Jafar Sadiq (asws) said:

"When you want to carry with you the clay of the grave of Hussain (asws), recite Sura Fatiha, Mu'awwazatain (Sura al Falaq and al Nas), Qul Huwallahu Ahad, Inna Anzalnah (Sura al Qadr), Ya Seen, and Ayatul Kursi. Then recite the following:

اللهم بحق محمد ﷺ عبدك و رسولك و حبيبك و نبيك و أمينك

O'Allah! I beseech You through the right of Muhammad (saw), who was Your servant and Messenger, Your beloved, Your Prophet, and Your Trustee.

و بحق أمير المؤمنين عليّ بن أبي طالبّ عبدك و أخي رسولك

And through the right of Ameerul Momineen Ali (asws) ibn Abi Talib (as), who was Your servant and the brother of Your Messenger (saw)

و بحق فاطمةّ بنت نبيك و زوجة وليك

And through the right of Fatima (sa) who was the Daughter of Your Messenger and the Wife of Your Wali

و بحق الحسنّ و الحسينّ و بحق الأئمة الراشدين

And through the right of Hasan (asws) and Hussain (asws) and through the right of the Rightly Guided Imams (asws)

و بحق هذه الترجة، و بحق الملك الموكل بها

And through the right of this dust and through the right of the angel devoted to it

و بحق الوصي الذي حل فيها، و بحق الجسد الذي تضمنت، و بحق السبط الذي ضمنت

And through the right of the Successor who is buried within it, through the right of His body, and through the right of the Grandson held within

و بحق جميع ملائكتك و أنبيائك و رسلك صل على محمد آل محمد، و اجعل لي هذا الطين شفاء من كل داء ولمن يستشفي به من كل داء و فقم و مرض، و أماناً من كل خوف

And through the right of all of Your angels, prophets, and messengers to send Your blessing on Muhammad (saw) wa Aal e Muhammad (asws) and to make this clay a means of cure for my every disease and for all who use it as a cure for any ailment. Also make it as a means of protection against all that which I fear

اللهم بحق محمد ﷺ و أهل بيته، اجعله علماً نافعاً ورزقا و اسعاً، و شفاء من كل داء وسقم و آفة و عاهت و جميع الأوجاع كلها، إنك على كل شيء قدير

O' Allah! I beseech You through the right of Muhammad (saw) wa Aal e Muhammad (asws) to make this clay as a source of knowledge and a source of rizq for me. And to make it a cure for my every ailment, sickness, disease, disability, and pain. For You are powerful over all things.

Then recite the following:

اللهم رب هذه التربة المباركة الميمونة، و الملك الذي هبط بها، و الوصي الذي هو فيها، صل على محمد ﷺ و آل محمد و سلم، و انفعني بها، إنك على كل شيء قدير

O'Lord of this blessed dust! O' Lord of the angel who brought it down with Him! O' Lord of the Successor who is buried within it! Send Your Salam and blessings upon Muhammad (saw) wa Aal e Muhammad (asws) and allow me to gain benefit from it (clay). For You are powerful over all things.

Chapter 94

Dua You Should Recite before Consuming the Clay from the grave of Hussain (asws)

HADITH 1

Imam Jafar Sadiq (asws) narrates:

"The clay of the grave of Hussain (asws) is a cure for every ailment. Recite the following before you eat from it:"

بسم الله و بالله

In the name of Allah and by Allah.

اللهم اجعله رزقاً و اسعاً، ع علماً نافعاً و شفاء من كل داء، إنك على كل شيء قدير

O'Allah! Make this the cause of my rizq (sustenance) and the source of beneficial knowledge and means of cure for my every ailment. For You are powerful over all things.

HADITH 2

Imam Jafar Sadiq (asws) narrates:

"Recite the following when you take from the clay of the Mazloom (Oppressed) (Imam Hussain asws) and place it in your mouth:

اللهم رب هذه التربة المباركة، و رب هذه الوصي الذي وارثه، صل على محمد ﷺ و آل محمد، و اجعله علماً نافعاً، و رزقاً و اسعاً، و شفاء من كل داء

O' Allah! I beseech You through the right of this dust, through the right of the Angel who held it (Jibrael as), through the right of the Prophet (saw) who embraced it and through the right of the Imam (asws) who is buried within it to send Your blessings upon Muhammad (saw) wa Aal e Muhammad (asws) and to allow this dust to be of benefit in curing me and act as a source of rizq (sustenance) for me, and to be my protection against every worry and ailment.

"If you recite this, Allah will cure you and bestow good health upon you."

Chapter 95

Consuming clay other than the clay of the
Grave of Hussain (asws) is Haram because
the clay of the Grave of Hussain (asws)
is Khak e Shifa

HADITH 1

Imam Jafar Sadiq (asws) narrates:

"Eating the clay is haram the way eating the flesh of the swine is haram. If a person dies
from having eaten clay other than the clay of the Grave of Hussain (asws), I will not pray
for him. For the clay of the grave of Hussain (asws) contains a cure for every ailment. But if
a person eats the clay of the grave of Hussain (asws) in order to satisfy a craving, he will
find no benefit in it."

HADITH 2

Sa'ad ibn Sa'ad narrates:

I asked Abul Hasan Imam Reza (asws) about eating clay.

Imam (asws) replied, "Eating clay is haram in the same way eating meetah (dead animal or
animal that is not slaughtered according to Islamic tradition), blood, and the flesh of the

swine is haram; except for the clay of the grave of Hussain (asws). For the clay of the grave of Hussain (asws) contains a cure for every ailment and acts as a protection against every worry."

HADITH 3

Imam Jafar Sadiq (asws) narrates:

"It is haram for mankind to eat clay except for the clay of the grave of Hussain (asws). Allah (swt) will cure those who eat from it in order to treat an ailment."

HADITH 4

Sama'ah ibn Mihran narrates:

Imam Jafar Sadiq (asws) said, "Eating clay is haram for mankind except the clay of the grave of Hussain (asws). Allah (swt) will cure those who eat the clay of the grave of Hussain (asws) as a means of treatment for illness."

HADITH 5

Imam Jafar Sadiq (asws) narrates:

"Anyone who sells the clay from the grave of Hussain (asws) has sold the flesh of Hussain (asws)."

Chapter 96

How to perform the Ziarat of the grave of Hussain (asws)
from a great distance

HADITH 1

Imam Jafar Sadiq (asws) narrates:

"If any from you lives far from Us, then you should go to the highest point of your house, perform two rakats of prayer, turn towards Our graves and say salam to Us. By doing this your salam will reach Us."

HADITH 2

Sadeer narrates:

Aba Abdullah Imam Jafar Sadiq (asws) said to me (Sadeer):

"O' Sadeer! How difficult is it for you to perform the Ziarat of the grave of Hussain (asws) five times on Fridays and once on every other day?"

I replied, "May I be sacrificed upon You! There is a great distance between us and His (Imam Hussain asws) grave."

Imam (asws) said, "Go to the roof of your house, look to the right and then to the left, raise your head towards the sky, and then face the direction of the grave of Hussain (asws) and say:

416

السلام عليك يا ابا عبد الله

Salam to You, O' Aba Abdullah (asws)!

السلام عليك ورحمة الله و بركاته

May the blessings and salam of Allah be upon You

"By doing this, one ziarat will be written for you. And it is equal to more than one hajj and one umrah."

Sadeer added, "After hearing this, there were times when I would perform this ziarat twenty times throughout the day."

HADITH 3

Sadeer narrates:

Aba Abdullah Imam Jafar Sadiq (asws) asked me (Sadeer), "O' Sadeer! Do you perform the Ziarat of the grave of Hussain (asws) once per day?"

I replied, "May I be sacrificed upon You! No."

Imam (asws) said, "How negligent the people are. Do you perform His Ziarat once per month?"

I replied, "No."

Imam (asws) asked, "Once per year?"

I replied, "Sometimes."

Imam (asws) said, "O' Sadeer! How negligent are the people regarding Hussain (asws)! Do you not know Allah has one million disheveled angels covered with dust, who mourn over Hussain (asws) and who perform His Ziarat continuously without ever stopping?

O' Sadeer! How difficult would it be for you to perform the Ziarat of the grave of Hussain (asws) five times on Friday and once on the other days?"

I replied, "May I be sacrificed upon You! There is a great distance between us and His (Hussain asws) grave."

Imam (asws) said, "Go to the roof of your house, look to the right and then to the left. Then raise your head towards the sky. And then face in the direction of the grave of Hussain (asws) and say:

السلام عليك يا ابا عبد الله

Salam to You, O' Aba Abdullah (asws)!

السلام عليك ورحمة الله و بركاته

May the blessings and salam of Allah be upon You

"By doing this, one ziarat will be written for you. And it is equal to more than one hajj and one umrah."

Sadeer added, "After hearing this, there were times when I would perform this ziarat twenty times throughout the day."

HADITH 4

Sulaiman narrates from his father, Isa, who said:

I (Isa) asked Aba Abdullah Imam Jafar Sadiq (asws), "How should I perform Your Ziarat if I am not able to visit You?"

Imam (asws) replied, "O' Isa! When you are unable to come to perform My Ziarat, on Friday you should perform ghusl or wudhu, then go to the roof of your house. Perform two rakats of prayer and then turn towards My direction.

Those who come to visit Me while I am still in this world are like those who have performed My Ziarat after I have left this world. Those who perform My Ziarat after I have left this world are like those who have visited Me while I was still in this world."

HADITH 5

Sadeer narrates:

Aba Abdullah Imam Jafar Sadiq (asws) asked me (Sadeer), "O' Sadeer! Why do you not regularly perform the Ziarat of the grave of Hussain (asws)?"

I (Sadeer) replied, "Because I am occupied."

Imam (asws) asked, "Would you like for me to teach you something which if performed, Allah will record the Ziarat for you?"

I replied, "Yes, may I be sacrificed upon You!"

Imam (asws) said, "Perform ghusl. Then go to the roof of your house and turn towards the grave of Hussain and say salam to Him. By doing this, the Ziarat of Hussain (asws) will be recorded for you."

HADITH 6

Abu Ahmad narrates from a companion who narrates:

Imam Jafar Sadiq (asws) said to me (companion), "If there is a great distance between you and Us, then you should go to the roof of your house, perform two rakats of prayer, turn towards Our graves, and say salam to Us. By doing this, your salam will reach Us."

HADITH 7

Abu Abdullah al Barqi narrates:

Hanan ibn Sadeer al Sairafee went to visit Aba Abdullah Imam Jafar Sadiq (asws) while a group of companions were with Him (Imam asws).

Imam (asws) asked Hanan, "O' Hanan ibn Sadeer! Do you perform the Ziarat of Aba Abdullah Imam Hussain (asws) monthly?"

Hanan replied, "No."

Imam (asws) asked, "What about once every other month?"

Hanan replied, "No."

Imam (asws) asked, "What about once per year?"

Hanan replied, "No."

Imam (asws) said, "Whoa! How negligent the people are towards their Master (Imam Hussain asws)."

Hanan said, "O' Son of RasoolAllah (saw)! I do not due my lack of finances and the great distance between us and Him (Imam asws)."

Imam (asws) said, "Then should I teach you a Ziarat which is accepted even from a great distance?"

Hanan said, "How can I perform this Ziarat, O' Son of RasoolAllah (saw)?"

Imam (asws) replied, "Perform ghusl on a Friday, or whatever day you wish, wear the most purified of your clothes, go to the highest place in your house or in a desert. Then face towards the Qiblah ; for Allah (swt) says, *"Wherever you turn, there is Wajullah (face of Allah)."* (Quran 2:115)

Then recite the following:

السلام عليك يا مولاي و ابن مولاي، و سيدي و ابن سعدي

Salam be upon You, O' my Moula, the Son of my Moula, my Master and the Son of my Master

السلام عليك يا مولاي الشهيد بن الشهيد، و القتيل بن القتيل، السلام عليك و رحمة الله و بركاته

Salam be upon You, O' my Moula, al Shaheed (martyr), the Son of al Shaheed (martyr), al Qateel (the slaughtered), Son of al Qateel (the slaughtered). May the salam and blessings of Allah be upon You

أنا زائرك يا بن رسول الله و لساني و جوار حي، و جوارحي، و إن لم أزرك بنفسي مشاهدة لقبتك

I perform Your Ziarat, O' Son of RasoolAllah (saw) with my heart, my tongue, and my body even though I have not physically come to Your Ziarat where I could see Your shrine.

فعليك السلام يا وارث آدم صفوة الله

Salam be upon You, O' inheritor of Adam (as), Safwatullah (the Chosen of Allah)

ووارث نوح نبي الله

And the inheritor of Nuh (as), the Prophet of Allah

ووارث إبراهيم خليل الله

And the inheritor of Ibrahim (as), Khaleelullah (friend of Allah)

ووارث موسى كليم الله

And the inheritor of Musa (as), Kaleemullah (the one spoken to by Allah)

و وارث عيسى روح الله

And the inheritor of Isa (as), Ruhullah (the spirit of Allah)

و وارث محمد ﷺ حبيب الله و نبيه و رسوله

And the inheritor of Muhammad (saw), Habeebullah (Beloved of Allah), His (Allah) Prophet and Messenger

420

و وارث عليّ أمير المؤمنين وصي رسول الله ﷺ و خليفته

And the inheritor of Ali (asws), Ameerul Momineen, the successor of RasoolAllah (saw) and His (RasoolAllah saw) Caliph

و وارث الحسنّ بن علي وصي أمير المؤمنينّ

And the inheritor of Hasan (asws). Son of Ali (asws), the Successor of Ameerul Momineen (asws)

لعن الله قاتليك، و جدد عليهم العذاب في هذه الساعة وفي كل ساعة

May the lanat of Allah be upon those who slaughtered You and may Allah continuously renew their chastisement in this hour and in every hour

أنا يا سيدي متقرب إلى الله جل و عز، و إلى جدك رسول الله ﷺ ، و إلى أبيك أمير المؤمنينّ، و إلى وُخيك الحسنّ، و إليك يا مولاي، بزيارتي لك بقلبي و لساني و جميع جوارحي، فعليك السلام و رحمة الله و بركاته

O' My Master (asws)! I seek the nearness of Allah, of Your Grandfather RasoolAllah (saw), of Your Father Ameerul Momineen (asws), of Your Brother Hasan (asws), and of You (asws), o' my Moula (asws), by performing Your Ziarat with my heart, my tongue, and my body. May the salam and blessings of Allah be upon You

فكن لي يا سيدي شفيعي لقبول ذلك مني

O' my Master (asws)! Intercede on my behalf so that this Ziarat of mine is accepted

و أنا بالبراءة من أعدائك و اللعنة لهم و عليهم أتقرب إلى الله و إليكم أجمعين

I seek the nearness of Allah and of all of You by disassociating myself from Your enemies and by sending lanat upon them

فعليك صلوات الله ورضوانه و رحمته

May the blessings, mercy, and pleasure of Allah be upon You

Then move slightly to the left and turn your face towards the grave of Ali (asws) ibn Hussain (asws) (Imam Zainul Abideen asws), who is buried at the feet of His Father Hussain (asws) and send salam upon Him (Imam Zainul Abideen asws) in the same way.

Afterwards ask Allah regarding the requests you have pertaining to your deen (religion), your life, and then pray four rakats of prayer.

The prayers of Ziarat can be done in either eight, six, four, or two rakats and the best of these is eight rakats.

After performing prayer, face the grave of Aba Abdullah Imam Hussain (asws) and say:

أنا مودعك يا مولاي و ابن مولاي، و يا سيدي و ابن سيدي

I bid farewell to You, o' my Moula, Son of my Moula, my Master, Son of my Master

و مودعك يا سيدي و ابن سيدي يا عليّ بن الحسينّ

And I bid farewell to You, o' my Master, Son of my Master, Ali (asws) ibn Hussain (asws)

و مودعكم يا ساداتي، يا معاشر السهداء

And I bid farewell to You, o' my masters, o' assembly of martyrs

فعليكم سلام الله و رحمته و رضوانه و بركاته

May the salam, mercy, blessings, and pleasure of Allah be upon You

Chapter 97

One who neglects performing the Ziarat of the Grave of Hussain (asws) is an oppressor

HADITH 1

A companion narrates:

Abu Jafar Imam Muhammad Baqir (asws) asked, "What is the distance between you and the grave of Hussain (asws)?"

I (companion) replied, "Sixteen parasangs (approximately 64 miles)."

Imam (asws) asked, "Do you not go to Him (Imam Hussain asws)?"

I replied, "No."

Imam (asws) said, "Woe how negligent the people are."

HADITH 2

Hanan ibn Sadeer narrates:

I asked Aba Abdullah Imam Jafar Sadiq (asws), "What do you say about performing the Ziarat of the grave of Hussain (asws)?"

Imam (asws) replied, "Perform His Ziarat and do not be negligent towards Him. For He is the Master of Martyrs and the Master of the Youths of Paradise. Yahya ibn Zakariya (as) is like Hussain (asws); for the heavens and the earth wept over those two."

HADITH 3

Ameerul Momineen (asws) narrates:

"May I sacrifice My Father (as) and Mother (sa) for Hussain (asws), who will be martyred on the outskirts of Kufa. I swear by Allah, it is as if I can see the various wild animals straining their necks to reach His grave and weeping over Him throughout the night until the dawn. When this occurs, be careful of becoming negligent of His grave."

HADITH 4

Sadeer narrates:

Aba Abdullah Imam Jafar Sadiq (asws) asked me, "O' Sadeer! Do you perform the Ziarat of the grave of Hussain (asws) daily?"

I (Sadeer) replied, "No."

Imam (asws) said, "Woe how negligent the people are. Do you perform His Ziarat weekly?"

I replied, "No."

Imam (asws) asked, "Do you perform His Ziarat monthly?"

I replied, "No."

Imam (asws) asked, "Do you perform His Ziarat yearly?"

I replied, "Sometimes."

Imam (asws) said, "O' Sadeer! How negligent the people are towards Hussain (asws). Do you not know Allah has one thousand disheveled angels covered with dust who mourn and weep over Hussain (asws), who perform the Ziarat of His grave continuously without any pause? The reward of their deeds is recorded for those who perform the Ziarat of Hussain (asws)."

HADITH 5

Hanan ibn Sadeer narrates:

I was with Abu Jafar Imam Muhammad Baqir (asws) when a man entered, said salam to the Imam (asws) and then sat down.

Imam (asws) asked the man, "Where are you from?"

The man replied, "I am from Kufa. I am one of Your muhib (lovers) and I believe in Your Wilayat."

Imam (asws) asked, "Do you perform the Ziarat of the grave of Hussain (asws) once a week?"

The man replied, "No."

Imam (asws) asked, "Do you once per month?"

The man replied, "No."

Imam (asws) asked, "Do you once per year?"

The man replied, "No."

Imam (asws) said, "You are deprived of the good."

HADITH 6

Fudail ibn Yasar narrates:

Imam Jafar Sadiq (asws) said, "O' Fudail! How negligent the people are! They do not perform the Ziarat of Hussain (asws). Are you aware there are four thousand disheveled angels covered with dust who continuously weep over Hussain (asws) and will do so without stopping until the Day of Judgment?"

HADITH 7

Zurara narrates:

Imam Muhammad Baqir (asws) asked, "What is the distance between you and the grave of Hussain (asws)?"

I replied, "Sixteen or seventeen parasangs (approximately 64-68 miles)."

Imam (asws) asked, "Do you visit Him (Imam Hussain asws)?"

I replied, "No."

Imam (asws) said, "Woe how negligent you are."

HADITH 8

Sulaiman ibn Khalid narrates:

I heard Aba Abdullah Imam Jafar Sadiq (asws) say, "It is strange how there are some people who consider themselves to be amongst Our Shia but they do not perform the Ziarat of the grave of Hussain (asws) even once in their lifetime due to either their negligence, carelessness, incompetence, or laziness regarding the Ziarat."

I asked, "May I be sacrificed upon You! What are the merits of the Ziarat of Hussain (asws)?"

Imam (asws) replied, "There are numerous merits and blessings in performing the Ziarat of Hussain (asws). The first blessing a person receives is the forgiveness of all of his past sins and he will be told to continue forth in performing good deeds."

HADITH 9

Sadeer narrates:

Imam Jafar Sadiq (asws) said to me (Sadeer), "O'Sadeer! Do you perform the Ziarat of the grave of Hussain (asws) once per day?"

I replied, "May I be sacrificed upon You! No."

Imam (asws) said, "How negligent the people are. Do you perform His Ziarat once per week?"

I replied, "No."

Imam (asws) asked, "Do you perform His Ziarat once per every month?"

I replied, "No."

Imam (asws) asked, "Do you perform His Ziarat once per year?"

I replied, "Occasionally."

Imam (asws) said, "O' Sadeer! How negligent the people are regarding Hussain (asws)."

HADITH 10

Abul Jarood narrates:

Imam Muhammad Baqir (asws) asked, me (Abul Jarood), "What is the distance between you and the grave of Hussain (asws)"

I replied, "One day if riding or more than a day if walking."

Imam (asws) asked, "Do you visit Him once per week?"

I replied, "No. I only go every once in awhile."

Imam (asws) said, "How negligent the people are. If His grave were that close to Us, we would have migrated in order to be near Him."

Chapter 98

Minimum Times Each Year the Wealthy or Poor Person Should Perform the Ziarat of Hussain (asws)

HADITH 1

Imam Jafar Sadiq (asws) narrates:

"It is wajib upon the wealthy to perform the Ziarat of the grave of Hussain (asws) twice per year and for those who are poor, once per year."

HADITH 2

Imam Jafar Sadiq (asws) narrates:

"Perform the Ziarat of the grave of Hussain (asws) once per year."

HADITH 3

See hadith 2

HADITH 4

al Halabi narrates:

I asked Aba Abdullah Imam Jafar Sadiq (asws) regarding the Ziarat of the grave of Hussain (asws).

Imam (asws) replied, "Go once a year."

HADITH 5

Imam Jafar Sadiq (asws) narrates:

It is necessary for those who are poor to perform the Ziarat of the grave of Hussain (asws) once per year and for those who are wealthy, twice per year."

HADITH 6

See hadith 4

HADITH 7

Abbas ibn Ameer narrates:

Abul Hasan Imam Musa Kazim (asws) said, "Do not be negligent regarding Hussain (asws). Those who are wealthy should perform His Ziarat once every four months. And as for those who are homeless, *"Allah does not impose upon any soul a duty but to the extent of its ability"* (Quran 2:286)

Abbas ibn Ameer added, "I do not remember if the Imam (asws) made this statement to Ali ibn Abu Hamzah or to Abu Nab."

HADITH 8

See hadith 4

HADITH 9

See hadith 2

HADITH 10

As ibn Qasim narrates:

I asked Aba Abdullah Imam Jafar Sadiq (asws), "Are there wajib prayers which should be performed after the Ziarat of the grave of Hussain (asws)?"

Imam (asws) replied, "There are no wajib prayers for Ziarat."

I asked, "How often should I perform His Ziarat?"

Imam (asws) replied, "As often as you can."

HADITH 11

Ali ibn Maymoon al Saigh narrates:

Imam Jafar Sadiq (asws) said to me, "O' Ali! I have heard there are some of Our Shia who allow one or years to pass without performing the Ziarat of Hussain (asws)."

I replied, "May I be sacrificed upon You! I know many people like this."

Imam (asws) replied, "I swear by Allah they have turned their backs on their own prosperity and have declined the rewards of Allah. They have distanced themselves from the nearness of Muhammad (saw)."

I asked, "May I be sacrificed upon You! How often should we perform the Ziarat of Hussain (asws)?"

Imam (asws) replied, "O' Ali! If you are able to perform His Ziarat once per month, then do so."

I said, "I am not able to do this because I'm a manual laborer. Others are dependent upon me completing my work. I cannot be absent for even a single day."

Imam (asws) replied, "You are excused, as are those like you. I was referring to those who are not like you, and who are able to perform the Ziarat of Hussain (asws) once per week. Such people will have no excuse before Allah and His Rasool (saw) on the day of Judgment for not performing the Ziarat of Hussain (asws)."

I asked, "Is it permissible for them to send someone on their behalf?"

Imam (asws) replied, "Yes, but it is better for them if they go themselves for they will receive a greater reward for going themselves due to the loss of sleep at night and tiredness in the day from traveling to perform the Ziarat of Hussain (asws).

Allah will look upon them in such a way that will cause them to be amongst those who shall reside with Muhammad (saw) and His Ahlul Bayt (asws) in the greatest of places in Firdoos. Therefore, you should encourage one another in performing the Ziarat of Hussain (asws) and be amongst those who adhere to its performance."

HADITH 12

See hadith 2

HADITH 13

Safwan ibn Mihran al Jammal narrates:

I asked Aba Abdullah Imam Jafar Sadiq (asws), "After a person has completed the Ziarat of the grave of Hussain (asws), how long should he wait before performing the Ziarat again? And how often should a person perform His Ziarat? What is the longest amount of time a person is allowed to go without performing His Ziarat?"

Imam (asws) replied, "For those who live near to His grave, it is not permissible for them to go longer than a month without performing His Ziarat. For those who live far from His grave, they should perform His Ziarat once every three years.

If three years pass and they do not perform His Ziarat, unless they have a valid excuse for not performing His Ziarat, then they are being ungrateful to RasoolAllah (saw), and have dishonored Him."

HADITH 14

Ubaidullah al Halabi narrates:

I said to Aba Abdullah Imam Jafar Sadiq (asws), "We perform the Ziarat of the grave of Hussain (asws) two to three times per year in order to be well known amongst the people."

Imam (asws) replied, "It is better for you if you perform Ziarat only once in the year if this is your niyyat (intention)."

I asked, "How should we send blessing on Him when we go for Ziarat?"

Imam (asws) said, "Stand behind the grave near to His shoulders and send blessings on RasoolAllah (saw) and then send blessings upon Hussain (asws)."

HADITH 15

Imam Jafar Sadiq (asws) narrates:

"Four thousand angels perform prayers next to the grave of Hussain (asws) everyday from dawn till dusk. Then they ascend to the heavens. At the same time another four thousand angels descend and perform prayer next to His grave from dusk till dawn.

A muslim should not refrain from performing the Ziarat of the grave of Hussain (asws) for longer than four years."

HADITH 16

Abu Naab narrates:

I asked Aba Abdullah Imam Jafar Sadiq (asws) about the reward for performing the Ziarat of the grave of Hussain (asws).

Imam (asws) said, "It is equal to performing an umrah. A person should not refrain from performing His Ziarat for a period of more than four years."

HADITH 17

Safwan al Jammal narrates:

While en route from Medina to Mecca, I asked Aba Abdullah Imam Jafar Sadiq (asws), "O' Son of RasoolAllah (saw)! Why do You as if You are distressed and full of sorrow?"

Imam (asws) replied, "If you were able to hear what I hear, then you would have been so distressed you would not have been able to ask Me this question."

I asked, "What is that You hear?"

Imam (asws) replied, "I hear the voices of the angels imploring Allah to send lanat upon those who slaughtered Ameerul Momineen (asws) and those who slaughtered Hussain (asws). And I hear the mourning of the jinn over Ameerul Momineen (asws) and Hussain (asws). As well as the intense grief of the angels who surround Them. Who could enjoy food and drink whilst hearing their voices?"

I asked, "After a person returns from the Ziarat of the grave of Hussain (asws), how long should he wait before performing His Ziarat again? How often should a person perform His Ziarat? And what is the longest amount of time a person should allow to pass before performing His Ziarat again?"

Imam (asws) replied, "Those who live near to His grave should perform His Ziarat no less than once per month. Those who live at a great distance should perform His Ziarat no less than once every three years.

If three years pass and they do not perform His Ziarat, or do not have a valid excuse for not performing His Ziarat, then they are considered amongst those who are selfish and unthankful to RasoolAllah (saw).

If the zawir (visitor) of Hussain (asws) knew how happy he made RasoolAllah (saw), Ameerul Momineen (asws), Syeda Fatima (sa), the Imams (asws), and the martyrs from amongst Our Family, and how They prayed for him (the zawir) and the rewards which They prepared for the zawir in this life and the rewards which will be preserved for Him before Allah in the hereafter, then the zawir would have wished for his house to be next to the grave of Hussain (asws) for as long as he lived.

When the zawir leaves Karbala to return to his home, his shadow does not fall upon anything without that thing praying for him. And when the sun shines down upon the zawir, it burns his sins like the fire burns the wood. The sun does not allow any of his sins to remain so he returns as a person without sin and his status will be elevated for him to a level that cannot be attained even by those who spilled all of their blood in the way of Allah.

Then an angel will be dedicated to the zawir who will (check translation pg 604 bottom) and who will seek forgiveness for the zawir until he returns to perform the Ziarat again or until three years pass; unless he dies before three years pass, then the angel will be with him until his time of death.

Chapter 99

Reward for performing the Ziarat of Imam Musa Kazim (asws) and Imam Muhammad Taqi (asws)

HADITH 1

Hasan ibn Ali al Washa narrates:

I asked Imam Reza (asws) if the reward for performing the Ziarat of the grave of Abul Hasan Imam Musa Kazim (asws) is the same as the Ziarat of the grave of Hussain (asws).

Imam (asws) replied, "Yes."

HADITH 2

Hussain ibn Yasar al Wasitee narrates:

I asked Imam Reza (asws), "Should I perform the Ziarat of the grave of Abul Hasan Imam Musa Kazim (asws) in Baghdad?"

Imam (asws) replied, "Yes, but if you go, perform the Ziarat behind a veil."

HADITH 3

Hasan ibn Ali al Washa narrates:

I asked Imam Reza (asws), "What are the rewards for those who perform the Ziarat of the grave of Your Father Abul Hasan Imam Musa Kazim (asws)?"

Imam (asws) replied, "The same as those who perform the Ziarat of the grave of Hussain (asws)."

HADITH 4

A companion narrates:

I asked Imam Reza (asws) about performing the Ziarat of the grave of Abul Hasan Imam Musa Kazim (asws).

Imam (asws) replied, "Perform prayers in the mosques beside the grave."

HADITH 5

Hussain ibn Yasar al Wasitee narrates:

I asked Abul Hasan Imam Reza (asws), "What are the rewards for those who perform the Ziarat of the grave of Your Father Imam Musa Kazim (asws)?"

Imam (asws) replied, "Its rewards are the same as the rewards for those who perform the Ziarat of His Father (RasoolAllah saw)."

I asked, "What if I am unable to enter near His grave out of fear?"

Imam (asws) replied, "Then say salam from behind the wall."

HADITH 6

Hussain ibn Muhammad al Ashari al Qummi narrates:

Imam Reza (asws) said to me, "Those who perform the Ziarat of the grave of My Father (Imam Musa Kazim asws) in Baghdad are like those who have performed the Ziarat of RasoolAllah (saw) and the grave of Ameerul Momineen (asws), except there are certain rewards associated only with RasoolAllah (saw) and Ameerul Momineen (asws)."

HADITH 7

Abdul Rahman ibn Abu Najran narrates:

I asked Abu Jafar Imam Muhammad Taqi (asws), "What is the reward for those who performed the Ziarat of RasoolAllah (saw) for the sole purpose of performing Ziarat?"

Imam (asws) replied, "Their reward is Jannah as well as those who perform the Ziarat of the grave of Abul Hasan Imam Musa Kazim (asws), their reward is also jannah."

HADITH 8

Imam Reza (asws) narrates:

"The Ziarat of the grave of My Father Imam Musa Kazim (asws) is the same as the Ziarat of the grave of Hussain (asws)."

HADITH 9

Raheem narrates:

I said to Imam Reza (asws), "May I be sacrificed upon You! We face many hardships when we perform the Ziarat of the grave of Abul Hasan Imam Musa Kazim (asws) in Baghdad. This is why we say our salam to Him behind a wall. What are the rewards for those who perform His Ziarat?"

Imam (asws) replied, "I swear by Allah that it is the same as the rewards for performing the Ziarat of the grave of RasoolAllah (saw). "

HADITH 10

Raheem narrates:

I said to Imam Reza (asws), "We face numerous hardships when we perform the Ziarat of the grave of Abul Hasan Imam Musa Kazim (asws) in Baghdad. What are the rewards for those who perform His Ziarat?"

Imam (asws) replied, "Its rewards are the same as the rewards for those who perform the Ziarat of the grave of Hussain (asws)."

After Imam (asws) said this, a man entered, said salam to the Imam (asws), and then sat down. He began speaking about Baghdad, how its people were inferior, and about the calamities which are expected to befall Baghdad, such as the collapsing of the earth the upheaval, and the bolts of lightning.

When I got up to leave, I heard Abul Hasan Imam Reza (asws) say, "As for Abul Hasan Imam Musa Kazim (asws), none of the calamities will affect Him."

HADITH 11

Ibrahim ibn Uqbah narrates:

I wrote to Abul Hasan the Third Imam Ali Naqi (asws) asking Him about the Ziarat of the grave of Aba Abdullah Imam Hussain (asws) and about the Ziarat of the graves of Abul Hasan Imam Musa Kazim (asws) and Abu Jafar Imam Muhammad Taqi (asws).

Imam (asws) replied, "Abu Abdullah Imam Hussain (asws) comes first, but the Ziarat of Imam Musa Kazim (asws) and Imam Muhammad Taqi (asws) is more complete and brings greater rewards."

HADITH 12

Abdul Rahman ibn Abu Najran narrates:

I asked Abu Jafar Imam Muhammad Taqi (asws), "What is the reward for those who perform the Ziarat of RasoolAllah (saw) with the sole purpose of performing His Ziarat?"

Imam (asws) replied, "Their reward is Jannah and the reward for those who perform the Ziarat of the grave of Abul Hasan Imam Musa Kazim (asws) is also Jannah."

Chapter 100

The Ziarat of Imam Musa Kazim (asws) and Imam Muhammad Taqi (asws)

HADITH 1

Imam Ali Naqi (asws) narrates:

When you are in Baghdad, recite the following:

السلام عليك يا ولي الله

Salam to You, O' Wali of Allah

السلام عليك يا حجة الله

Salam to You, O' Hujjatullah (Proof of Allah)

السلام عليك يا نور الله في ظلمات الأرض

Salam to You, O' Noorullah (Noor of Allah), the light in the darkness on the Earth

السلام عليك وا من بدا لله في شأنه

Salam to You, O' The One for Whom Allah altered His Will

اتينك عارفا بحقك، معاديا لأ عدائك ، فاشفع لي عند ربك يا مولاي

I have come to You with full marifat (recognition) of Your station. I am the enemy of Your enemies. Intercede on my behalf with Your Lord, O' my Moula (asws)

Then supplicate to Allah and ask for the fulfillment of your needs. After recite the same salam for the Ziarat of Abu Jafar Muhammad (asws) ibn Ali (asws) (Imam Muhammad Taqi asws)

HADITH 2

Imam Ali Naqi (asws) narrates:

When you desire to perform the Ziarat of Musa (asws) ibn Jafar (asws) (Imam Musa Kazim asws) and Muhammad (asws) ibn Ali (asws) (Imam Muhammad Taqi asws), perform ghusl, wear purified clothes, and then go to the graves of Abul Hasan Musa (asws) ibn Jafar (asws) and Muhammad (asws) ibn Ali (asws)

When you arrive at the grave of Musa (asws) ibn Jafar (asws) (Imam Musa Kazim asws), say:

السلام عليك يا ولي الله

Salam to You, O' Wali of Allah

السلام عليك يا حجة الله

Salam to You, O' Hujjatullah (Proof of Allah)

اتينك عليك يا نور الله في ظلمات الأرض

Salam to You, O' Noorullah, the light in the darkness on the Earth

السلام عليك وا من بدا لله في شأنه

Salam to You, O' The One for Whom Allah altered His Will

اتينك عارفا بحقك، معاديا لأ عدائك ، فاشفع لي عند ربك يا مولاي

I have come to You with full marifat of Your status. I am the enemy of Your enemies. Intercede on my behalf with Your Lord, O' my Moula (asws)

Then ask for the fulfillment of your needs. And then say salam to Abu Jafar Muhammad (asws) ibn Ali (asws) (Imam Muhammad Taqi asws), being sure that you have performed ghusl prior to arrival and say:

اللهم صل على محمدّ بن عليّ الإمام البر التقي النقي الرضي المرضي، و حجتك على من فوق الأرضين و من تحت الثرى

O'Allah! Send Your blessings on Muhammad (asws) ibn Ali (asws), al Imam, al bar, al taqi, al naqi, al reza, and the Hujjat (proof) on those who are on the earth and under the dust.

صلاة كثيرة تامة زاكية مباركة متواصلة متواترة مترادفة كأفضل ما صليت على أحد من أوليائك

O' Allah! Send an ever increasing, fully complete, purified, frequent and continuous blessing on Him that is greater than any of the blessings You have sent on any of Your Auwliya (friends).

السلام عليك يا ولي الله

Salam be upon You, O' Wali of Allah

السلام عليك يا نور الله

Salam be upon You, O' Noor of Allah

السلام عليك يا حجة الله

Salam be upon You, O' Hujjatullah (Proof of Allah)

السلام عليك يا إمام المؤمنين و وارث النبيين

Salam be upon You, O' Imam of Momineen (Believers) and Heir of the Prophets

السلام عليك يا خليفة النبيين و سلالة الوصيين

Salam be upon You, O' Caliph of the Prophets and O' Progeny of the Successors

السلام عليك يا نور الله في ظلمات الأرض

Salam be upon You, O' Noorullah (noor of Allah) in this oppressive earth.

أتيتك زائراً عارفاً بحقك، معادياً لأ عدائك، موالياً لأوليائك، فاشفع عند ربك يا مولاي

I have come to You to perform Your Ziarat while having the marifat (recognition) of Your rights I am the enemy of Your enemies and friend to Your friends. Intercede on my behalf with Your Lord, O' my Moula (asws)

Then ask for the fulfillment of your needs. InshaAllah they will be fulfilled.

HADITH 3

Masoom Imam (asws) narrates:

Recite the following near the grave of Abul Hasan Imam Musa Kazim (asws) in Baghdad. This can also be recited at all of the sites of the Masoomeen (asws):

السلام على أولياء الله و أصفيائه

Salam be upon You, O' Walis of Allah and His Chosen Ones.

السلام على امناء و أ حبائه

Salam be upon You, O' Ameenullah (trustees of Allah) and the Beloved of Allah

السلام على أنصار الله و خلفائه

Salam be upon You, O' Ansarullah (supporters of Allah) and His Caliphs

السلام على محال معرفة الله

Salam be upon the sources of marifat of Allah

440

السلام على مساكن ذكر الله

Salam be upon the houses in which Allah is remembered

السلام على مظاهر أمر الله و نبهيه

Salam be upon the Mahzer (manifestation) of the Amr (order) of Allah and His prohibitions

السلام على الدعاة إلى الله

Salam be upon the Ones who have called the people towards Allah

السلام على المستقرين في مرضات الله

Salam be upon the Ones who are firmly held within the pleasure of Allah

السلام على المخلصين في طاعة الله

Salam be upon the Ones who are loyal in Their obedience to Allah

السلام على الأدلاء على الله

Salam be upon the Ones who guided others towards Allah

السلام على الذين من والاهم فقد والى الله، و من عرفهم فقد عرف الله، و من جهلهم فقد جهل الله، و من اعتصم بهم فقد اعتصم بالله، و من تخلى منهم فقد تخلى من الله

Salam be upon the Ones whose followers are considered as the followers of Allah, those who anger You have angered Allah, those who know You know Allah, those who reject You also reject Allah, those who seek refuge with You have sought refuge with Allah and those who have forsaken You are amongst those who have forsaken Allah.

اشهد الله أني مسلم لكم

I take Allah as my witness that I have submitted myself unto You

سلم لمن سالمكم

I make peace with those who made peace with You

و حرب لمن حاربكم

And make war with those who have made war with You

مؤمن بسركم ع علانيتكم، مفوض في ذلك كله إليكم

I believe in You that which is secret and that which is apparent and on You I rely for all things

لعن الله دعو آل محمدّ من الجن و الإنس، و أبرء إلى الله منهم، و صلى على محمد صلى الله عليه وآله و آلة

May the lanat of Allah be upon the enemies from amongst men and jinn of Aal e Muhammad (asws) and I seek the nearness of Allah by disassociating myself from them (the enemies) May the blessings of Allah be upon Muhammad and His Family

Imam (asws) added, "This Ziarat is sufficient to be read in all of the sites of Masoomeen (asws). After reciting it, send as many blessings as you can upon Muhammad (asws) wa Aal e Muhammad (asws), name Them one after the other, and disassociate yourself from Their enemies.

Then recite supplications for yourself and the momineen from amongst the men and women."

Chapter 101

Reward for the Ziarat of
Imam Ali Reza (asws) in Tus

HADITH 1

Dawood al Sarmee narrates:

I heard Abu Jafar the Second (Imam Muhammad Taqi asws) say:

"Those who perform the Ziarat of the Grave of My Father (asws) will be rewarded with Jannah."

HADITH 2

See hadith 1

HADITH 3

Hamdan al Daywani narrates:

I went to Abu Jafar the Second (Imam Muhammad Taqi asws) and asked, "What is the reward for those who perform the Ziarat of Your Father (Imam Ali Reza asws) in Tus?"

Imam (asws) replied, "Allah forgives the past and future sins of those who perform the Ziarat of the grave of My Father (asws) in Tus."

Afterwards, I met with Ayub ibn Nuh ibn Durraj and said to him, "O Abul Hussain! I heard my Moula Abu Jafar Imam Muhammad Taqi (asws) say, "Allah forgives the past and future sins of those who perform the Ziarat of the grave of His Father (asws) in Tus."

Ayub said, "Should I tell you what I heard?"

I replied, "Yes."

Ayub said, "I heard Imam Muhammad Taqi (asws) say, "On the Day of Judgment, a mimbar (pulpit) will be placed beside the mimbar of RasoolAllah (saw) for those who perform the Ziarat of My Father (Imam Ali Reza asws). And they will sit upon this mimbar while the rest of the people face the hasab (accounting)."

HADITH 4

Imam Reza (asws) narrates:

"Those who come to My Ziarat even though My house is far and My grave is distant will be visited by Me on three occasions on the Day of Judgment and I will save them from its terrors. The first occasion is when the books will be distributed to the right and to the left, the second is on the Sirat (bridge), and the third is at the Mizan (scale)."

HADITH 5

Ali ibn Abdullah ibn Qutrub narrates:

One day when the children of Abul Hasan Imam Musa Kazim (asws) were gathered around Him, His Son Imam Reza (asws), who was still young at the time, passed by Him.

Imam Kazim (asws) said, "This Son of Mine (Imam Reza asws) will leave this world while being alone and in a distant land. Those perform His Ziarat while submitting their self to Him and while having the marifat (recognition) of His rights will be regarded by Allah (swt) as one of the martyrs of the battle of Badr."

HADITH 6

Hamdan ibn Ishaq narrates:

I heard Imam Muhammad Taqi (asws) say, "Allah forgives the past and future sins of those who perform the Ziarat of the grave of My Father (Imam Reza asws) in Tus."

After performing the Ziarat, I (Hamdan ibn Ishaq) went for Hajj where I met Ayub ibn Nuh. Ayub said to me, "Imam Muhammad Taqi (asws) said, "Allah forgives the past and future sins of those who perform the Ziarat of the grave of My Father (Imam Reza asws) in Tus and on the Day of Judgment Allah will set a mimbar for them beside the mimbar of RasoolAllah (saw) and the mimbar of Ali (asws). They will remain there while Allah finishes the hasab (accounting) of the creation."

Later, I met with Ayub ibn Nuh again. He (Ayub) had come for the Ziarat of Imam Reza (asws) and Ayub said, "I have come seeking the mimbar."

HADITH 7

Muhammad ibn Sulaiman narrates:

I said to Abu Jafar Imam Muhammad Taqi (asws):

If a person decides to perform a wajib Hajj after he had performed the umrah, and with the help of Allah, the person is able to complete the hajj and umrah. Then if he goes to Medina and says salam upon RasoolAllah (saw), then comes to You while having the marifat of Your rights; knowing that You (Imam asws) are Hujjatullah (proof of Allah) upon the creation of Allah and that You are Babullah (the door that leads to Allah) and says salam to You.

Then he goes to perform the Ziarat of Aba Abdullah al Hussain (asws) and says salam to Him. Then the person goes to Baghdad and says salam to Imam Musa Kazim (asws) and then returns to his home country.

If Allah provides the person with enough rizq (sustenance) so that the following year, he is able to go for hajj again, is it better for the person to repeat the hajj in the same way he did the year before or should he go to Khurasan for the Ziarat of Your Father Imam Ali Reza (asws) and say salam to Him?"

Imam (asws) replied, "It is better for him to go to Khurasan and say salam to Imam Reza (asws). However he should go in the month of Rajab, but at the moment, this is not applicable because there is fear for you from the King as performing Our Ziarat enrages him (the king)."

HADITH 8

Ali ibn Mahziyar narrates:

I asked Abu Jafar Imam Muhammad Taqi (asws), "What is the reward for those who perform the Ziarat of the grave of Imam Reza (asws)?"

Imam (asws) replied, "I swear by Allah their reward is Jannah."

HADITH 9

Nasr al Bizanti narrates:

I read the following in a letter from Imam Ali Reza (asws):

"Tell My Shia that performing My Ziarat is equal to performing one thousand hajj in the eyes of Allah."

I asked Imam Muhammad Taqi (asws), "One thousand hajj?"

Imam Taqi (asws) replied, "I swear by Allah, and the reward for those who perform His Ziarat while having the full marifat of His (Imam Reza asws) rights is one million hajj."

HADITH 10

Imam Musa Kazim (asws) narrates:

"Those who perform the Ziarat of This Son of Mine (Imam Kazim (asws) pointed towards Imam Reza asws) will be rewarded with Jannah."

HADITH 11

Ali check about this hadith pg 621)

HADITH 12

Yahya ibn Sulaiman al Mazini narrates:

Imam Musa Kazim (asws) said, "Allah will record seventy accepted hajj for those who perform the Ziarat of the grave of My Son Imam Reza (asws)."

I asked, "Seventy hajj?"

Imam (asws) replied, "Yes, or even seven hundred hajj."

I asked, "Seven hundred hajj?"

Imam (asws) replied, "Yes, or even seventy thousand hajj."

I asked, "Seventy thousand hajj?"

Imam (asws) replied, "Yes. Just because you go for hajj does not mean it is always accepted, but those who perform His Ziarat (Imam Reza asws) and spend the night beside Him are like those who perform the Ziarat of Allah on His Arsh."

I asked, "Like the ones who perform the Ziarat of Allah on His Arsh?"

Imam (asws) replied, "Yes. On the Day of Judgment, there will be four people from the previous nations and four people from the last nation at the Arsh (throne) of Allah. The four from the previous nations are Nuh (as), Ibrahim (as), Musa (as), and Isa (as). The four from the last nations are Muhammad (saw), Ali (asws), Hasan (asws), and Hussain (asws).

A barrier will be extended and only those who have performed the Ziarat of the graves of the Imams (asws) will sit with Us. The highest ranking ones and those closest to Us will be the ones who have performed the Ziarat of the grave of My Son, Imam Ali Reza (asws)."

Chapter 102

Ziarat of Imam Ali Reza (asws)

HADITH 1

Masoom Imam (asws) narrates:

"Recite the following when you perform the Ziarat of the grave of Ali (asws) ibn Musa (asws) al Reza (Imam Ali Reza asws):"

اللهم صل على عليّ بن موسىّ الرضا المرتضى، الإمام التقي النقي، و حجتك على من فوق الأرض و من تحت الثرى، الصديق الشهيد

O' Allah! Send Your blessings upon Ali (asws) ibn Musa (asws), al Murtaza, who is Taqi (virtuous) and Naqi (pious) and Your Hujjat (proof) upon the living and the dead of this earth, who is also al Sadiq (trustworthy), al Shaheed (witness)

صلاة نامية زاكية متواصلة متواترة مترادفة، كأفضل ما صليت على أحد من أوليائك

Send an ever increasing, bountiful, purified, and unending blessing upon Him (Imam Reza asws); one that is continuous and greater than any of the blessings You have ever sent upon Your Auwliya (friends)

HADITH 2

Masoom Imam (asws) narrates:

"When you decide to perform the Ziarat of the grave of Ali (asws) ibn Musa (asws) al Reza in Tus, perform ghusl before leaving your house, and recite the following while you are performing ghusl:"

اللهم طهرني و طهر لي قلبي، واشرح لي صدري، أجر على لساني مدحتك، و الثنآء عليك، فإنه لا قوة إلا بك

O' Allah! Purify me and purify my heart; expand my chest and make my tongue glorify and honor You. For there is no power except with You.

اللهم اجعله لي طهوراً و شفآء و نوراً

O' Allah! Make this ghusl a means of purification, a cure, and a shining light for me

Recite the following when the time comes for you to depart from your home:

بسم الله و بالله، و إلى ابن رسوله ﷺ ، حسني الله، توكلت على الله

I am performing this ziarat in the name of Allah, by Allah, to Allah, and for the Son of His Rasool (saw). Allah is sufficient for me and I rely only on Allah

اللهم إليك توجهت، و إليك قصدت، و ما عندك أردت

O' Allah! I have turned to You. I am coming towards You and I am seeking that which is with You

As you go out of your house, while standing beside your door, recite the following:

اللهم إليك وجهت و جهي، و عليك خلفت أهلي و مالي و ما خولتني، و بك و ثقت فلا تخيبني

O'Allah! I have turned my face towards You and I am leaving behind my family, my wealth, and all that which You have given to me. I leave all of this in Your protection. I have placed my trust in You so I shall not be distressed.

يا من يخيب من أراده، و لا يضيع من حفظه، صل على محمد ﷺ و آل محمد، و احفظني بحفظك، فإنه لا يضيع من حفظت

O' One whom those who seek Him are never disappointed and those who are protected by Him will never be lost! Send Your blessing on Muhammad (saw) wa Aal e Muhammad (asws) and protect me with Your protection; for those who are protected by You will never be lost.

Once you arrive safely in Tus, perform ghusl again and recite the following while performing the ghusl:

اللهم طهرني، و طهر قلبي، و اشرح لي صدري، و أجر على لساني مدحتك و محبتك و الثناء عليك، فإنه لا قوة إلا بك

O' Allah! Purify me and purify my heart. Expand my chest and allow my tongue to honor You, to glorify You, and to speak only of Your love. For there is no power except with You

و قد علمت أن قوة ديني التسليم لأمرك و الإتباع لسنة نبيك، و الشهادة على جميع خلقد

I understand the foundation of my religion is found in my submitting myself to Your decrees, following the traditions of Your Prophet (saw), testifying that You are the Creator of all of the creation

اللهم اجعله لي شفاء و نوراً، إنك على كل شيء قدير

O'Allah! Make this ghusl a means of cure and a shining light for me. For You have power over all things.

Then dress yourself in purified (pak) clothes, walk towards the grave barefoot with awe and serenity as you recite takbir (Allahu Akbar), tahleel (La ilaha illa Allah), tasbih (subhanAllah), tamhid (Alhamdulillah), and tamjeed (La hawla wala quwwata illa billah). Take short steps and recite the following as you enter the Haram:

بسم الله و بالله و على ملة رسول الله ﷺ ، أشهد أن لا إله إلا الله وحده لا شريك له، و أشهد أن محمداً ﷺ عبده و رسوله، و أن علياً ولي الله

I enter in the name of Allah, by Allah, and while I am part of the ummah (nation) of RasoolAllah (saw). I testify there is no god except Allah, who is One and has no partner. And I testify Muhammad (saw) is His servant and His Messenger. And I testify Ali (asws) is the Wali (representative) of Allah

Then face His grave while your back is towards the Qiblah. Look towards His face and recite:

أشهد أن لا إله إلا الله وحده لا شريك له، و أشهد أن محمداً ﷺ عبده رسوله، و أنه سيد الأولين و الآخرين، و أنه سيد الأنبياء و المرسلين

I testify there is no god except Allah who is One and has no partner. And I testify Muhammad is the servant and Messenger of Allah; He (Muhammad saw) is the Master of the first and the last and that He (Muhammad saw) is Syedul Nabieen wal Mursaleen (master of prophets and messengers)

اللهم صل على محمد عبدك و رسولك ونبيك و سيد خلقك أجمعين، صلاة لا يقوى على إحصائها غيرك

O' Allah! Send Your blessing—whose number can only be counted by You—upon Muhammad (saw) who is Your servant, Your Messenger, Your Prophet, and the Master of all of Your creation; a blessing which cannot be measured by anyone other than You (Allah)

اللهم صل على أمير المؤمنين عليّ بن أبي طالبّ، عبدك و أخي رسولك الذي انتجبته لعلمك، و جعلته هادياً لمن شئت من خلقك، الدليل على من بعثته برسالاتك، و ديان يوم الدين بعدلك، و فصل قضائك بين خلقك، و المهيمن على ذلك كله، و السلام عليه و رحمة الله و بركاته

O' Allah! Send Your blessing—whose number can only be counted by You—upon Ameerul Momineen Ali (asws) ibn Abi Talib (as); who is Your servant and the brother of Your Messenger (saw); whom You chose as the trustee of Your knowledge and whom You appointed as a guide upon Your creation and a guide for those upon whom You sent Your message, who is the Hujjat (proof) upon the one You sent with the risalat (prophet hood), and He is the one who will act as judge on the Day of Judgment for He is the absolute master over all things. May the salam and blessings of Allah be upon Him

اللهم صل على فاطمة بنت نبيك، و زوجة وليك، و ام السبطين الحسنّ و الحسينّ سيدي شباب أهل الجنة، الطهرة الطاهرة المطهرة، التقية الرضية الزكية، سيدة نساء العالمين و سيدة نساء أهل الجنة من الخلق أجمعين، صلاة لا يقوى على إحصائها غيرك

O' Allah! Send Your blessing—whose number can only be counted by You—upon Syeda Fatima (sa), the Daughter of Your Rasool (saw), the Wife of Your wali, the Mother of the two Grandsons of Your Prophet (saw), Hasan (asws) and Hussain (asws), the Masters of the Youth of Paradise, the one who is Tahera (purified), Mutahira (Purifier), Naqqiya (Pious), Razia (whose will is Allah's will), Zakia (Virtuous), who is Syedatul Nisa al Alameen and Syedatul Nisa al Jannah from amongst Your creation

اللهم صلى على الحسنّ و الحسينّ سبطي نبيك و سيدي شباب أهل الجنة، القائمين في خلقك، و الدليلين على من بعثت برسالاتك، و دياني الدين بعدلك و فصل قضائك بين خلقك

O'Allah! Send Your blessing—whose number can only be counted by You—upon Hasan (asws) and Hussain (asws), the two grandsons of Your Prophet (saw), the two masters of the Youths of Paradise, the representatives of Allah upon Your creation and the proof upon all of the Prophets You sent with Your message, and They administer Your divine justice and act as the decisive judges between Your creation

اللهم صل على عليّ بن الحسينّ سيد العابدين، عبدك و القائم في خلقك، و خليفتك على خلقك، و الدليل على من بعثت برسالاتك، و ديان الدين بعدلك، و فصل قضائك بين خلقك

O' Allah! Send Your blessings—whose number can only be counted by You—upon Ali (asws) ibn Hussain (asws) Syedul Abideen (master of worship), Your servant, and the representatives of Allah upon Your creation and the proof upon all of the Prophets You sent with Your message, and They administer Your divine justice and act as the decisive judges between Your creation

اللهم صل على محمدّ بن عليّ، عبدك و ولي دينك، و خليفتك في أرضك، باقر علم النبيين، القائم بعدلك، و الداعي إلى دينك و دين آبائه الصادقين، صلاة يقوى على إحصائها غيرك

O'Allah! Send Your blessings—whose number can only be counted by You—upon Muhammad (asws) ibn Ali (asws), Your servant and the Wali (representative) of Your religion, Your caliph upon the earth, the one through whom the knowledge of the prophets was revealed, the one who calls others to Your religion and the religion of His trustworthy Forefathers (asws)

اللهم صل على جعفرّ بن محمدّ الصادق، عبدك و ولي دينك، و حجتك على خلقك أجمعين، الصادق البار

O'Allah! Send Your blessings—whose number can only be counted by You—upon Jafar (asws) ibn Muhammad (asws) al Sadiq, Your servant and Wali of Your religion, Your Hujjat (proof) upon Your entire creation, al Sadiq (trustworthy)

اللهم صل على موسىّ بن جعفرّ الكاظم، العبد الصالح، و لسانك في خلقك الناطق بعلمك، و الحجة على بريتك، صلاة لا يقوى على إحصائها غيرك

O'Allah! Send Your blessings—whose number can only be counted by You—upon Musa (asws) ibn Jafar (asws) al Kazim, Abd-e-Saleh (virtuous slave of Allah), Your Lasan (tongue) amongst the creation, the representative of Your knowledge, the Hujjat (proof) upon Your creation

اللهم صل على عليّ بن موسىّ الرضا الرضي المرتضى، عبدك و ولي دينك، القائم بعدلك، و الداعي إلى دينك و دين آبائه الصادقين، صلاة لا يقدر على إحصائها غيرك

O'Allah! Send Your blessings—whose number can only be counted by You—upon Ali (asws) ibn Musa (asws) al Reza, al Raza, al Murtaza, Your servant and Wali of Your religion, the Just Imam of the time, , the one through whom the knowledge of the prophets was revealed, the one who calls others to Your religion and the religion of His trustworthy Forefathers (asws)

اللهم صل على محمدّ بن عليّ، عبدك و وليك، القائم بأمرك، و الداعي إلى سبيلك

O'Allah! Send Your blessings—whose number can only be counted by You—upon Muhammad (asws) ibn Ali (asws), Your servant and Wali of Your religion

اللهم صل على عليّ بن محمدّ، عبدك و ولي دينك

O'Allah! Send Your blessings—whose number can only be counted by You—upon Ali (asws) ibn Muhammad (asws), Your servant and Wali of Your religion

اللهم صل على الحسنّ بن عليّ، العامل بأمرك، و الوائم في خلقك، و حجتك المؤدي عن نبيك، و شاهدك على خلقك، المخصوص بكر امتك، الداعي إلى طاعتك و طاعة رسولك

O'Allah! Send Your blessings—whose number can only be counted by You—on Hasan (asws) ibn Ali (asws), the one who carried out Your amr (commands), the representatives of

Allah upon Your creation, Your Hujjat (proof) and representative of Your Prophet (saw), Your witness over Your creation, the one honored by You, and the one who calls others to Your obedience and the obedience of Your Rasool (saw)

صلواتك عليهم أجمعين، صلاة لا يقوى على إحصائها غيرك

May Your blessings—whose number can only be counted by You—be upon all of them

اللهم صل على حجتك و وليك، و القآئم في خلقك، صلاة نامية باقية، تعجل بها فرجه و تنصره بها، و تجعلنا معه في الدنيا و الآخرة

O'Allah! Send Your ever increasing and everlasting blessings—through which You hasten His reappearance, support Him and allow us to be with Him in this life and in the hereafter—upon Your Hujjat (proof) and Your Wali, Your representative upon Your creation

اللهم إني أتقرب إليك بزيارتهم و محبتهم، و اولي و ليهم، و اعادي عدوهم، فارزقني بهم خير الدنيا و الآخرة، و اصرف عني هم نفسي في الدنيا و الآخرة، و أهوال يوم القيامة

O'Allah! I seek nearness to You by performing Their Ziarat and by my love for Them. I make friends with Their friends and I oppose Their enemies. Through Them provide me with rizq (sustenance) and remove the worries of my soul in this life and in the hereafter. And through Them protect me from the terrors of the Day of Judgment.

Then sit beside His head and recite the following:

السلام عليك يا حجة الله

Salam be upon You, O' Hujjatullah (proof of Allah)

السلام يا ولي الله

Salam be upon You, O' Waliullah (representative of Allah)

السلام عليك يا نور الله في ظلمات الأرض

Salam be upon You, O'Nurullah (light of Allah) in the darkness of the earth

454

السلام عليك يا عمود الدين

Salam be upon You, O'pillar of the religion

السلام عليك يا وارث آدمّ صفوة الله

Salam be upon You, O' inheritor of Adam (as), Safwatullah (chosen of Allah)

السلام عليك يا وارث نوحّ نبي الله

Salam be upon You, O' inheritor of Nuh (as), Nabiullah (prophet of Allah)

السلام عليك يا وارث إبراهيمّ خليل الله

Salam be upon You, O' inheritor of Ibrahim (as), Khaleelullah (Friend of Allah)

السلام عليك يا وارث مسي كليم الله

Salam be upon You, O' inheritor of Musa (as) Kaleemullah (the one spoken to by Allah)

السلام عليك يا وارث عيسىّ روح الله

Salam be upon You, O' inheritor of Isa (as), Ruhullah (the spirit of Allah)

السلام عليك يا وارث محمد ﷺ حبيب الله

Salam be upon You, O' inheritor of Muhammad (saw), Habeebullah (beloved of Allah)

السلام عليك يا وارث أمير المؤمنين عليّ بن أبي طالبّ ولي الله

Salam be upon You, O' inheritor of Ameerul Momineen Ali (asws) ibn Abi Talib (as), Wali of Allah

السلام عليك يا وارث الحسنّ و الحسينّ سيدي شباب أهل الجنة

Salam be upon You, O' inheritor of Hasan (asws) and Hussain (asws), the two Masters of the Youths of Jannah

السلام عليك يا وارث عليّ بن الحسينّ زين العابدين

Salam be upon You, O' inheritor of Ali (asws) ibn Hussain (asws) Zainul Abideen

السلام عليك يا وارث محمدّ بن علي باقر علم الأولين و الآخرين

Salam be upon You, O'inheritor of Muhammad (asws) ibn Ali (asws), who is the inheritor of the knowledge of the first and the last

السلام عليك يا وارث جعفرّ بن محمدّ الصادق البار التقي النقي

Salam be upon You, O'inheritor of Jafar (asws) ibn Muhammad (asws) al Sadiq (trustworthy), al Bar (pious), al Taqi (virtuous), al Naqi (pure)

اسلام عليك يا واث موسي بن جعفر الكاظم

Salam be upon You, O'inheritor of Musa (asws) ibn Jafar (asws) al Kazim

السلام عليك أيها الصديق الشهيد

Salam be upon You, O' al Sadeeq al Shaheed (trustworthy, martyr)

السلام عليك أيها الوصي البار التقي

Salam be upon You, O' Successor, al Bar, al Taqi

أشهد أنك قد أقمت الصلاة، و آتيت الزكاة، و أمرت بالمعروف، و نهيت عن المنكر، و عبدت الله مخلصاً حتى أتاك اليقين

I testify that You established the prayer and gave zakat. You enjoined the good and forbade the evil. And You worshipped Allah alone until that which is certain came unto You

السلام عليك يا أبا الحسنّ ورحمة الل و بركاته، إنه حميد مجيد

May the blessings and salam of Allah be upon You, O'Abul Hasan (asws). For Allah is Hameed (the praised) Majeed (the glorious)

456

Then fall upon the grave and recite the following:

اللهم إليك صمدت من أرضي، و قطعت البلاد رجاء رحمتك، فلاتخيني، و لا تردني بغير قضاء حوائجي، و ارحم تقلبي على قبر ابن أخي نبيك و رسولك ﷺ

O'Allah! I have left my home for You and traveled across the land in search of Your mercy. Do not disappoint me and do not send me back without fulfilling my requests. Have mercy on me as I lay face down on the grave of the Son (asws) of the Brother (asws) of Your Prophet and Your Rasool (saw)

بأبي أنت و امي، أتيتك زائراً و وافداً، عائذاً مما جنيت به على نفسي و احتطبت على ظهري، فكن لي شفياً إلى ربك يوم فقري و فاقتي، فإن لك عند الله مقاماً محموداً، و أنت عند الله ع جية في الدنيا والآخرة

May my father and mother be sacrificed upon You! I have performed Your Ziarat while being Your guest and seeking refuge from the atrocities I committed against myself, and from the weight that I carry upon my back (sins). Intercede for me with Your Lord on the day of my need and poverty, for You have a praised position with Allah and You are distinguished in this life and in the hereafter with Allah

Then recite the following with your right hand raised while your left hand is placed upon the grave:

اللهم إني أتقرب إليك بحبهم و بموالاتهم، و أتولى آخرهم بما توليت به أولهم، و أبرء من كل وليجة دونهم

O'Allah! I seek nearness to You by loving and following Them (Imams asws). I follow the last of Them just as I followed the First of Them. I disassociate myself from any intimate friend other than Them.

اللهم العن الذين بداوا نعمتك، و اتهموا نبيك ﷺ، وجحدوا آياتك، و سحروا بإمامك، و حملوا الناس على أكتاف آل محمدّ

O'Allah! Send Your lanat upon those who denied Your blessings, accused Your Prophet (saw), denied Your Signs, ridiculed Your Imam (asws) and incited hostility amongst the people towards Aal e Muhammad (asws)

اللهم إني أتقرب إليك باللعنة عليهم و البرائة منهم في الدنيا و الآخرة، يا رحمن يا رحيم

O'Allah! I seek nearness to You by sending lanat on them and by disassociating myself from them in this life and in the hereafter. O' Rahman O'Raheem (All compassionate, all merciful)

Then move towards His feet and recite the following:

صلى الله عليك يا أبا الحسنّ، صلى الله عليك و على روحك وبدنك، صبرت و أنت الصادق المصدق، قتل الله من قتلك بالألسن

May the blessings of Allah be upon You, Your Ruh, and Your body, O' Abul Hasan (asws). You remained patient for You are al Sadiq al Masdiq. May Allah slaughter those who slaughtered You; either with their hands or their tongues

Then supplicate to Allah by sending lanat upon the killer of Ameerul Momineen (asws), by sending lanat upon the killers of Hussain (asws), and by sending lanat upon the killers of the Family of RasoolAllah (saw).

Afterward move towards His head from behind the grave and perform two rakats of prayer. Recite Sura Yaseen in one rakah after al Hamd and recite Sura al Rahman after al Hamd in the other rakah.

Then offer duas to Allah and pray for yourself and for your parents and your brothers in faith as much as you can.

Stay next to Him in Mashhad for as long as you wish and try to perform all of your prayers while being beside His grave.

Chapter 103

The Ziarat of Imam Ali Naqi (asws) and Imam Hasan (asws) al Askari in Samarra

HADITH 1

Masoom Imam (asws) narrates:

"When you want to perform the Ziarat of Ali (asws) ibn Muhammad (asws) al Jawad (Imam Ali Naqi asws) and Imam Hasan al Askari (asws), perform ghusl and then either go near to Their graves or you can perform the Ziarat by simply pointing towards Their graves from the door which opens to the street of Shubbak. Then you should recite the following:

السلام عليكما يا وليي الله

Salam be upon You, O Walis of Allah.

السلام عليكما يا حجتي الله

Salam be upon You, O Hujjatullah (proofs of Allah)

السلام عليكما يا نوري الله في ظلمات الأرض

Salam be upon You, O noors of Allah in the darkness of the earth

السلام عليكما يا من بدا الله في شأنكما

Salam be upon You, O He who possesses the attributes of Allah

السلام عليكما يا حبيبي الله

Salam be upon You O the beloved of Allah

السلام عليكما يا إمامي الهدى

Salam be upon You, O' Imams of Guidance

أتيتكما عارفاً بحقكما، معادياً لأعدائكما، موالياً لأوليائكما، مؤمناً بما آمنتما به، كافراً بما كفرتما به، محققاً لما حققتما، مبطلا لما أبطلتما

I come to You whilst knowing Your rights. I oppose Your enemies and make friends of Your friends. I believe in that which You taught and disbelieve in that which was taught by kafireen. I believe to be haq (true) those things that You said are haq and I believe to be batil those things that You said were batil (false)

أسأل الله ربي وربكما أن يجعل حظي من زيارتكما الصلاة على محمد ﷺ و آلّة، و أن يرزقني مرافقتكما في الجنان مع آبائكما الصالحين

I ask Allah who is my Lord and Your Lord to send His blessings upon Muhammad (saw) and the Family of Muhammad (asws) as my reward for performing this Ziarat and allow me to accompany You and Your Righteous Forefathers (asws) in jannah as my rizq

و أسأله أن يعتق رقبتي مان النار، و يرزقني شفاعتكما و مصاحنتكما، و يعرف بيني و بينكما، و لا يسلبني حبكما وحب آبائكما الصالين، و أن يجعله آخر العهد من زيار تكما، و يحشرني معكما الجنة برحمته

And I ask Allah to release me from the hellfire, to allow Your intercession and Your association be my rizq, and to allow me to meet You on the Day of Judgment. I beseech Allah to not remove my love for You and my love for Your Righteous Forefathers from my heart, to not make this Ziarat be the last Ziarat I perform and to resurrect me with You in Jannah by His mercy

اللهم ارزقني حبهما ي توفني على ملتهما

O'Allah! Preserve me with Their love and make me to die whilst believing in Their religion

اللهم العن ظالمي آل محمدّ حقهم و انتقم منهم

O' Allah! Send lanat on those who oppressed the rights of Aal e Muhammad (asws) and take Their revenge.

اللهم العن الأولين منهم و الآخرين، و ضاعف عليهم العذاب، و بلغ بهم و بأشياعهم و أتباعهم و محبيهم و متبعيهم أسفل درك من الجحيم، إنك على كل شيء قدير

O'Allah! Send lanat on the first of Their oppressors and the last and make your chastisement upon them be everlasting and ever increasing. Send Their oppressors, those who follow Their oppressors, those who love Their oppressors, and those who follow those who love Their oppressors to the lowest depths of hell. For You have power over all things.

اللهم عجل فرج وليك و ابن وليك، و اجعل فرجنا مع فرجهم، ياأرحم الراحمين

O'Allah! Hasten the reappearance of Your Wali, who is the Son of Your Wali and comfort us with Their support. O' Most merciful of the merciful

Then perform dua and prayers for yourself and your parents. If you are performing Ziarat near Their graves, then you should perform two rakats of prayer beside each of Their graves. But if you perform prayers inside the mosque which is next to Their graves, then you should pray for that which you need.

The mosque that is beside Their house is where They use to perform prayers.

Chapter 104

Ziarat for any Imam (asws)

HADITH 1

Ali ibn Hassan narrates:

"Imam Reza (asws) was asked regarding performing the Ziarat of the grave of Abul Hasan Imam Musa Kazim (asws). Imam (asws) replied:

Perform prayer in the mosques that surround Their graves and recite the following for this can be recited at any of the graves of Masoomeen (asws):

السلام على أولياء الله و أصفيائه،

Salam be upon the Walis of Allah and His Chosen Ones

السلام على امناء الله و أحبائه

Salam be upon the trustees of Allah and His Beloved Ones

السلام على أنصار الله و خلفائه

Salam be upon the supporters of Allah and His Caliphs

السلام على محال معرفة الله

Salam be upon the source of the marifat of Allah

السلام على مساكن ذكر الله

Salam be upon the houses in which Allah is remembered

السلام على مظاهر أمر الله و نهيه

Salam be upon the ones who are the mazher (manifestation) of the amr (commands) of Allah

السلام على الدعاة إلى الله

Salam be upon the ones who call the people towards Allah

السلام على المستقرين في مرضات الله

Salam be upon those who are firmly within the pleasure of Allah

السلام على المخلصين في طاعة الله

Salam be upon those who are loyal in Their obedience of Allah

السلام على الذين من و الاهم فقد و الى الله، و من عاداهم فقد عادى الله، و من عرفهم فقد عرف الله، و
من جهلهم فقد جهل الله، و من اعتصم بهم فقد اعتصم بالله، و من تخلى منهم فقد تخلى من الله

Salam be upon those whose friendship is the friendship of Allah and whose animity of the animity of Allah, whose marifat is the marifat of Allah, whose refuge is the refuge of Allah, and whose abandonment is the abandonment of Allah

أشهد الله أني سلام لمن سالمكم، و حرب لمن حاربكم، مؤمن بسركم و علانيتكم، مفوض في ذلك كله
إليكم

I take Allah as my witness that I am peaceful to those who are peaceful with You, that I oppose those who oppose You, that I believe in Your secrets including those which are batin (hidden) as well as the zahir (apparent), and that I rely upon You in all things.

لعن الله عدو آل محمدٍ من الجن و الإنس، و أبرء إلى الله منهم

May Allah send lanat upon the enemies of Aal e Muhammad (asws) from amongst the jinn and mankind. I seek the nearness of Allah by disassociating myself from them (enemies)

و صلى الله على محمد ﷺ و آلة

May the blessings of Allah be upon Muhammad (saw) wa Aal e Muhammad (asws)

Then Imam (asws) added:

This Ziarat may be performed for any of the Masoomeen (asws). After reciting it, you should send as many blessings upon Muhammad (saw) and His Ahlul Bayt (asws) as you can. Name Them one after the other and disassociate from Their enemies.

Then recite whatever duas you wish and pray for yourself and the momineen from amongst the men and women.

HADITH 2

Imam Jafar Sadiq (asws) narrates:

Recite the following Ziarat beside the grave of Hussain (asws) ibn Ali (asws). You may also recite this Ziarat beside the graves of all the Imams (asws):

السلام عليك من الله

May the salam of Allah be upon You

و السلام على محمد ﷺ بن عبد اللّٰة، أمين على وحيه وعزائم أمره، الخاتم لما وبق و الفاتح لما استقبل

May the salam of Muhammad (saw) ibn Abdullah (as) be upon You, for You are the trustee of the revelation (wahi) of Allah and of His will; of the things that have already come to pass and the things that are yet to come

اللهم صل على محمد عبدك و رسولك الذي انتجبته بعلمك، و جعلته هادياً لمن شئت من خلقك، و الدليل على من بعثته برسالاتك و كتبك، و ديان الدين بعدلك، و فصل قضائك بين خلقك، و المهيمن على ذلك كله، و السلام عليه و رحمة الله و بركاته

O'Allah! Send Your blessings upon Muhammad (saw), Your servant and Your Messenger; the one whom You chose through Your knowledge and whom You appointed as a guide for those amongst Your creation, the one You sent with Your Message and Your Book, the decisive judge of Your religion between Your creation, the one who rules Your religion with Your justice, and the absolute ruler over all things. Salam be upon Him and may the blessings and mercy of Allah be upon Him.

When reciting this Ziarat for Ameerul Momineen (asws), replace the first line (salawat upon Muhammad saw) with:

اللهم صل على أمير المؤمنينّ عبدك و أخي رسولك ﷺ

O'Allah! Send Your blessings upon Ameerul Momineen (asws), Your servant and brother of Your Messenger (saw)

When reciting this Ziarat for Syeda Fatima (sa), you should instead recite:

اللهم صل على فاطمةّ، أمتك و بنت رسولك ﷺ

O'Allah! Send Your blessings upon Fatima (sa), Your servant and Daughter of Your Messenger...

When reciting this Ziarat for any of the other Imams (asws), you should recite:

اللهم صل على أنباء رسولك ﷺ

O'Allah! Send Your blessings upon the Son of Your Messenger...

Then recite the following:

أشهد أنكم كلمة التقوى، و باب الهدى، و العروة الوثقى، و الحجة البالغة على من فيها و من تحت الثرى

I testify that You are the word of piety (kalamatul taqwa), and the door of guidance (babul hadi), the firmest handle (Quran 2:256), and the Hujjat (proof) which was declared to those which were on the earth and buried within it.

و أشهد أن أرواحكم و طينتكم من طينة و احدة، طابت و طهرت من نور الله و من رحمته

I testify that Your Ruh (spirits) and the clay from which You were created are pure and blessed with the noor of Allah and with His mercy

و اشهد الله و اشهدكم أني لكم تبع بذات نفسي و شرايع ديني و خواتيم عملي، اللهم فأتمم لي ذلك برحمتك يا أرحم الراحمين

I take Allah and You as my witness that I follow You in all of my affairs, in the rulings of my religion, and in my actions. O'Allah, O' Most Merciful of the Merciful fulfill this request for me

السلام عليك يا أبا عبد اللةّ، أشهد أنك قد بلغت عن الله ما امرت به، و قمت بحقه غير و اهن و لا موهن

Salam be upon You, O' Aba Abdullah (asws)! I testify that You conveyed everything, which was revealed to You from Allah, without any delay or hesitation

فجزاك الله من صديق خيراً عن رعيتك

May Allah reward You for Your struggle and bless You with the truth

أشهد أن الجهاد معك جهاد، و أن الحق معك و لك، و أنت معدنه، و ميراث النبوة عندك و عند أهل بيتكّ

I testify jihad is not jihad unless it is with You, that Haq is with You and that You are its (haq) source, and that the inheritance of the nabuwiyat (prophet hood) is with You and Your Ahlul Bayt (asws)

أشهد أنك قد أقمت الصلاة، و آتيت الزكاة، و أمرت بالمعروف، و نهيت عن المنكر، و دعوت إلى سبيل ربك بالحكمة و الموعظة الحسنة، و عبدت ربك حتى أتاك اليقين

I testify that You performed prayer, gave zakat, enjoined the good and forbade the evil, that You called the people towards the path of Your Lord with wisdom and good counsel, and that You worshipped Your Lord until that which is certain came to You

Then recite:

السلام على ملائكة الله المسومين

May the salam of Allah be upon the "*havoc-making angels*" (Quran 3:125)

466

السلام على ملائكة لله المنزلين

May the salam of Allah be upon the angels that descend upon Your shrine

السلام على ملائكة الله المردفين

May the salam of Allah be upon *"the angels following one after another, rank upon rank"* (Quran 8:9)

السلام على ملائكة الله الذين هم في هذا الحرم بإذن الله مقيمون

May the salam of Allah be upon the angels who reside within this Haram by the permission of Allah

اللهم العن اللذين بدلا نعمتك، و خالفا كتابك، و جحدا آياتك، و اتهما رسولك، احش قبور هما و أجو افهما ناراً، أعد لهما عذاباً أليماً

O'Allah! Send Your lanat upon the two who changed Your blessings, disobeyed Your Book, denied Your signs, and accused Your Messenger. Fill their graves and their stomachs with hellfire and prepare for them a painful chastisement

و احشرهما و أشياعهما و أتباعهما إلى جهنم زرقا، و احشرهما و أشياعهما و أتباعهما يوم القيامة على وجوههم عميا و بكماً وصماً، مأواهم جهنم كلما خبت زدناهم سعيراً

O'Allah! Resurrect the two of them along with their followers in Hell while being blind. And on the Day of Judgment, resurrect the two of them and their followers *"gather, them together, prone on their faces, blind, dumb, and deaf: their abode will be Hell: every time it shows abatement, We shall increase from them the fierceness of the Fire."* (Quran 17:97)

اللهم لا تجعله آخر العهد من زيارة قبر ابن نبيك ﷺ

O'Allah! Do not make this the last time I perform the Ziarat of the grave of the Son (asws) of Your Prophet (saw)

و ابعثه مقاماً محموداً تنتصر به لدينك و تقتل به عدوك، فإنك و عدته ذلك و أنت الرب الذي لا تخلف الميعاد

And resurrect Him in Muqm-e-Mahmood (highest place in jannah). You supported the religion with Him, and slaughtered Your enemies through Him. For this was Your promise with Him and You are the one who does not break His promise

You may recite the same beside the graves of all of the Imams (asws). Whenever you perform the Ziarat of any of the Imams (asws), you should also recite the following:

السلام عليك يا ولي الله

Salam be upon You O' Wali of Allah

السلام عليك يا حجة الله

Salam be upon You O' Hujjat (proof) of Allah

السلام عليك يا نور الله فى ظلمات الأرض

Salam be upon You O'Nurullah (light of Allah) in the darkness of the earth

السلام عليك يا إمام المؤمنين، و وارث علم النبيين، و سلالة الوصيين، و الشهيد يوم الدين

Salam be upon You, O' Imam of the momineen, the inheritor of the knowledge of the prophets, the descendant of the successors, and the witness on the Day of Religion

أشهد أنك و آبائك الذين كانوا من قبلك، و أبنآئك الذين من بعدك موالي و أوليائيو أئمتي

I testify that You, Your Forefathers (asws) before You, and Your Children (asws) after You are my Moulas, my Walis, and my Imams

و أشهد أنكم أصفياء الله و خزنته و حجته البالغة

And I testify that You are the Chosen Ones of Allah, His Trustees, and His Hujjat (proof) which has been declared before all

إنتجبكم بعلمه أنصاراً الدينه، و قواماً بأمره، و خزاناً لعلمه، و حفظة لسره، و تراجمة لوحيه، و معدناً لكلماته، و أركاناً لتوحيده، و شهوداً على عباده

468

Allah through His Knowledge chose You as the supporters of His religion, the executors of His affairs, the keepers of His knowledge, as the protectors of His secrets, the translators of His revelation, the sources of His words, the pillars of His oneness, and as the witnesses upon the creation

و استودعكم خلقه، و أورثكم كتابه، و خصكم بكر ائم التنزيل، و أعطاكم التأويل

Allah entrusted You with the affairs of His creation and made You the inheritors of His book. He honored only You with the revelation and gave only to You the batin (hidden) meanings of the Quran.

و جعلكم تابوت حكمته، و مناراً في بلاده، وضرب لكم مثلا من نوره

Allah made You as the vessels of His wisdom, the lighthouses in His land, and the examples of His Noor

و أجرى فيكم من علمه، و عصمكم من الزلل، و طهركم من الدنس، و أذهب عنكم الرجس

Allah placed His knowledge within You; protecting You from and not allowing any impurities near You

و بكم تمت النعمة، و اجتمعت الفرقة، و ائتلفت الكلمة

The blessings are completed through You, the words are united through You

ولزمت الطاعة المفترضة، و المودة الواجبة، فأنتم أولياؤه النجباء، ع عبده المكرمون

Allah made loving You and obeying You wajib (obligatory) for You are the chosen Auwliya and the most respected servants

أتيتك يا بن رسول الله ﷺ عارفاً بحقك، مستبصراً بشأنك، معادياً لاعدائك، موالياً لأوليائك

O' Son (asws) of RasoolAllah (saw)! I have come to You whilst having the marifat of Your rights and understanding of Your status. I am enemy of Your enemies and friend of Your friends.

بأبي أنت و امي، صلى الله عليك و سلم تسليماً

May my mother and father be sacrificed upon You. May the blessings and salam of Allah be upon You

أتيتك و افداً زائراً، عائداً مستجيراً مما جنيت على نفسي و احتطبت على ظهري، فكن لي وشفيعاً، فإن لك عند الله مقاماً معلوماً، و أنت عند الله وجيه

I have come as Your guest in order to perform Your Ziarat while seeking refuge from my crimes against myself and from the weight, which I carry upon my back (sins). Intercede for me with Your Lord for You have the highest status with Allah and are honored by Allah.

آمنت بالله و بما انزل عليكم، و أتولى آخركم بما توليت به أولكم، و أبرأ من كل و ليجة دونكم، و كفرت بالجبت و الطاغوت و اللات و العزى

I believe in Allah and in that which was revealed to You. I follow the last of You as I followed the first of You. I disassociate myself from and disbelieve in kafirat, Jibt (idolworship), Taghut (shaitan), Lat and Uzza.

Chapter 105

The Merits of Performing the Ziarat of the Shia (followers) of Ahlul Bayt (asws)

HADITH 1

Amr ibn Uthman al Razee narrates:

"I heard Abul Hasan the First Imam Musa Kazim (asws) say:

Those who are unable to come to Our Ziarat should perform the Ziarat of Our righteous momin instead. And the reward for performing Our Ziarat will be written for them. Those who are unable to meet with Us directly should meet with Our righteous momin and the reward for meeting Us will be written for them."

HADITH 2

Amr ibn Uthman narrates:

"I heard Imam Reza (asws) say:

Those who are unable to come to Our Ziarat should perform the Ziarat of Our righteous followers instead. And the reward for performing Our Ziarat will be written for them. Those who are unable to meet with Us directly should meet with Our righteous Followers and the reward for meeting Us will be written for them."

HADITH 3

Muhammad ibn Ahmad ibn Yahya narrates:

"I was in Fayd (a small town between Kufa and Mecca) with Ali ibn Bilal. We walked to the grave of Muhammad ibn Ismail ibn Bazi (a companion of Imam Musa Kazim (asws), Imam Reza (asws) and Imam Taqi (asws)). When we arrived at the grave Ali ibn Bilal said to me; "The owner of this grave said to me:

Those who go to the graves of Their brothers from amongst the momineen, place their hands on the graves, and recite the chapter of "Inna Inzulnah" seven times will be safe from the Day of Great Terror (judgment day)."

HADITH 4

See hadith 3

HADITH 5

Abdul Rahman ibn Aba Abdullah narrates:

" I asked Aba Abdullah Imam Jafar Sadiq (asws), "How should I place my hand upon the graves of the momineen?"

Imam (asws) faced towards qiblah , pointed to the earth, and then placed His hand upon it."

HADITH 6

Safwan al Jammal narrates:

"I heard Aba Abdullah Imam Jafar Sadiq (asws) say:

Every Thursday evening, RasoolAllah (saw)—along with a group of His companions— would go to Baqi of Medina. RasoolAllah (saw) would recite "Salam to you, o' people of the graves" three times. Then He would recite "May the mercy of Allah be upon you" three times.

Then RasoolAllah (saw) would turn to His companions and say, "They are better than you."

His companions would ask, "Why is that, O' RasoolAllah (saw)? They believed in Allah and we believe in Allah. They fought in the way of Allah and we fought in the way of Allah."

RasoolAllah (saw) would reply, "They believed in Allah without oppression. And I will testify for them that they died while believing in Allah. However you will live on after Me and will create bidah (innovations)."

HADITH 7

Imam Jafar Sadiq (asws) narrates from His Father Imam Muhammad Baqir (asws) who narrates from His Forefathers (asws) that:

"Ameerul Momineen Ali (asws)—along with some companions—entered a graveyard. Then Ameerul Momineen (asws) called out:

O' people of the dust! O' lonely people! O' those who are silent! O' deceased ones! We bear news that your wealth has been distributed amongst your heirs, your women have remarried, and your houses are inhabited by others. What news do you have?"

Ameerul Momineen (asws) turned towards His companions and said, "I swear by Allah that if they were given permission to speak, they would have said, "There is no provision better than guarding oneself; *for surely the provision is the guarding of oneself.*" (Quran 2:197)

HADITH 8

Ishaq ibn Ammar narrates:

"I asked Abul Hasan Imam Musa Kazim (asws), "Do the momineen know who visits their graves?"

Imam (asws) replied, "Yes, and they enjoy the company of their visitors while they are beside their graves, but as soon the visitors leave, they (momineen) will feel a sudden forlornness."

HADITH 9

Abdullah ibn Sinan narrates:

"I asked Aba Abdullah Imam Jafar Sadiq (asws), "How should I say salam to the people in their graves?"

Imam (asws) replied by reciting the following:

السلام على أهل الديار من المؤمنين و المسلمين

Salam be upon you; people of the graves from amongst the momineen (true believers) and muslims

أنتم لنا فرط و نحن إن شاء الله بكم لاحقون

You have preceded us and inshaAllah we shall join you

HADITH 10

Amr ibn Abul Miqdam narrates from his father who narrates:

"Abu Jafar Imam Muhammad Baqir (asws) and I passed by Baqi. We passed by the grave of a man who was from amongst the Shia of Kufa.

I said to Imam Baqir (asws), "May I be sacrificed upon You! This is the grave of one of the Shia."

Imam (asws) stopped beside the grave and said, "O'Allah! Have mercy on his isolation. Be near to him in his loneliness. Keep his company during his desolation. Make him feel safe during the time of fear. Descend Your mercy upon him in such a way he will not be in need of the mercy of any other and join him with his beloved. "

HADITH 11

Jarrah al Medini narrates:

"I asked Aba Abdullah Imam Jafar Sadiq (asws), "How should I say salam to the people in their graves?"

Imam (asws) replied by reciting the following:

السلام على أهل الديار من المؤمنين و المسلمين

Salam be upon you; people of the graves from amongst the momineen (true believers) and muslims

أنتم لنا فرط و نحن إن شاء الله بكم لاحقون

You have preceded us and inshaAllah, we shall join you

HADITH 12

In some books where Muhammad ibn Sinan narrates from Muffaddal who says:

"If a person recites, "Inna Inzulnah" seven times beside the grave of a momin, Allah will send an angel to that grave who will worship Allah. The rewards of this worship will be written for the one in the grave and for the person who came to visit the momin.

When this momin is resurrected, he will not have to face any terrors for Allah will remove all terrors from him through the angel who was devoted to his grave. He will enter jannah in the company of that angel.

Then he added, "When you go to the graves of the momineen, recite Sura al Hamd once, the chapter of Inna Inzulnah seven times, and then recite mu'awwazatain (Sura al Naas and al Falaq), Sura Qul Huwallahu Ahad, and Ayatul Kursi three times."

HADITH 13

Muhammad ibn Muslim narrates:

"I heard Abu Jafar Imam Muhammad Baqir (asws) say,

"When RasoolAllah (saw) passed by the graves of a group of momineen, He would say, "Salam be upon the dwellings of the momineen. InshaAllah we shall join you."

HADITH 14

ibn Ajlan narrates:

Abu Jafar Imam Muhammad Baqir (asws) stood beside the grave of a man and said:

"O' Allah! Be with him during his loneliness. Keep him company during his desolation. Descend Your mercy upon him in such a way that he will not be in the need of mercy from others."

HADITH 15

Ali ibn Abu Hamzah narrates:

"I asked Aba Abdullah Imam Jafar Sadiq (asws), "How should we say salam to the people of the graves?"

Imam (asws) replied, to recite the following:

السلام على أهل الديار من المؤمنين و المسلمين

Salam be upon you people of the graves—from amongst the momineen and mominaat and the muslims.

أنتم لنا فرط و نحن إن شاء الله بكم لاحقون

You have preceded us and inshaAllah we shall join you

HADITH 16

Asbagh ibn Nabata narrates:

"One day, Ameerul Momineen Ali (asws) passed by some graves. He turned to the right and said:

Salam be upon you, O' people who have moved from castles to graves

You have preceded us. InshaAllah we will follow and join you

Then Imam (asws) turned to the left and repeated the same statement."

HADITH 17

Imam Jafar Sadiq (asws) narrates:

"When you go to the graves, say salam and recite the following:

السلام على أهل القبور

Salam be upon the people of the graves

السلام على من كان فيها من المؤمنين و المسلمين

Salam be upon the momineen (true believers) and muslims in the graves

أنتم لنا فرط و نحن لكم تبع و إنا بكم لا حقون

You have preceded us and soon we shall follow and join you

و إنا الله و إنا إليه راجعون

From Allah we come and to Him we shall return

يا أهل القبور بعد سكنى القصور، يا أهل القبور بعد النعمة و السرور، صرتم إلى القبور، يا أهل القبور كيف و جدتم طعم الموت؟

O' those living in the graves who once lived in castles! O' people of the graves who once enjoyed blessings and pleasures! O' people of the graves! Now that you dwell within the graves how do you find the taste of death?

Then say, "Woe unto those who have gone to Jahannum". You should then weep and afterwards depart"

HADITH 18

Rabee ibn Muhammad al Musli narrates:

"When Aba Abdullah Imam Jafar Sadiq (asws) would enter a graveyard, He would say, "Salam upon the people of Jannah"."

Chapter 106

Merits of the Ziarat of Masooma e Qum
(Fatima (sa) daughter of Imam Musa Kazim asws)

HADITH 1

Sa'ad ibn Sa'ad narrates:

"I asked Abul Hasan Imam Ali Reza (asws) about the Ziarat of Fatima (sa), the Daughter of Imam Musa Kazim (asws).

Imam (asws) replied, "Those who perform Her Ziarat will be rewarded with Jannah.""

HADITH 2

The Son of Imam Muhammad Taqi (asws) narrates:

"Those who perform the Ziarat of My Aunt in Qum will be rewarded with Jannah."

Chapter 107

Special Ziarats and Narrations

HADITH 1

Abdullah ibn Hammad al Basri narrates:

"Aba Abdullah Imam Jafar Sadiq (asws) said to me:

"There is a blessing which is near that has not been given to anyone else. But you do not understand its true value nor do you adhere to it nor are you committed to it. There is a certain group of people—identified by their names—for whom Allah by His mercy and compassion has willed a good ending for them. He has bestowed this blessing upon them without them having to do anything."

I asked, "May I be sacrificed upon You! What is this blessing which You refer to but have not mentioned by name?"

Imam (asws) replied, "The Ziarat of My Grandfather, Hussain (asws) ibn Ali (asws). He is the desolate one in a remote land. Those who perform His Ziarat, mourn over Him. Those who do not perform His Ziarat, grieve over Him. Those who have not seen His grave are destroyed with anguish over Him. Those who look upon the grave—which is at His feet in that desert— of His Son, Ali Akbar (as), are filled with compassion for Him.

He (Imam Hussain asws) had no family nor friends in that land. The kafireen denied Him His rights, abandoned Him, and rose against Him. They slaughtered Him and left His body unburied to be scavenged by the beasts.

They (kafireen) denied Him (Imam Hussain (asws) to drink from the water of the River Furat even though they (kafireen) allowed their dogs to drink from this water. They abandoned their obligations towards RasoolAllah (saw); ignoring the orders of RasoolAllah (saw) regarding Himself and His Family (asws).

Eventually Imam Hussain (asws) was abandoned in His grave; struck down by layers of dust beside His family members and His Shia.

He is far from His Grandfather (saw) in Medina even though in life He (Imam Hussain asws) was very close to Him (RasoolAllah saw). He is alone in a House which is not visited except by those whose hearts Allah has tested for iman and whom He has allowed to know Our rights."

I said, "May I be sacrificed upon You! I used to perform His Ziarat until I was afflicted with having to serve this tyrant and to protect his wealth. Now I am well known to them. Therefore I no longer perform His Ziarat out of fear even though I'm well aware of its blessings."

Imam (asws) asked, "Do you know the merits of performing His Ziarat and the reward We have prepared for those who perform His Ziarat?"

I replied, "No."

Imam (asws) said, "Regarding the merits of His Ziarat, Allah exalts those who perform His Ziarat to the angels in the heavens. And We seek the mercy of Allah for those who perform His Ziarat every morning and evening. My Father (asws) narrated to Me that since the day of His (Imam Hussain asws) martyrdom, His burial site has never been deserted by those who send blessings on Him from amongst the angels, jinn, mankind, or beasts. Everything within the creation envies those who perform His Ziarat and tries to touch the zuwwar in order to receive blessings by looking at those who looked upon the grave of Hussain (asws)."

Then Imam (asws) said, "I have heard in the middle of Shabaan, some people from the suburbs of Kufa and various cities, go to perform His Ziarat. Their women grieve over Hussain (asws). The reciters recite poetry about Hussain (asws). The speakers narrate the story of Hussain (asws). The mourners mourn over Hussain (asws). And the lyricists recite marsiya about Hussain (asws)."

I replied, "May I be sacrificed upon You! I have seen some of that which You have described."

Imam (asws) said, "Praise be to Allah who appointed some to go for Our Ziarat, to glorify Us, and to recite Our accolades. And praise be to Allah who has made some of Our enemies to slander Our Shia for their nearness to Us while others insult them (Our Shia) and condemn their actions."

HADITH 2

Abdullah ibn Bukhair al Arjani narrates:

"I accompanied Aba Abdullah Imam Jafar Sadiq (asws) from Medina to Mecca. We stopped in an area called Usfaan (a village between Medina and Mecca). Then we passed by a mountain on the left side of the road which was black and formidable.

I said to Imam (asws), "O' Son of RasoolAllah (saw)! How formidable this mountain is! I have never seen anything like this."

Imam (asws) asked, "O' ibn Bukhair! Do you know which mountain this is?"

I replied, "No."

Imam (asws) said, "This mountain is called Kamad. It overlooks one of the valleys in Hell where the killers of My Father Hussain (asws) are. The melted materials of Hell flow under the killers of My Father Hussain (asws) in this valley. These materials include **GHISLEEN** (*"filth" Quran 69:36*), **SADEED** (*"festering water" Quran 14:16*), **HAMEEM** (*"boiling water" Quran 40:72*) , that material which emerges from the Putrid Well, that material which oozes from the sins (blood and pus) in **FALAQ** (lowest valley in Hell), that material which oozes out from the clay of **KHABAL** (pus), that material which oozes from Jahannum, that material which oozes from the blazing fires, that which oozes out from **HUTAMAH** (*"that which crushes into pieces Quran 104:4*), that which oozes out from **SAQAR** (*"burning hellfire" Quran 74:26*), that which oozes out from **HAWIYAH** (*"abyss" Quran 101:9*), and that which oozes out from **SA'IR** (*"burning fire" Quran4:55*).

Every time I pass by this mountain, I stop and see those Two seeking refuge with Me, and I look upon the killers of My Father (asws) and I say to them:

> "You established the foundation for what the killers of Hussain (asws) did. You showed Us no mercy during the time of Your rule. You slaughtered Us, denied and usurped Our rights. You oppressed Our affairs by dismissing Us. May Allah have no mercy on those who have mercy on the Two of you. Now taste the results of the evil that you (the two) brought forth. For Allah is not unjust with any of His servants."

Sometimes I climb the mountain of Kamad—where those Two are located. I stand there in order to soothe some of that which is in My heart. The second of the two begs and gives into despair more deeply."

I asked, "May I be sacrificed upon You! What do You hear when You climb this mountain?"

Imam (asws) replied, "I hear the voices of those Two. They cry out, "Come towards us so we may speak with You for we wish to repent." And then I hear the mountains cry out, *"Be ye driven into it with disgrace; speak not unto Me" (Quran 23:108).* "

I asked, "May I be sacrificed upon You! Who else is with them?"

Imam (asws) replied, "Every tyrant whose actions have been mentioned by Allah in Quran and everyone who taught kufr to the servants of Allah."

I asked, "And who are they?"

Imam (asws) replied,

> "Bulis who taught the Jews *"...the Hand of Allah is tied up"* (Quran 5:64)...
>
> Nastoor who taught the Christians that Isa (as) was *"The Messiah is the son of Allah"* (Quran 9:30) and that they are three...
>
> Firoan of Musa (as) who said, *"I am your lord, the most high"* (Quran 79:24)...
>
> Numrood who said, "I have overpowered all within the earth and killed those in the heavens"...
>
> the killer of Ameerul Momineen (asws)...
>
> the killer of Syeda Fatima (sa) and Mohsin (as)...
>
> the killers of Hasan (asws) and Hussain (asws)...
>
> as well as Muawiyah (la) and Amr ibn As, each has no hope of salvation...
>
> and anyone who incited hatred against Us, who helped Our enemies against Us—either with his tongue, wealth, or hand—will also be with them."

I asked, "May I be sacrificed upon You! You hear all of this and yet You do not feel anxious?"

Imam (asws) replied, "O' ibn Bukhair! Our hearts are not like the hearts of the people. We are the obedient, purified, chosen servants of Allah. We see that which people do not see and We hear that which people do not.

The angels come down to Us when We travel. They rest in Our beds. They watch Us when We eat. They attend Our funerals. They bring the news of that which will happen in the future to Us. They pray over Us and for Us. Their wings are placed over Us and Our children play under their wings. They prevent the animals from coming near Us. They bring various types of fruits to Us from various lands. They bring water from every land for Us and place it in Our vessels. There is not a day nor hour nor any prayer time that passes and the angels are not prepared to serve Us.

Every night the reports of every land and that which occurs in it, the reports of the Jinn, and the reports of all of the angels in the heavens are brought to Us.

We are informed when one angel departs from a place and another replaces him, We are also informed regarding the accomplishments of the new angel in comparison to the one he replaced.

The reports from all of the seven earths are continuously being brought to Us."

I asked, "May I be sacrificed upon You!" Where does the mountain end?"

Imam (asws) replied, "In the seventh earth, in a valley where Jahannum is at. There are many who keep watch over this valley. Their number is greater than the stars in the sky. the drops of rains, the inhabitants in the seas, and the bits of soil on the earth. Every one of these guards from amongst the angels has a sworn duty which he continuously performs and never abandons."

I asked, "May I be sacrificed upon You! The angels report to all of You (Ahlul Bayt asws)?"

Imam (asws) said, "No, the angels report to the Imam of each time. We are the caliphs over the matters which none of the slaves of Allah can rule on. Whenever a jinn denies Our ruling regarding a matter, the angels force him to carry out Our Will. If they are amongst the kafir jinn, the angels put shackles on them and torture them until they submit to Our order in those matters."

I asked, "May I be sacrificed upon You! Can the Imam (asws) see everything; from the East to the West?"

Imam (asws) replied, "O' ibn Bukhair! How can He be Hujjatullah (Proof of Allah) over the entire earth but not be able to see the entirety of that which He is caliph over? How can He be the Hujjat (proof) over the people if they are not in His presence, cannot reach Him nor does He possess power over them? How can He be the Hujjat on the people if He is unknown to them especially when He has been appointed as the intermediary between the slaves of Allah and Allah Himself?

Allah says, *"And have We not sent You but to all of mankind"* (Quran 34:28). This ayah refers to all of the creation on earth. The Hujjat (proof) after RasoolAllah (saw) performs the duties of RasoolAllah (saw) after RasoolAllah (saw) has departed this world. He (Hujjat) serves as the judge between the ummah on the matters they are in dispute over. He (Hujjat) is the one who ensures the people are given their rights. He (Hujjat) carries out the amr (commands) of Allah, and He (Hujjat) is the one who rules justly between the people.

How can these words of Allah be fulfilled if the Imam (asws) is not amongst the people? For Allah says, *"Soon will We show them our Signs in the (furthest) regions (of the earth), and in their own souls,"* (Quran 41:53). What sign other than Us did Allah use to show the people in the furthest regions?

Allah also says, *"And We did not show them a sign but it was greater than its like,"* (Quran 43:48). What sign is greater than Us?

I swear by Allah that Bani Hashim and Quresh are well aware of all that has been bestowed upon Us (Ahlul Bayt asws) but they were overcome by jealousy; just as Iblees was overcome by jealousy. When they (Bani Hashim and Quresh) find themselves in turmoil and need, they come to Us (Ahlul Bayt asws). So that We (Ahlul Bayt asws) may clarify the matter for them and remove their fear. They (Bani Hashim and Quresh) will say to Us (Ahlul Bayt asws), "We (Bani Hashim and Quresh) testify that You (Ahlul Bayt asws) are truly the people of knowledge.", but after they leave Our presence, they (Bani Hashim and Quresh) say to others, "We have not seen any who are more astray than those who follow the Ahlul Bayt (asws) and accept Their (Ahlul Bayt asws) words."

I asked, "May I be sacrificed upon You! If the earth of the grave of Hussain (asws) were to be opened, would there be anything in it?"

Imam (asws) replied, "O' ibn Bukhair! You always ask questions of great importance. Hussain (asws) along with His Father (asws), His Mother (sa), and His Brother, Hasan (asws), are in the House of RasoolAllah (saw) with RasoolAllah (saw) Himself. They are glorified and sustained the same way RasoolAllah (saw) is.

If the grave of Hussain (asws) had been exhumed during His time, then He would have been found there. But today Hussain (asws) is alive and in the presence of His Lord. He sits looking upon His resting place and the Arsh until the time comes when He is ordered to take it up. Hussain (asws) is sitting on the right side of the Arsh and says, "O' My Lord! Fulfill Your promise to Me.

Hussain (asws) looks upon and knows those who perform His Ziarat. He knows their names, the names of their fathers, their status, and their status before Allah. Hussain (asws) knows that which they carry with them better than you know your own sons. Hussain (asws) looks upon those who mourn over Him and seeks forgiveness for them as an act of mercy. Hussain (asws) also asks His Father (asws) to seek forgiveness for them.

Hussain (asws) says to those who mourn over Him, "O' those who cry over Me! If you knew what had been prepared for you, your happiness would be greater than your sorrow."

All of the angels in the heavens and at the Ha'yr (burial place of Hussain asws) who hear those who mourn over Hussain (asws) seek forgiveness for the mourners, and the zuwwar (visitors) return to their homes with no sins."

HADITH 3

Imam Jafar Sadiq (asws) narrates:

"No prophet or successor remains on the earth for more than three days after being buried. Their souls, their bones, and their flesh are taken up to the heavens. When a person goes to those places which possess Their signs and says salam to Them, They (prophets and successors) hear the salam as if it had been said close to Them even though it was in reality said from a distance."

HADITH 4

Safwan ibn Mirhan al Jammal narrates Imam Jafar Sadiq (asws) said:

"The least reward a zawir of Hussain (asws) receives is that for every good deed he performs a million good deeds are written for him. And his every bad deed will be written only once. Then what is the value of one million compared to only one.

Then Imam (asws) said, "O'Safwan! Rejoice, for Allah has appointed some angels who carry shafts of light and when the Keepers (angels who record good and bad deeds) are about to record a bad deed for the zawir of Hussain (asws), these angels order the Keepers to stop. And the Keepers will not write the bad deed. Then when the zawir performs a good deed, these angels tell the Keeper, *"Record it now "for Allah will change their evil deeds to good deeds"* (Quran 25:70)."

HADITH 6

Imam Jafar Sadiq (asws) narrates:

"There is a graveyard near you known as Buratha. One hundred and twenty thousand martyrs like the martyrs of Badr will be resurrected from this graveyard."

HADITH 7

Muhammad ibn Fadl narrates:

"I heard Imam Jafar Sadiq (asws) say:"

"Those who perform the Ziarat of the grave of Hussain in the month of Ramadan and die while on the way will not be judged, their book of deeds will not be announced, and they will be told , "Enter Jannah.""

HADITH 8

Aban ibn Taghlib narrates:

Imam Jafar Sadiq (asws) asked me, " O'Aban! When was the last time you performed the Ziarat of the grave of Hussain (asws)?"

I replied, "I swear by Allah, O' Son of RasoolAllah (saw)! It has been a long time since I performed His Ziarat."

Imam (asws) said, "Glory be to Allah, the Most Great! You are one of the Chiefs of the Shia and you neglect the Ziarat of Hussain (asws). With each step the zawir takes, Allah will record one good deed and erase one bad deed for those who perform the Ziarat of Hussain (asws) and Allah will forgive all of their past and future sins.

O'Aban! When Hussain (asws) was martyred, seventy thousand angels descended to his grave. They were disheveled and covered with dust. They continuously mourn and weep over Him and will do so until the Day of Judgment."

HADITH 9

Hasan ibn Jahm narrates:

I asked Abul Hasan Imam Reza (asws), "Which is better; going to Mecca but not going to Medina or going to the Ziarat of the Prophet (saw) but not going to Mecca?"

Imam (asws) replied, "Which do you think is better?"

I said, "We believe performing the Ziarat of RasoolAllah (saw) is wajib, the same as performing the Ziarat of Hussain (asws) is wajib ."

Imam (asws) replied, " Now that you have said this, you should know that one Eid day when Aba Abdullah Imam Jafar Sadiq (asws) was in Medina, He went to the grave of RasoolAllah (saw) to say Salam to Him.

Imam (asws) told those with Him, "We have been elevated above all people in every land including Mecca and every other city for having said salam to RasoolAllah (saw)."

HADITH 11

Imam Jafar Sadiq (asws) narrates:

"When RasoolAllah (saw) ascended to the heavens on the night of Miraj, He was told, "Allah (swt) will test You with three hardships to see how patient You will be."

RasoolAllah (saw) replied, "I submit to Your will, O' Lord. And I have no power to be patient except through You. What are the three hardships?"

RasoolAllah (saw) was told, "The first is hunger and giving preference to the needy over Yourself and Your Family."

RasoolAllah (saw) replied, "I accept, O' Lord. I am pleased with Your will and submit to it. I seek success and patience only through You."

RasoolAllah (saw) was then told, "The second is You will be denied and Your life will always be in great danger. You should spend Your wealth, Your blood, and Your ruh fighting against the people of kufr. You should remain patient when You are harassed by the kafireen and the munafiqs. You should remain patient when You will be injured and wounded in the battles."

RasoolAllah (saw) replied, "I accept, O' Lord. I am pleased with Your will and submit to it. I seek success and patience only through You."

RasoolAllah (saw) was then told, "The third is that Your Family will be martyred after You. As for Your brother, Ali (asws), Your ummah will slander and admonish Him. They will be violent against Him. They will deny Him and usurp His rights. They will oppress Him and finally they will slaughter Him."

RasoolAllah (saw) replied, "I accept, O' Lord. I am pleased with Your will and submit to it. I seek success and patience only through You."

Then RasoolAllah (saw) was told, "As for Your Daughter (sa), She will be oppressed and deprived. The rights that You gave Her will be usurped. She will be beaten while pregnant. Her holiness will be violated. Her house will be entered against Her will. Then She will be disgraced and dishonored. She will have no one to protect Her. She will miscarry due to being beaten and will die as a result of that beating."

RasoolAllah (saw) replied, *"Surely we are Allah's and to Him do we return"* (Quran 2:156) I accept, O' Lord. I am pleased with Your will and submit to it. I seek success and patience only through You."

Then RasoolAllah (saw) was told, "She will have Two Sons with Your Brother. One of whom Your ummah will loot, stab, and slaughter maliciously."

RasoolAllah (saw) replied, *"Surely we are Allah's and to Him do we return"* (Quran 2:156) I accept, O' Lord. I am pleased with Your will and submit to it. I seek success and patience only through You."

Then RasoolAllah (saw) was told, "As for Her Second Son (asws), Your ummah will invite Him for jihad but then they will slaughter Him while He is defenseless. They will also slaughter His children and His family members who will be with Him. They will ravage the women. He (Hussain asws) will ask for help from Me but I have already willed His martyrdom and the martyrdom of those with Him.

His martyrdom will be the hujjat (proof) against everyone from the creation. The inhabitants of the heavens and the earths will weep and lose patience over Him. The angels who will not have permission to help Him will mourn over Him.

But I shall raise a Man from His Progeny whose shadow is with Me under the Arsh. Through Him I shall support Him (Hussain asws). He will fill the earth with justice and equality. The dread from Him will travel with Him. He will slaughter so many people that it will cause doubt amongst the people against Him."

RasoolAllah (saw) replied, "Surely we are Allah's."

Then RasoolAllah (saw) was told, "Raise Your head."

Imam (asws) added, "Then RasoolAllah (saw) said, "I looked up and saw a man who was more beautiful and aromatic than any other. He had blessed features and was wearing clothes made of noor. Noor was emanating from His forehead, from above Him, and below Him. He was surrounded by angels—whose number was so great they could only be counted by Allah (swt).

I (RasoolAllah saw) asked Him to come near to Me. He came and kissed My (RasoolAllah saw) forehead.

Then I (RasoolAllah saw) said, "O'Lord! Who will this man avenge and against whom will He show His anger? For what reason have You arranged these angels?"

Then Allah said to RasoolAllah (saw):

"Regarding Your Brother (Moula Ali asws), *for remaining patient, He will enter the "gardens of retreat"* (Quran 32:19) On the day of resurrection, I will establish Him as a hujjat (proof) upon the creation. I will decree for Him to stand by the Pool of Kauthar and distribute water to Your Auwliya (friends) and prevent Your enemies from drinking from it. Jahannum will become cool and safe for Him so that He may enter and bring out anyone who has even an atoms weight of love for You. I will make all of You (Ahlul Bayt asws) to dwell in the same part of Jannah.

Regarding Your Son who will be abandoned and martyred (Hasan asws), and Your Other Son who will be betrayed and martyred (Hussain asws), I will adorn My Arsh with Them; for the sufferings which They endured. They will be glorified and honored in way which mankind cannot even imagine. Trust in Me.

I will bless those who perform the Ziarat of His (Hussain asws) grave because those who perform His Ziarat are like those who have performed Your (RasoolAllah saw) Ziarat and those who have performed Your (RasoolAllah saw) Ziarat are like those who have performed My (Allah) Ziarat and I always bless and glorify those who perform My Ziarat.

Regarding Your Daughter (sa), She will stand beside My Arsh and I (Allah) will tell Her (sa), "I have appointed You as the judge over My creation. You may decree whatever You like over those who oppressed You and Your Children, and Your decree will be executed."

Then She (sa) will go to the courtyard where judgment takes place and She will order those who oppressed Her to be taken to Hell.

The oppressor will wish he could be given his life back and say, *"'Ah! Woe is me!- In that I neglected (my duty) towards Allah,"* (Quran 39:56). Then *"the unjust one shall bite his hands saying: O! would that I had chosen a way together with the messenger (of Allah) O woe is me! would that I had not taken such a one for a friend !* (Quran 25:27-28). And *"Until he comes to Us, he says: O would that between me and you there were the distance of the East and the West; so evil is the associate! it will not profit you this day that you are sharers in the chastisement."* (Quran 43:38-39)

The oppressor will say, *"You alone judges between Thy servants as to that wherein they differ."* (Quran 39:46)"

They will be told, *"the curse of Allah is on the unjust. Who hinder (people) from Allah's way and seek to make it crooked, and they are disbelievers in the hereafter"* (Quran 7:44-45)."

Imam (asws) continued and said,

"The first judgment will be between Mohsin (as) ibn Ali (asws) and the one who killed Him (Mohsin as)—the second usurper (la). Then he (second usurper la) will be brought forward along with his servant qunfuz (la) and together they will be lashed with whips of fire. The whips will be such that if one of them were to hit the oceans, then all of the oceans from the east to the west would boil. If just one of the whips were to touch the mountains, then they would all be destroyed and turn to ash.

Then Ameerul Momineen (asws) will kneel before Allah in order for Allah to judge between Him and the fourth usurper—muawiyah (la).

Then the second usurper (la), qunfuz (la), and muawiyah (la) will be thrown in a well of fire, which will be covered so none can see them, and they will not be able to see anyone.

Those who followed them in this life will say, *"Our Lord! show us those who led us astray from among the jinn and the men that we may trample them under our feet so that they may be of the lowest."* (Quran 41:29)

Allah (swt) will reply, *"it will not profit you this day that you are sharers in the chastisement."* (Quran 43:39) *"Then they will cry out in distress and they shall there call out for destruction."* (Quran 25:13)

The Two—imprisoned by the angels of Hell— will come to the Pool of Kauthar and say to Ameerul Momineen Ali (asws), "Forgive us, give us some water and save us."

The Two will be told, *"But when they shall see it nigh, the faces of those who disbelieve shall be sorry, and it shall be said; This is that which you used to call for."* (Quran 67:27) by attributing the title of commanders of the believers to yourselves. Return to Hell thirsty. The only drink you two shall receive is **HAMEEM** (*"boiling water" Quran 40:72*) and **GHISLEEN** (*"filth" Quran 69:36*). And *"the intercession of intercessors shall not avail them."* (Quran 74:48)."

HADITH 12

Abdullah ibn Abdul Rahman al Asam narrates from his grandfather who said:

I asked Aba Abdullah Imam Jafar Sadiq (asws), "May I be sacrificed upon You! Which is greater—going for Hajj or giving sadqa (charity)?"

Imam (asws) asked, "The answer depends on if there are sufficient funds to go for Hajj or not?"

I replied, "No."

Imam (asws) said, "If the money is sufficient for going for Hajj, then going for Hajj is better than giving sadqa. However, if it is not sufficient then giving sadqa is better."

I asked, "What about jihad (fighting in the way of Allah)?"

Imam (asws) replied, "Jihad is not accepted unless it is done with an Imam (asws)."

I asked, "What about performing ziarat?"

Imam (asws) replied, "Performing the Ziarat of RasoolAllah (saw), The ziarat of Hamzah (as), the Ziarat of the Successors (as), and the Ziarat of Hussain (asws) in Iraq are greater."

I asked, "What are the rewards for performing the Ziarat of Hussain (asws)?"

Imam (asws) replied, "Those who perform the Ziarat of Hussain (asws) will be immersed in the mercy of Allah and will have gained His pleasure. Evil will be kept away from them, their rizq will increase, and the angels will surround them. They will be surrounded with a noor that will allow the angels to identify them. They will not pass by the angels without them (angels) praying for them (zuwwar)."

HADITH 13

Abdul Rahman ibn Muslim narrates:

I went to Imam Musa Kazim (asws) and asked, "Which is greater; performing the Ziarat of Hussain (asws) ibn Ali (asws) or performing the Ziarat of Ameerul Momineen (asws) or ... —I named each Imam (asws) one by one."

Imam (asws) replied, "O'Abdul Rahman! Those who perform the Ziarat of the First of Us are like those who perform the Ziarat of the Last of Us. Those who perform the Ziarat of the Last of Us are like those who perform the Ziarat of the First of Us.

Those who follow the First of Us are like those who follow the Last of Us. Those who follow the Last of Us are like those who follow the First of Us.

Those who fulfill the needs of one of Our Shia are like those who have fulfilled the needs of all of Us, Imams (asws).

O'Abdul Rahman! Love Us, love those who love Us, love for Our sake, and cause others to love for Our sake. Befriend Us, and befriend those who befriend Us. And hate those who hate Us.

Beware! Those who oppose Our words are like those who oppose the words of Our Grandfather, RasoolAllah (saw). Those who oppose the words of RasoolAllah (sa) are like those who oppose the words of Allah.

Beware, o' Abdul Rahman! Those who oppose Us, oppose Muhammad (saw). And those who oppose Muhammad (saw), oppose Allah. And those who oppose Allah (swt) truly deserve to be burned in the fires of Hell by Allah. And there will be none to help them."

HADITH 14

al Halabee narrates:

Aba Abdullah Imam Jafar Sadiq (asws) said:

"When Hussain (asws) was martyred, Our Family in Medina heard a crier call out, "Today torment has descended upon this ummah. You shall not see any pleasure until your Qaim (Imam e Zamana atfs) rises and pleases you by killing your enemies and avenging the One (Hussain asws) who was slaughtered by the many."

They (Our family) were frightened after hearing this and said something has surely happened, yet we are unaware. After some time had passed, they heard the news of the martyrdom of Hussain (asws). When they counted the days, they realized He had been martyred on the same day they had heard the crier."

I (al Halabee) said, "May I be sacrificed on You! How long will You (Ahlul Bayt asws) and we (Shia) remain under this intense fear and bloodshed?"

Imam (asws) replied, "When the seventieth tyrant appears, and the tyrants before him have passed, at that time you will see many strange and perplexing signs. When this time comes, you will be pleased to see the signs."

Then Imam (asws) adds, "When Hussain (asws) was martyred, a person went near the camp of the enemies and condemned them. He said, "How can I not cry out when RasoolAllah (saw) is standing and looking upon this earth and you. I fear He (RasoolAllah saw) will beseech Allah against you. Then I will be destroyed along with you."

The soldiers looked at each other and said, "This man has lost his mind."

The repenters said, "By Allah! What have we done to ourselves? We slaughtered the Master of the Youth of Paradise for the son of Summayyah (ubaidullah ibn ziyad la)." Then the repenters rose against ubaidullah ibn ziyad (la)."

I asked, "May I be sacrificed upon You! Who was the one who called out to them?"

Imam (asws) replied, "We do not believe he was anyone other than Jibrael (as). If He (Jibrael as) had been given permission, He would have cried out to them in such a way their souls would have left their bodies and immediately entered Hell. But they were given respite so that they may increase their sins and will have a painful chastisement."

I asked, "May I be sacrificed upon You! What do you say about one who has the ability to perform the Ziarat of Hussain (asws) but does not?"

Imam (asws) replied, "He has abandoned RasoolAllah (saw) and Us. He has belittled a matter that is wajib on him.

Allah will look after the needs of those who perform the Ziarat of Hussain (asws) and He (Allah) will take care of every matter that is important to them in this life.

Performing the Ziarat of Hussain (asws) increases the rizq of the servants of Allah. They will be reimbursed for the money that they spent in performing the Ziarat.

Fifty years of sins will be forgiven and they will return to their families having every sin and misdeed erased from their book. If they die while performing Ziarat, the angels will descend and perform their ghusl. The doors of Jannah will be opened for them and its fragrance will surround them until the day they are resurrected.

If they do not die while performing Ziarat, the door from which their rizq descends will be opened and they will be reimbursed with ten thousand dirhams for every dirham they spent performing their Ziarat and their reimbursement will be kept secure for them.

When they are resurrected, they will be told, "You have ten thousand dirhams for every dirham you spent for Allah has kept it safe with Himself for you."

The Mission of Wilayat

As followers of Masoomeen (asws), we have been ordered by Allah to spread His commands to those "who were not present". If one hears of the command of Allah and does not convey it to others, then no excuse will be accepted from him and he will be thrown into hell. It is wajib upon all to convey the message of wilayat e Ali (asws) as this is the command of Allah.

However there are so few books of hadiths and sayings of Masoomeen (asws) that have been translated that it makes it very difficult for momineen to share the words of Masoomeen (asws) with others. We hope that our mission will not only make it easy for momineen to fulfill their duties and obey the command of Allah to spread wilayat e Ali (asws), but that we will have also fulfilled our obligation in spreading this command of Allah and gained the pleasure of Masoomeen (asws) instead of Their anger. We pray that not only will our iman and marifat be increased but that of every person's as well. We pray to our Imam (atfs) to help us and guide us so that we do not go astray and do not lose sight of our true mission which is;

Spreading the true religion of Allah

Wilayat e Ali (asws)

Previously Published Books include:

Names & Titles of Ameerul Momineen (asws)

Tawheed al Mufaddal

Ana Howa (I am That)

Glorious Sermons & Sayings of Ameerul Momineen (asws)

Basairul Darjaat vols 1-2 (urdu)

Mashariqul Anwar al Yaqeen (urdu)

Join the Wilayat Mission mailing list at

http://www.wilayatmission.org/contact.html

to receive email updates of all future publications.

www.ingramcontent.com/pod-product-compliance
Lightning Source LLC
Chambersburg PA
CBHW081422090426
42740CB00017B/3152